<u>Of Little Faith</u>

Religion and Politics Series
John C. Green, Ted G. Jelen, and Mark J. Rozell, series editors

The Christian Right in American Politics: Marching to the Millennium
John C. Green, Mark J. Rozell, and Clyde Wilcox, Editors

Of Little Faith: The Politics of George W. Bush's Faith-Based Initiatives
Amy E. Black, Douglas L. Koopman, and David K. Ryden

School Board Battles: The Christian Right in Local Politics
Melissa M. Deckman

Of Little Faith

The Politics of George W. Bush's
Faith-Based Initiatives

Amy E. Black, Douglas L. Koopman,
and David K. Ryden

GEORGETOWN UNIVERSITY PRESS ■WASHINGTON, D.C.

Georgetown University Press, Washington, D.C.
© 2004 by Georgetown University Press. All rights reserved.
Printed in the United States of America

10 9 8 7 6 5 4 3 2 1   2004

This book is printed on acid-free recycled paper meeting
the requirements of the American National Standard
for Permanence in Paper for Printed Library Materials.

Library of Congress Cataloging-in-Publication Data

Black, Amy E.
   Of little faith : the politics of George W. Bush's faith-based initiatives / Amy E.
Black, Douglas L. Koopman & David K. Ryden.
      p. cm.—(Religion and politics series)
Includes bibliographical references and index.
   ISBN 1-58901-012-4 (cloth : alk. paper)—ISBN 1-58901-013-2 (pbk. : alk. paper)
   1. Federal aid to human services—United States.   2. Human services—Contracting
out—United States.   3. Church charities—Government policy—United States.   4. Church
charities—United States—Finance.   5. Church and state—United States.   6. Bush, George
W. (George Walker), 1946–   7. United States—Social policy—1993–   I. Koopman,
Douglas L.   II. Ryden, David K.   III. Title.   IV. Religion and politics series (Georgetown
University)
   HV95.B585 2004
   361.2′5′0973—dc22

                                                                              2003019469

Contents

List of Focal Points

Preface

In all likelihood, this project began in the basement of the Longworth House Office Building, when Doug Koopman and I met for a quick cafeteria lunch. Doug was in Washington, D.C., with a group of Calvin College students and working with the House Republican Conference, and I was on Capitol Hill for a year serving as an American Political Science Association (APSA) congressional fellow, after which I was moving to the Chicago area to begin a new teaching position at Wheaton College. We met a few times for a quick (and greasy) lunch, compared notes about our time so far on the Hill, and brainstormed about new research projects.

As political science professors observing and participating in the life of the House of Representatives, we had many stories to share with one another. We soon discovered common interest and a mutual fascination with H.R. 7, the House legislative piece of President George W. Bush's faith-based initiative. In my work for Representative Melissa Hart (Pennsylvania, 4th district), I attended meetings with staff from the White House Office of Faith-Based and Community Initiatives and followed the progress of H.R. 7 through a very contentious Judiciary Committee. As part of his work for Representative J. C. Watts (Oklahoma, 4th district), Doug assisted in the plans for a House Republican Conference–sponsored "faith-based summit" and observed the internal politics of H.R. 7 from the office of its key House sponsor. Off Capitol Hill, David Ryden was following the developments with great interest, wondering about the implications of proposed changes for constitutional law. In April 2001, the three of us participated in the summit, moderating panels and watching the story of the faith-based initiative begin to unfold. We each followed the legislation with great interest as the political battles intensified and sometimes turned into partisan shouting-matches. As the views on faith-based partnerships polarized, we realized we were witnessing a public policy story in progress that needed to be told.

Soon we had assembled a team, bringing together three different perspectives and viewpoints that we believe shed light on different facets of the story. Each of us brings special expertise to explore various dimensions of this initiative and practical experience that helps bridge the gap between theory and practice. Doug has extensive practical political experience and focuses his research on Congress and religion and politics. As a former APSA congressional fellow in 2000–2001, I have experience in interest-group politics and political behavior. David, for six years a practicing lawyer, has written extensively on how faith-based initiatives relate to constitutional questions and on the role of the black church.

Each of us entered this project with some degree of ambivalence about the idea of increasing government partnership with religious organizations. Although generally sympathetic to the positive role religion can and should play in civil society, we had reservations about the extent to which current law should or would change. By bringing together a team of researchers with different ideological perspectives and areas of expertise, we hoped to check one another's potential biases and, to borrow a biblical metaphor, allow iron to sharpen iron.

Watching the rising levels of partisan rancor, the dissemination of much misinformation on both sides of the debate, and noticing a general confusion about the purposes and potential of faith-based initiatives, we began this project with the goal of bringing some clarity to a very muddled debate. As political scientists who work outside the political process, we hoped to provide a more objective and informed analysis of the events. This project also allowed us to explore how faith traditionally shapes policy and provided an important case study on the role of religion in society.

In particular, the political and legislative odyssey of faith-based initiatives presents a special opportunity to illustrate with a real-life example many important issues in the study of American politics and public policy. The following chapters examine the legislative, administrative, legal, and political aspects of the initiative from the 2000 election campaign through the end of the 107th Congress. The story highlights the tensions inherent in the constitutional separation of powers, offers a direct contrast of the procedures and folkways of the House and the Senate, illustrates the role of the modern presidency in action, and reminds readers of the influence and reach of the Supreme Court. In the course of the book, we raise many questions just as we provide answers to others. In the end, however, we hope that you will find the story as rich and intriguing as we have.

Amy E. Black

Acknowledgments

The authors wish to express their gratitude to the people and institutions that have made this work possible. To everyone who agreed to give of their time to speak with us about these issues, we are grateful. So many individuals told us their stories and were open and forthright in sharing both their triumphs and disappointments. We could not have written this book without the support and assistance of so many men and women working on the front lines of the battle over the faith-based initiative.

We owe a special debt of gratitude to the past and present staff members of the White House Office of Faith-Based and Community Initiatives (WHOFBCI) who agreed to talk with us. We appreciate Jim Towey and David Kuo and their willingness to share their vision of the office's work, and we owe much thanks to former WHOFBCI staff, including John DiIulio, Don Eberly, Don Willett, and Stanley Carlson-Thies. Their willingness to relive the events and provide insights on the establishment of the office was critical for our research. Our interaction with so many dedicated and talented professionals on all sides of the faith-based issue renews our faith in the political process and those working in it.

We also want to thank Richard Brown, John Green, Ted Jelen, Mark Rozell, and everyone at Georgetown University Press who believed in this project and offered constructive advice. Gayle Boss helped us all find our voice with her careful editing.

AMY E. BLACK: I wish to thank several people who helped me with the project. Joe Loconte, Chip Hauss, and Roger Conner provided guidance and direction as I was beginning the research; their suggestions for interviews opened many doors. None of this would have been possible without Representative Melissa Hart and the APSA Congressional Fellowship Program who gave me the opportunity to learn about Congress and participate in the process from the inside. I must also thank my friends in Washington, D.C., especially Kristine Cornils, whose hospitality and open door offered me a much appreciated home away from home.

This book benefits greatly from the capable research assistance of Kristin Brostrom, Dawn K. Crowell, and Christopher Upham, all of whom approached their work with professionalism and good humor. I greatly appreciate the assistance of Jan Miller and all my Wheaton colleagues whose encouragement made this book possible. I owe special thanks to the Wheaton College Alumni Grant and the G. W. Aldeen Fund, whose generous support allowed me to conduct interviews that were absolutely crucial for understanding the politics of the faith-based initiative.

Douglas L. Koopman: I would like to especially thank the House Republican Conference, then headed by J. C. Watts, for the time I was allowed to participate as a legislative fellow while supervising Calvin College's Paul Henry Semester in Washington, D.C., program. The fellowship provided the germ of the idea for this book and the opportunity to participate in many of the events related to the House faith-based bill. I would also like to thank Calvin College for the opportunity to pursue the writing of this project during my sabbatical year at Calvin. The extensive time to conduct research and write during that sabbatical made this book possible. During that time I was greatly aided by two young women at the college. Melissa Keeley, an undergraduate student and my research assistant for the summer of 2002, took notes during interviews I conducted and wrote much of what is now chapter 4. Melissa Fritsch, research assistant at the Calvin College Center for Social Research, tracked down source documents, drafted and revised short portions of several chapters, and generally helped keep me on track throughout the sabbatical year. Most important, I would like to thank my wife Gayle for her editing assistance and, especially, for her understanding and encouragement during a difficult two years from the conception of the project to its completion. She and the boys, Kai and Cotter, were a great source of comfort and, when necessary, pleasant distraction while I brooded over this task.

David K. Ryden: I would like to thank a number of individuals for their support and assistance in this project. Sally Smith of the Hope College Political Science Department deserves the label of "saint" for her cheerful willingness to accommodate any request, large or small. Her technological acuity goes far in making up for my shortcomings in that area. Several Hope College students—Elizabeth Van Houwelingen, Jim Plasman, and

Jeremy Brieve—provided valuable assistance by proofreading, polishing notes, running down citations, conducting research, and carrying out any number of other sundry tasks. Thanks to my professional colleagues and coauthors, Amy Black and Doug Koopman, for the genesis of this book and for inviting me to come aboard. It has been a pleasure working with you both.

My participation in this project would not have been possible without the generous support of the Towsley Foundation of Midland, Michigan. Their award of the Towsley Scholarship several years ago and the sabbatical that accompanied it provided me with the time to launch a wholly new research path into the fascinating subject of faith-based social services. I also want to thank Hope College and its administration for its institutional support in the form of a summer grant. I am especially appreciative of the extra measure of grace extended to me by my wife, Jennifer, especially as little Theo entered our household during the final stages of the project.

Introduction

The Faith-Based Initiatives
through Three "Lenses"

In December 2002, retiring U.S. representative J. C. Watts was closing down his congressional offices when the national media called on him to comment on two breaking stories—controversial comments Senate Republican majority leader Trent Lott had made at Strom Thurmond's one hundredth birthday party about Thurmond's 1948 Dixiecrat presidential race, and President Bush's executive order to create a more favorable environment for faith-based groups seeking to gain government contracts. Watts expected the calls. He had been the key sponsor of H.R. 7, the House faith-based bill, in the last Congress, and almost since the start of his congressional service in 1994 he had been a Republican spokesperson on issues of race.

Watts, the only African American Republican in Congress, would leave the House in a few weeks, giving up his position as chair of the House Republican Conference, the fourth-ranking leadership post. He had come to Congress after an impressive sports career as a college quarterback at the University of Oklahoma and then as a professional quarterback in the Canadian Football League, spurning the NFL because no interested team seemed to want him to play his college position. An ordained minister, Watts returned to Oklahoma after his professional football career ended in 1986 to pastor churches and begin public service. In 1989 he changed his party affiliation from Democrat to Republican and was elected to his first public office one year later. Rising fast, he successfully sought a seat in the U.S. House in 1994. While serving in Congress, Watts took time to preach regularly in churches near Washington, D.C., and, more often, throughout the state of Oklahoma. Athletically fit and handsome, Watts soared to congressional prominence, pushed by a party conference sensitive to accusations it was a white male bastion. Watts ran for and was elected conference chair after the 1998 congressional elections. He had been in the House just four years, an astoundingly quick rise to leadership.

As the only African American Republican elected to a national office, Watts quickly became the de facto spokesperson for the GOP on issues

1

of race. It was not a role he particularly relished, but it was thrust upon him by a party that felt the need to respond to such issues with a person of color. Watts thought this role stereotyped him as *the* black Republican, rather than as a leading Republican who happened to be African American. Making him the party's spokesperson on racial issues, he thought, frequently let the GOP too easily distance itself from some of its past and current positions.[1]

Commenting on television and in the newspapers on Trent Lott's alleged sympathy for segregation was not Watts's idea of a pleasant or effective use of his last few days in Congress. But he accepted media requests, suggesting at first that Lott did not need to resign. On December 19, the Associated Press quoted Watts saying that Lott's statements were as "serious as the venue in which they were delivered—a birthday party," a type of "complimentary humor that often accompanies personal tributes."[2]

Quickly, however, Watts joined the growing chorus calling for Lott to step down from his leadership post. In imploring Lott to quit the fight to save his position, Watts acknowledged that Lott had "served his state . . . [and] his country well," but wondered aloud if Lott wanted "to put [his] family [and] grandkids through this, and the party?" He went on to say that "if it was me, I just would not put my family through it."[3] In a later *Meet the Press* interview, Watts called Lott's remarks "indefensible" and said that Lott needed to do more than apologize if he wanted to mend fences with the African American community.[4]

In the 107th Congress of 2001–2002, Watts had also become a regular spokesperson on faith-based initiatives, one of President Bush's priorities and the centerpiece of the Texan's compassionate conservative agenda. Watts had been tapped by House speaker Dennis Hastert and Republican whip Tom DeLay to sponsor the House faith-based bill and guide it to House passage. The bill's major provision was a broad expansion of charitable choice, which encouraged many intensely and vocally religious groups to apply for and receive federal funds to deliver social services. Charitable choice had already passed Congress four times, first as part of the massive 1996 welfare reform law. The new bill in the 107th Congress also included charitable giving incentives for individuals and businesses and individual development accounts for the poor.

Managing "faith-based," as the bill and the issue frequently became known, was a role more to Watts's liking. As a preacher at inner-city black churches, Watts had seen firsthand the work that such churches were doing with limited funds. The chief objective of the faith-based initiative—getting more financial assistance to such churches and helping them effectively use these funds—fit well his legislative interests. In Congress Watts had championed innovative ways to empower and assist the poor, advocating individual development accounts, empowerment zones, school choice, and closer cooperation between government and small community-based social service providers. Leading the House legislative effort on faith-based initiatives was a far better fit for J. C. Watts's natural interests than being a party spokesperson on race.

Linking Race and Faith

There was a political side to faith-based that linked the legislation to Watts's uncomfortable role in the party. With the GOP at the forefront of a drive to channel more aid to faith-based ministries—frequently inner-city groups operated by and serving African Americans—a slight shift of black voters toward Republicans seemed at least plausible. Watts was skeptical of any short-term Republican gains from the faith-based initiative alone. To attract any significantly higher proportion of African American voters, Republicans needed a more comprehensive strategy on issues of interest to that community, and the party needed to work at these issues over the long haul. A quick faith-based victory could and should be only a start if Republicans were serious about winning minority votes. Some Republican operatives, apparently seeing the limitations of faith-based to attract minorities, thought the initiative would be more useful as a payoff for the party's white conservative evangelical core. This opinion was a serious mismatch between the effects of the initiative, which would help mainly the poor and minorities, and the priorities of conservative religious interest group leaders, who wanted to gain more space for traditional religion in the public square. Working with currently established core supporters, however, would simplify the legislative path in the House.

For years Watts had pushed a broad legislative agenda that appealed to much of black America. Those issues ranged from recognizing the contribution of slave labor in building the U.S. Capitol, to funneling more federal aid to historically black colleges, to developing better U.S. trade relations with African nations. He was sincere in these efforts, but many in the GOP establishment seemed more interested in symbolism.

The party still depended on a few prominent black conservatives to defend it, rather than addressing what many inside and outside the party saw as far deeper problems. Watts had been a tireless but quiet worker within the party for a more substantive strategy. His faith-based leadership might give him more influence inside the party on the broader issue of creating a racially inclusive GOP.

Legislative Failure

Getting right to work in early 2001, Watts pushed H.R. 7, the major faith-based bill, through the House, dutifully completing this legislative task for the president by August. It had been a partisan push the entire way, despite efforts by some in the White House and Congress for bipartisanship. The bill quickly became portrayed as a sop to the "religious right," a gross oversimplification of the bill. This was probably inevitable, however, given the poisoned political atmosphere after the 2000 presidential election and the way faith-based legislation was wrapped up in both race and religion. The Republican Senate had done nothing in the early months of 2001, waiting for the House to proceed on H.R. 7 and hoping Pennsylvania Republican Rick Santorum and Connecticut Democrat Joseph Lieberman could develop a bipartisan bill. Then Vermont Senator James Jeffords switched his affiliation from Republican to Independent and shifted the Senate to Democratic control. The switch, and the House's partisan debate, doomed any expansion of charitable choice and made even minor faith-based aid a long shot for the entire 107th Congress.

Then came September 11, 2001. Congress focused on terrorism and war, and faith-based fell out of the news and down the priority list of its supporters and its opponents alike. By the time J. C. Watts was packing his congressional belongings almost two years after George W. Bush came to office, there was no significant faith-based legislative success. Only a meager $30 million in "compassion capital funds" had been attached to a larger spending bill in late 2001, with most of those funds allocated in small grants late in fiscal year 2002. There were no new big tax incentives for charitable giving and no expansion of charitable choice.

Senate supporters of faith-based legislation worked hard, if sporadically, through all the distractions and partisan distortions to find common ground. Senators Santorum and Lieberman jointly introduced the CARE Act in early 2002, a much different bill from H.R. 7. It had more generous tax provisions and compassion capital funds, but no expansion of charitable choice. Instead, CARE contained brief religious nondiscrimination language—a few specific clarifications of which faith-based groups could apply for federal funds that would slightly expand the eligibility pool. CARE had a broad spectrum of support, but little deep interest beyond its two principal authors. To charitable choice proponents, CARE was little better than nothing. To charitable choice opponents, CARE was completely unnecessary but not quite harmless. Its chief supporting interest groups were nonprofits seeking its generous new tax breaks. In June 2002, CARE squeaked through an uninterested Senate Finance Committee, and in the fall of 2002 it awaited floor action. Dwindling time and lingering controversies doomed CARE, however. Committed opposition by a handful of senators and a few liberal civil liberties interest groups prevented the bill from moving ahead. CARE finally died in the waning days of the lame-duck Senate following the 2002 elections, after several failed attempts to consider it under expedited procedures.

Executive Action

Frustrated by inaction on even a mild Senate bill, President Bush issued two executive orders on December 12, 2002, that addressed the faith-based issue. One added two new faith-based satellite offices in two more executive departments. The other, far more controversial, unilaterally implemented the religious nondiscrimination provisions contained in CARE. Opposition to the latter order by interest group foes such as Americans United for Separation of Church and State and the American Civil Liberties Union (ACLU) was strong. Barry Lynn of Americans United stated, "Bush is on a crusade to bring about an unprecedented merger of religion and government," and promised to "explore every opportunity to challenge this in the courts."[5] He went on to say that "[u]nder this scheme, taxpayers will be forced to support churches they don't believe in, and workers will be denied publicly funded jobs because they don't conform to religious mandates."[6] ACLU legislative counsel Christopher Anders said of Bush's actions, "You could not strike a more core civil rights protection," and characterized the orders as "a tremendous rollback to civil rights."[7]

Most legislators involved in the issue supported the move, including Senator Lieberman, who called it "a constructive step forward."[8] Lieberman praised the fact that the White House had dropped the provision of the House bill that would have preempted local gay-rights laws, and said that the orders appeared to present "a sound plan for realizing the principle of equal treatment for faith-based groups."[9] Representative Watts had long ago abandoned hopes for H.R. 7, agreeing in October 2002 to support the CARE Act if it ever passed the Senate.[10] He supported the president's executive order reluctantly, as a small but "excellent step toward the full deployment of the armies of compassion."[11]

Objections were heard from several officeholders, including the key House Democrats who fought H.R. 7, representatives Bobby Scott of Virginia and Chet Edwards of Texas. They used the occasion to repeat their general concerns about faith-based initiatives. Edwards told reporters that he opposed the order because "[n]o American citizen should have to pass someone else's religious test to qualify for a federally funded job."[12] Scott saw this as one more step toward Bush's ultimate goal of allowing all types of religious organizations to directly receive government grants; this, he argued, violated the establishment clause of the First Amendment. Scott reminded the public of the earlier House bill on which Bush's executive order was partially based, calling it the "ugliest" piece of legislation he could recall in public life.[13] Further congressional opposition was articulated by several Democrats prominent in the legislative debates. Representative Jerry Nadler of New York accused the president of "legalizing government-funded religious discrimination."[14] Senator Edward Kennedy of Massachusetts stated that while he shared Bush's goal of "strengthening community-based services through faith-based organizations," he was troubled that Bush issued an order that effectively "permit[ted] federally funded discrimination." "Under the new rule," Kennedy pointed out, "organizations can accept public funds and then refuse to employ persons because they are Jewish, Catholic, unmarried, gay or lesbian."[15]

The president's faith-based initiative, launched with great fanfare two years before, had stalled in the Senate after Representative Watts had pushed it through the House. Because the president had power to act unilaterally in the executive branch, the policy fared better there. And some sympathetic court decisions had improved its prospects in the judicial branch. But overall, by December 2002 the president's faith-based initiative had achieved nothing close to what one might have expected from the rhetoric of the 2000 campaign and the early predictions of its supporters.

The Faith-Based Story

The story of President George W. Bush's first efforts on faith-based initiatives is one marked by both failures and successes—most of the former quite public, many of the latter hidden. Depending upon which part of the political system one examines, this centerpiece of the president's compassionate conservative agenda has either gained important new ground or failed miserably. And depending upon one's view of the initiative and the men and women who supported it, those advances and retreats are cause for either great concern or great joy for the American political system and the place of religion in American public life.

The uneven journey of President Bush's faith-based initiative during the 2000 election campaign and the 107th Congress offers insight into important issues in American government, politics, and public life. Further, the story is both accessible to average citizens and relevant to those interested in our nation's public life. What exactly happened in President Bush's first two years in office to this signature domestic initiative, one that appeared in the campaign and in the early months of his presidency to be central not only to his political agenda but to him personally? What does the story of the faith-based initiative say about American political institutions and American public life in general?

This book is largely a narrative of the ups and downs of the faith-based issue from the 2000 election campaign to the end of the president's first two years in office, telling a story in loose chronological order. But as the authors, we have found an analytical framework helpful in understanding and writing the story—a framework that views the faith-based issue through three lenses: a public policy lens, a political party lens, and a lens of religion in the public square. We believe that these three lenses will bring order and understanding to the narrative and help the reader follow the complexity of the faith-based story, offering a chance for relating the case study to larger issues in American public life.

Public Policy Process

Normally a new idea grows for years and years before manifesting itself. With charitable choice, it's the complete opposite. It just sort of passed into law.

Carl Esbeck, in National Journal

The faith-based story is, first, a story of policymaking. The textbook treatment of policymaking separates the process into several sequential steps.[16] The process begins with an identification of a problem suitable for government action, as opposed to a problem that, however severe or important, cannot be handled by government. The next phase is getting that problem on the public agenda, so that governments, voters, and the media will see it as suitable for a government-directed response. In the third step, a wide range of political actors formulate potential solutions. Out of this variety of possibilities, one potential solution is selected and legitimated—this fourth step is marked by a new law enacted after an open and accessible legislative process that subjects the problem and its proposed solutions to public scrutiny. Executive branch agencies implement these new laws in the next step, and, in time, the policy enters the sixth and final step as laws undergo evaluation by the agencies and a wide range of other actors, including Congress, the media, and the public at large.

Textbook public policy theory explains how the basic elements of American government and politics interact. Elections theoretically ratify the policy choices of the winners, providing a list of agenda items. The president and Congress develop potential solutions to items on the agenda. In its open and accessible legislative process, Congress studies, debates, and eventually selects one of those solutions, a critical step in legitimization. Congress, too, theoretically plays a role in policy evaluation once the chosen solution has been tried for a sufficient length of time so that an assessment can be made.

The president is regularly involved at all times. He campaigns on a policy agenda. He repeatedly promotes proposals while in office; he participates in the legislative process; and under his authority the executive branch implements a legislated solution. The federal courts legitimate policy by stating that proposed solutions do or do not conform to constitutional guidelines. Courts also open up new policy avenues for exploration by making declarations about the constitutionality and suitability of related approaches in different fields. For example, the *Zelman* decision of 2002 declared that private school vouchers funded by state governments were constitutional.[17] It opened up the possibility that other levels of government could subsidize other privately delivered social services besides education.

Theory in Real Life

Of course, life isn't like even the best textbook model. Sometimes policies skip steps; other times a particular issue is involved in several steps simultaneously. The real-life story of the faith-based initiative, seen through the policymaking lens, is a case in point. The Bush administration's first two years with faith-based involved the White House, simultaneously, in two steps of the policy process. There was a difficult *legitimization* process attached to new legislation and an unusually transparent *implementation* process for previously enacted faith-based provisions that had been ignored by the Clinton administration.

On January 21, 2001, President Bush's first day in office, the federal government was already authorized to implement charitable choice language in four different laws, the keystone of past faith-based initiatives and a part of the new president's own plans to promote faith-based organizations. Charitable choice had first become federal law in the 1996 welfare reform act. The specific charitable choice language of that act had barely been debated in Congress because welfare reform was dominated by much larger issues such as overall spending levels and ending welfare as an entitlement. Charitable choice language was added fairly late in the years-long legislative process, avoiding almost entirely the legislative and public scrutiny that is supposed to characterize the first several steps of policymaking. Similar charitable choice language was later added to three other pieces of legislation enacted in the Clinton years; each time the provision attracted only slightly more attention. Because President Clinton had done little to encourage federal or state compliance with charitable choice provisions in any of these laws, the new Bush administration was faced with the unusual opportunity of being free to implement a virtually dormant current law that they supported and on which the president had campaigned. It was a daunting task, but at least it was near the end of the policy process and, for lawmaking purposes, a *fait accompli*. The four politically tougher policy tasks, from problem identification to policy legitimization, were completed for several federal programs, including huge expanses of federal welfare policy.

But that, of course, is not the whole policy story. *Candidate* Bush had campaigned on ending what he described as long-standing, pervasive, and severe government discrimination against faith-based organizations seeking like other nongovernmental groups to provide government-funded services. Ending such antireligious discrimination in order to unleash and empower "armies of compassion" was the critical component of candidate Bush's compassionate conservative agenda. By all indications it was a fitting policy initiative. As governor of Texas, Bush had been a champion of including faith-based groups as government service providers, speedily implementing federal charitable choice policies already on the books and mimicking their provisions in state law. Governor Bush's personal life reinforced his public policy; by his own account, the younger George Bush had his life turned around with a sudden and deep personal religious commitment.

In a political world where successful candidates must turn campaign promises into legislative proposals, *President* Bush thus had to offer a faith-based initiative the size and implications of which seemed proportional to his campaign rhetoric. Conventional political wisdom forced the president and his allies in Congress to begin a new faith-based policy process, whereas the facts of the issue indicated that the executive branch should focus on implementing current law. But campaign promises suggested a new policy process: the new administration had to identify a problem for which faith-based initiatives were a solution, argue for its place on the agenda, propose their mostly predetermined solution as the best available alternative, and then get it legitimated in legislation.

The new process did not go well. Republicans in the House and Senate had different interests and objectives from the White House and from each other; the Senate soon came under Democratic control; internal decisions were poorly made; and external events slowed and eventually stopped momentum for a faith-based bill. The House Republican leadership was able to ram an ambitious faith-based bill through in mid-2001, but Senate supporters of faith-based action could not exert enough internal or grassroots pressure to get even a watered-down faith-based bill to the Senate floor. The faith-based legislative effort started with a bang and ended with worse than a whimper—silence. President Bush had to resort to an executive order, in the middle of the 2002 religious holiday season, to implement only a small portion of the original faith-based plan—relatively weak guidelines to make sure federal agencies would not discriminate against a narrowly defined set of faith-based groups when contracting for services. By the end of 2002, the White House had not yet succeeded in expanding charitable choice, increasing tax benefits, or distributing much compassion capital funding.

The rough, lengthy, and ultimately futile legislative road impeded the implementation of existing laws, because it heightened congressional, media, and interest-group awareness of charitable choice's controversies. Staff in the White House Office of Faith-Based and Community Initiatives and its five satellite offices knew that any sudden moves to implement prior laws would be lightning rods for negative publicity. So legitimization of new provisions and implementation of old provisions became politically codependent. Even the small steps of the December 2002 executive order were taken after Congress adjourned, before a large sympathetic audience in Philadelphia (where the order was announced), and a handful of days before the Christmas holiday.

Political Party Competition

> By an almost two-to-one ratio, the public is more likely to associate Republicans with "faith in God." ... [T]he most secular-oriented voters support Democrats by more than two to one, but the more numerous regular churchgoers support Republicans by a like ratio.
>
> *Stanley and Anna Greenberg, in* The American Prospect

> GOPers now tout the [faith-based] initiative as a way to attract black support.
>
> *Jeffrey H. Birnbaum, in* Fortune *magazine*

The faith-based story is also a story about competition—competition between Republicans and Democrats for blocs of voters, and competition within each party for policy priorities and public images. The two major political parties are at virtual parity today at the national level, and have been so for nearly three decades. Such an extended time of parity is actually quite unusual in American politics. For the almost 150 years that Republicans and Democrats have been America's major parties, one or the other has been for a time a fairly reliable majority. From after the Civil War until the early decades of the twentieth century, the Republican Party dominated; the Depression of the 1930s ushered in a Democratic majority until the late 1960s, when fissures caused by the Vietnam War and civil rights legislation started to fracture the once solid Democratic South.

History implies that the GOP should have reestablished itself in the 1970s as a reliable majority party. That did not happen, in part because of Richard Nixon and Watergate, and then either because of, or in spite of (depending on one's political views), Ronald Reagan and his legacy of purer social and economic conservatism. Republicans have dominated the presidency since 1968, but the Democrats held the Congress from the 1950s to the 1990s. Then the sides seemed to switch. Bill Clinton survived a full eight years in the White House, and in 1994 Republicans won House and Senate majorities for the first time in forty years. In 2000, Republicans were once again trying to establish themselves as the nation's majority—what they saw as a too-long-delayed natural order of things. Democrats, on the other hand, were trying to continue their hold on the White House and gain back the Congress they had controlled almost always since World War II.

Each side tried a slightly new strategy to achieve its objective, and the faith-based initiative was an element of the strategy on both sides. Republican elites thought that faith-based might allow them to attract a few more highly religious African American and Hispanic voters; gaining only a few more percentage points in these groups would assure a GOP majority. In addition, Republican support for social services might attract a few more ethnic white Catholic voters and keep in the fold upper-income suburban women, the "soccer moms" who were starting to vote Democratic by significant margins because they saw the GOP becoming too socially conservative. The initiative seemed a good idea to Republican strategists trying to change the caricature of their party as one beholden to white evangelical Protestant males, without actually offending any members of that group. The initiative's overt support for intense and vocal religion seemed consistent with the views of the white Protestant base, yet its emphasis on aiding the poor would help with moderate whites, Catholics, and even racial minorities who would be the prime beneficiaries of faith-based funds.

Some Democratic elites, mostly from the moderate Democratic Leadership Council (DLC), thought that supporting faith-based initiatives was a good idea for their party, too. It might help inoculate the Gore–Lieberman ticket from lingering character concerns about Bill Clinton.

In addition, a frequent internal critique of the Democratic Party was that the public was becoming increasingly convinced that national Democratic leaders seemed uncomfortable with religious language and with issues important to voters, including many traditional Democrats who held deep religious beliefs.[18] A Democratic presidential ticket with a faith-based plank might also address this more systemic problem.

The political party lens also helps illuminate some intra-party competition on faith-based issues, showing how campaign consensus can deteriorate into congressional stalemate. Each major political party has become more ideologically uniform in the past few decades. New recruits at both the mass and the elite level have made Republicans more uniformly conservative and overtly religious, and Democrats more uniformly liberal and secular. Simultaneously, party officials and other party elites such as convention delegates, elected officials, and grassroots leaders, tend to be more ideologically extreme than the average party voter. That is, newer Democratic Party elites and leaders of their closely aligned interest groups have more extremely liberal views and looser ties to traditional religion than typical Democratic voters and older activists, while newer Republican Party elites and their closely aligned interest groups are more extremely conservative and religious than typical Republican voters and older GOP activists.[19]

These differences within and between the parties are muted during campaigns as each party attempts to appeal to undecided middle-of-the-road voters. The faith-based initiative's popularity in the campaign, and much of its unraveling afterward, can be explained by the change of venue—its moving from the outside-the-Beltway campaign arena where each party's message is simplified and targeted at the same group of moderates, to the inside-the-Beltway policymaking arena that is controlled by more extreme party and interest-group leaders.

Another part of the partisan story is the conflict between old, new, and potentially ascendant elites within each political party. Most of the recent GOP fights have been between economic conservatives with long ties to the party who emphasize economic and size-of-government issues, and social conservatives with shorter historic ties to Republicans who focus on cultural issues such as abortion, homosexuality, and the family. At first glance, the faith-based initiative seems to be another issue pushed by the social conservatives, inspiring initial skepticism from GOP economic conservatives. Upon closer examination, however, it is clear that the initiative does not advance the core interest of cultural conservatives: its view of government is more sympathetic and its intended beneficiaries, the poor and those who serve them directly, are not exactly traditional Republican voters.

The biblical book of Hebrews defines faith as "the substance of things hoped for, the evidence of things not seen." Bush's faith-based initiative clearly was an act of faith trying to form a new political coalition. It was targeted to a hoped-for element of an emerging GOP rainbow coalition of conservatism—no evidence for which could be seen in the election of 2000.

The Public Square and Religion

Many Federal policies and practices—including regulations, guidelines, program materials, decision-making criteria, awards-committee viewpoints, etc.—go well beyond sensible constitutional restrictions and what the courts have required, sharply restricting the equal opportunity for faith-based charities to seek and receive Federal support.

White House Office of Faith-Based and Community Initiatives

Bush's plan is the single greatest assault on church-state separation in modern American history. The First Amendment was intended to create a separation between religion and government, not a massive new bureaucracy that unites the two.

Barry Lynn, Americans United for Separation of Church and State

A third important lens through which to understand the faith-based story looks at a philosophical question: What is the proper place of religion and faith in the American public square? There is much dispute over what the Constitution permits, and even more disagreement over what is good for the American political system. Seeing how these grand-scale philosophical questions are linked to the rather modest faith-based proposal requires knowing some additional details about the proposal and about current law and regulation.

Three-Part Initiative

President Bush's faith-based initiative is, in fact, many proposals intended to expand the variety of religiously affiliated social services that receive financial help from the federal government. It has three basic objectives. The first two emphasize two major but different barriers to increasing the variety of religious groups that get direct and indirect government support. A third objective is to help charitable groups far more generally.

The first objective is to change current government practices—sometimes explicit but more often hidden—that exclude certain groups from getting government support because these groups are, in a variety of ways, "too religious." Sometimes faith-based groups are discouraged by government from even applying for federal funds because, for example, their name or location is deemed too religious. Proponents of current practices say these processes help preserve the wall of separation between church and state; opponents say they perpetuate discrimination against religion.

FOCAL POINT I.1

"Religiously Affiliated" Catholic Charities

Catholic Charities has the unusual distinction of being cited by both detractors and proponents of President Bush's faith-based initiatives. Proponents cite Catholic Charities as an example of how religious groups can successfully operate social service programs, and they go on to argue that all faith-based groups should have the chance to do so. Detractors of the initiative agree that Catholic Charities is a fine example of a faith-based group doing effective work. Because it and similar faith-based groups already receive federal funds, however, they argue that the president's new ideas are not needed.

Catholic Charities has existed in the United States for nearly three hundred years. It is the largest faith-based provider network in the country and has been contracting with the federal government for over a century. In 2000, the Charities provided services for over seven million individuals through more than 1,600 branch agencies. The range of human needs met by Catholic Charities included the basics of hunger, shelter, and clothing, and more complex services such as disaster response, socialization, refugee resettlement, counseling, education, health care, adoption, treatment for substance addiction, and the prevention of child abuse and neglect.

Defenders of the status quo in faith-based service provision describe Catholic Charities as an organization able to provide necessary social services while maintaining its religious core, despite abiding by prohibitions against proselytization and worship in the social services it provides. Catholic Charities and groups like it that abide by such restrictions are usually called "religiously affiliated" groups and are not part of the "faith-based" groups brought into play by President Bush's proposals. Richard Mockler, the executive director of Catholic Charities of California, does not feel that the Charities' position contradicts the Catholic faith, but is rather an "expression of respect for the dignity of each person that we serve."

Catholic Charities does more than simply provide social services. National leaders are quite forthcoming about the group's three-pronged mission to provide services for people in need, to advocate for justice in social structures, and to call the church and other people of good will to do the same. Former Charities president Fred Kammer, S.J., has identified certain "essentials" that keep the organization loyal to the Catholic faith. The first essential is the biblical concept of justice: the Charities continue to help the "widow, orphan, and stranger" for whom the ancient Jewish peoples were commanded by God to care. Catholic Charities continues to primarily aid poor women, children, and marginalized individuals who are outside the mainstream of society because of their foreign origin, race, or disability.

Kammer argues that the absence of religious proselytization in Catholic Charities programs reflects a faith-formed determination to serve everyone in need. He quotes Pope John Paul II, who in his address to the Pontifical Council in 1997 described appropriate Catholic giving this way: "Actions of aid, relief, and assistance should be conducted in a spirit of service and free giving for the benefit of all persons without the ulterior motive of eventual tutelage or proselytism."

Catholic Charities also secures its religious basis by requiring member organizations to be bound by a Code of Ethics explicitly grounded in "Scriptures, papal encyclicals, synodical and other documents." Member organizations must hold to "sanctity and dignity of human life, . . . a preference for serving the neediest and most vulnerable, . . . [and a commitment to] be faithful to Biblical values, the social teaching of the Church, and the relevant sections of the code of Canon Law."

One claim made about faith-based organizations receiving government funding is that these organizations might temper their criticism of government in fear of losing access to funds. Catholic Charities appears not to have responded that way. It repeatedly makes pronouncements on government policies especially in the domestic arena. One of its statements against President Bush's 2003 economic stimulus proposal, for example, stated that "another round of tax cuts may leave governments . . . unable to play their essential roles in promoting the common good and preserving essential community services and supports. . . . "

Catholic Charities has broad support in the public and among the centrists in the faith-based debate. But it also draws some fire from the extremes on the left and the right. Some on the left dislike its obviously religious name and the religiously based arguments it uses for its work. Some on the right accuse Catholic Charities of compromising its faith by limiting its expression in the services it delivers. In the midst of it all, Catholic Charities perseveres in its work and its leaders actively participate in the political system.

—Melissa Fritsch

Sources

Catholic Charities website. www.catholiccharitiesusa.org (accessed 21 January 2003).

Catholic Charities of California website. www.cccalifornia.org/articles/10131.html (accessed 21 January 2003).

The legislative proposal that President Bush pushed to combat what he viewed as antireligious discrimination was to expand charitable choice to more federal programs. Charitable choice would require federal administrators of covered programs to allow almost all religious organizations to apply to provide federally funded services on the same basis as other providers, without compromising the religious viewpoint and character of the newly applying religious organizations. Three types of providers were targeted for help. Highly evangelical providers—groups that seek to tell clients about a particular religious faith and urge them to join it—composed one set of groups that President Bush wanted to make eligible. Many service providers that treat clients by urging upon them traditional moral beliefs and behaviors, rather than applying modern professionally developed techniques, were a second group Bush wanted to aid. Typically these providers are staffed by clergy and other religiously credentialed persons delivering services that a secular agency might provide through staff trained more specifically in a particular helping profession. Third, the president also wished to support otherwise professional and nonevangelical social services provided by church staff and based in houses of worship. Many churches provide office space for professional social service providers and some place professionally credentialed service providers on church payrolls. Many of these groups are currently not eligible for federal funds. Charitable choice made clear that churches hosting all types of providers—evangelical, those urging traditional morality, and professional secular groups—could apply for federal aid without changing their names or organizational structures or "scrubbing" their buildings to remove religious imagery. They merely needed to offer a program that addressed the social problem the government was targeting and to ensure that no direct federal funds would go to inherently religious activities like worship. To charitable choice proponents, the new proposals help end bigoted and constitutionally unnecessary government discrimination against intensely and vocally religious groups. To charitable choice opponents, current practice screens out groups that would likely misuse federal funds for worship or recruitment, would operate inferior programs, or would run roughshod over constitutional guidelines.

A second objective of the president's faith-based initiative was to lessen the disadvantages that smaller, less established, and less credentialed social service providers confront when they do compete for federal funds. He wished to provide "compassion capital funds" to small community and faith-based groups so they could develop or hire the expertise to apply for federal funds. Compassion capital funds would be targeted to smaller, newer, and volunteer-intensive groups—provider categories full of faith-based entities and often located in houses of worship. In the eyes of those who support this objective, the federal government should actively assist these service providers to get the most effective and efficient social services and, when faith-based groups are involved, to avoid antireligious bias. Advocates of compassion capital funds claim that such funds help "level the playing field," making fairer the competition between current (usually large) federal contractors and those who are not yet (but ought to be) providing services with government help. Opponents argue that compassion capital is a direct and impermissible government subsidy of religion.

A third objective of the faith-based initiative is to provide assistance to all charitable groups—not just faith-based and not just those involved in social services—through new tax incentives. The most costly element of this third emphasis would be a charitable contribution tax deduction for taxpayers who do not itemize deductions; under current practice, only taxpayers who complete and return a separate itemized deduction page with their tax returns can take such deductions. Other tax code changes benefit corporations or individuals in special circumstances, such as individuals who hold large retirement savings and would like to help charitable groups.

President Bush described the entire bundle of proposals with these three objectives as his faith-based initiative, even though the objectives and proposals are quite distinct from each other and address different problems facing nongovernmental groups that might provide government-supported social services.

Why Controversy?

How this trinity of faith-based proposals turned into a three-headed political monster is, at first impression, puzzling. Many of the ideas, such as expanding charitable tax breaks, are without controversy if only money can be found. And few people object in principle to providing technical assistance that would enable smaller and newer social service providers to tap into the federal funding process, so long as the technical help is distributed without regard to the religious character of providers.

Likewise, the scope of the controversial charitable choice proposal in the faith-based initiative is quite narrow. Charitable choice tinkers with federal government contracting practices—a part of policymaking that rarely gets a newspaper mention or television news blurb, much less focused media attention or rallies in Washington, D.C. And while the controversial provision makes numerous faith-based and community-based social service programs newly eligible to apply for federal support, there is no guarantee that any such group would get money.

Charitable choice and, to a lesser extent, the compassion capital fund have, however, broad implications for the interaction between government and religion. In the faith-based debate of President Bush's first two years, both supporters and opponents moved quickly to discuss these broader implications, simultaneously deepening and distorting what was at stake. Expanding charitable choice by welcoming a broader array of religious groups into federally funded programs would clearly mean closer cooperation between government and religion. The underlying premise of expansion is that America should welcome more religious voices in the public square—new voices more openly religious than those now accepted. And the compassion capital part of the faith-based initiative assumes that small social service providers, often operated by faith-related groups and even houses of worship, are worthy of receiving federal funds.

Thus, the small proposed changes lead to large policy questions. Some questions involve cooperation between religion and government: What are the benefits and liabilities to government and religion in moving toward closer cooperation? Is it prudent or even constitutional to give religious beliefs and groups more official sanction and support than they now enjoy? Will faith-based groups be satisfied with a small corner of the public square or will they soon take it over? Does helping faith-based groups in the short run harm them in the long run—for example, by reducing their effectiveness and independence? Other questions involve the effectiveness and efficiency of the groups that might become newly eligible for federal support: Are such organizations as effective as or more effective than groups currently receiving federal aid? How do we know? If faith plays a visible role in a program, is that a key to its performance or an unnecessary addition that can be made optional for program participants without any decline in quality or effectiveness? If faith-based social service providers are more successful and religion is the key to that success, does the Constitution or common sense allow federal funds to flow to these groups? Why should scarce federal funds be diverted to these new providers without compelling constitutional and empirical evidence?

Controversial Types of Religious Organizations

In large part, charitable choice and compassion capital are controversial *not* because they provide government funds to religious social services for the first time. They raise hackles because they would allow *new types* of religion into the public square by means of government subsidies for their operations.

Since the founding of the Republic, the federal government has cooperated with religious groups that provide social services. Direct and indirect government financial support has grown in the twentieth century as government has played a growing role in providing social services. In 1996, as a typical year, Catholic Charities USA received $1.3 billion (or 64 percent) of its income from government sources. That same year the Salvation Army received $245 million (16 percent) of its income from the government, and the YMCA $203 million (8 percent). Nationwide, Lutheran Social Ministries received 92 percent of its revenue from government in a recent year.[20]

Conviction, Circumstances, Content

For the most part, however, the government has funded services provided by only certain types of religious providers, and that is the root of the controversy. For purposes of understanding the faith-based debate, it is useful to characterize religious providers by the depth of their religious *conviction* in operating a program, by the transparency of the religious *circumstances* of the program, and by the *content* of the program itself.

The federal government has no interest in the depth of conviction to religious faith of a social service provider. The government regularly funds social service providers that are managed by and staffed with persons of deep religious conviction, even if the services purchased are without religious content. What matters is that the conviction must remain hidden—the program must be secular, whether it is run by a secular agency or by one with a religious affiliation. To argue that President Bush's faith-based initiative would for the first time open federal programs to religiously committed groups (as both proponents and opponents have sometimes argued) belittles presently funded service providers whose unannounced but deeply held religious convictions compel them to provide social services.

The federal government has, however, been quite interested in the religious circumstances of programs. By circumstances we mean elements like the location, physical surroundings, and organizational affiliations of a program provider, and not the content of the program itself. Generally, the government has been unwilling to fund programs operated in explicitly religious locations such as churches, or by groups easily identified as religious by their names, staff or board members, or organizational affiliation. The government has feared that such groups have a pervasively religious atmosphere and that providing them with federal funds would indicate that, regardless of the content of the service, government supports religion generally and the particular religious faiths being funded. In addition, current policy takes into account that a religious atmosphere or an obvious if unstated religious commitment by the provider might pressure the beneficiary to adopt the same religious commitment. In situations like these, the chance of violating many persons' understanding of the appropriate church-state relationship is high. As such, federal contracting procedures have generally not encouraged, and often explicitly prohibited, the provision of funds to church-based groups or highly confessional groups housed in any location. President Bush's faith-based initiative sought to open federal funding to such groups. The CARE Act proposed in the Senate, and the president's December 2002 executive order, essentially tell executive agencies to ignore the circumstances of social service delivery in making contracts for social services.

FOCAL POINT I.2

"Pervasively Sectarian" InnerChange Freedom Initiative

The InnerChange Freedom Initiative (IFI) is a prisoner rehabilitation and antirecidivism program of Prison Fellowship Ministries. Prison Fellowship is itself an evangelical Christian organization founded in 1975 by Watergate villain turned born-again Christian Charles Colson, a favorite speaker on the politically and religiously conservative circuit and a strong advocate for evangelical Christianity in the public square.

InnerChange works to bring down recidivism rates by working intensely in prison with prisoners who are scheduled for later release. Patterned after a similar program Colson first discovered while visiting prisons in Brazil, IFI is the first program of its kind in the United States. Bringing the Christian message of God's boundless love and grace is at the core of IFI's program content. Under a rigorous schedule that runs from 5:30 a.m. to 10:00 p.m. each day, participating convicts study the Bible and learn biblical principles for living responsibly from trained IFI staff. The program is more comprehensive than just Bible study, including such elements as job training, community service, reconciliation with crime victims, restitution for crimes, and mentoring of prisoners by Christians from nearby churches. The primary goal of the IFI program is to effect a lasting personal transformation in inmates through a religious conversion experience based in orthodox evangelical Christianity. If the conversion experience is lasting and true, IFI claims that prisoners will not return to their previous life of crime. As such, the religious goal of conversion meets the secular goal of reducing recidivism.

The central focus of the InnerChange program—personal religious conviction—is a prime example of a "pervasively sectarian" program, since (as journalists Hanna Rosin and Terry Neal note) it "embodies all the potential of the faith-based movement, as well as its complications. From its name to every class it sponsors, the program is explicit about its proselytizing mission," to bring prisoners to a religious faith based in Christianity. IFI is an explicitly religious group, and it would not be possible to remove or separate out the program's religious elements, or make them optional for clients, and still retain the program's identity.

As Texas governor, George W. Bush strongly supported Inner-Change's work in Texas prisons. It was under his leadership that the first Texas IFI program began in 1997, when Prison Fellowship Ministries partnered with the Texas Department of Criminal Justice to open an IFI "pod" in the Carol S. Vance Unit near Houston. Other IFI programs have since opened in Iowa, Kansas, and Minnesota. As governor, Bush demonstrated his personal commitment to the program early on, visiting the Texas pod in October 1997 with Charles Colson and singing "Amazing Grace" with the inmate choir. As reported by the *Washington Post*, Bush "helped shepherd Inner-Change into his state when no other state would accept it. On the 2000 campaign trail, Bush regularly praised Texas's work with IFI as a prototype for church-state cooperation that he would apply to a range of federal services if elected president."

The essence of the IFI movement is the idea that individual faith experiences can reduce the ills of society. The program's purpose of "inner change" is expected to have the subsequent benefit of lower rates of recidivism, and preliminary studies suggest this is the case. The most comprehensive research on the program to date, Byron Johnson's study that followed Houston participants at least two years after their release from prison, found that IFI graduates are significantly less likely than nonparticipants to be rearrested or reincarcerated. Not everyone is convinced by these data, however. Critics look at these same studies, raise methodological concerns, and suggest further research is needed before making any firm conclusions about IFI.

Under the terms of most partnerships with state-run prisons, Prison Fellowship, and not the state government, pays IFI staff. Inmates are given an informed choice to enter the IFI program or choose nonreligious alternatives. The state government continues to provide the inmates in IFI with the basics for living (food, housing, and clothing) in a prison setting. Some IFI programs, such as those in Kansas and Iowa, also receive government funding for additional nonreligious elements, such as job training or substance abuse treatment.

As president, George W. Bush has remained one of IFI's strongest supporters, frequently citing InnerChange as the type of program that would benefit most from his faith-based initiatives. Bush's specific references to IFI frighten some critics of faith-based, who point to the program's intense religiosity. Other observers raise the concern that the focus on pervasively sectarian programs might lead to overlooking the many less intensely religious, and less controversial, programs that would also benefit from the president's faith-based ideas.

—Dawn K. Crowell

Sources

InnerChange Freedom Initiative website. www.ifiprison.org (accessed 19 July 2002).

Johnson, Byron. "The InnerChange Freedom Initiative: A Preliminary Evaluation of a Faith-Based Prison Program." Center for Research on Religion and Urban Civil Society at the University of Pennsylvania, Philadelphia, Pa., June 2003.

Jones, Jim. "Unique Prison Program Serves as Boot Camp for Heaven." *Christianity Today* 42, no. 2 (9 February 1998): 88.

Marks, Alexandra. "A Spiritual Approach to Time Behind Bars." *Christian Science Monitor*, 16 April 2001. www.csmonitor.com/durable/2001/04/16/fp1s4-csm.shtml.

Rosin, Hanna, and Terry M. Neal. "Converting Convicts to Christians: Texas Blesses Use of Strict 'Christ-Centered' Agenda at Small Prison." *Washington Post*, 27 November 1999, A1.

The federal government has also been concerned about program *content* and has, as a rule, barred funds to explicitly religious programs. Whether particular content is religious or not, however, is quite subjective. A program might be infused with religious principles but not focused on religious conversion. A remedial reading program, for example, might use stories from the Bible as readings but do nothing to encourage beneficiaries to convert to a biblical faith. Religious content, in another case, might be more evangelical, explicitly urging persons to convert to a religious faith that, for example, calls one to depend upon Jesus for aid in treating an infirmity. The former example is probably constitutional; the latter most likely not. The Supreme Court is clear that the government cannot directly fund social service programs that seek *with those funds* to convert individuals to particular religious beliefs. Even when it is administratively possible to separate government and private funds and thus fund the nonreligious parts of an evangelical program, the federal government has almost always chosen not to do so because the risk of perceived endorsement of religion is too high. This is one reason why programs such as the InnerChange prisoner rehabilitation program are so controversial. President Bush's faith-based initiative would allow the funding of such religious programs and would simultaneously prohibit federal funds from being spent for "inherently religious activities" like worship or scripture study. But it is not clear exactly how, or whether, such a guideline could work in the case of a program such as InnerChange. Essentially, Bush's proposals trust the funded group to separate funds and programs between sacred and secular purposes and use government funds only for secular purposes.

Public Square Theory in Practical Terms

Some faith-based initiative proponents argue that many social service providers described as "nonreligious" actually seek to convert their clients to secular ways of behavior and thought that are functional equivalents of religion.[21] All social service treatments, so this argument goes, begin with a fundamental worldview that makes assumptions about human nature, the roots of social problems, the relevance of the supernatural, and related matters. If the federal government only funds nonreligious programs, it is really funding a particular, secular*ist* view of reality. To be truly nondiscriminatory toward religion, this argument contends, federal programs must be open to self-identified religious providers as well as these "functional-equivalents" providers.

Opponents generally did not engage this philosophical point in the rough and tumble of legislative jockeying and administrative rulemaking. The point is somewhat obscure intellectually, and the everyday limitations of American political debates do not lend themselves well to subtleties. These limitations are inevitable and understandable, but we think they are regrettable because this philosophical point is at the root of the religion-in-the-public-square question. However, two major controversies that have been extensively aired in the faith-based debate are related to the underlying philosophical question about what constitutes religion; these and related questions help get at the deeper content.

Is Traditional Religion Uniquely Dangerous or Vulnerable?

The first controversy is whether traditional religion is a particularly, perhaps uniquely, dangerous or vulnerable element in public policy debates and government activities. Most opponents of faith-based initiatives assume, consciously or unconsciously, that robust traditional religion is dangerous in the public square of American politics and policy. Barry Lynn of Americans United has characterized the leading figures of politically conservative religious groups as "media-dominating far-right activists" who "seek to end democracy, real moral choice, and true religious freedom, and replace them with a theocracy."[22] From this perspective, religion is by nature, or at least frequently in practice, intolerant, coercive, and imperialistic. Traditional religion, because it makes claims about ultimate truths, cannot be committed to liberal pluralism, the starting point for democratic politics. Rather, from this view, religion operates as an exclusivist ideology that is inconsistent with America's secular and tolerant public arena, where decisions are made democratically, pragmatically, and provisionally. Once religion, as religion, gets in the public square, so the argument goes, it will inevitably seek dominance for its truths and silence its critics. To the extent that the president's faith-based initiative gives greater government respect to and support for religion, it ought to be opposed, for that is the beginning of the end for American democratic pluralism.

Other opponents of the faith-based initiative have almost the opposite view of religion—that it is too vulnerable to thrive in the public square debates. They seek to protect organized religion from involvement in government and politics, fearing that such entanglements will sap religion of its central, spiritual power and divert it from its main tasks of worshipping God and saving individuals' souls. These opponents, smaller in number but no less sincere than those worried about the dangers of religion, have joined with the larger group to form a powerful and persuasive coalition against the president's faith-based initiatives.

On the other side of the debate, faith-based proponents tend to believe religion invigorates public square debates about politics and policy.[23] To them, religion brings essential elements of conviction and clarity. Religious talk resonates with most of the American public, which is still highly religious, helping to explain issues in language the public understands and to bind the American people to public structures. And while religion does make claims about ultimate truth, most religions emphasize that, at least in this present, imperfect world, knowledge of absolute truth is partial and incomplete. Religion, even more than secular ideologies in this view, provides a check on intolerance because it is ultimately humble about human abilities to know right from wrong. Proponents argue that there is no greater arrogance than that of secular intellectuals who irrationally believe that they alone are rational and nonreligious. In contemporary American politics, this argument contends, persons of faith speaking as such have been essentially excluded from public debate. All religion wants and deserves is a more secure place in the almost completely secularist public square; taking over the public square is neither possible nor desirable. In fact, from this perspective religious persons are less likely to be tyrants than secular ones precisely because religion sets limits on politics and worldly affairs. A successful faith-based initiative, according to this view, would help to secure at least a small place for religion in the public square, enhancing pluralism, diversity, and even tolerance.

Is Traditional Religion Inferior?

Whether one agrees with the arguments of one side or the other, it is important to note that the faith-based debate involves actors with biases for or against a larger place for religion in public debates. A second and related disagreement is whether social services mixed with strong doses of religion are inferior or superior to social services with no religion. Most faith-based opponents tend to believe that intensely faith-based social services are inferior in theory and practice—likely to be unscientific, ineffective, and unprofessional. The faith-based initiative, so it goes, invites quackery and abuse, especially if it allows the government to fund social services that do not have all the oversight and credentialing requirements that apply to present providers. To preserve the quality of social services in general, and those funded by government in particular, one should oppose the president's faith-based initiative. Other opponents of the faith-based initiative support the work of faith-based groups, but think that government contracts would sap much of the vitality and power of key social ministries. They worry that faith-based social services would become preoccupied with the narrow quantifiable measures that concern government overseers—how many clients were served in a day, how was each government dollar used, how was every federally funded minute spent, and so on—rather than the more essential task, in their view, of (for example) converting people to a life of religious faith. Again, these two sets of faith-based initiative opponents, with quite different motivations, have aided each other in the fight against the president's ideas.

On the other side, faith-based proponents argue that intensely religious treatments are effective and even superior supplements to or replacements for conventional secular treatments. Adding a religious dimension to more traditional treatment methods may more completely address the causes of many social problems, they say. Further, religious conversion may help some individuals who might not otherwise be helped. Overtly religious persons may deliver services more effectively or efficiently than others by, for example, bringing a greater understanding of the problem or deeper dedication to service. Thus, this side of the argument goes, even if one is only concerned about effectiveness, faith-based treatments should be welcomed and at least given a chance to prove their value.

The Controversy of Group Rights

These two controversies introduce a third and much less noticed aspect of the faith-based debate and one that complicates its proponents' arguments: the implied assertion of group rights. In the faith-based debate, proponents argue for a religious group's right to undertake services, for religious reasons, that the modern American welfare state has typically assigned to government.

America does not have a well-developed language of group rights; our jurisprudence and political discussions focus on the individual. The Bill of Rights has been interpreted to guarantee primarily the freedom of persons. The First Amendment freedom of religion, especially, has been most readily recognized and easily secured for lone individuals, not groups.

Proponents of group rights have not fared well in American politics, even when advocating for groups widely acknowledged as subjects of discrimination. Affirmative action, a sort of "group right" for racial and ethnic minorities, has always been controversial. In the 1992 election, for example, candidate Bill Clinton felt it necessary to distance himself from this policy. And one need only remember the unhappy fate of his early choice for attorney general, Lani Guinier, who favored group rights in some racial and ethnic voting situations, to realize that even thoughtful discussions of group rights are open to misunderstanding and ridicule. Between the two major parties, group rights have been far less attractive to Republicans and conservatives who, more frequently than Democrats and liberals, hold to individualistic assumptions. In many ways, the faith-based debate is about allowing religious groups to define the scope of their religious calling and to be rewarded like any other group if that calling compels them to deliver social services.

Religious Group Rights

Asserting rights for religious groups combines the controversies of group rights with widely held concerns about religion. Faith-based proponents essentially argue for the right of religious persons to band together as an openly religious group to perform social services that arise out of religious conviction, and to receive government support and sanction on those terms. The argument here is that religion is not mere individual belief; it is also a belonging, a group belonging. Religious individuals and groups express their faith in public action, not merely in private belief and action. Religious conviction about social problems requires group effort and organization. From this view, a religious community providing social services is appropriate and often even required by religious faith. Additionally, supporters of this side of the debate contend that beneficiaries of social services are also often religious, and these persons should have the option to receive services infused with religion. Surely, they conclude, the government should treat fairly these individual wishes and corporate expressions of faith, especially if they are wanted and useful. Such supporters would say that failure to fund openly religious social services discriminates against religion and religious adherents.

In contrast, opponents sometimes argue that faith-based social services are often little more than schemes to convert target populations to dangerous sectarian views. Bush's faith-based initiative would, on this view, fund religion and religious conversion with federal dollars. Each religion's goal, so this argument goes, is to promote its belief system and discredit the belief systems of others. Faith-based social services, then, appear from this position to be deceptive weapons in religious wars, not corporate callings of the faithful. Government's primary domestic obligation, on the other hand, is to deliver social services evenhandedly. It should deliver those services directly or, if it does so indirectly by funding others, then providers should deliver the social services in the same way as the government would. Groups that want government funds but refuse to secularize, this argument concludes, must really have religious conversion, not social service, as their primary goal.

The faith-based debate is thus also tied up in questions of group rights: rights of groups to operate in the public square as religious groups and to define the form, scope, scale, and justification of practices that they say come from religious conviction. On the one side is the argument that religion is an individual and private matter of belief. On the other side is the argument that religion is also often corporate and public and that religious persons and groups should have the freedom to define for themselves the form and expression of their faith and to be treated fairly by government in so doing.

For these and other reasons, we think that seeing the faith-based story through the religion-in-the-public-square lens is important. It helps address three underlying questions that rarely raise themselves openly in the faith-based debate: Does religion have unique characteristics that should prevent it from getting space in the public square? Are social services that are infused with religion inherently of different quality than those without religious elements? Are religious adherents' claims to group rights legitimate?

The rest of this book views the recent pieces of the faith-based story through these three lenses of public policy, partisan politics, and the public square. Most chapters offer narratives that follow chronologically the faith-based story from the campaign of 2000 through the end of 2002. Chapter 1 sets the stage for the narrative, providing important policy, judicial, administrative, and legislative history behind the major faith-based idea of the Clinton years—charitable choice. Chapter 2 chronicles the use of the faith-based initiative in both the Gore and Bush campaigns during the 2000 election. Chapters 3 and 4 tell the story of faith-based legislation in the House and the Senate, respectively, in 2001 and 2002. Covering the same period from a different angle, chapter 5 turns to the executive branch, reviewing the manifold changes in the personnel and strategy of the White House Office of Faith-Based and Community Initiatives and its five satellite offices. Chapter 6, focusing on the federal judiciary and constitutional considerations, deviates from the narrative style, commenting on important church-state developments in this "least dangerous" branch of government. The concluding chapter returns to the three lenses of analysis introduced here, discussing the lessons to be learned from the faith-based story about American government, policy-making, and the relationship between faith and politics.

One

Before the Faith-Based Initiative

Background and Disputes

Everyone was so engaged on so many issues, it started off as a blip.
Dan Katz, Americans United for Separation of Church and State, July 2002

Part of why it passed before is that the people who voted for it didn't think it would be taken seriously.
White House official involved in the faith-based initiative, December 2002

One is struck, upon meeting Carl Esbeck for the first time, by the depth of his thought, the seriousness of his purpose, and the caution and care of his speech. Ask the lanky law professor with thick graying hair and a thin moustache about faith-based initiatives and he is likely to spend the next ten minutes or more asking you to restate the query in several ways, probing how much you know about the initiatives, church-state law, and a host of related matters. The unassuming Professor Esbeck, the primary author of the original charitable choice language in the 1996 welfare reform bill, does not seem interested in showing how much he knows; to the contrary, the impression is that he wants only to say precisely the right thing with precisely the right intellectual complexity to be rightly understood. Only after Esbeck has sized up his inquisitor does he provide a response, prefaced by a long contextual introduction and illustrated at each important step by references to cases and court decisions. He seems to talk in the form of entire journal articles, footnotes included.

The Centrality of Charitable Choice

Faith-based developments in the three branches of government between 1996 and 2000 focus around charitable choice legislative language—its legislative consideration, its impact on the administration of federal programs, and its improving chances for favorable judicial consideration.

Reviewing these issues is a key to understanding the faith-based story of campaign 2000 and the 107th Congress of 2001–2002. Important, too, is seeing how faith-based initiatives fit in the history of the changing relationship between government and private entities in social service delivery. The faith-based initiative is not simple politics, law, or social science. Grasping its nuances and subtleties means understanding both the theory and the reality of constitutional lawmaking, political strategizing, public policy making, and social science evaluation. Professor Esbeck, who teaches at the University of Missouri Law School and thus hails from the same state as charitable choice's first chief Senate advocate, John Ashcroft, has been at the center of faith-based developments since charitable choice arrived on the scene in 1995. His name will surface regularly as we review the relevant history.

President Bush's push for faith-based initiatives would not be possible without prior changes in social policy that moved from centralized federal control to localized, and often faith-based, service delivery. Reaching back to the 1970s, the federal government's involvement in social service delivery has been changing. To its proponents, the national faith-based initiative looks plausible because it is a logical next step in a longer history of transformed government services, building on precedents in place at state and local levels of government. The faith-based initiative is a threatening policy development to its opponents for the same reason. To them, it cloaks in religious righteousness a trend they have opposed from its beginning three decades ago.

The faith-based initiative also tries to take advantage of the opportunity presented by the currently murky status of the First Amendment's religion clauses. The First Amendment states that "Congress shall make no law respecting an establishment of religion, or prohibiting the free exercise thereof." The first phrase is considered the "establishment clause" and the second phrase the "free exercise clause." Thomas Jefferson wrote that together the clauses required a "wall of separation" between church and state: few other Founders thought the same, nor did the federal courts for about a century and a half. Since approximately 1940, however, a Supreme Court majority has adopted Jefferson's terminology. The Court's position appeared to be changing again by the late 1980s. For faith-based advocates, that is good news. There would be no use in pursuing a closer relationship between church and state, religion and government, if it seemed unlikely that the federal courts would allow it. There are wider cracks today in the wall of separation between church and state than there have been in two generations, and proponents such as Professor Esbeck want to widen these cracks through faith-based initiatives. For faith-based opponents, the initiative serves as one battleground in a longer and larger war to return to a stricter separation of church and state.

The legislative and administrative history of early faith-based efforts, centered on implementing the charitable choice language Carl Esbeck developed, is important. The 2001–2002 debates about George W. Bush's faith-based initiatives were more prolonged and public restatements of points made while Bill Clinton was president. While the earliest charitable choice provision had been law four and a half years before the younger Bush came to office, and Clinton signed three other laws with similar provisions, by early 2001 none had been significantly implemented. This is one reason the Bush debates were both heated and inconclusive. Proponents could argue that charitable choice was virtually settled law; opponents could say that it was a new idea. Proponents could claim that there had been no implementation problems; opponents could postulate hypothetical wrongs that faith-based invited. Neither side could point to much evidence to support its claims; such evidence simply did not exist.

This chapter summarizes several key areas of background that put in context President Bush's faith-based initiative—the history of the federal government's changing involvement in social services, the changing constitutional picture, and the rise of charitable choice as an idea and as law.

Recent Trends in the Federal Government's Involvement in Social Services

Religious organizations have operated human service programs throughout our nation's history.[1] Many faith traditions assert that caring for one's neighbor is a religious obligation, and America's churches and religious voluntary organizations have always responded to that obligation. When problems related to industrialization, mass immigration, and racial tension became more complex in the late nineteenth century, religious groups answered with larger and more durable organizations. But fighting social problems alone was a losing battle. In the early and mid-twentieth century, America's religious organizations called on government to assist them in human service tasks too large and complicated to be addressed solely by private efforts.

In response, some local and state governments moved quickly to meet the growing needs in industrial America, but the federal government did not formally involve itself in welfare programs until the Great Depression of the 1930s. The Social Security Act of 1935 established the federal Aid to Dependent Children program, which gave states matching federal funds to "assist, broaden, and supervise existing mothers' aid programs." The middle decades of the twentieth century saw a marked expansion of government-funded social welfare programs, with thousands of workers and billions of dollars devoted to the cause. While government programs grew from nothing, religious efforts increased from preexisting levels.

There was no obvious end of human needs to be met. Old social problems persisted and new issues were making their way into public consciousness and onto government agendas. The late 1950s brought the civil rights movement and growing national awareness of poverty in the South, in Appalachia, and in industrial cities. Pressure built to expand government social services. In response, President Lyndon Johnson declared an "unconditional war on poverty" in his 1964 State of the Union address. More new federal social service programs, such as Job Corps, Head Start, and Medicaid, followed. A steadily improving economic climate and growing spending by these and other federal programs reduced the poverty rate significantly throughout the remainder of the 1960s and kept it fairly level until the mid-1970s. Some social problems, like poverty and illness among the elderly, saw steep declines.

Religious groups and government were often partners, formally and informally, in these Great Society efforts. But because the federal role was new and growing, the long-standing role of churches and other religious organizations was largely overlooked in academic literature and public debates. Differences among religious groups providing social services were becoming more apparent. Those religious organizations that did partner with government were of a particular stripe; those that did not were of another. The politics of most of the partnering groups tended to be liberal and their theology ecumenical and humanitarian, which made such groups more willing to be junior partners to government in providing services supported by government dollars. They were more willing, for example, to tone down the religious content of their programs in order to meet concerns of government about supporting religion. These liberal and ecumenical groups established nonsectarian and even nonreligious governing boards, applied for and received tax-exempt status, partnered with secular nonprofits, and became more sophisticated organizationally and more directly involved politically. Such groups, like Lutheran Social Services and Catholic Charities, became categorized as *religiously affiliated* social service agencies. They are usually established groups with decades of experience in dealing with the government agencies that fund a large share of their programs.

More theologically conservative and evangelical groups also continued to provide social services that mixed those services with religious messages. To meet growing needs and provide economies of scale, many became multichurch efforts or separate faith-based organizations. Generally, these conservative evangelical groups did not seek government funds nor rearrange their management and staff to meet the criteria of potential government overseers. These groups now tend to be smaller and more independent from each other, and they often exist within a church structure, not outside it. In some cases, intensely and overtly religious groups do receive direct support from government, which may ignore the religious content and affiliations of programs because they provide quality social services. But such relationships are on shaky constitutional grounds related to First Amendment church-state issues.

Waning Enthusiasm

Just as Great Society programs became established in the early 1970s, large changes in the political environment came to threaten them. The energy crisis and the dual wars on poverty and in Vietnam stalled the post–World War II economic boom, sharply limiting the natural rise in federal revenues that had been partially spent on antipoverty programs. Good manufacturing jobs became scarce as competition from the rebuilt economies of Japan and Western Europe increased. There was more indifference to the rights and social situation of minorities as the peak events of the civil rights movement faded from memory. Widely circulating stories of waste in government social service programs eroded public support. The progress against poverty and deprivation stalled, if not reversed, by the late 1970s.

This new environment fostered three distinct but related criticisms of government-funded social services, and each criticism created a policy reaction. First, critics charged that the federally directed war on poverty was excessively detailed and restrictive. Central control, they said, stifled the creativity, knowledge, and participation inherent in locally run programs. They argued that the federal government should pull back to release the energies of local governmental and nongovernmental organizations. Second, some claimed that federal spending on social services was too high given shrinking federal revenues and the unique obligations of the central government for national defense and foreign affairs. They argued that the federal government could not afford to fund social services; state and local governments and the nongovernmental sector would have to carry the burden. Third, the leveling off of social improvement led to the argument that the root cause of poverty was moral, not economic. Spending more money, the argument went, at least in the same places with the same programs, did not do much good.

These three criticisms from the late 1970s have influenced federal social service policy down to the present. Social service spending as a share of the federal budget has declined and federal policy has called for state and local governments, nonprofit organizations, and aid recipients themselves to do more. These changes have come in three successive waves. The first wave of change during the Reagan administration simply reduced the federal share of social service spending. As an alternative or supplement to cuts, a few policymakers discussed increasing state and local flexibility to manage federal programs and thus save some overhead costs. There was some program consolidation and devolution, but this era was characterized chiefly by fewer federal dollars. No one yet urged that this money be channeled to a wider variety of religious service providers, although many critics argued that intensely religious social service providers were more effective and could meet needs with their own resources.

The next wave of federal social service reform gave states and localities a freer hand in running programs. In the mid-1980s, the federal government began to give states and localities waivers of many administrative details so that they could try new economic and behavioral incentives. This induced state and local governments to contract with or otherwise purchase services from private, mostly nonprofit, agencies. Ever since, state and local governments have taken increased management responsibility for federally funded social welfare, and private organizations have increasingly delivered social services as a sort of government-by-proxy.

The nation is now in a third wave of reform, which began with the passage of the 1996 welfare reform law. This wave is characterized by an "all hands on deck" approach to government-by-proxy service delivery, with government soliciting even more types of providers. The paradigm, for better or worse, appears to be free-market competition in the contracting of government-funded social services. The major push is to expand as widely as possible the marketplace of providers that bid for government funds in the hope that increased competition among providers will bring greater efficiency and effectiveness. Supporters of competition claim that the most helpful thing government can do is to create a "level playing field" on which all providers compete. Opponents attack the very idea of competition, arguing that it is disruptive, duplicative, and wasteful. To their eyes, the most helpful thing would be to increase the amount of government dollars going to current providers.

The George W. Bush administration, partly after the example of innovative states and partly at the urging of those states, continues the market mentality of reform's third wave. It wants the provider market to be less dominated by large secular and nominally religious providers and more open to smaller, community-based, and more intensely religious providers. The Bush administration has offered no more money in this more competitive market, but argues that more potential providers will lead to more effective and efficient social services, serving more needy people with the same number of dollars.

Each element of President Bush's faith-based proposal—tax benefits for non-itemizers giving to charity, compassion capital funds to help small organizations navigate government regulations, and charitable choice—is based on the marketplace model. The proposal's motivating idea continues decades-old trends in government-funded social service provision as much as it departs from those trends in turning to religious groups. Thus, opponents of Bush's faith-based initiative now include two groups: an established group that opposes the market model, and a new group that opposes the initiative on religious grounds.

The Constitutional Backdrop: A Short History

The changes in federal policy depend upon and interact with new legal uncertainties—possible changes in constitutional interpretation that allow greater church-state cooperation.[2] From this viewpoint, the president's faith-based initiative and the charitable choice laws that preceded it were tools to clarify, to the advantage of faith-based proponents, the extent to which federal courts, particularly the Supreme Court, would allow religious players in making and administering public policy based on First Amendment establishment clause interpretation. In recent years, many Court rulings have suggested that there is a new climate in the courts, more friendly to laws increasing religious-government cooperation. Esbeck and others more closely tied to electoral politics and public policy making have used these rulings to help spur the charitable choice movement (and later the faith-based movement).

The Pre-Incorporation Era of Inactivity (1789–1940s)

One need not go back very far in time to put the Bush faith-based initiative in its legal context, since the active history of establishment clause litigation is very recent.[3] Before the New Deal of the 1940s, the federal government's reach into social services was almost nonexistent. Because of this, there was little cooperation between government and religion in any kind of social service provision that reached any significant constitutional issue, and federal church-state legal cases essentially do not exist before the mid-twentieth century. Before the New Deal, however, several states were quite active in social services. When national constitutional questions started to be applied to states and local governments— through the "incorporation" doctrine formulated by the Supreme Court's reading of the Fourteenth Amendment—church-state controversies arose quickly.

The dramatic change came with the Court's 1947 ruling in *Everson v. Board of Education*, which stated that the establishment clause applied to state action. The change was almost overnight: the First Amendment now came into play when states, and all local governments, funded social service programs. Suddenly there was a new prohibition against state and local establishment of religion. This new prohibition found life and detailed definition in a myriad of cases about government financing of private schools and about the long-standing and widespread tradition of religious exercises in public schools. These cases created an active and controversial stream of Supreme Court jurisprudence that has been hotly contested for the last half-century.

The Era of No-Aid Separationism (1947–1980s)

The Court's establishment clause history has several distinct phases, each of which helps explain the current debate. The first phase was the era of strict separation—also referred to as "no-aid separation"—that flowed out of *Everson*. What the Court actually decided in *Everson* was far less important than the language it employed; the result certainly did not foreshadow the strict partitioning of things religious and governmental. The Court agreed that a municipal New Jersey government could reimburse families for the cost of transporting their kids on public buses to and from their school of choice, including religious schools. The separationist language the Court used, however, presaged a future where direct public aid to sectarian schools was highly unlikely to survive constitutional scrutiny.

More typical than *Everson* of what was to follow was the Court's decision one year later in *McCollum v. Board of Education* (1948), in which it struck down a program of religious instruction conducted by religious school teachers on public school grounds during school hours. *McCollum* ushered in an era of no-aid separation, defined by three characteristics. First, most of the important cases the Court faced involved public aid to parochial elementary and secondary schools, virtually all Catholic. The education of young children, and the perceived hierarchy and authority of the Catholic faith, both played into the details of Court decisions. Second and third were two other developments that assisted the doctrine of no-aid separation—the *Lemon* test and the notion of "pervasive sectarianism." With some exceptions along the way, these concepts, melded together, demanded a fairly consistent line of separation between public funds and private parochial school activities.[4]

The Lemon *Test*

The *Lemon* test was devised by the Supreme Court in *Lemon v. Kurtzman* (1971) and provided the key intellectual framework for later establishment clause cases. In *Lemon*, Chief Justice Warren Burger articulated three "prongs," all of which had to be met for a program of aid to a parochial school to survive constitutionally. First, the program in question required a secular purpose; second, its principal or primary effect could be neither to advance nor to inhibit religion; finally, the government aid was not to foster an excessive government entanglement with religion. A violation of any one prong would make a program unconstitutional.

The three-part *Lemon* test led to the high point of separationist doctrine in the 1970s because the second and third elements of the test produce something of a Catch-22 for aid programs to religious schools. The second prong meant that a program could not *substantially* aid a school's religious mission or activities, absolutely prohibiting public financing of religious indoctrination or instruction of any particular faith. Direct public assistance to religious institutions had to be "secular, neutral, and nonideological."[5] To satisfy the test of secularity, religious organizations had to purge themselves of their religious character or, at the very least, separate their secular functions and services (which could get government support) from their religious ones (which could not). But the level of oversight and regulation necessary for the state to confirm this separation brought into play the third prong, which insisted that an aid program must not "excessively entangle" the state in the schools' business. That is, to be sure that no religious purpose was being advanced, the state would have to provide an unacceptable (i.e., excessive) level of presence (i.e., entanglement) in school affairs. The practical result of the *Lemon* test was to ensure that most programs of school aid would be found unconstitutional. The logical option for states was to stop any and all public aid to religious schools.

Pervasively Sectarian Institutions

Equally important was the third development, the Court's creation of the idea of "pervasively sectarian" institutions. The Court concluded that the establishment clause did not allow government funds to find their way to pervasively sectarian organizations—those organizations that were so religious in character and so permeated by religious attributes that nonreligious services could not be assured. By definition, the interweaving of the religious and nonreligious aspects of their services made it impossible, the Court thought, to limit public aid solely to the pursuit of nonreligious ends. Since the funding of the nonreligious dimension would inevitably result in the funding of the religious as well, the Court reasoned that funding pervasively sectarian entities violated the nonestablishment principles of the First Amendment.

As the Court confronted this issue time and again in cases of public aid to private religious elementary and secondary schools, it became clear that its presumption was that such schools were pervasively sectarian. Program after program of aid to such schools fell before the Court, its *Lemon* test, and the standard of pervasive sectarianism. In *Levitt v. Committee for Public Education* (1973), *Meek v. Pittenger* (1975), and *Wolman v. Walter* (1977), the Court struck down programs that provided for religious schools to receive and use instructional materials of one sort or another. In some cases, textbooks for standard courses could be provided to parochial schools by the state, but any materials or supplemental instruction that might assist the religious mission—like overhead projectors and field trips—were prohibited. The Court was wary of any program that could risk government aid being put to religious use, and the only way to protect against that risk was through monitoring, supervision, and oversight of a magnitude that would, in turn, violate the excessive entanglement prohibition.[6] The guiding principle of this era was what George Washington University law professor Ira Lupu has called "money separation": a relatively firm limitation on state aid to private religious schools at the elementary and secondary levels. The ultimate result was distance and disconnection between religious institutions and government agencies.

The Era of Transition: From No-Aid Separation to Neutrality (1980s to Today)

Few judicially created standards have suffered as much criticism and derision in the last two decades as has the *Lemon* test. Still, the three-part test survives, albeit in an altered state. The Court's jurisprudence on cases involving aid to religious schools has undergone a gradual but not insignificant evolution. The separation standard became more flexible during the last years of the Burger Court and the gradual rise of a more conservative Rehnquist Court.

A competing idea of *neutrality* began to appear in Court opinions in the early 1980s. In *Mueller v. Allen* (1983), the Court allowed parents a state income tax deduction for expenses directly related to all types of elementary and secondary education, including the costs of tuition payments to private religious schools. In so doing, the Court emphasized that the state scheme was formally neutral in its treatment of religious as opposed to public schools because aid went directly to families rather than to the schools. The Court said that the benefit to families was primary and the benefit to schools incidental, thus passing constitutional muster. That decision was followed by *Witters v. Washington Department of Services for the Blind* (1986), a case in which the Court unanimously upheld vocational rehabilitation payments to a blind person who then used the funds to pay tuition for pastoral training at a Christian college. As in *Mueller*, five concurring justices emphasized that the program was formally neutral, noting that the decision that directed the aid to the religious institution was made solely by the program beneficiary and not the government.

The Bowen *Decision of 1988*

Neutrality as an alternative to strict separation was gaining currency, but the path of money-based establishment cases toward neutrality and accommodation has been neither straight nor unbroken.[7] Nevertheless, the trend away from strict separation accelerated with the Rehnquist Court. *Bowen v. Kendrick*, decided in 1988, would prove to be the springboard for the charitable choice idea. In *Bowen*, the Supreme Court approved of a federal program that included religious social service providers among its potential grantees. The Adolescent Family Life Act (AFLA) authorized federally funded services to teens on matters of teenage pregnancy and sexuality. The statute authorized funds for counseling, education, and other services to unwed mothers, and specified that religious service providers were to be included among those competing and qualifying for grants. The Court rejected the establishment clause challenge to the AFLA, holding that the act was neutral "on its face" toward religion. The Court noted that religious organizations were only one of a long list of possible nonprofit and private sector actors. The statute did not require or favor religious grantees, nor did it require that programs or services be inherently religious. It only included religious groups among those entitled to consideration in grant applications.

Bowen was a bellwether for the coming storm of charitable choice and questions of constitutionality that would grow out of its passage. It was an especially encouraging sign to those who would ultimately draft the charitable choice legislation. First, *Bowen* was the first modern case to take the constitutional issues out of the context of education and into the social service arena. As the lone decision to directly confront a federal subsidy of social services, it applied directly to charitable choice. Second, the decision clearly bolstered a new trend favoring formal neutrality over strict separation. The opinion rejected the automatic presumption that *any* financial aid to *any* religious institution would automatically result in a constitutional violation. Rather, the Court decided that the AFLA statute *on its face* was neutral, since it included grants to both secular and religious nonprofits. That there might be the *possibility* of advancing religion in some funded programs was not enough for the law to fall. The Court instead required that such improprieties be demonstrated as existing in fact in actual funded programs, essentially shifting the burden of proof from those supporting aid to those opposing it. The question of constitutionality depended upon actual implementation facts, not generalized theories of what was likely or possible. In sum, *Bowen* provided a road map for the future drafters of charitable choice as they tried to anticipate the extent to which the Court might allow government-religion partnerships in social services.[8]

The overall message of the relevant cases of the 1980s was stronger than the message of any one opinion. In each separate case, the majority continued to give lip service to the "pervasively sectarian" standard that usually demanded no aid, but the combined result was something far different—a loosening of the constraints on church-state financial cooperation. *Bowen* was especially encouraging to charitable choice supporters because it allowed religious groups to counsel teens on sexuality, pregnancy, and reproduction, highly charged and value-laden matters. The Court allowed religious organizations to provide government-funded services in an area that implicated matters of fundamental religious significance. These were programs that, presumably, could easily blur the lines between the religious, moral, and secular dimensions of teen pregnancy and sexual activity.

Related Political Developments

In addition to *Bowen*, intellectual and political movements helped create a new policy environment sympathetic to charitable choice legislation. A few years after *Bowen*, Marvin Olasky wrote *The Tragedy of American Compassion* (1992), a book that provided some intellectual heft to a growing political movement. Olasky was critical of what he saw as the government's secularization of social services, contending that religious institutions historically had been the most effective vehicles of service and compassion. In the next few years, the book would catch the eye of an array of political conservatives, including two stars of the Republican Party rising to new levels of leadership in the 1994 elections: George W. Bush, just elected governor of Texas, and Newt Gingrich, the new Speaker of the U.S. House.[9] Early in his first term Governor Bush met with Olasky and like-minded others to consider the public policy implications of his book: soon Texas would have the most aggressive implementation of faith-based policy of any state.[10]

FOCAL POINT 1.1

Early Friends

The Center for Public Justice (CPJ) and Company

The Center for Public Justice is a "civic education and policy research organization" in Annapolis, Maryland, that is "committed to public service that responds to God's call to do justice in local, national, and international affairs." Another way to describe CPJ is as a Christian "mini-think-tank" in the Reformed Protestant tradition, hard to place on a simple right-left political spectrum. Long before charitable choice appeared on the policy scene in 1995, CPJ was working with a handful of individuals and groups to develop the intellectual rationale for its promotion. Groups such as the Christian Legal Society and individuals such as Carl Esbeck and Marvin Olasky worked with CPJ on finding a more welcome place for Christian groups and ideas in the public square. Together, they are the core of early faith-based friends that drew the attention of policymakers and politicians, including Texas governor George W. Bush. Unsurprisingly, CPJ president James Skillen has stated that the organization is "almost whole-heartedly" in favor of President Bush's faith-based plans.

The Center for Public Justice's view of good public policy is based on the belief that every social institution, such as family, school, voluntary club, and church, bears responsibility to advance a particular form of justice appropriate to that institution. When this is done well, these institutions work together to form a flourishing common good. CPJ's ultimate objective is to do no less than "transform public life" by creating "the proper relationship between government and nongovernmental responsibilities and society, and uphold[ing] equal access for and treatment of all faiths in the public square." Openly Christian, CPJ has some views common to other politically and religiously orthodox interest groups in the Washington, D.C. area, such as a general support for smaller government. CPJ is quite unlike these groups, however, in urging government to sometimes force society's other institutions to live up to their various justice obligations.

One consequence of its position is that CPJ believes religious groups should have the power to define the extent of their social obligations and activities and be respected by government for these decisions. For example, if a group of religious believers want to establish a religious school, CPJ argues that the government should treat such schools on par with public schools. Similarly, if coreligionists want to provide social services, CPJ believes government should honor those efforts. In the early 1990s, CPJ started to promote its ideas more aggressively in the public policy arena. Stanley Carlson-Thies of CPJ headed what turned into the Center's charitable choice project, which soon caught the attention of politicians such as Governor Bush in Texas.

Skillen and Carlson-Thies (who worked in the White House Office of Faith-Based and Community Initiatives from its beginning until mid-2002) had known legal scholar and charitable choice creator Carl Esbeck for many years before 1995. Then and now a professor at the University of Missouri Law School, Esbeck has also worked for the Christian Legal Society (CLS) and its Center for Law and Religious Freedom (CLRF), headquartered in northern Virginia. CLRF advocates for free religious expression in the courts, dedicated to "protecting the religious freedom of all Americans," pursuing this mission through "legislative advocacy, 'test case' litigation, friend-of-the-court briefs, and providing information to CLS members and the general public." In the words of the CLRF website: "Much of the Center's litigation activity is designed to remove obstacles to propagation of the Good News of Jesus Christ." CLRF, often with Esbeck in the lead, has regularly joined the proreligious parties in key church-state court cases. And under CPJ sponsorship, Esbeck has written a guide to charitable choice to help faith-based organizations decide whether to participate in providing services funded by federal welfare block grants.

Marvin Olasky was instrumental in advancing faith-based ideas in the early 1990s and providing links between early supporters and politicians like George W. Bush. A journalism professor at the University of Texas–Austin and editor of the Christian newsweekly *World*, Olasky's 1992 book *The Tragedy of American Compassion* is a defining document for many conservatives in the faith-based movement. The book argues that localized and religiously inspired charities of the nineteenth century worked more effectively than government bureaucracies to help people and to address social ills, a central tenet of today's advocates for faith-based initiatives. In the early 1990s, U.S. Representative Newt Gingrich read and promoted the book, reflecting Olasky's views in the welfare policy theory encapsulated in the 1994 Contract with America. Olasky met as early as 1993 with George W. Bush, as the Texas governor was developing his own welfare reform ideas, and has remained influential in GOP political circles.

—Dawn K. Crowell

Sources

The Center for Public Justice—About the Center. www.cpjustice.org/about.html (accessed 15 April 2003).
The Center for Public Justice—Our Purpose. www.cpjustice.org/purpose (accessed 15 April 2003).
The Christian Legal Society—Center for Law and Religious Freedom—Litigation. www.clsnet.org/clrfPages/litigation/litigation_Overview.php3 (accessed 15 April 2003).

The political push attracted sympathetic constitutional scholars and lawyers who helped the politicians fashion legal arguments to support greater cooperation between the government and religious providers of social services. One of the groups deeply involved in these efforts was the Center for Public Justice (CPJ), a Christian think tank whose founding principles fit well the arguments for charitable choice. CPJ drew upon the expertise of sympathetic legal scholars, chief of whom was Professor

Esbeck, to promote these ideas among national and state-level policy-makers.

Years before George W. Bush became president, a network of politicians, policymakers, think-tank representatives, and constitutional scholars who advocated more direct interaction between church and state was coalescing. These efforts to bring religious institutions further into making policy and delivering services would likely not have gone far but for the 1994 elections. The Republican takeover of Congress changed Washington politics. Less noticed was that the 1994 elections seemed to be an important tipping point in government generally, with Republican gains in state and local elections hinting of broader conservative influence. With conservatism's openness to traditional morality and religious language, its ascendancy provided the opportunity to address the perceived mistreatment of religious social service agencies that Olasky had asserted. The new Republican congressional majority, in particular, welcomed religious social service agencies as potential partners with government. Sealing newly possible religious-government alliances with legislation like charitable choice was the logical next step.

The Establishment Clause in Flux

While Congress began contemplating and eventually passing legislation, the judicial branch was continuing to remold the establishment clause into a more accommodationist shape. The Court appeared to close the door on the era of strict separation in *Agostini v. Felton* (1997), overruling an earlier decision and upholding remedial educational services provided by public school employees at religious schools. The Court further softened the *Lemon* test by collapsing the second "primary effect" and the third "excessive entanglement" prongs into one that asked whether or not the program served to promote religion. The Court became concerned only about whether a program allocated assistance on religiously neutral criteria: remedial instruction that went to schools public and private, sectarian and otherwise, was acceptable.

The final constitutional development that pre-dated the Bush White House's push for faith-based initiatives was the *Mitchell v. Helms* decision in the summer of 2000. The drafters of charitable choice assumed that the Court had already, by 1995, moved away from a standard of strict separation of church and state. At the same time, there was no decision that completely substantiated this view. In other words, charitable choice assumed a degree of accommodation of religion that the Supreme Court seemed likely to permit but to which it had not given firm standing by 2000.

Mitchell v. Helms appeared to confirm the hopes of charitable choice proponents. It upheld a federal program distributing money to state and local educational agencies that would then lend the money to schools to purchase educational materials and equipment such as library and media materials and computer software and hardware. The funds would be available to public and private schools alike, and their use was limited to purchases that were "secular, neutral, and non-ideological" in nature. The four-justice plurality approving the statute invoked a broad vision of neutrality. It required only (1) formal neutrality in the distribution of aid to sectarian and other private and public schools, and (2) that the state itself was not directly in the business of religious indoctrination. The plurality opinion stated that it was constitutionally permissible for public aid to be diverted to religious purposes by the recipient school, as long as the aid itself was secular in nature and distributed on the basis of religiously neutral criteria. Even better for charitable choice supporters, four justices explicitly rejected the pervasively sectarian standard the Court had once advanced so strongly. *Mitchell* demonstrated just how permissive four members of the Court were prepared to be in allowing aid to religious institutions. There was little doubt that these four would reliably uphold charitable choice law.

Nevertheless, the *Mitchell* plurality could not secure a fifth vote either for the decisive burial of "pervasive sectarianism" or for the broad application of formal neutrality. The concurring opinion of justices Sandra Day O'Connor and Stephen Breyer, who joined with the four plurality judges in the basic opinion but not in the reasoning behind it, represents the new position of the Court concerning direct monetary aid to religious institutions. Written far more cautiously, this concurring opinion gave some ammunition to both sides. For the benefit of separationists, the opinion did not accept the neutrality standard as sufficient. To pass constitutional muster for O'Connor and Breyer, any aid or program with federal funds must also be secular in nature and restricted to secular activities. On the side of those wanting more accommodation between church and state, the O'Connor-Breyer opinion required that anyone challenging a program on constitutional grounds must show that the aid actually is or has been used for religious purposes, not merely argue that it could be or probably would be.

The split verdict of *Mitchell* was crucial in shaping the debate that enveloped President Bush's faith-based initiative. As then-Governor Bush prepared to launch his presidential campaign with the promise of a faith-based initiative, the constitutional atmosphere relevant to the initiative's charitable choice element was undeniably more favorable than it had been in a half-century. The constitutional news seemed to be getting better for charitable choice friends with every decision, yet even the Court's pronouncements in *Bowen* and *Mitchell* were sufficiently guarded to ensure plenty of counterarguments for opponents. Foes could contend quite convincingly that there was no conclusive or authoritative constitutional answer to the question of whether intensely and vocally religious groups could provide publicly funded services. Each side still had significant legal arguments at its disposal; the legislative battle would be difficult.

Charitable Choice Arrives: The Legislative Moment

Legislative friends of closer church-state cooperation felt confident enough in court decisions by 1995 to move ahead on legislation.[11] In the middle of the 1995 Senate debate on comprehensive welfare reform, Senator John Ashcroft of Missouri proposed a package of charitable choice provisions. As governor of Missouri from 1985 to 1993, Ashcroft had seen many faith-based organizations do successful work in a range of social service programs, often without government aid. New to the Senate, Ashcroft asked one of his staff, Annie Billings White, how he could get welfare reform to help faith-based organizations working with the poor. According to Billings White, the interest started with the senator: "No organizations came to John to ask him to do this. It was his desire; he wanted to increase the states' flexibility. He knew about programs like Teen Challenge and others. That was his motivation."[12]

Billings White had graduated from the University of Missouri–Columbia School of Law, and there had studied under Professor Esbeck, whose main scholarly interest is church-state law. He was focusing at this particular time on the way government funds secularized religious agencies that provided government-funded social services, and had written a paper on that issue for an academic conference in early 1995. To illustrate his position and generate discussion, Professor Esbeck circulated draft legislation to correct the problems he had identified.[13] After the conference, Esbeck adjusted his draft legislative language in consultations with James Skillen and Stanley Carlson-Thies at the Center for Public Justice, as well as with staff members of the Christian Legal Society and others. Professor Esbeck eventually sent Billings White a copy of the paper and legislative proposal. In a matter of a few months, the essence of Esbeck's suggestions became the charitable choice proposal that the junior Missouri senator and his staff started to promote in the Senate. Reflecting later on the serendipitous nature of events, CPJ's Skillen noted: "If Carl hadn't given [the proposed language] to Annie, [charitable choice] would not have come up."[14]

The newly Republican House wanted to do welfare reform quickly. It had rushed through an omnibus welfare reform bill in the spring of 1995 to fulfill a promise in the Contract with America to complete action on ten key bills within 100 days after the 104th Congress convened in January 1995. The Senate got started on welfare reform only after the House was completely done. There was no charitable choice language in the House welfare bill, but in the Senate a very short legislative provision, two sentences long, got into a bill introduced by Senator Bob Dole in early August. The provision provided that religious organizations who participated in welfare reform's new state block grant program were to retain their independence from government, and that organizations could not deny aid to needy families with children "on the basis of religion, a religious belief, or refusal to participate in a religious practice."

Legislative Debut

Senator Dole did not include fully developed charitable choice language in the original Senate welfare reform bill before his committee, nor did he add it during committee markup, the standard legislative procedure. Rather, Senator Ashcroft successfully lobbied Dole to add more lengthy and detailed charitable choice provisions to the bill during the August 1995 recess, between the time of committee consideration in the summer and the floor discussion that was to begin in early September. Thus, charitable choice language first appeared as part of the "chairman's substitute" amendment to the committee-approved bill. The chairman's substitute, a frequent legislative device, makes corrections and incorporates newly negotiated deals among senators made after formal committee approval but before floor consideration. Such a deal between Ashcroft and Dole got charitable choice into the 1995 Senate floor version with almost no notice.

It did not take long for an ACLU lobbyist reading through the massive chairman's substitute to discover a "weird thing"—the full charitable choice language.[15] Most interest groups lobbying on welfare reform were not prepared for a debate on church-state issues, and didn't quite know how to react to the new language. Later, an Ashcroft staff person would recall an ACLU memo in late summer 1995 raising questions about the language's church-state constitutionality. Supportive Senate staff encouraged the conservative Institute for Justice to answer the ACLU memo with legal counterarguments.[16]

In the overall context of welfare reform, charitable choice was a small side issue. There was no congressional record about the provision's meaning, no speech or position paper for or against it, and no readily available legal context to begin an informed debate. Some lobbyists later questioned whether Senator Dole even knew the implications of the charitable choice provisions he put in his chairman's substitute. Daniel Katz, then with the ACLU and now with Americans United for Separation of Church and State, noted that Dole had recently criticized a Housing and Urban Development agreement with the Nation of Islam to provide security at a federal housing site. Dole questioned whether this particular religious group should receive federal dollars. "Clearly," Katz said later, "Dole didn't know what the hell he was doing" in including the charitable choice language in the chairman's substitute. Almost immediately, the Working Group for Religious Freedom in Social Services, a coalition of opponents led by Katz of the ACLU, and Julie Segal of Americans United, organized itself to draw attention and opposition to the provision.[17]

But it was an uphill battle to get legislators and staff even to notice the short and off-point provision. According to Katz, even though there were many "religious groups working with us—Baptist Joint Committee, Jewish groups, mainstream Protestant denominations—it was difficult to get their attention. Each was working on fifty other things in the bill. There were not enough resources to get the attention of coalition partners. It was way too difficult in that environment."[18]

Senators spoke about welfare reform's charitable choice provisions in floor debate on two occasions in the 104th Congress, the first in the September 1995 debate, only a few weeks after the ACLU lobbyist first found the language in the bill. Congress usually recesses from early August until just after Labor Day every year. Nearly all senators and representatives leave the city, as do many key staff members. In 1995, Labor Day fell on September 4; the Senate leadership had set September 8 as the deadline to file amendments to welfare reform. Thus, in a matter of days the groups that opposed charitable choice had to find Senate staff persons not on vacation to whom they could explain their concern and convince them their bosses should offer amendments that would delete or modify charitable choice.

Several senators were sympathetic, but most of them already had written amendments on other matters. These other provisions seemed of more consequence. Further, the opportunities to offer amendments were limited and most senators wanted to focus on their original amendments. Opposition groups finally convinced Republican senator Bob Packwood of Oregon to offer an amendment to strike charitable choice from the welfare bill. Unfortunately for him and the opponents of charitable choice, Senator Packwood's political career was collapsing at just this time. Packwood had become embroiled in a sexual harassment scandal in which nearly twenty women charged that, over several years, the Senator had made unwanted sexual advances. On September 6, the Senate Ethics Committee voted to recommend that Packwood be expelled; the next day Packwood announced his resignation. With the deadline for amendments looming, charitable choice opponents had little time to find another senator willing to offer the amendment to strike charitable choice, although Senator Edward Kennedy of Massachusetts finally agreed to file such an amendment under his name.

FOCAL POINT 1.2

Early Foes

The Working Group for Religious Freedom in Social Services

Some accounts of charitable choice contend that the provision went unnoticed for months or even years after it first appeared in summer 1995. That is not true. Almost as soon as its language was inserted in Senate welfare reform, its opponents organized. By the time of the first Senate floor debate in September 1995, a collection of groups under the awkward heading "The Working Group for Religious Freedom in Social Services" had formed to lobby against the provision. The key early members of this working group were Americans United for Separation of Church and State (AU) and the American Civil Liberties Union (ACLU), soon joined by the Baptist Joint Committee on Public Affairs (BJC), People for the American Way (PAW), and others. Although organized in opposition to charitable choice, the working group was not an especially effective lobbying force in the early years. Once President Bush announced his high-profile faith-based initiative, however, these groups built the momentum and political interest to bring other civil liberties, religious, and public employee groups into a formidable coalition. Renamed the Coalition Against Religious Discrimination, they became a powerful force raising public concerns about the danger of charitable choice expansion.

AU has been the most outspoken faith-based opponent. Originally founded in 1947 by members of Christian faiths such as Seventh-day Adventists and Baptists and nonreligious groups such as the American Secular Humanist Association and the American Ethical Union, AU started out as essentially an anti-Catholic organization. It retains some religious ties, but the bulk of its current support is from those seeking a secular public square and a strong separation between religion and government. No longer specifically anti-Catholic, AU fervently opposes groups that it identifies as part of the "religious right" and whatever might be on those groups' agendas. Its current executive director, Barry Lynn, is a seasoned and articulate spokesperson, never hesitant to provide a memorable quote for the media. During the 2002 campaign, he described then-governor and presidential candidate George W. Bush's charitable choice initiative as "nothing short of government subsidized bigotry." Throughout its history AU has engaged in public advocacy, litigation, grassroots mobilization, and public education around issues of church and state. Immediately after charitable choice passed in 1996, AU went to court to stop its enactment. Julie Segal, then legislative counsel for the group, thought that charitable choice clearly violated the First Amendment's establishment clause: "Nothing advances a religious mission more than paying someone to walk into a church," she argued. "There will be some element of coercion there, even if it's subtle coercion."

The Baptist Joint Committee on Public Affairs is about sixty years old and based in Washington, D.C. It is an umbrella Baptist organization claiming to represent several Baptist groups including the Alliance of Baptists, American Baptist Churches in the U.S.A., Baptist General Conference, Cooperative Baptist Fellowship, National Baptist Convention of America, National Baptist Convention U.S.A., National Missionary Baptist Convention, North American Baptist Conference, Progressive National Baptist Convention, Religious Liberty Council, and the Seventh-Day Baptist General Conference. The BJC has been dedicated to "protecting religious liberty by keeping church and state separate," from a "uniquely Baptist witness." It represents what most would categorize as more liberal Baptists; conspicuous in its absence from the BJC is the very large and conservative Southern Baptist Convention, whose leaders were important supporters of House faith-based legislation.

The ACLU was founded in 1920 and has grown from a "roomful of civil liberties activists" to an organization of over 300,000 supporters with branches in almost every state. Throughout its history, the ACLU has sought to ensure that the Bill of Rights is more than "just a 'parchment barrier' against government oppression and the tyranny of the majority." In its mission to fight violations of civil liberties wherever they seem to occur, its lawyers have appeared before the Supreme Court more often than any organization except the U.S. Department of Justice. The ACLU was part of the early challenge to the 1996 welfare reform law that included charitable choice, and the organization strongly opposed then-Senator John Ashcroft's Charitable Choice Expansion Act of 1999, the first legislative attempt to broadly apply charitable choice in federal programs.

Americans United, the Baptist Joint Committee, and the ACLU have opposed charitable choice since 1995, calling it unconstitutional because, in their view, it ignores the "pervasively sectarian" standard and subsidizes religious discrimination. Melissa Rogers, formerly BJC's associate general counsel, has also warned about the enervating effects of charitable choice on deeply faithful groups:

"Religion is a 'prophetic critic' of government, and if it is subsidized, it will be less likely to bite the hand that feeds it." Together, these groups have helped define the lines of argument against faith-based initiatives—arguments used both by groups that are friendly and by those that are unfriendly to deep religious sentiment.

—*Melissa Fritsch*

Sources

American Civil Liberties Union website. www.aclu.org/about/aboutmain.cfm (accessed February 2003).

———. www.aclu.org/Files/OpenFile.cfm?id=10740 (accessed February 2003).

Baptist Joint Committee on Public Affairs website. www.bjcpa.org (accessed February 2003).

Quaid, Libby. "Welfare Provision Challenge Planned." Associated Press Online, 9 January 1998.

Senator William Cohen of Maine, another Republican, was active on this issue as well. He agreed to offer, and on September 13 did offer, an amendment modifying charitable choice in two ways. First, Cohen's amendment allowed states to require churches and other intensely religious social service providers to set up a nonprofit organization such as a 501(c)(3) as a condition of receiving a contract, striking the language that explicitly prevented states from setting this requirement. Cohen argued on the Senate floor that to require faith-based groups to set up separate nonprofits actually encouraged, not discouraged, them to deliver social services—a plausible argument, but one not widely shared by charitable choice proponents. Cohen also claimed that prohibiting states from requiring separate nonprofits ran counter to constitutional guidelines under the "pervasively sectarian" standard. The other portion of the Cohen amendment added language that required charitable choice to be implemented "consistent with the Establishment Clause," a redundant but politically appealing phrase. After a division of Senator Cohen's amendment into two portions, a part requiring establishment clause compliance was adopted by voice vote; a portion letting states require separate nonprofit entities passed fifty-nine to forty-one. Although both parts of Cohen's amendment succeeded, Billings White noted later that these defeats "didn't hurt us much."[19]

When the bill went to a House-Senate conference committee in November 1995 to reconcile differences between House and Senate versions, Ashcroft faced two major opponents there: moderate Republican senator John Chaffee of Rhode Island and moderate Republican congresswoman Nancy Johnson of Connecticut. House Speaker Newt Gingrich pushed the sides to negotiate, and eventually a compromise that favored Ashcroft was worked out. Rather than completely override state laws against the commingling of government and religious funds that Ashcroft desired, the final language preempted only those state and local programs that included federal dollars as part of a program's funding. States could manage solely state-funded programs in their own way. Other details strengthened the power that beneficiaries had to receive nonreligious services, and weakened the legal relief that faith-based groups could seek if they felt they had been unfairly excluded from bidding on welfare programs. The conference committee finished its work near the end of 1995 and sent the bill to President Clinton, who vetoed it early in 1996.

Election Pressures

The presidential election summer of 1996 brought new political pressures on President Clinton to support comprehensive welfare reform. In the president's many public comments on welfare reform, he often advocated the benefits of faith-based approaches to social service delivery without detailing his views on what particular kinds of faith-based groups should receive federal aid. With many members of Congress also facing the voters, the legislature worked steadily on a new welfare reform bill. July 23 was the last day of Senate debate on a revised welfare reform bill that President Clinton had just announced he would sign. Once again, charitable choice was buried in the text. On a parliamentary maneuver questioning the germaneness, or relevance, of charitable choice, the Senate parliamentarian ruled that charitable choice should be stripped from the bill because it was not germane. Under Senate rules, however, a supermajority of sixty senators could reverse this ruling. In a brief and chaotic debate, Senator Ashcroft moved to overturn the parliamentary judgment. Ashcroft won by sixty-seven to thirty-two, a vote that reinstated the charitable choice language. Three liberal Democrats voted with him and three moderate Republicans against, evidence that there was at least some confusion over the subject of the vote. With election campaigns in high gear, Clinton quickly signed the bill, an act that caused consternation within his administration but earned him widespread approval among swing voters.

After winning in November, President Clinton tried to address liberal worries over the charitable choice language. First, he proposed that Congress delete charitable choice from welfare reform as part of a large "technical corrections" bill he wanted. Congress did pass some corrections to the law, but did not remove charitable choice. As further evidence that the most concerned groups had not given up the fight, Clinton used his administrative powers to essentially void charitable choice, writing a guidance letter to federal administrators that prohibited "religiously-affiliated organizations that are pervasively sectarian" from eligibility to compete for federal funds.[20]

Additional Federal Charitable Choice Legislation

Three other bills with charitable choice language became law in the years between 1996 and 2001. In 1998, the 105th Congress reauthorized the community services block grant program, which sends funds to states for a variety of community service programs. Senator Dan Coats of Indiana introduced the reauthorization bill, and he included new charitable choice provisions similar to those in welfare reform. These provisions were affirmed in committee discussions. Revised charitable choice language that even more strongly protected the religious rights of faith-based groups was added between committee approval and floor debate. Floor debate on the bill was brief and without overt controversy; the bill passed on voice vote. In the House-Senate conference on the bill, the House, which had a shorter version of charitable choice language in its community services bill, essentially adopted the Senate language. On October 27, President Clinton signed this bill into law, but simultaneously issued an opinion that again virtually negated its charitable choice provisions, restating his view that it would be constitutionally impermissible to fund "pervasively sectarian" institutions.[21]

The 106th Congress of 1999–2000 enacted two more laws with charitable choice provisions. The Children's Health Act of 2000 authorized block grants to the states for substance abuse prevention and treatment programs, and the Community Renewal Tax Relief Act of 2000 extended similar programs operated by the federal government's Substance Abuse and Mental Health Services Administration. The former bill was signed into law just before the 2000 election; the latter bill became law on December 21, 2000, nine days after the Supreme Court intervened in the Florida recount to declare George W. Bush the forty-third president of the United States.

Congress paid sporadic attention to charitable choice in its passage of these latter three laws. The most extensive discussion was in October and November 1999, when the Senate was debating the Youth Drug and Mental Health Services Act (which would become part of the Children's Health Act of 2000). In committee, senators Jack Reed of Rhode Island and Edward Kennedy of Massachusetts offered an amendment restricting the hiring discretion of religious groups, discretion they had been granted in prior civil rights laws. Their amendment lost on a strictly party-line vote of eight to ten. The committee then approved the entire bill almost unanimously. The majority views in the committee report defended the charitable choice language by citing the exemplary work of faith-based groups in treating substance abuse problems. Seven of the eight committee Democrats signed additional views objecting to the charitable choice language. They criticized the assumption of charitable choice proponents that faith-based approaches effectively treat substance abuse. The dissenters believed, rather, "that successful substance abuse programs must have a strong link to clinical care and that treatment for addiction should be based on the latest scientific information to ensure the best possible care. . . . [M]ore peer-reviewed research should be conducted to evaluate the effectiveness of programs involving untrained non-scientific methods and . . . clear scientific information [should] be provided when claims are made regarding the effectiveness of such programs."[22] Despite this dissent, the full Senate approved the bill by voice vote on November 3, 1999. Although no further action on this bill was taken, most of its contents, including its charitable choice provisions *in toto*, were added to the Children's Health Act that was enacted late in 2000.

The Early Players and Issues

Briefly tracing the legislative history of the four enacted charitable choice provisions helps identify key congressional proponents and opponents, and reveals almost all the concerns that arose more prominently in the

2001–2002 debates. Several key players in the House and Senate emerged. Then-Senator John Ashcroft initiated charitable choice in the Senate, with Bill Frist of Tennessee prominently supporting him. Emerging as key opponents were senators Reed, Kennedy, and Christopher Dodd of Connecticut. The charitable choice champion in the House was Mark Souder of Indiana, although the provision was much less discussed there than in the Senate. The most vocal House critics of charitable choice were Representatives Bobby Scott of Virginia, Chet Edwards and Sheila Jackson-Lee of Texas, Nancy Pelosi of California, and Barney Frank of Massachusetts.

The most common argument against charitable choice in these first debates was the idea that if the government funded intensely and vocally religious providers, it could be funding the recruitment of new members by these groups. Interestingly, the major argument of the Bush years, that protecting the hiring discretion of faith-based groups would let them discriminate against groups such as gays and racial minorities, was not made frequently or forcefully before 2002, although it became slightly more prominent each time charitable choice went through the legislative process.[23]

Opponents of charitable choice legislation never succeeded in blocking it during the Clinton years. When House opponents offered amendments to delete or scale back charitable choice language, they lost. The margins were usually in the range of seventy to ninety votes, with thirty-five to fifty House Democrats voting with nearly all Republicans to keep charitable choice. The strength of the Democratic vote was misleading, however. In several of our interviews for this book, both Democratic and Republican sources stated that many House members voted for charitable choice only because they knew that the Clinton administration would not enforce its provisions. This quote from an anonymous source is typical: "Members of Congress told me outright that they knew the Clinton administration wouldn't enforce it, so they could vote for [charitable choice] without fear."

Senate floor votes on charitable choice do not exist. The only related Senate floor vote was an indirect procedural vote that was not well understood by senators. The few Senate committee votes indicate that, to the extent faith-based funding was an issue, it divided along partisan lines.

But interest groups and their congressional allies attacking charitable choice in the Clinton years had yet to find a winning strategy that could gain attention and traction.

Implementing Charitable Choice

By the time President Bush took office in January 2001, four charitable choice laws were on the books. Only the 1996 welfare reform and the 1998 community services block grant programs had been law long enough to expect any steps toward implementation. Because the Clinton administration had relied on the "pervasively sectarian" distinction of older Supreme Court decisions in interpreting charitable choice provisions in these two laws, the federal bureaucracy had done almost nothing to implement them.

That is not to say charitable choice had no effect. Because charitable choice is a logical extension of decades-long trends to push actual social service delivery onto private groups, some states were already working with intensely and vocally religious groups before 1996; they saw the 1996, 1998, and 2000 charitable choice provisions as endorsements of their earlier work. Other states did not work with faith-based groups before 1996 and, despite the new charitable choice laws, received no prodding by the federal government to change. Absent federal action, states that had been moving toward working with faith-based groups kept moving; those that lagged, lagged farther.

The lack of congressional debate on charitable choice also discouraged implementation. An open and extended legislative debate about a policy usually generates interest and creates a coalition of supporters. The legislative process itself, if successful, both responds to those supporters and recruits new supporters who want to see the law implemented. The nearly subterranean charitable choice process limited support. There was almost no organized grassroots constituency or D.C.-based lobby prodding federal, state, and local governments toward implementation.

Another reason that an interest group coalition did not form quickly behind charitable choice is that it does not fit traditional religious lobbying alignments in Washington, as Stanley Carlson-Thies of CPJ has argued.[24] In his view, liberal religious lobbies believe the proper political objective of churches in social service policy debates is to *advocate for the poor*. They see themselves urging more federal funding and control of welfare programs, not more contracting out of these services to small, local, unregulated providers. Politically conservative religious groups, on the other hand, tend to see the church as a preferred *alternative to government* in providing social services. Their main goal is to cut domestic spending, and let churches that can capably discern between deserving and undeserving deal with the needy. This view, too, does not square with charitable choice laws that assume close cooperation between government and religious groups; rather, it envisions churches working independently from government. With no preexisting constituency clamoring for charitable choice, and no fit between its premises and the two standard perspectives on the relationship among social services, government, and religion, there was almost no outside pressure for implementation.

There was also a faction of the intensely and overtly religious social service providers that saw danger in a charitable choice debate. Throughout American history the practice of federally supported social services provided by religious groups has deviated significantly from the theory of federal rules and constitutional law. For his 1996 book *When Sacred and Secular Mix*, Stephen Monsma surveyed nearly 800 child service agencies, international relief groups, and religious colleges and universities. He found in this pre–charitable choice period that many quite intensely and vocally religious groups received federal funds. The survey indicated that some aid recipients were violating constitutional norms, standard practices, and policymakers' assumptions. Most nonprofits surveyed, including the intensely religious, reported little pressure from government overseers to tone down their religious practices. The book's chief finding was not that intensely religious providers are uniformly excluded or harassed but, rather, that their participation is legally insecure. As Monsma explained already in 1996, the problem is not widespread exclusion, but rather inconsistency due to constitutional, legislative, and administrative ambiguity.[25]

An extensive public debate on charitable choice cuts both ways for these intensely and vocally religious groups—pervasively sectarian groups already receiving federal funds. The eventual codification in law of provisions like charitable choice would assure most of these providers that their funding was stable and secure. A highly visible policy debate, however, in which existing arrangements attract attention, immediately threatens them.

Some social scientists and interest groups have tracked state implementation of faith-government partnerships throughout the early charitable choice years. In a 1998 study by Amy Sherman for CPJ, Texas, Michigan, and Virginia were cited as the most aggressive states pursuing church-state partnerships both within and outside charitable choice programs.[26] Other than these three states, however, there was not much cooperation. A follow-up study a year later told a significantly different story. In it, Sherman examined nine selected states (California, Illinois, Massachusetts, Michigan, Mississippi, New York, Texas, Virginia, and Wisconsin) and found that 125 new government and faith-based collaborations had been set up after 1996. Eighty-four collaborations were financial; the other forty-one were nonfinancial agreements in which, for example, faith-based volunteer groups had written agreements with funded nonreligious agencies. The size of financial collaborations ranged from $5,000 to $350,000, with more contracts at the lower end of the scale. Most collaboration was with new provider groups, and nearly all these new collaborations seemed to arise when state administrators noticed the federal charitable choice provisions.

Many new faith-based providers used federal funds to expand programs that had not previously received government funds. Other groups were able to expand their programs from those that met only short-term needs to those that addressed longer-term needs in the same areas of concern: for example, from providing an overnight homeless shelter to finding longer-term housing for the formerly homeless. Even though many contracts seemed to stem from state administrators taking notice of federal charitable choice laws, neither they nor new participants were well informed about either their general guidelines or their application to specific programs.[27]

Some states showed a dramatic increase in faith-based contracting in the year between Sherman's 1998 and 1999 studies. Indiana, under Democratic governor Frank O'Bannon and Republican mayor of Indianapolis Steven Goldsmith, put great effort into faith-based outreach. State agencies invited thousands of groups to workshops on government contracting, efforts that in less than a year resulted in about fifty new contracts for a total of $3.4 million. Texas under George W. Bush aggressively promoted federal charitable choice, adopted similar rules in all of the state's human service programs, and directed state agencies to appoint liaisons to religious groups.[28] The state established a new and separate funding pool, "the Local Innovations Project" grant, to which faith-based and community organizations were encouraged to apply under simple and expedited procedures. The state also issued alternative licensing and credentialing guidelines so that a greater variety of groups could be eligible to receive funds.[29]

The Center for Public Justice issued one final report before the 2000 presidential election, an August 2000 "report card" on state compliance with federal charitable choice law. That report used a fairly rigid definition of compliance, noting whether grant guidelines had explicit protections for the religious identity of groups and whether they clarified that groups needed to serve all clients, allow offended beneficiaries to opt out of the religious elements of a program, and not use public funds for inherently religious activities. Twelve states received passing grades of "C" or above on the report card, with George Bush's Texas receiving an A+; Indiana, Ohio, and Wisconsin received A's, while Arizona, Arkansas, California, Illinois, Michigan, North Carolina, Pennsylvania, and Virginia were the other eight states that passed.

In March 2001, the Associated Press (AP) produced one of the few studies of charitable choice implementation not sponsored by charitable choice advocate CPJ. The AP study found that only five states aggressively used federal charitable choice provisions—Arkansas, Indiana, Missouri, Ohio, and Texas—and a few others made small steps toward compliance. The combined impression created by these studies is that, when the faith-based debate commenced in early 2001, both sides lacked significant evidence to defend or refute their concerns about effectiveness, church-state violations, and other matters. Despite having been law for more than four years, charitable choice was unimplemented, its rules untested, and its effects undocumented.

Summary: Critical Areas of Dispute

The idea of religion and government sharing the social service burden is not new. More than a century ago, religious groups called upon government to assist them in funding and providing social services. Before 1996, however, the general rule was that only those religious agencies that were not pervasively sectarian were supposed to be eligible to participate in government-funded welfare support programs, although actual practice deviated frequently from the general rule. Because the Supreme Court seemed to drift away from excluding pervasively sectarian groups from direct federal support, the shift created an opportunity to encourage more religious groups to compete for federal funds in more social service delivery areas. Charitable choice ignores the "pervasively sectarian" distinction, stating that faith-based social service agencies of any religious intensity or organizational structure can contract with government agencies. Under charitable choice, all types of religious groups must be allowed to participate on the same basis as any other group in federally funded social service programs. And they must be allowed to participate without government impairing their religious character. In congressional and interest group debate during the Clinton years, when four charitable choice provisions became law, a host of issues arose. All these issues resurfaced in the Bush administration debate. As a conclusion to our review of the pre-2000 issues, and as an introduction to the 2001–2002 debate, it is helpful to organize and discuss these controversies in four major categories.

The Level Playing Field

The first general category of controversies is the meaning of treating pervasively sectarian or intensely and vocally religious groups "on the same basis" as other groups: that is, how to achieve the so-called level playing field. Proponents of charitable choice argued for a new law that would ensure equity for intensely and vocally religious groups wanting to compete with groups that have long-standing financial arrangements with the government. But opponents of charitable choice claim that the "level playing field" phrase really aims to secure special protections and promotions for religion.

One specific issue is whether the government should even give attention to the religious aspects of potential service providers. Charitable choice suggests that government should cast a blind eye to a group's religious characteristics. Its provisions prohibit the government from taking the religious character of the organization into account when making grants or contracts, shielding from the government any knowledge about the religiosity of the potential provider. Proponents say that the government should only be interested in program performance, not religious character, and that ignorance about the religious elements of a provider ensures that funds will be distributed on the basis of merit only and not on the basis of government administrators' religious biases. Opponents of this argument say that the government must know all the religious specifics of a potential provider so that administrators can be sure that government is not promoting religion either in appearance or in fact.

Another level-playing-field question is whether faith-based groups need to prove their worth before becoming eligible to compete for government funds. Charitable choice proponents say they should not; evaluations should come in the actual review of grant or contract proposals and in the initial performance of groups getting first awards. While most charitable choice proponents think faith-based groups are superior and would be proven so under objective standards, they question the objectivity of most government evaluation criteria. They argue that it is unfair to hold religious groups to pre-eligibility performance standards that current fund recipients do not themselves meet. Charitable choice opponents say that credible evidence is needed before current policy should be changed; otherwise broadening eligibility is merely instituting a proreligious bias based on ideological opinion, not scientific evidence.

A third level-playing-field issue is whether to allow faith-based groups to have different employee and practitioner qualifications. Proponents of separate standards argue that many faith-based treatment regimens require their practitioners to have different types of background, training, and practice than secular regimens. According to this view, many current licensing and credentialing requirements unfairly bar religious groups from providing publicly funded social services. The requirements artificially prop up secular treatments of questionable effectiveness, shutting out competition from alternative treatments that are highly successful. Opponents argue that qualification guidelines promote the best professional practices and training and introduce no antireligious bias; attempts to avoid qualification guidelines will invite inferior services and abuse of clients. In one case, the proponents' arguments have become law: the charitable choice provisions in the federal substance abuse prevention and treatment block grants allow for alternative credentialing.

A fourth controversy under this heading involves different standards for different types of federal assistance. The federal government supports social services in three ways: indirectly through *vouchers* to beneficiaries and directly through *contracts* that purchase goods or services and through *grants* to particular organizations for that organization's projects. Vouchers for a particular service (child care, for example) are sent to individual beneficiaries, who can redeem them at eligible child-care providers. The providers can turn these vouchers in for cash reimbursement for services they have provided to voucher holders. Federal court decisions have made it clear that vouchers are not direct aid to groups providing services, but aid to individuals seeking services and, at best, only indirect aid to service providers. Therefore, the reach of the federal government's laws about church-state relations, hiring discretion, and other matters do not typically apply to providers of voucher services. Thus, charitable choice proponents generally like voucher programs because faith-based organizations can easily participate.

Federal contracts are written agreements between the government and organizations to provide federally funded services. This is a form of direct aid, but it is a payment *for* a service, rather than a payment *to* a group. The government is "shopping" for services and should, according to market principles, want many providers bidding. Although it would be within the federal government's power to attach conditions to its shopping demands, fewer restrictions tend to produce more bids. Thus, conceptually at least, the federal government would not want to restrict the market for providers by erecting barriers to bids by religious groups.

A grant, in contrast to a contract, is a direct financial contribution to a group, usually for a particular program of the group to address an area of the government's concern. Compared to contracts, grants are driven more by an organization's interest and less by a government's specific service demand. Because grants are income to a provider group, government typically inquires into the structure, capability, and program details of grant seekers to ensure funds are used effectively. Doing so allows the government to ask detailed questions about the organization, including its religious aspects. Federal grants are either directly administered by the federal government or, more frequently, administered on the federal government's behalf by state or local governments. With indirect grants, state and local governments often insist that recipients abide by the locality's regulations, as well as the regulations of the federal government.

A final level-playing-field issue is whether the government should create different oversight rules for faith-based providers than for other providers. Charitable choice legislative proposals usually permit more limited oversight of faith-based groups: for example, such proposals some-times allow self-certification by the group that it complies with all require-ments. The chief defense for this difference in oversight involves church-state concerns—the First Amendment's free exercise clause implies less rigorous government oversight of religious providers than nonreligious ones. Opponents of differential treatment argue that to avoid proreligious bias in oversight, faith-based groups must comply with exactly the same standards as non-faith-based groups—perhaps tougher standards given establishment clause concerns.

The Church-State Boundary

A second broad category of controversy is how to define the boundaries of the church-state relationship in an environment in which social services are contracted out. Government must draw a fine line to not officially support religion while supporting social services that religious groups provide. One item under this heading is whether to separate or commingle funds received from governments and from other sources. What can groups do with federal dollars and what can they do with other dollars in the same federally supported program? Most charitable choice laws bar the direct use of federal funds for "inherently religious activities" of worship, instruction, or proselytization. This restriction applies only to federal money directly received by groups. It does not apply to vouchers that beneficiaries receive and then use at a service provider. This limitation is also restricted to federal finances: the limits on federal dollars do not apply to other dollars given to the group or to voluntary services provided by the group. Supporters say these limits are the most government can ask; opponents say these limits are almost meaningless. Because new federal dollars free up private money previously spent on services, the private money can be used for religious activities conducted by the same persons with the same clients in the same place.

A related narrow church-state issue is preemption: whether federal regulations override any conflicting or more comprehensive state and local laws. Charitable choice implies that, in programs completely or partially funded by federal dollars, state and local provisions are voided. Proponents of charitable choice generally support the preemption of state and local laws; opponents do not. The stance of each side is somewhat contradictory. One typical argument of faith-based proponents is that the decisions of local leaders should be respected; their support for preemption language thus seems contradictory. At the same time, one typical argument of faith-based opponents is that national standards should apply everywhere uniformly; their argument to respect state and local laws in this instance runs counter to their general lines of argument.

Another church-state controversy is whether to require groups that receive federal funds to separately incorporate their service component, usually by mandating nonprofit, 501(c)(3) status. This would most often take the shape of a service provider sponsored by a church incorporating separately as a nonprofit group, a sometimes costly and administratively complex step. Opponents say that this is a largely unnecessary barrier to faith-based groups wanting to enter the marketplace of service provision. Good accounting procedures, this side argues, should be sufficient. Proponents say that separate incorporation is necessary to monitor the use of funds and keep intact the wall between government and church. Both sides seem to ignore the fact that 501(c)(3) status does nothing to ensure secularity. There are many deeply religious nonprofits; the issues of overt religiosity and official nonprofit status are unrelated.

Which religious groups would actually get public money for their social services is another church-state issue. This concern comes from many points on the ideological spectrum. Orthodox believers, usually political conservatives with connections to Republicans, worry that programs of "weird" religions such as Scientology or even devil worship might receive federal funds. Others, usually political liberals with connections to Democrats, are sure that Republicans want to use charitable choice to fund politically conservative and religiously orthodox faith traditions. Charitable choice provisions make clear that funding the social services of faith-based groups does not constitute and should not be seen as an endorsement of the religious views of the groups that receive funds. Indeed, charitable choice language appears to remove the religious nature of a group from any consideration. But both sides tend to ignore that principle in the policy debate. Charitable choice supporters tend to want certain religions to get official sanction; opponents point out that endorsements of specific faith traditions almost certainly violate the Constitution.

Finally, there is the concern over the present constitutional interpretation. Charitable choice proponents want to write into law the maximum proreligious rules they believe today's Supreme Court will accept. Opponents want to buttress the weakening "pervasively sectarian" standard. One peculiarity is that some charitable choice laws explicitly state that the affected program must be consistent with the establishment and free exercise clauses of the First Amendment. The statement is superfluous. All laws must be consistent with relevant Supreme Court decisions. The constitutional questions about charitable choice are not over whether these clauses apply, but rather what their application means.

Religious Freedom and Vitality

A third category of controversies centers on religious freedom: the concerns of potential faith-based service providers that their religious character could be impaired by a closer relationship to the federal government. One issue under this heading is how much government can control an organization's structure and location. Charitable choice law usually states that the group receiving government funds can control the definition, development, practice, and expression of its religious beliefs overall and in the program receiving funds. Proponents state that in the interest of free expression the government must not control these things. Opponents argue, on the other hand, that the government must be able to influence these things to avoid government promoting religion. Charitable choice provisions also usually prohibit government from requiring a grant recipient to alter its governing structure or its service location by, for example, removing religious art or symbols from its walls. Again, proponents say that an agency's structure or location says almost nothing about the quality and content of its program and that such requirements are discriminatory barriers to entry. Opponents argue that church-state separation requires the government to make sure that services it pays for do not appear to support religious faith.

Hiring, one of several religious freedom controversies in earlier charitable choice debates, has evolved into the faith-based initiative's largest controversy in the Bush administration. Charitable choice laws state clearly that receiving federal funds does not diminish a religious group's power to take religion into account when hiring employees. Proponents say that groups need hiring discretion for two reasons. The first is on church-state separation grounds: religious groups must be able to define for themselves their conditions of employment. The other reason is to ensure the continuation of service quality—which they contend depends on the faith commitment of practitioners. Opponents counter with the argument that a group becomes an agent of the federal government when it takes federal dollars. The government can apply whatever rules it wants when it pays for services, and it should especially apply employment-based civil rights protections. Advocates on each side claim constitutional support: proponents say that the Constitution clearly protects religious groups regardless of where funds originate, and opponents argue that accepting federal funds clearly requires compliance with civil rights laws. Disinterested constitutional scholars usually disagree with both sides, arguing that Congress could impose by simple statute its views either way.[30] In the absence of legislative direction, however, it seems most likely that the courts would rule in favor of a religious group's right to make decisions about employees.

Charitable choice proponents have held that religiously based hiring freedoms are vitally important. Because they abide by all other federal antidiscrimination laws, this side argues that preserving the religious exemption results in essentially equal treatment—it allows religious groups to hire fellow believers on religious criteria but not to discriminate in any other ways. Secular groups, this side contends, engage in a similar form of viewpoint discrimination; one does not, for example, require a federally funded Planned Parenthood group to hire pro-life employees or an environmental nonprofit receiving a government grant to hire proponents of strip mining. The other side argues that *all* federal, state, and local civil rights and nondiscrimination laws should apply. In their view, religious groups that insist on a religious exemption really want to discriminate on any basis, especially on the basis of race and sexual orientation, under the cover of religious doctrine and religious freedom.

An additional, although less prominent religious-freedom issue is whether it is in the best interest of religious groups to receive federal funds. Perhaps religious organizations need protection from the temptation to depend upon federal funds, by being prohibited from applying for them in the first place. Charitable choice sympathizers say that religious groups should have the freedom to choose for themselves whether or not to apply. No one forces a group to seek government funds. To them, a preemptive prohibition is at least paternalistic, if not bigoted. The other side essentially argues that many groups will not judge wisely, will eventually become too dependent upon federal dollars, and will lose their religious voice, independence, and effectiveness. There is evidence that religious groups modify their missions in the pursuit of government dollars; indeed, such tendencies were the subject of Professor Esbeck's research when he first proposed the language of charitable choice.

Beneficiary Freedoms

A fourth category of controversies centers on the beneficiaries—on how to protect the clients of federally funded programs from religious offense when receiving services. Ironically, the original meaning of "choice" in charitable choice referred to expanding the options for beneficiaries so they could choose between services offered by religious and secular agencies. Most charitable choice laws require that intensely and vocally religious groups serve everyone who enters their programs; groups cannot refuse to provide services based on a beneficiary's belief or unbelief. Second, even strong charitable choice advocates agree that clients who object to the religious character of a faith-based group that is providing them a service have a right to an acceptable and accessible alternative.

A more controversial aspect related to beneficiary freedom is whether a religious provider must allow someone to opt out of the religious parts of a program while participating in nonreligious parts. Some supporters of faith-based programs argue that this "opt-out" ability dilutes the quality of treatment faith-based groups provide and should not become law. Other supporters of faith-based programs argue that this opt-out might be acceptable but its application should be considered on an individual basis. Strong proponents of an opt-out argue that it is required to ensure that clients' religious rights are fully protected. This debate over opting out, which became labeled a "secondary opt-out," to distinguish it from the ability of beneficiaries to opt for an entirely different program before beginning treatment, became a serious point of controversy within Republican and conservative ranks during the 2001–2002 debate about faith-based legislation.

All these disputes were aired in charitable choice debates before the 2000 election campaign. But because both major-party presidential candidates supported faith-based initiatives, almost none of these disputes became widely known. A new and more intense round in the faith-based fight, however, was about to begin, hinted at in the 2000 presidential election.

Two

On the Trail

Campaigning on Faith-Based Issues

Think of [faith-based] as the opposite of a wedge issue. On this question, Gore doesn't mind if he and Bush sing from the same hymnal. "I don't think this should be a political fight," he says.

E. J. Dionne, Washington Post, *May 28, 1999*

Nothing put forth in the first 100 days of his administration has sparked as much passion, discord, and suspicion as President Bush's proposal to make it easier for faith-based groups to get federal dollars to deliver social services to the nation's needy.

Mary Leonard, Boston Globe, *April 29, 2001*

On May 24, 1999, a presidential candidate visited the Salvation Army's Adult Rehabilitation Center in Atlanta, Georgia, and delivered a speech announcing an important plank of his presidential campaign. In one of his first major policy addresses of the campaign, he devoted half an hour to a discussion of the importance of faith-based organizations:

Ordinary Americans have decided to confront the fact that our severest challenges are not just material, but spiritual. Americans know that the fundamental change we need will require not only new policies, but more importantly a change of both our hearts and our minds. . . . For too long, national leaders have been trapped in a dead end debate.

As Mother Teresa put it, "Plant the act, reap the habits. Plant the habits, reap the virtue. Plant the virtue, reap the character. Plant the character, reap the destiny."

I am here today because I believe government should play a greater role in sustaining this quiet transformation—not only by dictating solutions from above, but by supporting the effective new policies that are rising up from below.

Today I give you this pledge: if you elect me President, the voices of faith-based organizations will be integral to the policies set forth in my administration.

Which presidential candidate spoke these promissory words in May of 1999? Who was the first to make a campaign pledge to use the White House to support faith-based organizations? Vice President Al Gore.

Two months later, candidate George W. Bush delivered the first policy speech of his campaign, an address in Indianapolis that, in outlining his goals for faith-based initiatives, echoed many of the themes in Gore's speech:

The American Dream is so vivid, but too many feel: The dream is not meant for me.... [T]he places where these problems are concentrated, from North Central Philadelphia to South Central Los Angeles, have become the ruins of communities. Places where despair is the easy path, and hope the narrow gate.

For many people, this other society of addiction and abandonment and stolen childhood is a distant land, another world. But it is America. And these are not strangers, they are citizens, Americans, our brothers and sisters.

In their hopes, we find our duties. In their hardship, we must find our calling, to serve others, relying on the goodness of America and the boundless grace of God. Real change in our culture comes from the bottom up, not the top down. It gathers the momentum of a million committed hearts. So today I want to propose a different role for government. A fresh start. A bold new approach.

As both of these excerpts illustrate, candidates George W. Bush and Al Gore gave major policy speeches early in their campaigns announcing support of expanding opportunities for faith-based organizations to partner with the federal government.

The apparent consensus quickly turned to conflict once campaign promises became presidential proposals. By the time H.R. 7, the House version of President Bush's faith-based initiative, reached a vote on the floor of the House of Representatives, opposition to the proposal had grown fierce. After an emergency move by the Republican leadership saved the bill from likely defeat, behind the scenes strong-arming led to passage of a tempered version of the original bill by a thirty-five-vote margin, with members casting votes generally along party lines. Reflecting the growing intensity of opposition to faith-based legislation, a much less dramatic Senate bill, the CARE Act, failed to make it to the floor of the Senate by the end of the 107th Congress, even though it did not include the policy provisions that had created the most rancor in the House debate.

How did the apparent bipartisan policy consensus from the campaign turn so quickly into a bitter partisan conflict? Why did the policy environment shift so dramatically? To begin to unpack this puzzle, we will first consider some of the reasons for Bush and Gore's support of faith-based initiatives in their campaigns. We will then analyze the role of the faith-based issue in the campaign to uncover the differences in the two candidates' rhetoric and focus. Finally, we will chart the movement from consensus to confrontation, describing the political context in which Bush would work to implement the faith-based policies promised in his campaign.

Common Ground in the Campaign: Bush and Gore's Faith-Based Politics

Campaign 2000 was the campaign of faith-based politics. Although their proposals varied in emphasis, details, and focus, candidate George W. Bush and both Democratic contenders, Bill Bradley and Al Gore, all announced campaign positions in favor of some sort of increased government partnership with faith-based organizations. To most outside observers, the two major-party nominees appeared to agree on the fundamental principle of encouraging government partnerships with faith-based organizations. However, consensus on the issue was shallow and, in certain ways, more rhetorical than substantive. To understand the role of faith-based policy in the two campaigns, we first explore some of the reasons, both general and candidate-specific, that Bush and Gore advocated their faith-based policies.

Looking Ahead to the General Election

Since the 1970s the results of state primary elections and caucuses have determined the major-party nominees for president. During the primary season, candidates compete against fellow partisans, tailoring their appeals to the party faithful while attempting to persuade voters that they best represent the ideals and values of their party. As a consequence, Republican contenders usually move to the political right, advocating conservative policies that appeal to core Republican voters. Democratic contenders, in turn, promote more liberal policies that appeal to core Democratic supporters. Prospective nominees from each party hope to secure their party's nomination as soon as possible so they can end the interparty attacks, focus instead on confronting the other party's nominee in the November general election, and build a campaign designed to appeal more broadly to the American people.

In 2000, however, both Bush and Gore had clear advantages within their parties going into the primary season. Having served two terms in a successful Democratic administration, Vice President Gore was Bill Clinton's heir apparent. Republicans, determined to take back the White House from an administration scarred by impeachment, rallied quickly around then-Governor Bush as their best hope. Although both candidates did have to compete in caucuses and primaries to secure their nominations, neither candidate expected a strong primary challenge; both campaigns assumed they would win. Thus, instead of waiting until after the party conventions to fight for the general election swing voters, both candidates, in large part, began to fight the general election battle during the primaries.

In such a political context, it makes sense to appeal to general election voters earlier in the campaign season. Strategically, the faith-based issue gave each candidate a chance to make a moderate move. Bush's support of these policies moved him to the left of traditional Republicans because he embraced the work of both government and community organizations in meeting human needs. This focus provided the core of his "compassionate conservative" philosophy. As one of Bush's campaign policy advisers explained: "We weren't so concerned about drawing distinctions with Gore. This was about transforming the Republican party."[1] Whereas many conservative voices within the party advocated a more libertarian approach to social welfare programs, Bush argued that government needed to be involved in programs serving the poor. By calling upon the government to partner with churches and faith-based organizations to provide those services, however, he promoted a new policy approach that appealed to conservatives with its promise of less "big government" involvement and more attention to religion. At the same time, this compassionate conservative approach gave Bush the freedom to address social policy issues more typically associated with the political left.

FOCAL POINT 2.1

Democrats, Republicans, and Faith-Based Proposals

Political scientists offer a variety of explanations why political parties change issue positions. One such explanation, issue ownership, con-tends that voters connect Democrats and Republicans with different issues. In recent decades, for example, Democrats have earned a reputation as being better on education, health care, and social welfare policies. Republicans, in contrast, "own" issues such as na-tional security, defense, and tax policy.

Scholar Geoffrey Layman has applied this theory to politically relevant religious issues and America's two major political parties. Most broad faith traditions have long been tied to one party: Protes-tants to the Republicans, and Catholics and Jews to the Democrats. Layman argues that in the past thirty years, Democrats have been captured by groups and leaders who sponsor a "soft" form of cultural relativism based on a secularist, or at least private and politically irrelevant, view of religion. Republicans, in turn, have been captured by politically conservative and religiously orthodox groups. Recent research affirms Layman's views. People highly committed to a par-ticular religion tend to be more politically conservative and Republi-can than their less committed co-believers. Politically, this implies that the Republican Party can hope to gain crossover votes from more observant Catholics and Jews, and the Democrats from less devout Protestants.

Centrists in each party can try to counteract what they see as extremist trends within their parties by pushing new issues. In theory, centrist Democrats and Republicans could both identify the same issue as a moderating force. In practice, the faith-based initiative is one such issue. As noted in *The New Republic*, "Gore and Bush are only two of the growing number of politicians who have called for increased government reliance on the social welfare activities of churches and religious charities. . . . The list includes presidential hopefuls—from Bill Bradley to Lamar Alexander—plus countless governors, mayors, and state legislators."

Reasons Republicans Have Supported Faith-Based Proposals

For years, Republicans have recognized that religion is a fault line in the Democratic Party. White Democrats are the most secular group in America, but black Democrats are the most religious. Faith-based offered Republicans an opportunity to expand their supporting coalition and reshape the party's image on social welfare. By appealing to traditionally Democratic voting blocs such as African Americans by showing a more compassionate side, Republicans might draw some votes away from Democrats. As Al From, the president of the Democratic Leadership Council, noted: "In 2000, the Republicans are going to try to steal our politics. . . . They have to become credible on compassion issues, just as in 1992 we had to be credible on fiscal discipline, toughness on crime, and welfare." The emphasis on compassionate conservatism moved the GOP toward the political center, but strategists were confident that traditional conservatives would stay within the fold: conservative religious voters were unlikely to find a political home with the Democrats.

Reasons Democrats Have Supported Faith-Based Proposals

The Democratic Party also had many reasons to support policies to increase partnerships between religious organizations and the government. According to a recent study published by the Brookings Institution, religion is important to most Americans and they expect their politicians to, at a minimum, pay deference to God and religion. A majority of Americans say that religion is very important. Approximately two in five say that they attend church weekly: nearly one in three believes the Bible is literally true and claims to be born again. Understanding the important role religion plays in many Americans' lives, many Democrats have advocated reaching out to religious voters. Bill Clinton followed this strategy in 1992 to win office by advocating a "Third Way" of governing centered on a conservative view of individual responsibility that resonated with the traditionally religious. In 2000, Gore sought to reach religious voters by selecting Senator Joe Lieberman, an orthodox Jew who speaks openly of his religious beliefs, as his running mate and by embracing, for a time, faith-based initiatives.

The Democratic strategy of signaling moderation on religious issues appeared to be wise. Although secular voters are a strong voting bloc within the Democratic Party, the Gore team thought that dissatisfied secularists would not find political refuge in Republican proposals. As the campaign progressed and Green Party candidate Ralph Nader began to pose a threat of peeling away left-leaning Democrats, however, the Gore campaign moved to a more populist strategy and began to downplay issues, like faith-based, that appealed to more conservative Democrats.

—Amy Black

Sources

Hacker, Jacob S. "Faith Healers." *The New Republic*, 28 June 1999: 16.
Klein, Joe. "The Men in the Mirror." *New Yorker*, 14 June 1999: 33.
Kohut, Andrew, John C. Green, Scott Keeter, and Robert C. Toth. *The Diminishing Divide: Religion's Changing Role in American Politics.* Washington, D.C.: Brookings Institution, 2000.
Layman, Geoffrey. *The Great Divide: Religion and Cultural Conflict in American Party Politics.* New York: Columbia University Press, 2001.

Gore also made a move toward moderation with his support of faith-based initiatives, using a tactic Ron Brownstein described as "competing for ground usually claimed by Republicans."[2] Traditional Democrats see government as the solution, not the problem, so they advocate for the government to play an activist role on social welfare issues. In addition, secular voters and advocates of the separation of church and state are relatively small but vocal Democratic constituencies. By legitimizing the role of religious institutions and conceding that government may not always offer the best solutions to problems, Gore's faith-based proposal moved him slightly to the political right, a tactic Clinton mastered in securing his two election victories. One author described Gore's strategy on faith-based as "a Clintonian compromise," noting that "with his 'new partnership' vision, Gore erased what could have been a major difference between [2000's] presumptive Republican and Democratic presidential nominees."[3]

Shifting Public Opinion on Religion and Politics

While Gore and Bush were seeking ways to appeal to moderate voters, both campaigns also recognized that the changing political environment created new opportunities to discuss religion and politics. Both candidates thought that appeals combining religion and public policy would be attractive to the independent, moderate swing voters whose votes determine which party wins the White House. What trends led them to embrace such a strategy? What does the public think about politicians using religious themes in political campaigns? One excellent source on the subject is *The Diminishing Divide*, a book by a quartet of respected scholars and pollsters.[4] Analyzing survey data from the 1960s through the mid-1990s, the researchers identified trends in the changing public view of religion and politics that help explain why the political environment was right for faith-based campaigning.

First, religion is an important and broadly accepted influence on contemporary American politics. While a strong majority of Americans embrace the general concept of the separation of church and state, they do not endorse the complete separation of religion from any influence on government. Rather, a majority of the public thinks that religious views and values, on balance, bring good things to politics. In addition, Americans have grown increasingly supportive of linking religion and politics. In the 1960s, a majority of Americans thought that it was improper for clergy to speak out on political issues; by the 1990s, public sentiment had reversed. Most Americans now accept religion in the public square even while maintaining stated support for the separation of church and state. This apparent paradox is not due to a lack of public understanding, the authors of *The Diminishing Divide* suggest. Rather, many Americans distinguish between improper interaction between religious organizations and governments and proper religion-based moral reasoning about public issues.[5]

Second, the researchers found no evidence of a spiritual reawakening in America in the past thirty years, suggesting instead that increased public support for religion is better understood as a reaction to growing secularity and the decline of a dominant Protestant value system. The public supports religious people and messages in politics to restore some sense of order and meaning to an arena they perceive as too secularized and amoral. Religious voices are also prominent in politics because the political agenda has changed in recent decades to include more cultural and sexual issues such as abortion and school prayer, issues for which religious arguments are more obviously germane.

In addition, this research finds growing connections between religion and politics at the grassroots level as more religious people enter the political realm. That is, long-term political activists are not necessarily becoming more religious, but churches and religious organizations are increasingly educating their members on the importance of politics, engaging and mobilizing them on political issues, and drawing them into the public square. As a result, the more religiously committed members of major religious traditions are also more active in politics; the less committed within each tradition are less active in politics.[6]

In this changing political climate, in which increasing numbers of religious adherents were entering the public square, presidential candidates in 2000 appeared more comfortable raising religious themes. Al Gore's selection of Joe Lieberman, a devout Orthodox Jew, as his running mate signaled Gore's ease with some mixing of religion and politics and opened new doors for direct religious appeals during the campaign. Almost all of the candidates raised some religious themes and issues on the campaign trail, and Bush and Gore gave prominent attention to faith-based initiatives early in their campaigns. Such policies symbolically and substantively linked religion and government more closely, tapping into the transformed political environment and growing popular support for such connections.

Although the American public has grown more receptive to the inclusion of religion in the public square, elites have been less supportive of such policies. Research comparing the views of the general public and elites in the academy, media, business, and government reveals great differences between the two groups on matters involving religion and politics. Differences between the general public and elites are greatest when members of each are asked about media fairness to religious groups and whether the religious right is a threat to democracy; differences narrow on more abstract questions about church-state relations. The more specific or concrete an example, however, the greater the division between the public and elites. For example, only one in five respondents from the general public would ban a moment of silence in public schools compared with about half of the media and government elites and three of four academics surveyed.[7]

FOCAL POINT 2.2

Mixing Faith and Politics

Elite vs. Public Opinion

Not all campaign issues—even popular ones—make their way into policy once election day passes. One reason is the different audiences: campaigning plays to the masses but governing works with the elites. The religious beliefs and behaviors of the American voting public differ greatly from those of the elites who conduct, shape, and report on public policy. Not surprisingly, these differences about religion and its role in public life affected the transition of the faith-based initiative from a "no-brainer" campaign strategy to a highly contentious legislative initiative.

One useful source investigating differences between elites and the masses on religion is Ted Jelen and Clyde Wilcox's *Public Attitudes toward Church and State.* This 1995 book combs through opinion surveys conducted among members of the general public and among four different elites—government, business, media, and academic—presenting contrasts on religious views. Because public policy making involves at least the three elites of government, media, and academia, the book provides some explanation for the difficulty of the faith-based initiative in the Washington policy world.

Basic religious affiliation and its importance is one area of division. The public is roughly divided about one-third evangelical Protestant, one-fourth mainline Protestant, one-fourth Catholic, and only one-eighth with no religious preference. Among elite categories, however, evangelical Protestants comprise only one-seventh of government, less than one-tenth of the media, and almost no one in academia. About 40 percent of government and media elites and 30 percent of academic elites identify with mainline Protestant churches, and almost one-sixth of government, one-fifth of media, and half of academic elites claim no religious preference at all.

Half the members of the public rate religion as "very important" to themselves personally and almost half report that they attend church weekly. In contrast, about two-fifths of government, one-third of media, and one-ninth of academic elites feel that religion is "very important," with approximately the same proportions reporting weekly church attendance. The importance of religion to a person's life also varies. Only one-tenth of the public reports that religion is "not important" to them personally, compared to almost one-fourth of government, one-fifth of media, and one-half of academic elites surveyed.

Given these differences, it is not surprising that differences exist in key common religious beliefs. Almost one-third of the members of the public believe in the literal truth of the Bible and describe themselves as "born again," compared to only one-tenth of government and media elites and barely any academics surveyed.

These differences in affiliation and belief translate into differing views about the interaction between religion and government. More than a majority—60 percent—of the public agrees that there should be a "high wall" of church-state separation. The three elite groups, however, believe this much more strongly, with more than 80 percent of government, 90 percent of media, and 95 percent of academics surveyed advocating such a "high wall." On the more general question of "government help to religion," the divide is greater. Just under half of the public agrees that government should not help religion, but nearly 70 percent of the media, 80 percent of the government, and 90 percent of the academic elites surveyed believe in the "no aid" principle.

Specific issues demonstrate an even wider chasm between public and elite views about religion and government. Seventy percent of the public believes that it is important for the president to "have religion," while a little less than half of the media and only 20 percent of academic elites concur. To the extent that the faith-based initiative was cast in the media as attractive to a "religious right," further problems are suggested. Overwhelming majorities of the public agree with specific issues traditionally supported by evangelicals and the religious right, and few see the religious right or evangelicals as a threat. To illustrate, only 12 percent of the public would describe the religious right or evangelicals as a "threat to democracy." In contrast, almost one-third of the government and media elites surveyed feared the religious right/evangelicals, as did three-fourths of academic elites. Public prayer at high school sporting events shows a similar divide. Only one-third of the public feels that prayer is inappropriate at such events, but 60 percent of government, three-fourths of media, and almost nine-tenths of academic elites believe it to be inappropriate.

Given the stark contrast between the mass public and politically involved elites on religious issues that these numbers suggest, it is little wonder that the president's faith-based initiative encountered difficulty in the legislative process.

—Amy Black and Melissa Fritsch

Source

Jelen, Ted G., and Clyde Wilcox. *Public Attitudes toward Church and State.* Armonk, N.Y.: M. E. Sharpe, 1995.

The differences between elites and the general public on issues of religion and politics suggest that faith-based initiatives would have far greater difficulty inside Washington than out on the campaign trail. Influential elite groups that would debate the issue have far more skeptical views about the wisdom and propriety of more closely mixing religion and politics than do typical American voters.

The General Political Climate

Just as popular opinion on religion and politics was shifting in 2000, so, too, did factors outside the campaigns themselves create a political environment conducive for advancing faith-based proposals in both parties. Because the candidates were campaigning in the midst of relative peace and prosperity, traditional presidential issues such as the economy and foreign relations were not major issues on voters' minds. As National Public Radio's campaign correspondent Elizabeth Arnold explained: "The economy's good and crime is down, so you have a whole lot of candidates running around out there right now scrambling for meaningful themes, looking for that core message that will excite the crowd."[8]

In addition, the 1999 school shootings at Columbine High School that left fourteen students and one teacher dead began a nationwide conversation about the need for values and morality at the beginning of the presidential campaign season. Referring to remarks made by political scientist John Green, the *Boston Globe* described the political context: "With the shootings at Columbine and the disgust over President Clinton's sexual escapades, Green said there is a vast hunger for spirituality, meaning, and morality in everyday life."[9] Indeed, the political conditions were well suited to candidates calling for a return to traditional values and invoking religious imagery.

Other factors helped create an ideal political climate for presidential candidates to advocate that faith-based organizations offer social services previously provided by the government. National polls indicated a declining trust in government and many signs that Americans were disengaging from the political process. In the words of one commentator: "Although Bush and Gore are sure to disagree on programmatic details, their substantial agreement is significant. Government has become so toxic politically that presidential candidates are reluctant to say a government program might be a good thing."[10] Hailing the effectiveness of religious and community organizations, the candidates could respond to this growing malaise by advocating new ways of providing social services.

At the same time that trust in government was declining, consensus was growing in the policy community and the general public that religious organizations might provide better solutions to enduring problems: "Political leaders, academics and policy analysts from across the ideological spectrum more and more see initiatives sponsored by churches and led by people of faith as a promising approach to the nation's social problems. And they say government—which almost everyone agrees will remain the primary financial support for poor Americans—should aid these efforts."[11] In this political context it is not surprising that both major-party nominees took positions that promoted an increased role for religion.

Specific Reasons Bush Supported a Faith-Based Initiative

Just as general political conditions affected the candidates' decisions to promote faith-based policies in their campaigns, so, too, did each candidate have specific reasons for taking his position.[12] Bush's support of a national faith-based initiative was in large part an extension of work he had begun as governor of Texas. Under his leadership, Texas moved to the forefront in aggressive implementation of charitable choice provisions. In addition, Governor Bush's staff worked diligently to remove regulations and liability provisions that were seen as barriers to faith-based groups. When discussing the campaign decision-making process, Bush advisers quickly connect Bush's Texas experience with his early and forceful promotion of faith-based initiatives, noting that it was a deliberate choice for the governor to highlight the faith-based issue in the first policy address of his official candidacy, the August 1999 speech in Indianapolis.[13]

Although the opponents and supporters of Bush's faith-based proposals find few points of agreement, there is one on which almost every one involved with this issue concurs: the faith-based initiative is of great personal importance to George W. Bush. As one of Bush's advisers explained: "He sees this all through the prism of his own conversion. . . . His conversion experience is a point of commonality, a point of understanding with people in crisis and difficulty."[14] Bush often speaks of the power his religious conversion supplied to help him overcome his drinking problem, and he believes faith-based groups can help transform the lives of others seeking help.

For supporters of faith-based partnerships, Bush's personal connection to the issue is both a sign of the depth of his commitment to the issue and an indicator that he truly understands the goals and motivations of faith-based providers. For many of those who oppose increased government partnership with faith-based groups, however, the connection between this policy and Bush's faith experience is a matter of serious concern. If Bush credits religious conversion for changing his own life and behavior, the argument goes, what will keep him from expecting that everyone undergo a similar religious experience? As Meg Riley of the Unitarian Universalist Association of Congregations noted: "Once [Bush's] personal story of salvation was attached to it, this was very frightening."[15] Bush's support, grounded in personal experience, appears solid and unwavering— providing encouragement to supporters and eliciting fear from religious pluralists.

Although Bush's steadfast support of the faith-based initiative clearly originated in his religious experiences and personal belief in the effectiveness of faith-based organizations, he and his advisers also saw political reasons for supporting this policy. In recent decades, strong religious commitment has defined large voting blocs, separating the religious from the secular. According to Douglas Laycock of the University of Texas Law School: "The alignment today is the religiously intense against the secular, and with respect to that fight, evangelicals and conservative Catholics are now on the same side."[16] The Bush team hoped to appeal to the core Republican constituency of evangelical voters and attract new support among conservative Catholics, traditionally Democrats, by promoting a policy to encourage the work of faith-based groups.

In addition, faith-based policies offered an opportunity for the Bush campaign to reach out to minority voters, especially the traditionally Democratic voting blocs of urban African Americans and Latinos. Described by *The New Republic* as the "first Republican initiatives in decades that capture the spirit of black, as well as white, Christianity,"[17] faith-based proposals to increase government partnerships typically receive strong support from black and Latino congregations. Although Republican pollster Frank Luntz downplayed the possible political motivations behind Bush's proposal, he noted the potential political power of faith-based policies:

> I don't believe he is doing it for political purposes, but I will tell you absolutely that if he continues on this road of faith-based assistance, that is the first successful effort I have seen to penetrate the black mind-set that has worked. . . . They are the most faith-based segment of the population there is. And they not only appreciate what Bush is doing but they support it.[18]

More than any other issue in Bush's platform, faith-based proposals offered the best hope for courting minority voters.

Specific Reasons Gore Supported a Faith-Based Initiative

Unlike Bush, who had an established track record of aggressively promoting faith-based initiatives as governor of Texas, Gore lacked a clear public record on these issues. Although Gore is a professing Christian and former seminarian, religion and faith were not common topics in the vice president's public speeches. As political scientist John Green noted in a public forum after the election: "Although Al Gore is actually a very religious man, most people did not know that about him. Then his faith suddenly appeared on the radar screen, and it surprised a lot of people, including journalists."[19] Indeed, Gore's relative silence on religious issues during his time as vice president led one reporter to remark after the Salvation Army speech: "Perhaps most interesting this past week was Gore's foray into religion and faith in politics after six years of saying little on the subject."[20]

Gore's record in public office did not provide a clear indicator of his position on government partnerships with religious groups, so Gore could have reasonably justified a campaign stance either favoring or opposing such policies. The one option not politically feasible for him, however, was silence. Even before the Texas governor officially declared his candidacy, Bush's support of faith-based initiatives had received significant national attention, and everyone expected the issue to be important in his campaign. Thus, in the spring of 1999, Gore had an opportunity to take a public position on faith-based policies before his presumed rival officially began his campaign.

Campaign adviser Bill Galston described Gore's decision-making process. The Gore campaign debated the merits of faith-based proposals, forming two teams of policy advisers making their best arguments for each side of the debate. They then presented the arguments to the vice president, who ultimately decided to embrace a policy expanding charitable choice. The next step was a public announcement, for, as Galston explains, "having made his decision, [Gore] didn't want to hide it. We set forth in an organized way to explain what his views were on a subject clearly of importance to the country and to the voters."[21] On May 24, 1999, Gore did just that, delivering an impassioned speech at the Salvation Army in Atlanta calling for a "new partnership" between government and faith-based organizations and advocating the expansion of charitable choice.

Like the Bush campaign, Gore and his advisers realized the potential political benefits of his decision to support faith-based initiatives. Recognizing the pattern of eroding support for Democrats among religious adherents, Gore's policy advisers were very open about their appeal to religious voters. In an often-quoted phrase, senior policy adviser Elaine Kamarck trumpeted: "The Democratic Party is going to take God back this time."[22] When asked why Gore supported faith-based initiatives in his campaign, adviser Galston explained: "One, he believed it was the right position to take. Second, he wants to do something to counteract the impression that the Republicans are favorable to religion and the Democratic Party is hostile to religion in public life. This is not a useful perception for the American people to have."[23]

In addition to fighting the public's perception of the Democratic Party as hostile to religion, Gore also found political benefit in promoting faith-based initiatives as a way of distancing himself from Clinton. Gore needed to build his reputation as a moral man and a person of faith to counteract his connection to an administration marred by scandals. The faith-based issue offered a good opportunity. As one reporter noted: "For Gore, the political benefit of religious talk is twofold; it sneaks some ground out from under Republicans who have long dominated the morals debate; and, less overtly, it may serve to disassociate him from Clinton's personal scandals."[24] Dan Katz, one of the conveners of a coalition to fight charitable choice, offered a more blunt interpretation of Gore's motivation: "For Gore it was a pathetic attempt to portray himself as not Clinton."[25]

A Shallow Consensus: Differences in Bush and Gore's Faith-Based Proposals

As we have noted, both Bush and Gore had compelling reasons to support faith-based initiatives in their presidential campaigns. Although both candidates expressed general support for this policy, the two campaigns varied significantly in their policy proposals and in their emphasis on faith-based issues. Upon closer examination, the apparent consensus was relatively shallow.

Perhaps the distinction between the two candidates' proposals is best summarized in a report of the Progressive Policy Institute: "While Vice President Gore was more measured in his support of [faith-based organizations], Bush's promise to rally the 'armies of compassion' was integral to his philosophy of 'compassionate conservatism.' "[26] Indeed, Bush's faith-based proposals throughout the campaign offered specificity and detail, highlighted by the candidate's fervency and impassioned rhetoric. The call for leveling the playing field for faith-based groups was part of compassionate conservatism, a larger plan for repositioning the Republican Party on social welfare issues. Gore, in contrast, advocated a more general sense of partnership, calling for the expansion of charitable choice while at the same time emphasizing the need for secular alternatives and the importance of protecting the separation of church and state. Promotion of faith-based partnerships was one of Gore's many policy positions; other campaign issues received far more of the vice president's attention and emphasis.

Comparing Faith-Based Proposals

Both Bush and Gore delivered substantive policy speeches early in their campaigns devoted specifically to the promotion of faith-based issues. Despite the basic similarities, however, the two speeches differed in the scope and detail of their policy proposals.

Gore called for a "new partnership" between the government and faith-based organizations. After commending the work of faith-based groups, Gore advocated the expansion of current charitable choice provisions:

> I believe we should extend this carefully tailored approach to other vital services where faith-based organizations can play a role, such as drug treatment, homelessness, and youth violence prevention.
>
> Of course, any extension must be accompanied by clear and strict safeguards: Government must never promote a particular religious view, or try to force anyone to receive faith. We must ensure that there is always a high-quality secular choice available. We must continue to prohibit direct proselytizing as part of any publicly-funded efforts. And we must establish the same clear accountability for results we would expect of anyone who does the public's business. But we must dare to embrace faith-based approaches that advance our shared goals as Americans.[27]

In this speech, candidate Gore reminded the audience of his past commitment to working with faith-based groups, outlined the significant differences that religious charities can make in people's lives, and made clear his openness to greater partnership between government and faith-based organizations. At the same time, he reiterated the importance of maintaining the separation of church and state: "The separation of church and state has been good for all concerned, good for religion, good for democracy, good for those who choose not to worship at all. It is our freedom from persecution, our absolute and unassailable choice of whether to and how to worship, that keeps religion strong."[28] Explaining Gore's perspective on the role of faith-based groups, campaign adviser Elaine Kamarck said: "He sees faith as an addition, a supplement."[29]

Like his opponent's speech, Bush's address introducing his faith-based proposals devoted significant time to praising the work of religious charities and showcasing success stories. But Bush's speech included more detailed policy proposals and advocated much more sweeping change in the way government relates to religious organizations. Outlining the goal of his faith-based initiative, Bush promised:

> In every instance where my administration sees a responsibility to help people, we will look first to faith-based organizations, charities and community groups that have shown their ability to save and change lives. We will make a determined attack on need, by promoting the compassionate acts of others. We will rally the armies of compassion in our communities to fight a very different war against poverty and hopelessness, a daily battle waged house to house and heart-by-heart.[30]

He further explained his proposal, outlining "three broad areas" of government action: promoting charitable giving, expanding the role and work of faith-based organizations, and implementing legal and regulatory reform to ease burdens on nonprofit organizations.

Some reporters who covered Bush's speech directly compared the two candidates' faith-based proposals. Referring to a policy "white paper," a document the Bush campaign provided to the press corps on the day of the speech that outlined specifics of the proposed policy, Ron Brownstein observed: "Bush's speech went notably further [than Gore's] in detailing an agenda to bolster these groups. . . . Bush buttressed his speech with a 10-page list of specific proposals."[31] In a statement that would prove to be prophetic, the *Washington Post* compared and contrasted the two proposals:

> Both President Clinton and Vice President Al Gore, the likely Democratic nominee, have also called for a greater public role for faith-based groups. But Bush's speech is sure to generate discussion and

perhaps controversy as the most extensive set of recommendations for how government could work directly with religious institutions to solve social problems.[32]

Whereas Gore promoted a revised model of caregiving, supporting a policy that would expand service choices to include moral and religious groups as well as secular ones, Bush advocated an entirely new philosophy of social services. As religion and public life commentator Joe Loconte explained, Bush's proposal "signified a paradigm shift in the way we provide social services in this country from a top-down, secular government model to one that is deeply infused by faith commitment."[33]

Campaigning on the Faith-Based Issue

Just as Bush and Gore's campaign positions varied in their content and scope, so, too, did they place different degrees of emphasis on the faith-based issue during the months of campaigning. Gore announced his position with a high-profile speech early in his campaign, but, over time, other issues took center stage. Bush, on the other hand, began his campaign discussing faith-based initiatives and continued to emphasize the issue among his top policy priorities throughout the campaign season. For Gore, faith-based was one issue of many. For Bush, faith-based initiatives revealed the heart of his philosophy of governance—compassionate conservatism.

Because both candidates were on the record in support of some increase in government partnership with faith-based groups, the issue was not a source of major contention in the campaign. One would expect, then, that the faith-based issue would fade into the background. As Gore adviser Bill Galston noted: "Events conspired to lower the profile of the issue. If the candidates agree, that takes it off the table for most of the press. After a few stories, if they agree, what more can you say? Conflict is news. That's the oldest song in the business."[34]

With both candidates expressing general agreement, the campaigns knew that most reporters would have little incentive to devote time and effort to unpacking the nuances in the candidates' views on faith-based partnerships. Thus, in order for faith-based issues to receive much press coverage, the campaigns knew they would need to move the issue to the

Table 2.1. Articles Highlighting Both Candidates and
Faith-Based Issues

	Highlighting the views of		
	Both	*Gore*	*Bush*
Total number of articles	**40**	2	**40**
Type of article			
Editorial/opinion	18	0	4
Straight news	20	2	35
Other	2	0	1
Primary subject			
Faith or faith-based	27	0	5
Campaign analysis/candidate comparison	9	0	16
Compassionate conservatism	0	0	0
Other	4	2	19

forefront, staging events and planning speeches that could command media attention.

To compare how often the two campaigns succeeded in capturing media attention on faith-based policies, we analyzed newspaper coverage looking for how often major newspapers discussed some aspect of faith-based initiatives in articles mentioning candidate Bush or Gore. We searched the Lexis-Nexis major newspapers database for all articles that appeared from January 1, 2000, until election day, searching for the term "faith-based" and a mention of either Bush or Gore.

The results of the search were clear: Media reports were much more likely to connect the faith-based issue with Bush than with Gore. Of the 207 articles retrieved in the search, eighty-two mentioned both Bush and Gore and the faith-based issue, and about half of those articles (forty) discussed both candidates' positions on the issue. In the remaining articles that mentioned both Bush and Gore, forty of the articles only discussed Bush's stance on the faith-based issues, compared with two articles that spoke only of Gore's position on faith-based.

More than half of the articles retrieved in the search focused specifically on one candidate or the other. In this set of articles, the results are

Table 2.2. Articles Highlighting a Single Candidate and
Faith-Based Issues

	Candidate	
	Gore	*Bush*
Total number of articles	**5**	**120**
Type of article		
Editorial/opinion	0	24
Straight news	4	87
Other	1	8
Primary subject		
Faith or faith-based	1	25
Campaign analysis/candidate comparison	0	17
Compassionate conservatism	0	14
Other	4	63

striking. Of the 125 articles that reference faith-based and only one of the presidential candidates, Bush is the subject of 120 articles (96 percent), compared with a mere five articles that discuss Gore and a reference to faith-based policies. Although Gore may have discussed faith-based initiatives on some of his campaign stops, reporters rarely mentioned the issue in stories focusing exclusively on the vice president.

Most of the major newspaper articles discussing the faith-based issue and George W. Bush offer only a short reference to the policy, with almost one in four describing a campaign appearance at a faith-based organization. Seventeen articles connecting Bush and faith-based provide substantive discussion of the issue, with five articles referencing campaign stops. Bush's strategy of highlighting his support for faith-based initiatives by visiting religious organizations on the campaign trail succeeded in getting him media coverage for this issue.

Although candidates cannot completely control what the media will cover of their campaigns, they do devote significant time and resources to developing a communications strategy, planning appearances and speeches that call attention to issues the campaign hopes the media will report. Analysis of campaign stories shows which messages succeeded in capturing the attention of reporters, and, as such, offers a good measure of the central themes and ideas of a campaign. This analysis of the campaign coverage suggests that the faith-based initiative was reported as a centerpiece of the Bush campaign. In contrast, the faith-based issue was reported as one of many issues for Gore and did not appear to the media and thus to the public to be a central part of his message in 2000.

Faith-Based Policies over the Course of the Campaign

What factors might account for the vast differences in media coverage of the two candidates and the faith-based issue? The evidence suggests that Bush and Gore campaigned differently on faith-based issues.

Throughout the campaign season, Bush's support for faith-based groups was central to his campaign. Outside observers at any point in the primary or general election would recognize that the faith-based initiative was one of Bush's top policy priorities. As a Bush adviser explained: "For Bush, it was a theme from the first day in Cedar Rapids, Iowa. Bush was saying he was proud to be a compassionate conservative. This was a main theme at the convention; it was a main theme in the last weeks of the campaign."[35] During both the primary and general election seasons, Bush made appearances across the country at churches and faith-based organizations where he championed the role of religious groups. The topic often surfaced in interviews and in major speeches. Consistently, the Bush campaign emphasized faith-based initiatives and the larger theme of compassionate conservatism.

In his speech before the Republican convention, for example, Bush raised the theme that prosperity must have a purpose. Chiding the Clinton administration for its general failures, Bush called for a change in vision in a speech that focused more on broad themes than specific policy proposals. With references to faith and collective responsibility sprinkled throughout the speech, Bush spoke of the "unfinished struggle for human dignity," connecting this struggle to compassionate conservatism. Bush highlighted the work of a Christian ministry and then concluded: "Government cannot do this work. It can feed the body, but it cannot reach the soul. Yet government can take the side of these groups, helping the helper, encouraging the inspired. My administration will give taxpayers new incentives to donate to charity, encourage after-school programs that build character, and support mentoring groups that shape and save young lives."[36]

In contrast, Vice President Gore's support of faith-based partnerships appeared to wane over time. His discussion of faith-based began with great fanfare in the Salvation Army speech and was most pronounced in the primary. By the time of the Democratic convention, however, Gore's faith-based rhetoric had disintegrated into vague references and no specific policy promises. Clearly, the faith-based issue was no longer a central policy priority; Gore's campaign strategy instead appeared to shift to a focus on more traditional populist themes. In an impassioned convention speech rich with policy proposals, Gore began by spotlighting four major issue areas: health care, education, retirement security, and tax cuts. The remainder of the speech advocated twenty-seven specific policies ranging from gun control to universal preschool but made no direct mention of expanding faith-based partnerships.

Several post-election commentators noted the shift in Gore's campaign strategy. John DiIulio, for example, described the policy shift in a post-election forum:

> That May [Salvation Army] speech by Gore was a bold speech for a Democrat, at least as bold as Governor Bush's speech in July. . . . But as the Democratic convention drew nearer, there was a fight, apparently, about whether even to keep the language favoring charitable-choice expansion in the party's official talking points. . . . Gore had a problem in that his appeals were episodic and rather sketchy; he was never able to flesh out the implications, even when Senator Lieberman was nominated and it seemed like a perfect moment to put flesh on the bones of these sentiments. It never happened.[37]

Apparently under attack from some key constituency groups, Gore backed away from his earlier rhetoric on the faith-based issue and moved to more traditional Democratic territory. When asked about the faith-based issue in the Gore campaign, New Democrat spokesman Will Marshall recalls: "He didn't develop it; he didn't show commitment; he seemed to have abandoned it. . . . Undoubtedly, campaign strategists saw this as an irrelevant, or worse, Bush issue. 'If Bush is talking about it, why are you?' So they get on solid Democratic turf and off the Bush turf."[38]

In conclusion, Bush and Gore's apparent agreement on faith-based policies was more surface than substance. The two candidates defined and prioritized the issue very differently. Gore made a strong policy statement supporting expansion of existing charitable choice early in his campaign, but his issue focus shifted to other policies with more importance for his election bid. In contrast, Bush began and ended his candidacy calling for a series of policy changes that would create a fundamental shift in the relationship between government and faith-based groups, placing this issue at the center of his larger strategy of compassionate conservatism.

The Road to Confrontation:
Postelection Faith-Based Politics

Though the two major-party candidates advocated positions on the same "side" of the policy debate, they disagreed substantially on the extent to which government policy should change. So it is less than surprising that the apparent bipartisan agreement during the campaign quickly turned to discord once George W. Bush assumed the presidency. This section introduces some of the central factors that help explain how "consensus" became confrontation in the months following the election.[39] The chapters that follow will trace the movement of faith-based proposals through the legislative process and the executive branch, detailing the unfolding and building confrontation.

Divisiveness of the Election Outcome

Gore's popular-vote victory and the prolonged battle over the Florida recount created a polarized political environment in which many Democrats believed that Bush stole the election from Gore. Although Gore won a slim majority of the popular vote nationwide, the thirty-six-day election aftermath culminated in a Supreme Court decision that ended the battle over electoral votes and created a highly charged partisan climate. An aide to Representative Tony Hall, the Democratic sponsor of H.R. 7, in recounting how difficult it was to build Democratic support for the president's faith-based legislative priorities in early 2001, explained that "the water in the well [had been] poisoned by the post-election hangover."[40] The bitterness of the election aftermath had destroyed bipartisan accord and trust, vanquishing most hope of working smoothly and harmoniously across party lines.

Distrust of the newly inaugurated president was likely highest among African Americans. Nine out of ten black voters chose Gore over Bush, and surveys following the election decision revealed the significant mistrust of the election outcome: "Eighty-seven percent of African-Americans still don't think Bush won the election legitimately."[41] During the Florida recount, civil rights leaders convened in Florida to protest. African American turnout had reached historic highs in Florida, and the precincts in Florida with the most voting irregularities were also the precincts with the highest percentages of African Americans: "The errors were overwhelmingly in black precincts—and in the region of 10 percent. The most likely reason is that vast numbers of new inexperienced voters were probably in need of more help than most—and didn't get it."[42] Although faith-based initiatives generally draw great support from the black community, the suspicion and mistrust following the election severely damaged the likelihood that African American leaders would rally to the president's side.

In an atmosphere of intense partisanship and distrust over the election outcome, Bush faced an additional political obstacle. The congressional elections had resulted in the slimmest of margins in both chambers. Vice President Cheney provided the tie-breaking vote to maintain Republican control of the evenly divided Senate (a victory that would quickly prove hollow when Senator Jim Jeffords left the Republican Party, giving the Democrats a majority in and control of that chamber). Republicans maintained a slim majority in the House, but a handful of defectors could easily block legislation. With another congressional election less than two years away, Democratic leaders on the Hill realized that the opportunity to regain control of both chambers was in their grasp. In such a polarized and partisan environment the new president lacked both the electoral mandate and the political strength to pass legislation quickly.

Latent Opposition Waiting to Surface

Even though both candidates supported faith-based policies, neither Republican nor Democratic proposals received unanimous support within either party. Bush faced opposition from the right wing of the Republican Party, just as Gore's position was unpopular with the left wing of the Democratic Party. In both parties, however, most critics of faith-based policies kept their opposition on this issue quiet during the campaign. As Galston explains: "Partisans didn't have an incentive to weaken their own candidate. After the election the differences came to the surface. Lots of

Democrats swallowed their doubts because they didn't want to weaken Gore's candidacy. Lots of conservatives who agreed in principle disagreed with the Bush approach in practice."[43] Once the election was decided, opponents who had looked the other way during the campaign were now free to voice their concerns in public.

Ironically, the president's strong personal commitment to this issue played a powerful role in energizing the opposition. As noted in chapter 1, all five existing charitable choice laws had passed without these new provisions receiving much attention from lawmakers or the media. When Senator Ashcroft originally introduced charitable choice in the 1996 welfare reform, the opposition was unable to engage enough interest to defeat the policy. The political environment in 2001 was far different. Propelled by a mood of sharp partisanship and Bush's high-profile attention to the issue, a broad coalition of groups opposed to faith-based initiatives quickly mobilized. When asked what factors were most important for energizing opposition to faith-based provisions during the 2001–2002 legislative battles, interest group leaders often pointed to the president himself. By giving national attention to the faith-based initiative and promoting a stand-alone bill to expand government partnerships with religious and community organizations, the president gave opponents a ready and high-profile target to attack. As Dan Katz of Americans United for Separation of Church and State explained: "This year, the stars are really aligned. The president is making this his biggest issue. The civil rights groups are engaged as well as state and local [governments]. This time we have a much more powerful set of allies."[44] By shining a spotlight on faith-based initiatives, the president's proposals received sustained and significant attention from the media, interest groups, and scores of legislators for the first time.

Opposition or Tepid Support from Traditional Conservatives

While opponents were successfully organizing and building a strategy to fight the faith-based initiative, many traditional conservative organizations and leaders expressed their resistance to the plan. Clearly many conservatives had significant reservations about the president's proposals, with some opposing faith-based legislation outright. As political reporters Dana Milbank and Thomas Edsall summarized:

The White House expected church-state separation groups to object to the program. But it didn't expect a chorus of doubts from religious conservatives such as Pat Robertson, Jerry Falwell, Richard Land, Michael Horowitz, and even Marvin Olasky, one of the program's early architects. They worry that churches would be corrupted by government regulations or that objectionable sects would be rewarded.[45]

Although some administration officials said they expected opposition from some conservatives, and several sources maintain that the president himself was aware of potential fallout from the right, it is clear that at least a portion of White House political advisers miscalculated how traditional conservatives, particularly religious conservatives, would respond to the faith-based initiative.

Several conservative groups raised fears that government partnership would threaten the autonomy of religious organizations: that is, acceptance of government dollars would come with "strings attached" that could compromise the work or mission of the organization. As Richard Land of the Southern Baptist Convention said: "[W]ith the king's shillings come the king's shackles."[46] Still others argued that the faith-based plan might funnel government dollars to "dangerous" religions. Pat Robertson, for example, expressed his concern about the proposal, describing what he deemed an "intolerable situation": that "the same government grants given to Catholics, Protestants, and Jews must also be given to the Hare Krishnas, the Church of Scientology, or Sun Myung Moon's Unification Church—no matter that some may use brainwashing techniques, or that the founder of one claims to be the messiah and another that he was Buddha reincarnated."[47] Making money available to religious organizations was only good policy, these critics implied, if it went to religions acceptable to them and stayed out of the hands of "fringe" religious groups.

Not all conservative groups opposed the faith-based initiative outright, but the support of those who favored the policy lacked strength and vibrancy. As Ralph Benko, a lobbyist hired to promote the faith-based agenda in Congress, explained: "Ultimately, there was a conservative base for [the Senate faith-based bill], but it is not at the top of their agendas. . . . [T]hey are no longer mobilizable on [the bill]. Why? They are passionate about specific issues, and this is not on their list. They are favorably disposed but not active."[48] For most traditional conservative groups, the faith-based issue never became a high priority. With limited staff and resources, multi-issue groups must choose which issues they will empha-size. Enough conservatives had reservations about the faith-based initiative that it was difficult to find conservative organizations willing to devote significant resources and political capital to fight a battle not fully sup-ported within their ranks. Instead, activists devoted much of their time to abortion politics, an issue that often rallies conservative consensus and grassroots support. Their front-and-center concerns in 2001 included advocating for the appointment of pro-life officials and against embryonic stem-cell research. At the same time, many conservative groups were monitoring the president's education reform proposal—pushing for the inclusion of school vouchers while raising concerns about increased federal control over school assessment. Lauren Noyes, a former Hill staff member who used to organize weekly meetings for the Values Action Team, a coalition of conservative groups promoting family values, remembers only tepid support for the faith-based initiative. From her recollections, pro-family groups saw other issues as greater priorities, and many had reserva-tions about government involvement with faith-based groups.[49] In short, many conservative groups lacked both the political will and the resources to advocate strongly for the faith-based initiative.

Potential Political Power of the Message

Another factor influencing the conflict over the faith-based initiative was Democratic concern about losing key voter support. Faith-based proposals are popular among African Americans, a Democratic constituency that comprises an important part of the party's base. As John DiIulio explained: "Black Americans are in many ways the most religious people in America."[50] Current research suggests that African American congrega-tions already benefit from charitable choice provisions and would be much more likely than predominately white churches to apply for additional federal grants to help support their work. If black churches would benefit from a high-profile Bush initiative, Republicans hope—and Democrats fear—that African American voters might respond with greater support for the Republican president and his party.

Clearly, Bush's advisers hoped that faith-based proposals would attract black support. In a campaign press release, the Bush team trumpeted the support of black ministers, quoting one pastor who contended: "African Americans will no longer be taken for granted. It can no longer be what someone wants to do for us, we want to participate in our own destiny."[51] After the election, the White House continued to court African Americans with faith-based proposals, hoping to rebuild trust lost in the election aftermath and broaden the party's appeal to minority voters. When the new president signed two executive orders initiating his faith-based program, several prominent African American religious leaders participated in the public ceremony. Two months later, Bush invited fifteen black religious leaders to the White House to enlist their support for the faith-based program. One reporter described the spectacle as "one of the more unlikely alliances of the new administration," expressing fascination as "prominent black ministers filed out of the Oval Office on Monday declaring their support for President Bush's faith-based initiatives program."[52]

Although some African American leaders rallied to support Bush's initiative, others viewed the plan with great skepticism, casting the policy as a political ploy. For example, John Hurst Adams, a leader in the African Methodist Episcopal Church, compiled a list of "questions to which you should have a satisfactory answer before entering faith-based initiatives" and distributed it to those expressing an interest in the policy. As reporter Ken Herman observed: "The final question gets right to the politics. 'Is there a strong political agenda attached, namely a way to recruit blacks to Republican Party and thinking?' Adams asks. 'This could mean abandonment of the masses of black folk,' he answers."[53] Such a description of masses of African American voters abandoning the Democratic Party seems exaggerated, but most observers agree that if a faith-based initiative were ever successful it would likely help President Bush make some political gains with an overwhelmingly Democratic constituency.

Well aware of the potential danger of faith-based policies attracting black voters, Bush's critics discovered a way to rally the civil rights community against faith-based initiatives, framing the legislative debate as a discrimination issue. By focusing on an exemption in the Civil Rights Act that allows religious organizations to hire employees who share their religious values and beliefs, opponents argued that faith-based legislation would use taxpayer dollars to fund "religious discrimination." Under this act, employers may not discriminate on the basis of sex, race, or religion. Religious organizations, however, may use religious criteria when making hiring decisions. Kevin Hasson of the Becket Fund described this argument as a "blunt instrument to bludgeon something into submission," noting further the political power of this argument: "They like it because they can call it discrimination, a bad thing in the American lexicon. No bill will pass with this poison pill."[54] Once opponents linked charitable choice with a discrimination argument, proponents of faith-based policies lost almost any hope of receiving public support from black Democratic legislators. Time will tell if the framing of the debate also erodes support for faith-based policies in the African American community at large.[55]

Political Mistakes by Supporters of the Faith-Based Initiative

An additional factor—strategic miscalculations—helps explain the movement from consensus to conflict. A combination of political missteps and unwise strategic decisions contributed to the rancor over faith-based legislation and severely inhibited bipartisan efforts to pass it. As will be detailed in the next three chapters, the Bush administration and other supporters of faith-based initiatives made several strategic errors in their work to promote the president's plans. Perhaps most significantly, legislation was introduced too quickly, without enough attention to details and without consideration of potential political problems and backlash. Although the concept of government partnership with religious organizations appears straightforward at first glance, the practical reality of implementing any such policy raises complex constitutional, practical, and legal questions. Echoing Senator Joe Lieberman's oft-repeated quip, "The devil is in the details," lobbyist Dan Katz summarized: "An abstract political issue is political peril."[56] Several former occupants of the White House Office of Faith-Based and Community Initiatives lamented in interviews that they did not have enough time to educate the public and build consensus in favor of legislative action. Without months to lay the political groundwork, such sweeping and complex political change was difficult if not impossible to achieve.

Consensus, Confrontation, and Partisan Politics

As evidence from the 2000 presidential campaign demonstrates, candidates Bush and Gore agreed in their general support of faith-based policies, yet the possibilities for bipartisan cooperation quickly evaporated. Consensus turned to confrontation, and partisanship reigned.

One insight from the complicated and still unfolding story of the faith-based initiative is this: George W. Bush's support for faith-based proposals is resolute. In the midst of such a political firestorm, many other elected officials would have retreated. But Bush continues his call for faith-based legislation even as the partisan battle rages. Anyone who might have doubted Bush's personal commitment to this issue during the election is likely convinced by now. Although faith-based legislation ultimately failed in the 107th Congress, the impetus and determination to open more access for religious organizations remains strong and will remain a central presidential concern throughout Bush's time in office.

In addition, this story is a reminder that parties and elections matter. Normally, newly elected presidents enter office with political capital built up by winning the election. Since Bush lost the popular vote, he could not claim the electoral mandate that typically follows a November victory. An environment as polarized as Washington, D.C., makes bipartisan consensus difficult to achieve and extremely fragile at any time. In the aftermath of the bitter 2000 election, with razor-thin party margins in Congress, Democrats and Republicans had even less interest in working together and many incentives to retreat to their respective party bunkers.

One of the greatest ironies of the conflict over faith-based proposals so far is that both parties could have reaped political benefits from a bipartisan initiative. Following an election in which the major-party candidates both supported government partnerships with faith-based groups, Democrats could have embraced the goals of Bush's faith-based initiative, insisted upon revisions to moderate the policy in ways that would appeal to their core supporters, and forced Republicans to share the political victory. Instead, providing yet another example of what cynics decry as "politics as usual," the process was characterized by partisan rancor and legislative stalemate. It is to that rancorous process, the legislative battle, that we now turn.

Three

Partisan Appeal

Faith-Based in a Republican House

We actually "jammed" [the White House faith-based staff] when we introduced the bill.

House Republican staff person on the introduction of H.R. 7

Democrats fear that this bill is payback to conservative Christians for their support and see this as a GOP ploy to attack the Democratic base.

House Democratic staff person sympathetic to H.R. 7

Democratic representative Tony Hall of Dayton, Ohio, had an impeccable reputation among his colleagues.[1] Known on Capitol Hill as "Mr. Hunger," Representative Hall chaired the House Select Committee on Hunger from 1989 until it was abolished in 1993. Protesting the committee's elimination that year as part of cost-cutting and congressional reform, Hall went on a hunger strike. He ended his strike about three weeks later, but only after the World Bank and the U.S. Department of Agriculture promised to call hunger conferences and Congress set up a hunger issues clearinghouse. First elected in 1978, Hall served in the House until 2002, when he was nominated by President Bush to be the nation's ambassador to three United Nations food-aid programs with offices in Rome. Upon Senate confirmation, Hall resigned from Congress and moved to Italy to take up his new post.

An evangelical Presbyterian, Hall's deeply held religious beliefs informed the positions he took in Congress: concern for the poor and others at the margins of society, opposition to abortion and the death penalty, and the need for America to come to terms with its slave-owning past. He voted against permanent normal trading relations with China, for example, more because of his opposition to that nation's record on coerced abortions and religious freedom than over concerns about labor competition. On the other hand, he supported the 1999 air bombing campaign in Yugoslavia because he believed it to be the best means available to relieve the suffering of refugees fleeing Slobodan Milosevic.

This cluster of convictions does not fit nicely within the boundaries of either of today's political parties. The Democratic son of a Republican local officeholder, Hall's congressional voting record was usually described as "moderate" and his thinking as "independent." More accurately, Hall sought to apply his religious convictions to issues with less regard than most of his colleagues for partisan or interest group considerations. Hall could sometimes sound like a naïve idealist when he justified a vote against a popular bill, but those close to him asserted that his style was based in a determined refusal to succumb to the cynicism that infuses Washington politics and policymaking.

Hall's independence often made him one of a handful of Democrats voting on the Republican side of a bill. That independence encouraged Republicans to work with him on issues when the GOP wanted bipartisanship. When the Bush administration went looking in early 2001 for a Democratic cosponsor of House faith-based legislation, Hall was an obvious person to ask. Recommended by Virginia congressman Frank Wolf and former House Republican leadership staffer Billy Pitts, Hall was soon "invited to be the lead Democrat" on House faith-based legislation that Republicans assumed would draw significant support from members of both parties.[2]

Hall was willing to give the invitation strong consideration. He had been pleased when the president selected John DiIulio to head the White House Office of Faith-Based and Community Initiatives (WHOFBCI) over other candidates more closely aligned with religious and political conservatives. After the invitation and before Hall's response, President Bush invited the Ohio congressman to join him on a January 2001 visit to the Fishing School in northeast Washington, D.C., a faith-based community center for inner-city children known for its after-school and summer mentoring and tutoring programs. Everything Hall said at the school favored an expansive faith-based bill like the one that had been described by candidate Bush. In a statement issued by his office that day, Hall argued that "faith has been a defining characteristic of our communities' life throughout our nation's history, and people who serve God by serving those in need remain one of America's greatest strengths. This [faith-based] initiative will draw on these traditions and bring them to bear on some of our most difficult social problems. . . . To those who worry that we are in uncharted territory, I would point to the work American charities do overseas. . . . Many of these organizations are closely affiliated with religious groups; many of their projects grew from missionary roots."[3]

Bush and Hall did not know each other; the Fishing School visit was, in fact, only the second time they had met. But a Hall staff person noted that in their three-mile car ride back to the White House from the school, Bush and Hall "hit it off. They talked about Jesus. Tony was impressed and touched."[4] Hall's ride with President Bush clinched his decision to be the lead Democratic sponsor of the House version of the faith-based initiative.

The ride in the presidential limousine started a friendship between the two evangelical politicians. But "car ride" is also a cautionary metaphor for the way the faith-based initiative worked its way through the House. While Hall worked closely on the text of H.R. 7 before its introduction, he was taken for a ride on the bill's road, a passive passenger on a vehicle steered by Republicans and conservative interests. To his credit, Congressman Hall never jumped out of the faith-based car. Privately critical of several strategic decisions, publicly he did all he could to get Democrats to support H.R. 7—conducting briefings for Democratic members and staff, and urging them to give the GOP the benefit of the doubt on controversial strategic moves.

The appearance of bipartisan support that Hall helped provide for the president's faith-based initiative on that January 2001 day at the Fishing School soon wore off. H.R. 7 passed the House less than six months later with almost no Democratic votes and no broad coalition to help it through the Senate. The bill's road to passage was determined by the House Republican leadership and the interests most closely aligned with the strongly conservative majority of that party. The faith-based initiative was conceived as a way to improve the lot of poor and ethnic minorities, but House Republicans reshaped it into a poorly fitted and little appreciated payoff to the GOP's traditional religious base.

The Overall Political Context of Early 2001

House Republicans anticipated good relations with George W. Bush, the first Republican president since their party had won a majority in both houses of Congress in 1994. Bush seemed a bit left of the House GOP's center, although not by enough to foreclose cooperation. House Republicans were also encouraged by the legislative style that Bush had used in Texas and pledged to continue in Washington: outline an idea's general objectives, let the legislature work out the details, and then come back into the legislative process in the late stages to claim joint credit.

The president's issue agenda was limited and clear. The number one priority was tax reform, centered in large income tax reductions. A second priority was educational reform. Faith-based was a close third. In January 2001, it looked like tax reform would be mostly partisan, although many Democrats were finding tax cuts too appealing to oppose. The White House was running education as a bipartisan exercise; indeed, one of the more controversial and, to House Republicans, irritating moves of the early Bush administration was its decision to work with Democratic senator Edward Kennedy on the education bill. The choice to be bipartisan on education inclined the White House to be more conservative on the faith-based initiative. As one White House staff person summarized it later: "The strategy [was] on taxes, go to the right. On education, work with Kennedy. [So] we can't afford to hurt the right [on faith-based legislation]. Faith-based can't be another moderate thing."[5] A key part of the "right" strategy on faith-based was to let the House proceed with its legislation before the Senate.

Among House Republicans, no one member was deeply committed to faith-based legislation. In prior congresses, Representative Mark Souder of Indiana had led House charitable choice debates, but the key legislative champion, Senator John Ashcroft, had been defeated in his bid for reelection and was soon to be Bush's attorney general. Because of the president's interest, however, faith-based had to be a House leadership issue in the 107th Congress. This meant that the House Republican leaders would decide the key strategic moves without having strong personal interest and experience in the faith-based issue. To many of these leaders the faith-based initiative seemed useful mostly for political purposes—primarily to reward their politically conservative and religiously orthodox key interest groups, and secondarily to reach out to deeply religious ethnic minorities.[6]

Faith-based was one of President Bush's personal priorities for reasons quite different from the purely political. The president wanted to encourage intensely and vocally religious groups to provide more social services because such groups, in his experience, worked wonders. Effectiveness and efficiency, not partisan calculation, seemed his primary motivation—a conclusion reinforced by nearly all of our interviews. Friend and foe alike did not doubt the president's sincere belief in the effectiveness of faith-based programs. The president seemed to think faith-based was an issue that could and should attract all reasonable people of whatever race, party, or interest group.

In contrast, views among most of the new staff in other White House offices more closely matched those of House Republicans and key traditional constituencies, because they all came from the same pool. As one close observer later noted: "They are all 'inside' people—within the West Wing and with each other. They are cliques who hang out. They know each other from the campaign."[7] To these staff members, the faith-based initiative was useful as a tool to reward politically and religiously conservative groups seeking greater access to the public square and to political power, and as part of a strategy to appeal to deeply religious ethnic minorities. But they lacked the president's deep belief in the efficacy of faith-based social services. As one WHOFBCI staff person asserted: "Nobody in the administration except George W. Bush [had] any time at all for the faith-based issue; it is, for them, symbolic politics. . . . There is a disconnect between the president and his staff."[8] One close observer of the White House's relationship with Congress on the issue summarized it this way in early 2003: "[V]ery few people in the White House made it a priority. Some wanted to use [the failure to pass faith-based legislation] as a club to beat up on Democrats."[9]

Fashioning the President's Proposal into Legislative Language

Legislative efforts got off to a muddled start. The president rushed out his executive orders creating the faith-based offices on January 29, 2001, the same day he announced DiIulio as director of the WHOFBCI. The next day, the president unveiled his faith-based legislative agenda in "Rallying the Armies of Compassion," a seventeen-page paper issued by the Executive Office of the President.[10] "Rallying" was both ambitious and ambiguous. The paper boldly called for government to promote new and better ways to meet the needs of poor Americans by directly and indirectly encouraging faith- and community-based social service organizations. Administratively, the WHOFBCI and its satellites would take every step they could under existing law to make the federal government more hospitable to partnerships with a wider range of faith-based groups seeking to meet human needs. They would completely enforce existing charitable choice laws and identify and remove other barriers to faith-based participation in federal programs.

Legislatively, the president's call to arms was broader but murkier. "Rallying" proposed five major tax changes to encourage charitable giving and suggested a joint public-private technical assistance and start-up fund called the "compassion capital fund." It only indirectly suggested that charitable choice be applied to new programs, and those were only small pilot programs for after-school literacy and the children of prisoners. One reporter described the president's proposed legislative plan as "a low-key approach that could make it easier for his proposals to be enacted."[11]

Other than the size of the tax breaks for charitable giving and the introduction of the compassion capital funds, President Bush's faith-based legislative proposal was so modest that the discrepancy between his campaign rhetoric and his governing document created confusion. One wire service misreported that the WHOFBCI would "distribute billions of dollars to religious groups and charities over the next ten years," helping create a misperception that led to weeks of phone calls to the office from groups seeking money.[12]

The White House's particular legislative preference for charitable choice was as murky as it was important. The four charitable choice provisions in previous laws differed from each other. The major differences were in the intensity of government oversight, the freedom of faith-based recipient groups to define the practices and qualifications of their staff members, and the ability of objecting beneficiaries to opt out of parts of a funded program. Most interest groups in early 2001 were grappling with the broad idea of faith-based, but the strong supporters and opponents, previously involved in the issue, were examining the detailed differences among previous charitable choice versions and wanted to know which one the new president would support.

"Rallying the Armies of Compassion," however, offered no insight into the administration's view. Later interviews with involved White

House staff suggest two explanations for the ambiguity. First, most staff persons at the six faith-based offices did not want more charitable choice legislation right away, although they planned to seek legislative expansions eventually. As one WHOFBCI staff person stated later: "DiIulio wanted to wait, pinpoint the problems, and then address those" in a later bill.[13] Implementing prior charitable choice law would take effort and generate public controversy, and a simultaneous legislative fight on new faith-based initiatives would only complicate an already daunting task. An executive branch official put it this way: "Dropping the bill early was a terrible mistake. Pursuing legislation was a mistake, but the Hill was forcing it."[14] Some suggested that his ambiguous faith-based proposal reflected the new president's basic legislative style—outline general principles and leave it to Congress to fill in the details.[15] One White House source involved in crafting the legislative strategy advanced that theory: "'Armies of Compassion' . . . outlines the principles and basic reform. We let the legislative process take form around it, leaving room for discussion and negotiation." The same source claimed that this strategy was "a consistent policy across the administration."[16] Others doubted that explanation, citing several instances, such as comprehensive tax reform, where White House officials were intimately involved from the beginning in legislative details.[17]

The administration's ambiguity was immediately exploited. Within days, a wide set of disagreements and concerns arose. Faith-based groups already funded with federal dollars, such as Lutheran Services of America, Catholic Charities, and the United Jewish Communities, were concerned about losing present funds to new and perhaps unqualified and poorly monitored competitors.[18] Steve Selig of the United Jewish Communities' Human Services and Social Policy Pillar cited a widespread concern: "For sectarian institutions receiving public dollars, the challenge will be to provide non-sectarian and non-discriminatory service and be open to the same standards of accountability as those offered by" currently funded groups.[19]

Others suggested that the president wanted faith-based to be a payoff to the religious right. David Saperstein of the Religious Action Center of Reform Judaism worried about government-sponsored proselytization, warning representatives of large Jewish organizations that "if money goes to such groups as the Southern Baptist Convention, which has 'targeted us for conversion,' federal grants will 'free up their money to come after us.' "[20] Joanne Negstad of Lutheran Services of America worried that faith-based groups providing government services might force participants to take part in religion. "We really believe [religious activities] need to be voluntary," she stated in a wire service report on the initiative.[21]

Legislative Leaders

The White House could, of course, move administratively by itself, but it had to find House and Senate sponsors for legislation. Due partly to the indifference of White House faith-based staff to getting a bill, recruiting members to sponsor bills was done at higher and more political levels. While the president courted Representative Tony Hall, Speaker Dennis Hastert (R-Illinois) and others in the House GOP leadership decided in late January that Republican Conference chair J. C. Watts should be the primary House sponsor and that Hastert would be the first Republican cosponsor.[22] Hastert's office would be intimately involved in drafting the legislation, but Watts's office would be its public face. That strategy would have consequences for the legislative journey. The Hastert office was committed to a "purer" version of charitable choice language, a version that appeared in the most recently enacted laws of late 2000.[23] Watts was not a legislative detail person but had excellent communication resources, and this bill seemed a good complement to his larger agenda in seeking GOP support among African Americans.[24]

These key sponsorship decisions were political, but not exclusively so. Both Hastert and Watts were sincere in wanting social services delivered more effectively. As one Democratic staffer put it later: "Watts and Hastert had a heart for this. Hastert was interested in community renewal—it was for real."[25] Originally, House leaders thought that the faith-based initiative could be a bipartisan bill and the legislative equivalent of a slam dunk in basketball. Whereas most bills go through many months of waiting even for committee consideration, in early February 2001, Watts thought he could have a bill ready for final House votes by mid-April.

Conservative Division:
Pragmatic Pluralists vs. Purist Preferentialists

Internal and external conflicts, however, soon foreclosed speedy bipartisan favor. Concerns by some conservative religious spokespersons and interest group leaders, strains between the WHOFBCI and the Republican House leadership, and the outside political environment all worked to quickly make House consideration of the faith-based proposal highly partisan, and the content of the legislation quite different from the guidelines the president put forth in the "Rallying" document.

FOCAL POINT 3.1

Conservative Rift

Purists vs. Pragmatists

Early friends of the faith-based initiative, such as the Center for Public Justice, Marvin Olasky, and the Institute for Justice, cooperated closely before George W. Bush became president. But they started to divide into rival camps as the Bush administration turned its faith-based campaign promise into personnel and legislative decisions. On one side were the purists and preferentialists who wanted daring and bold strokes. On the other side were the pragmatists and pluralists who wanted caution and care.

Purists

Purists wanted legislation primarily to help intensely and vocally religious groups, resisting compromise. Marvin Olasky, a key faith-based player while Bush was governor of Texas, felt that the WHOFBCI position on legislation did not really "level" a "playing field" tilted against faith. Rather, he felt that it was perpetuating discrimination against the most effective, and intensely religious, groups. "Unless an organization can strictly segment its religious and non-religious work," Olasky said about the emerging WHOFBCI position, "it would not be eligible to participate. And that seems to be patently discriminatory." Another problem with the faith-based office's view was the possibility that faith-based funds would support fringe religions. Citing groups such as Scientologists and Hare Krishnas, Pat Robertson described that possibility as "an intolerable situation." Jerry Falwell similarly feared that "bigoted" religious groups would be funded under the faith-based initiative.

Robertson shared Olasky's concern that the Bush administration might "cave" to separationist pressure and overly regulate, or even prohibit funding to, evangelistic programs. Terrence Scanlon of the Capital Research Center warned that these intensely religious organizations could be sapped of their vitality in much the same way that the old welfare system "undermined individual initiative among the poor." Michael Horowitz of the Hudson Institute felt that an "administrative headache" would result from religious organizations' efforts to segregate their programs into religious and nonreligious components.

Pragmatists

Other faith-based supporters found the WHOFBCI's views quite tolerable. These pragmatists differed from the purists in their vision of civil society and a healthy public square. Ronald Sider of Evangelicals for Social Action described Robertson and Falwell as "confused about the First Amendment," and claimed that the positions they took were playing into the hands of those who accused them of promoting "theocracy." Some African American pastors also joined the pragmatists. These pastors saw an opportunity in the initiative to renew their neighborhoods and better control the resources that had previously been controlled from afar by government or large nonprofits. "The benefit is real clear to us," said Rev. Alice Davis of the Shiloh Baptist Church in Washington, D.C. "We need the money" and hope to have a greater say in how it is spent. Other pragmatic supporters saw compromise as necessary for the initiative to be constitutional. While Olasky derided late amendments to H.R. 7 as a "valentine" for Supreme Court justice Sandra Day O'Connor, most pragmatists saw them as necessary if the bill was to withstand legal challenge.

Some administration pragmatists seemed to welcome purist criticism. At a gathering of the National Association for Evangelicals, WHOFBCI director John DiIulio bluntly stated that "predominantly white, ex-urban, evangelical and national para-church leaders should be careful not to presume to speak for any persons other than themselves and their own churches. . . . [U]rban African American and Latino faith communities have . . . histories that make them generally more dedicated to community-serving missions." His provocative statement was intended to publicly position the faith-based bill as middle-of-the-road, but it also drew a firestorm of criticism from the purists.

Bridging the Gap

Some early faith-based friends tried to bridge the growing gap. The conservative Southern Baptist Convention and the mostly liberal

Call to Renewal network supported the introduced version of H.R. 7 while simultaneously working for pragmatic changes. President Bush himself spoke positively of H.R. 7, but his intense desire for a successful bill indicated that he wanted constitutionally sound legislation and not just an ideological statement. On his first lobbying trip to the Hill regarding H.R. 7, he stressed the pragmatists' argument about faith-based effectiveness, describing how he personally "saw it work . . . in places where hope had been lost." One representative quoted Bush as glossing over the details of H.R. 7 that purists opposed, saying, "[The idea] is so important to me that I want you to overlook some of the details and get it done."

The disputes between purists and pragmatists operated almost exclusively within the inner circles of conservative activists and Republican politicians. They were obscure and trivial to most of the media, which reported them as such, framing the entire faith-based debate for the policymaking community and the public at large as one of far-right infighting over the spoils of a Bush presidential victory.

—Melissa Fritsch

Sources

Edsall, Thomas B. "Robertson Joins Liberals in Faulting Bush's 'Faith-Based' Plan." *Washington Post*, 22 February 2001, A5.

Edsall, Thomas B., and Dana Milbank. "Blunt Defense of 'Faith-Based' Aid." *Washington Post*, 8 March 2001, A8.

Fransley, Arthur E., II. "Faith-Based Action." *Christian Century*, 14 March 2001: 12–15.

Goodstein, Laurie. "For Religious Right, Bush's Charity Plan Is Raising Concerns." *New York Times*, 3 March 2001. www.nytimes.com (accessed 3 March 2001).

Loconte, Joseph. "Faith-Based Skepticism." *The Weekly Standard*, 26 March 2001, 10–12.

Milbank, Dana. "Defending 'Faith-Based' Plan." *Washington Post*, 6 March 2001.

Olasky, Marvin. "Rolling the Dice." *World* 16, no. 29 (4 August 2001).

Witham, Larry. "Faith-Based Plan Shows Cultural Split." *Washington Times*, 26 March 2001, 4.

Conservatives supporting the faith-based initiative had always been divided into two camps, and the ambiguity of the president's legislative wishes brought that division into legislative play. On the one side were the purists who wanted greater official support for orthodox religion in the public square. Some of these purists wanted government to give explicit preference to evangelical Christianity and block "fringe" religious groups from receiving funds. Reviewing the faith-based initiative for the first time in some detail, religious broadcaster Pat Robertson called it "appalling" that the plan could result in government contracts for programs run by minority religions such as the Church of Scientology and the Unification Church.[26] Purists had always had mixed reactions to charitable choice, appreciating its implied endorsement of religious treatments for social ills but worrying about the government regulation that might intrude upon them if they received government funding. Because charitable choice had not been implemented on any significant scale, however, there was little evidence of its impact. What purists did want under a Republican president was a faith-based initiative that clearly protected their right to operate programs in the way they thought their faith required: few reporting requirements, full hiring discretion, and freedom to operate programs in and as part of a church.

The purists also wanted a new government attitude toward religion: a neutral view to replace what they thought was a prevailing antireligious position. They wanted government to fund entire programs, no matter how religious, as long as a secular alternative was available to complaining beneficiaries. They argued that only this freedom to be fully religious would keep a program effective, the very reason government was looking their way. Marvin Olasky seemed worried that regulations infringing in any way on this freedom would "sap the vitality of religious social programs," much like welfare undermined individual initiative.[27] Purists had made headway on the legislative front: the late-2000 version of charitable choice in a drug treatment law had been written to their liking. Their most important legal claim was that at least four conservative Supreme Court justices—Clarence Thomas, William Rehnquist, Antonin Scalia, and Anthony Kennedy (but probably no more)—would be with them if their version of charitable choice became law and was challenged in court. If President Bush had the opportunity to name one or two replacements for Court retirements that did not favor their position, perhaps their view of neutrality might enjoy a majority. Purists had friends within the White House and Congress, and their views were most strongly held among the House Republican leadership.

Another conservative faction was more pragmatic and pluralistic. This group agreed with the purists that religion should be more active in the public square, but they did not take it quite as far. The pragmatists were not explicit preferentialists, looking for government to support religion generally or a particular form. Rather, they were pluralists, happy if government agencies would be merely blind to or ignorant of the religiosity of a provider, rather than hostile to it. If under charitable choice religious treatments generally or even a particular religious treatment came to be preferred, so be it, but the government should choose which services to fund without regard to religion. Groups that might receive funds, they argued, should compete on merit alone, on a level playing field that neither advanced nor discouraged religion.

The pragmatists were also sensitive to arguments that government might appear to be endorsing religion by supporting a program that closely integrated faith with treatment. They were willing to separate government funds from private contributions, and religious program elements from nonreligious elements. They were also willing to let beneficiaries opt out of the religious elements of a program in which they otherwise participated.

These pragmatic and pluralistic conservatives also made strong arguments for their views: the most frequent point was that their pluralistic approach would almost assuredly pass constitutional muster with the existing Supreme Court, since Justice Sandra Day O'Connor could be counted on to join the four purist justices to create a majority. Pragmatists had friends within and beyond the Republican Party, but their strongest support inside the policymaking system was in the administration's faith-based offices.[28]

These controversies between purists and pragmatists defined the infighting among the Republicans in the House of Representatives and the White House who were writing the House bill. Press leaks about the disputes framed much of the larger public debate.

Disagreements between Purists and Pragmatists

Three controversies between the purists and the pragmatists dominated discussions. The first centered on which new groups or programs might be likely to get federal help. Many of the purists held views like Rev. Pat Robertson's: they wanted charitable choice to be used as a means to purposely advance a particular religious faith—usually politically and theologically conservative evangelical Protestantism. Robertson warned his *700 Club* television audience on February 20, 2001, that Bush's faith-based plan might allow fringe groups such as the Hare Krishnas and the Church of Scientology to "all become financial beneficiaries" of the federal government.[29] If the faith-based plan could be designed to support traditional beliefs and discourage others, Robertson and other purist conservatives would support it. Pragmatists, however, who had more closely followed judicial decisions, argued that such overt government support for particular faiths and their services would be held unconstitutional.

The second debate was whether to seek legislation that allowed federal dollars to subsidize religious messages. Federally funded social services vary greatly in what they do, and the admixture of service with religion is even more varied. For some services—providing emergency food, for example—the religious content of a program is easily separated from the immediate aid it offers. For other services, such as drug or alcohol rehabilitation, the religious content of the program may be integral to and inseparable from the way the program achieves its ends. Purists, given their definition of neutrality, argued that the federal government could and should directly fund even the most integrally religious programs with minimal program oversight. In early March, Olasky worried that the administration's legislative proposal might "backpedal and refuse to finance programs that are the most overtly evangelistic." If that happened, Olasky warned, the administration would be "shot at by the right."[30] Pragmatists, whatever their personal preferences, argued that direct support would ultimately fail in court because it violated judicial guidelines then operative about government neutrality.

The last dispute between purists and pragmatists was over the religious freedom of program beneficiaries. Both sides saw that the law required beneficiaries to be able to choose a clearly nonreligious program rather than a faith-based one. Once a beneficiary was in a program, purists argued, he or she should have to accept all of its religious content and programming. Pragmatists disagreed. They wanted what came to be termed a "secondary opt-out," a provision that allowed a beneficiary in a faith-based program to opt out of the religious parts of the program while participating in the rest.

Purists and pragmatists also differed over strategy. Most purists thought that a House bill to their liking would rally public support for faith-based initiatives. A strong advocate of this view was Marvin Olasky, a faith-based advisor for Governor Bush who had not found a place in the Bush White House. Criticizing the pragmatists, Olasky wrote: "I see the faith-based initiative as something that could be taken directly to the people of what remains a religious country."[31] Confident in the public appeal of the initiative, purists seemed unconcerned about the political realities of a closely divided House and Senate, a skeptical media still learning about faith-based issues, and the Supreme Court's still cautious and fragile majority. Pragmatists had these larger political realities fully in mind, and wanted House legislative language that would more easily pass in the Senate and that would be more likely to receive favorable court decisions.

Of key political importance in these disputes was the range of ideology in each group. Purists were nearly all politically and religiously conservative activists. Pragmatists ranged more broadly, with members from the right end of politics to the left of center, and they had been named to the key faith-based positions in the Bush administration. John DiIulio, a moderate to liberal Democrat, was director of the White House Office of Faith-Based and Community Initiatives; Carl Esbeck, the conservative creator of charitable choice, was in the Department of Justice's faith-based office and on the administration's team charged with negotiating legislative language.

The private disagreements between purists and pragmatists complicated internal legislative negotiations. The faith-based office's legislative preferences were clear—grant large tax incentives and create the compassion capital fund now; expand charitable choice later. This implied at least a two-bill strategy, dividing the initiative between immediate requests and longer-term needs. White House staff in the more political offices had a different view, identical to most purists. They wanted one major faith-based legislative push to show that the president really believed in the idea, and to match campaign rhetoric with legislative content. Most House Republicans, notably the leadership, seemed to side with the White House political offices.

Infighting during House Bill Negotiations

These disagreements soon manifested themselves in negotiations over the House bill. Already in early February, internal dissent was apparent, with each side going its own way. The House Republican leadership staff was depending for advice on its traditional set of mostly purist interest group allies such as the Family Research Council, the Capital Research Group, and the Free Congress Foundation. These groups wanted pure charitable choice language, and provided information to House staff that defended their arguments. Other parts of the president's proposals, such as the compassion capital fund, were less interesting to them. The priorities of DiIulio and others in the faith-based offices were directly opposite. Purists took their disagreements with DiIulio to House Republicans and to other offices in the White House staffed by more familiar faces, and got some action. By mid-February, the higher-ups in the White House explained to the faith-based staff that, if House Republicans and the purists wanted it, broad charitable choice expansion would be in a forthcoming comprehensive House bill.[32]

The pragmatists' fallback position was to insist on a charitable choice approach that would clearly pass constitutional muster with the Supreme Court. Pushing their legal case with the purists, pragmatists first saw this strategy apparently backfire. Conservative religious leaders like Pat Robertson and Marvin Olasky went public with their criticisms of faith-based policy options. Robertson warned: "This thing could be a real Pandora's Box, and what seems to be a great initiative can rise up to bite the organizations as well as the federal government."[33] Olasky became more public with his worries that the Bush administration would backpedal on the initiative's details.[34] He criticized those in the faith-based offices who focused on "placating Sandra Day O'Connor"; rather, he wanted a bill that assured faith-based groups that they would not have to give up "any of their theological distinctiveness, such as a commitment to worship and evangelism."[35]

February 2001: Private Disagreements Go Public

In the weeks between mid-February and the House bill's introduction in late March, these concerns spread among purists. Many began to doubt the whole idea of charitable choice, especially as applied to direct funding.[36] The purists' now public doubts gave permission for other White House staff and House Republicans to rein in or ignore WHOFBCI director DiIulio and discount the legislative ideas that he was pushing in discussions with more sympathetic policymakers such as Senator Lieberman.

The actual situation was a bit more complicated. Conservative Carl Esbeck in the Justice Department's faith-based office was strongly committed to the constitutionally safe path on charitable choice. He was constantly pushing House staff to write legislation that provided more separation of funds and programs between religious and nonreligious, and to add a secondary opt-out provision. House Republicans, however, wanted the approval of purist groups, whose ideology they knew, more than they wanted the approval of the WHOFBCI, whose staff they did not entirely trust. The relevant House negotiators agreed with the purists on the need to expand the "right kind" of charitable choice regardless of where the Supreme Court might stand, writing legislative language that would be "tighter and better" than the 1996 welfare reform law.[37] To these House staffers, reports of conflicts between conservative groups and the WHOFBCI reinforced what they already thought: that they were on the right track and that the WHOFBCI was poorly staffed and of doubtful loyalty to the cause.[38]

March 2001: Pragmatists Lose the Internal Battle

By early March, most of the details of the House bill were set, although WHOFBCI negotiators were not ready to give up on the pragmatic approach. Disputes over the timing of the bill's introduction and the pace of its consideration added to behind-the-scenes disarray. At a series of mid-March meetings among pro-faith-based staffers from both parties and legislative chambers, a host of disagreements were aired, fueled by a recent DiIulio speech to the National Association of Evangelicals. Many purists interpreted as a personal attack DiIulio's remark that "predominantly white, ex-urban evangelical and national para-church leaders, should be careful not to presume to speak for any persons other than themselves and their own churches."[39] They distrusted DiIulio even more—both his go-slow strategy and his reaching out to Democrats. Key House Republican offices also wanted to move a House bill fast. As part of a strategy to attract blacks to the GOP, Representative Watts had started planning a "faith-based summit" of African American clergy for mid-April.[40] He wanted a faith-based bill that was far along in the legislative process by that time to prove Republican sincerity to this group. Speaker Hastert's office agreed with Watts, and seemed ready to put the bill on the fast track with the apparent backing of top White House officials.

Some other Republican offices represented at the mid-March meetings wanted to go more slowly. House whip Tom DeLay's office had concerns with the purist language, preferring the older 1996 version of the bill— a position attacked as too "liberal" by more purist congressional staffers in a later e-mail. Other friends of faith-based not directly involved in legislative negotiations also preferred a slower pace. Representative Mark Souder of Indiana, for example, argued that a quick and comprehensive bill would only serve to unify the opposition and ultimately stall progress on faith-based, a position that caused one House Republican staff person to characterize him in an e-mail as "a jerk."[41]

Many persons outside of the House wanted to go slowly, too. Joe Lieberman and Rick Santorum had been forced into such a strategy in the Senate, partly in response to the controversies growing out of the disputes between the House and White House. Lieberman had formed a small group of Senate Democrats willing to discuss a charitable choice expansion bill among themselves, and he was concerned that unsettling news about the House bill was disturbing those efforts. The WHOFBCI, like other White House offices, was still understaffed because of a slow and budget-conscious transition. Most of its staff wanted a go-slow approach in order to get the office up to speed, concentrate on implementing current law, identify barriers to faith-based and community-based participation, and educate Congress, the media, and outside constituencies in the initiative's complexities.[42] A quick legislative push was one more unnecessary thing on a plate already too full.

There were even divisions among the key House sponsors. Representative Hall supported the bill's content but adopted much of the WHOFBCI's critique about a quick pace. He argued for a series of field hearings across the nation on the good work that faith-based groups were doing and other strategies to broaden the proposal's appeal.[43] The two Republican sponsors, Hastert and Watts, argued that the public would support the bill as they saw it making progress through Congress.

Why the Difficulties?

Why didn't other offices in the White House settle disputes between the House purists and WHOFBCI pragmatists? According to interviews conducted later, White House faith-based staff often had difficulty getting other White House offices to attend to the details of their concerns in House legislative negotiations. The WHOFBCI was staffed with experts who understood the complexities of constitutional law and welfare policy, but not the personal politics of Capitol Hill. Stanley Carlson-Thies, formerly of the WHOFBCI, explained: "The White House already has publicity, congressional liaisons, public communications, and so on in other places with professional staffs. The professionals at the faith-based office were best at other things."[44] Another faith-based staff person offered, in a later interview, a less sympathetic view: "The White House lobbying people [were] worthless on this whole thing."[45]

Virtually all other White House offices wanted sweeping legislation to pass quickly and with the full support of the religious groups traditionally aligned with Republicans. One critic of the strategy called it "red meat for the partisans."[46] Others more sympathetic to the strategy pointed out that it was important for any administration to push legislation on behalf of the groups and interests at the core of its support.[47] In the view of most of the administration's faith-based staff, few of the relevant White House staff persons understood the details of the issue or wanted to take the time to learn.

Besides faith-based pragmatists, opponents of faith-based initiatives also wanted delay. Racially tinged questions from the 2000 election controversy filled the political air of early 2001. Most Republicans were eager to reverse what they said were misperceptions of them, and they thought faith-based would help.[48] House Democrats also saw the rapid pace of the ambitious faith-based bill in racial terms—as a clear attempt to grab a piece of their party's African American electoral base.[49] These Democrats tried to use the faith-based debate to twist Republican enthusiasm for the idea back on itself, casting it as a blatant manipulation of African Americans for electoral gain.

Most key internal players wanted to go quickly, and so they did. The pragmatists' calls for delay were portrayed by some purists as fundamental disloyalty, according to an e-mail from one of the House offices supporting the purists' point of view. On March 20, approximately forty representatives of politically and religiously conservative interest groups met at the Free Congress Foundation offices to probe, and eventually endorse, the faith-based language upon which Watts, Hastert, and Hall had settled only days before.[50]

The next day, the three congressmen unveiled an outline of their bill at a Capitol Hill news conference. They still did not have a final text in legislative form, but Watts and his cosponsors wanted to take advantage of the simultaneous introduction of a faith-based tax bill in the Senate by senators Santorum and Lieberman. Reports about the House news conference hinted at the behind-the-scenes disagreements among faith-based supporters. Mark Souder indicated he wanted to hold hearings on the initiative in a Government Reform subcommittee that he chaired, a possibility that would considerably slow down the bill. At a separate news conference on the different legislative tack that he and Senator Santorum were taking, Senator Lieberman hinted that the White House faith-based office was on his side of an internal dispute: "I think there's a shared conclusion, and I believe it's shared by the White House ... that we ought to take some time, work out the questions [on charitable choice]."[51]

Official Introduction: Start of the Legislative Process

On March 29, 2001, Representative Watts finally formally introduced H.R. 7, the Community Solutions Act, with Speaker Dennis Hastert and Representative Tony Hall as his two original cosponsors. The bill included broad charitable choice expansion along the lines urged by purists and an expensive set of charity tax breaks. One aspect of the bill that came as a great disappointment to the WHOFBCI was that it contained no compassion capital fund, because House staff had considered such a fund a "new spending program." According to one of the House negotiators: "[W]e were not comfortable with a new social welfare program yet, and weren't sure the caucus would support it."[52] None of the few pilot projects supported by the president and DiIulio was included, which surprised some in the WHOFBCI—they had not even seen the bill's text until it had been completely drafted. As interpreted by one WHOFBCI staff person: "The Republicans in the House [felt they] didn't have to get approval; they didn't want to just do the White House's bidding" and so introduced a bill without getting full White House support for each provision.[53]

Representative Watts pledged quick and favorable House action on H.R. 7, predicting an "overwhelming majority of the House of Representatives" would support it when it came to a vote, presumably in the near future.[54] The White House publicly expressed gratitude for Watts's introduction of the bill, issuing a statement of thanks for continuing to advance the initiative.

But all was not well, even that first day in the life of H.R. 7. That day at the White House, an uncomfortable moment arose at a faith-based coalition meeting. According to a meeting account e-mailed later by an attendee, WHOFBCI staff members criticized H.R. 7 for omitting the secondary opt-out, while House GOP staff members angrily defended the bill, saying it was supported by unnamed "constitutional scholars" who had reviewed the text.

April 2001: Something to Shoot At

H.R. 7's introduction gave everyone something to shoot at or defend. Support from purists for the faith-based initiative was already cooling. They had started to question adding charitable choice language to programs directly aiding faith-based providers, and were getting more interested in voucher-type social services. In voucher programs, federal funds go to individual beneficiaries in the form of vouchers or certificates that the beneficiaries can use at many different service providers. Because vouchers are aid to beneficiaries and not to service providers, the providers are mostly free from government control. This lets them avoid most federal regulations and constitutional questions about church-state involvement.

In the broader faith-based debate, opposition was growing. News reports about the disputes between purists and pragmatists had framed the issue very narrowly in the public mind as the obsession of right-wing factions. The only interesting question to the media and the attentive public was how much, not whether, the bill catered to the concerns of the "far right." The text of the new bill did not help calm those fears. As one WHOFBCI staff person noted: "The moment [H.R. 7] was filed it would polarize debate. Instantly, people would retreat to their bunkers and lob rhetorical missiles back and forth. . . . We just knew it would corrupt our ability to rally broad support."[55] The absence of certain provisions—a secondary opt-out, separation of religious and nonreligious program elements, and compassion capital funds—in the unveiled H.R. 7 fueled the impression that the legislative exercise was about appeasing politically and religiously conservative interest groups and not about reaching out to small, poor, and inner-city service agencies.

The bill's text and media interpretation of the intramural conservative battles encouraged the rest of the interest group community to express its concerns, to get those views wide publicity, and, eventually, to have those views reflected in public opinion. Critics of faith-based were now regularly mentioning two themes: hiring discretion and funding proselytization with government dollars. "We are going to fight this very hard," said a spokesman for a public employees' union, drawing attention to the hiring discretion issue as a top priority.[56]

Especially frustrating to most staff in the administration's faith-based offices was that most commentators and news reporters were incorrectly equating H.R. 7 with President Bush's full faith-based plan, even though faith-based staff members had several concerns with the bill and were actively seeking changes.[57] They continued their efforts to convince the House and its allies that all direct grant recipients should be required to fully separate and segment by place, time, and funding source the religious and nonreligious elements of a program. The separation would make a secondary opt-out plausible as well, because religious and nonreligious program elements and funds would already be segregated. And with additional advice coming in from legal experts, House Republicans and some aligned interest groups were starting to back off their claim that a secondary opt-out was completely unnecessary from a constitutional perspective. They seemed willing to revise the provision later in the legislative process. But that pragmatic accommodation was not showing up in media reports.

Meanwhile, the left and center of the political spectrum were lining up to oppose H.R. 7. On April 11, representatives Bobby Scott and Chet Edwards held a briefing for Democratic staff, assisted by the Baptist Joint Committee, the NAACP Legal Defense Fund, the National Abortion Rights Action League, the Interfaith Alliance, and public employee unions. About 150 Democratic congressional staff attended, according to an e-mail by a staff person who attended—an indication of the depth of Democratic interest in and likely opposition to faith-based initiatives.[58] Interest in arguments against H.R. 7 was far higher than Scott and Edwards had thought it would be.

FOCAL POINT 3.2

The Dynamic Duo

Representatives Scott and Edwards Rally the Opposition

No legislators did more to derail President Bush's faith-based initiative in the 107th Congress than Democrats Robert C. "Bobby" Scott of Virginia and Chet Edwards of Texas. Opponents of faith-based could not have asked for two better members of Congress to be on their side. Scott is a reliably liberal member of the Congressional Black Caucus but sometimes votes against the party to get defense dollars for Virginia or when his interpretations of the Constitution's free speech and government takings provisions are at stake. Edwards will split with Democrats on some social and economic issues, but as a signal that he is a team player, he has also found a place in the Democrats' whip system.

An African American representing Richmond and southeast Virginia, Bobby Scott linked the faith-based issue to civil rights. Funding religious social services would, in his view, invite federally funded bigotry based on religion, race, and sexual preference. Scott's views are shaped by his youthful experience in Virginia where "Christian academies" sprouted up in the 1960s as local residents avoided government steps to integrate public schools. Scott worries that the faith-based initiative's hiring provisions would repeat that sad historical chapter, this time in social services.

Chet Edwards is an active Methodist who represents the area around Waco, Texas, home to Baylor University, the world's largest Baptist university. Waco is also known as the city nearest to the tragic 1993 standoff between federal agents and David Koresh's Branch Davidian sect. As one political handbook summarizes, Edwards's "principal legislative concern is to preserve the separation of church and state." In 1998 and 1999, Edwards led House opposition to a school-prayer constitutional amendment. His work has been encouraged by officials at Baylor, whose Baptist heritage includes a strong church-state separationist theme.

Edwards's main fear about Bush's faith-based initiative is that it will contribute to unhealthy competition among American religious groups for funding preference, enervating religious faith. "The separation of church and state has worked magnificently well," Edwards has noted. "Our churches are filled. And their social outreach programs are great successes. The state-subsidized churches of Europe are empty. Why would we want to be like them?"

Scott and Edwards fought charitable choice long before George W. Bush became president, leading the opposition each time charitable choice language came to the House floor. Before 2000, Scott and Edwards lost every vote by large margins. In the first two years of the Bush administration, however, they met with far greater success, getting nearly all Democrats to vote against H.R. 7 and forcing House GOP leaders to scramble mightily to avoid defeat.

In many ways, Scott and Edwards's best allies were H.R. 7's advocates. As a Scott staff person explained later: "The [administration] talked about faith-based legislation so much that the press was forced to ask questions about it." The duo would then go to members of the press and suggest that they "ask this" and "ask that" about its details. The purist version of H.R. 7 helped its opponents as well. As an Edwards staff person stated later: "Because [H.R. 7's supporters] were so overreaching in so many ways, we were able to bring [House Democrats who had previously supported charitable choice] our way."

The best success Scott and Edwards achieved was with the Congressional Black Caucus (CBC). Scott brought in leaders of the NAACP Legal Defense Fund and the Leadership Council on Civil Rights to argue that the faith-based initiative brought no new money and that the hiring language allowed federally funded white churches to hire only "their kind." Reportedly "relentless" in their arguments, Scott, Edwards, and the newly activated civil rights groups convinced all CBC members to oppose H.R. 7, even though a few had earlier pledged support.

This dynamic House duo took their case to the Senate after H.R. 7's narrow House victory. Many Senate insiders believe that Scott and Edwards were the key to derailing the Senate CARE Act, with one Senate Democratic staff person calling their activities "intense" and a House staff person declaring that "the Senate had never seen [such intense lobbying by House members] before."

Edwards and Scott were sometimes joined by other House members such as Judiciary Committee Democrats Barney Frank of Massachusetts, Jerry Nadler of New York, and John Conyers of Michigan, who would buttress one or more of the two leaders' arguments. While the help of these members was useful, Scott and Edwards clearly deserve the most credit, or blame, for the faith-based initiative's legislative demise.

—*Melissa Fritsch*

Sources

Barone, Michael, Richard E. Cohen, and Charles E. Cook, Jr. *Almanac of American Politics 2002*. Washington, D.C.: National Journal, 2002.

Broder, David S. "More Risk Than Reward?" *Washington Post*, 11 July 2001, A19.
Available at www.house.gov/scott/c_choice/more_risk_than_reward.htm
(accessed 20 July 2003).
Congressional Quarterly's Politics in America 2002. Washington, D.C.: Congressional
Quarterly Press, 2002.
Interviews with Denise Edwards, Max Finberg, Dan Gerstein, and Theresa Tilling
Thompson.

H.R. 7 supporters made a few countermoves. Representative Hall, for example, organized a briefing with WHOFBCI director DiIulio on April 18 to present the bill in a better light. House committee staffers were circulating arguments refuting many of the opponents' claims. The executive branch faith-based offices joined in these efforts as they simultaneously lobbied for more than a dozen changes to the bill in order to, as one faith-based staff person characterized it in an e-mail, "improve the odds when [charitable choice] is litigated."

Summit Complications

Watts's upcoming April 25 summit for black clergy, however, was making it difficult for anyone outside of the reliable right to think of supporting faith-based. Watts had organized a similar summit in 2000 for the heads of historically black colleges, an event that Republicans had judged important for making contacts with some African American leaders. Watts was planning a similar summit or two for each of the following several years on various issues as part of his strategy to recruit a slice of the African American vote for the GOP. The April 25 summit was mostly an open forum between Republicans and African American clergy, with its chief purpose a dialogue on how government and local faith-based groups could work more cooperatively to provide for social needs.

However, Watts and his Senate sponsor, Rick Santorum, planned to restrict the invitations to Republican members of the House and Senate and grassroots faith-based workers nominated by those members. For weeks, the White House faith-based office was concerned about the partisan tone of summit planning, and as an apparent expression of its displeasure barely cooperated with Watts's office on the summit.

Opponents soon saw that they could use the summit to make two charges: that faith-based was a partisan ploy and that it introduced great danger to the public square. On the latter charge, for example, Americans

United for Separation of Church and State attacked the summit's thirty-two-member honorary advisory committee, which Watts had set up, for including individuals who had "made insulting and intolerant comments about religious, ethnic, and other minority groups."[59] A few steering committee members resigned in the ensuing but short-lived controversy. The charge that faith-based was a partisan ploy had a longer and deeper impact. The invited summit delegates were largely African American clergy, and virtually all were the constituents of Republican congresspersons who had invited them. Given Watts's purposes for the summit, few Democratic congresspersons would have invited constituents to attend even if they could have. The exclusive invitation list that resulted lent credence to the partisan charge.[60] Pressured by both parties, Representative Hall broke publicly with his Republican friends on the summit's wisdom. He decried its partisan nature, hoped that it would not be repeated, and noted that its main effect would be to harm prospects for the legislation.[61] Later, a Hall staffer would call the summit a "disaster" that made any greater bipartisanship impossible.[62]

Much of the summit's partisanship seemed unnecessary. Because Watts saw the bill and the summit as separate, he had been willing to accommodate the faith-based office's concerns about the summit even as he insisted on a purist version of the legislation. But the faith-based office rarely even responded to Watts's request for input on the summit. The hard feelings of the legislative negotiations had spilled over into the summit, to the detriment of all faith-based supporters. As one Democratic staff person put it: "In nobody's mind but their [Watts's office] own was the summit distinct from the faith-based initiative. [The summit] was the spark that ignited the tinder already dry from the election. There was no trust [of the president] in the Democratic Party, and they perceived the summit as having the full Bush blessing. . . . Without the summit, we would have gotten thirty to forty Democrats on H.R. 7."[63]

May and Early June 2001: Desperately Seeking Democrats

With the summit behind them, the three House sponsors and the Bush faith-based staff together sought a more bipartisan course for H.R. 7, even as disputes over the text remained. House Republicans were optimistic that the partisan tenor of the summit would be quickly forgotten; Democrats were sure it would not be.[64] Whereas Watts had first thought that the

House could have H.R. 7 ready for floor consideration by April, the earlier difficulties in drafting the legislation and holding the summit led him to think that June was the soonest possible date and early fall was more likely. Other Republicans, more worried about the partisan atmosphere, predicted even later consideration.[65]

New events further complicated a quick timetable. On April 26, the day after the summit, DiIulio appeared at a congressional hearing on charitable choice held before Representative Souder's Government Reform subcommittee. He was peppered there with pointed questions from Representative Scott about how the White House and H.R. 7 wanted to deal with hiring discretion, religious establishment, and proselytization. Reports about the director's responses implied both that he had conceded some ground to the purist conservatives on direct government funding and that not all the consequences of charitable choice had been thoroughly examined. In response to a press inquiry earlier that day, DiIulio said that it was "more appropriate" for pervasively religious groups to seek vouchers, but if they wanted to apply for direct grants it would be "fine" with him. Before the congressional committee, DiIulio reportedly "never answered the question" when asked about proselytization in programs receiving direct government funds, and did not know the answer to a technical question about the classification of workers potentially funded by federal dollars.[66]

Coalition Politics

With the summit over, Watts's office could devote attention to the legislative coalition for H.R. 7 that they had started to build before the event. The week that the bill was introduced, Watts's office began to assemble an interest group coalition to push it, seeking both purists and pragmatists. A few small groups like the Center for Public Justice and the National Center for Neighborhood Enterprise were ready to join up. Others were waiting to see the final text of the bill because of what they were hearing about certain provisions. The Southern Baptist Convention (SBC), for example, wanted the secondary opt-out, but when the provision was omitted from the original text the SBC joined the coalition and decided to argue internally for the change. The coalition formally commenced its lobbying activities the week after the summit. The coalition was described by one lobbyist as "a relatively small number of groups, a fraction of the potential galaxy of support."[67] Many members of the group were most interested in the tax provisions of H.R. 7—they were nonprofits who would benefit from the charitable-giving provisions, and local community development groups that supported H.R. 7's individual development accounts. A smaller set of groups was interested in charitable choice. This set concentrated on that provision, to be reviewed by the Judiciary Committee, while pushing for the whole bill.

Democratic support was needed quickly. In early May the coalition thought that perhaps fifty Democrats might vote for H.R. 7 if there could be a fairly immediate sea change in how it was being portrayed. But no one had good ideas about how to change the bill's portrayal and the public's perception of it without drastically changing the text, which none wanted to do. The coalition struggled throughout the rest of the House legislative process with that conundrum. Later, an outside critique claimed of the coalition: "[T]here was no mechanism to mobilize. There didn't seem to be a link to the right members of Congress at the right time."[68]

Members of Congress opposing H.R. 7, especially representatives Scott and Edwards, were in high gear, creating and solidifying a new and more dangerous image of the legislation in the minds of a host of Democrats who had voted for earlier versions of charitable choice.[69] Given the differing levels of activity by the pro–H.R. 7 coalition and opposing Democrats, the prospects of bipartisanship on H.R. 7 were worsening by the day.

Questions of legislative timing made bipartisanship even less likely. Responding to the president's personal interest, the political offices of the White House wanted H.R. 7 to pass quickly. That would require some pressure by the House leadership on committee chairs and Republican rank-and-file, a partisan appeal that would do nothing to change the bill's already partisan image. It was also in many groups' interest to maintain H.R. 7 as first written whether it passed or not, and then to blame the controversies it would thus create on the ineptitude of DiIulio, other pragmatists, and Democrats. Except for faith-based pragmatists in the Bush administration and anyone concerned about the fate of faith-based in the Senate and later, no one really wanted a bipartisan strategy.

Other events within the Congress gave further ammunition to faith-based critics. One important event was the Bush administration's tepid support for $90 billion worth of charitable-giving tax incentives, which were first included in the president's tax reform bill and then deleted.

The decision to drop these provisions near the end of congressional negotiations, combined with the administration's insistence on repealing the federal estate tax, meant a combined loss to the charitable sector of $21 billion in contributions over several years.[70]

House Republican staff said that the charitable deduction was not high on the White House's priority list and, because it did not have a powerful interest group coalition behind it, was dropped without much objection. While the White House still claimed that it supported the charity tax breaks and would fight for them in the faith-based legislation, another large tax break—such as H.R. 7's deductions—after tax reform was highly unlikely. Congressional Republicans supporting faith-based admitted that they "probably missed [the] window" of opportunity for the charity tax breaks. White House staff seemed less concerned about the loss. To Democrats and other opponents of faith-based, however, the willingness to drop these tax breaks provided further evidence that Republicans were not interested in truly aiding charities or faith-based groups. As one House Democratic staff person put it, when the charitable tax deductions were dropped from tax reform, "it was obvious the rest of the White House apparatus wasn't fighting for this."[71] Combined with the absence of compassion capital funds, the elimination of charity tax breaks in tax reform indicated for many observers that Republicans firmly supported only purist charitable choice language and not the other elements of the faith-based initiative.

The larger political environment also got much worse very fast for faith-based supporters. The Senate shifted control from Republican to Democrat when, on May 24, Republican senator Jim Jeffords of Vermont declared himself an Independent caucusing with Democrats. Overnight the Bush administration lost the certainty of getting any form of faith-based legislation on the Senate agenda. The highly partisan cast of H.R. 7 in the House suddenly was much more detrimental to later consideration in the Senate, because Senate Democrats would be loath to advance an initiative so strongly associated with conservative Republicans.[72]

Despite these developments, purist conservatives were intent on giving H.R. 7 their particular signature. Because they had become gradually persuaded that direct grants would require segmentation and separation, by early summer they were seeking wider use of vouchers and other indirect funding measures for the evangelical Christian programs about which they were most concerned.[73] Many media reports incorrectly linked these new demands to the Bush administration's desire to quickly push the bill through the House, implying that the White House was cooperating even more closely with House Republicans and exacerbating partisan tensions with Democrats.[74]

Watts's efforts at coalition-building among interest groups seemed to be going reasonably well, although Democratic support was still virtually nonexistent. According to the e-mail of a Watts staff person at the time, by early June Habitat for Humanity and the Salvation Army had endorsed H.R. 7, and the Catholic Conference, the U.S. Conference of Mayors, and the National League of Cities were about to jump onboard. Still, President Bush asked conservative activist and philanthropist Michael Joyce to better organize faith-based lobbying efforts for the House bill. In early June, Joyce organized a new group, Americans for Community and Faith-Centered Enterprise (ACFE), explicitly for that purpose. While ACFE eventually played a large role in developing a Senate coalition, for the most part House Republican staff resented its late entry in the House debate and saw its creation as counterproductive to building a bipartisan coalition.[75] According to one House Republican source, ACFE and Joyce were too identified with the conservatives and, in the daily fight for votes on the floor, the group did not "put any real pressure on congressmembers to pass the bill."[76]

The Official Legislative Process Begins

By the time formal House hearings and markups were scheduled, the fate of H.R. 7 seemed set. President Bush's opponents had successfully defined H.R. 7 as an extremist bill that had the president's full support. As such, passage would require a partisan push. In mid-June two House Ways and Means subcommittees held a joint hearing on H.R. 7.[77] The Ways and Means Committee's jurisdiction ranges widely over both taxes and welfare, so the hearings brought out the full range of arguments for and against H.R. 7. Several interest groups supporting H.R. 7 endorsed it because they claimed that prior charitable choice laws had operated well. Amy Sherman of the Hudson Institute testified that there was almost no evidence that the troubling scenarios of opponents were borne out in practice. Several groups opposed to the bill raised the range of objections discussed here, focusing on the potential discrimination issues behind hiring discretion.

Several members of Congress also testified. The key supporters were Watts and Hall; the key opponents were Chet Edwards, Bobby Scott, and Jerry Nadler. Hall and Watts tried to cast the legislation as opening up opportunities for small service providers to compete with large groups already getting federal funds. Opponent Edwards took up the separationist argument, defending a strong proreligion view of church-state separation that "does not mean keeping people of faith from being involved in government but rather . . . keeping government from being involved in religion." He warned that H.R. 7 "will provide tax dollars to religious groups and open the door to government review of church activities [and] . . . invasive government monitoring, regulation, and accounting." In addition, Edwards claimed that the law would "force the government to pick and choose which religions it funds," generating "outright religious infighting, intolerance, and discrimination."[78] Representative Nadler of New York spoke about the hiring discretion issue, arguing that H.R. 7 did not prohibit discrimination or defer to state and local antidiscrimination laws.[79]

Of all those testifying, Representative Scott presented the most detailed criticism of H.R. 7. First, he attacked the usefulness of the bill for small charities. The absence of compassion capital funds, he asserted, meant that the bill "does absolutely nothing to increase participation by small religious organizations in social service programs. They still have to navigate the grant process . . . without adequate technical assistance." Next, he questioned the motivation of those supporting the purist charitable choice language. The key purposes of charitable choice, he thought, were to allow groups to proselytize and to discriminate in hiring employees while receiving federal funds.[80] Taking advantage of the purist language in H.R. 7, Scott noted that the bill seemed to allow full funding of pervasively religious approaches to treatment that would turn "the federal program into a virtual worship service."[81] Scott highlighted the ministerial exemption of present case law that allows churches to ignore federal civil rights laws in hiring key personnel. He raised the specter that all hires under charitable choice could be covered under this exemption, resulting in virtually unchecked federally funded bigotry.[82]

The hearing, like many hearings, consisted mostly of a series of individual statements with little opportunity for dialogue between opponents and supporters. As such, the structure of the hearing did not allow supporters of H.R. 7 to engage the well-publicized arguments Scott and other opponents made. Scott's staff later identified the hearing and news reports about it as a "big victory" for their side.[83]

June 28, 2001: Judiciary Committee Markup

Behind-the-scenes maneuvering over H.R. 7 had been constant since it was first introduced. The top House sponsors were negotiating a legislative timeline with Representatives Bill Thomas and James Sensenbrenner, the chairmen, respectively, of the Ways and Means and Judiciary committees. After several early June dates had been agreed to and later postponed, Sensenbrenner finally settled on a Judiciary Committee markup for June 28. Several of the delays were due to Sensenbrenner's concerns over the constitutionality of some of the original provisions of H.R. 7.[84] Essentially he found two things wrong with the bill. First, he believed that without a secondary opt-out for beneficiaries participating in a federally funded program, the bill violated the Supreme Court's current reading of relevant constitutional law. Second, Sensenbrenner thought that language about separating funding and programming into religious and nonreligious categories should be strengthened. New to the Judiciary chairmanship, Sensenbrenner wanted to be careful that his committee not approve legislation that would later be overturned in the federal courts.

Most faith-based staff in the administration, as we have seen, agreed with Sensenbrenner's concerns. Other administration officials dismissed those concerns and wanted to move ahead with something close to the original text of H.R. 7. Sensenbrenner even received a phone call from Vice President Cheney urging the committee to approve the original H.R. 7. Sensenbrenner recalled the conversation this way: "I told him there were legal problems and I didn't think the administration had done its homework on broadening its base so that it had bipartisan support. Having a partisan bloodbath is not going to achieve what the administration wants, and I told him that."[85]

Watts, Hastert, and Hall were frustrated with Sensenbrenner's position. But the chairman was insistent, and eventually the House sponsors agreed to the modifications he wanted. After several days of tense high-level negotiations, the committee approved in markup an amended bill along the lines supported by the chairman and by White House faith-based pragmatists, adding a secondary opt-out, stronger requirements about separating funds and program elements, and a $50 million Department of Justice compassion capital fund.[86] Virtually all the changes to the bill had been on the pragmatists' agenda for a long time. As one administration faith-based staffer exulted in an e-mail, the faith-based office "got its way" in the committee battle.

These changes, however, disturbed the purists and did nothing to mollify critics on the center and the left. The committee also included broad language encouraging agencies to "voucherize" programs covered under the bill, trying to pacify the conservative purists. While the voucher language did please the purists, most of them expressed only lukewarm support for the overall bill. Marvin Olasky called the revised H.R. 7 only a "slight improvement over the status quo," adding that under it "many of the most effective compassionate conservative groups will not be helped."[87]

The hiring freedoms allowed to funded faith-based groups were only slightly reined in during Judiciary markup. Because this was becoming the most noted controversy in charitable choice, the other changes to H.R. 7 that moderated the bill brought no Democratic support. At the end of markup, the Judiciary Committee approved H.R. 7 by a party line twenty-to-five vote, with most Democrats abstaining. Any hope of bipartisanship was already gone, and the committee's changes made purist support for H.R. 7 more tepid.

July 2001: Markup and Meltdown

After the Judiciary Committee markup many supporters of H.R. 7 consoled themselves by looking to the large tax incentives still in the bill, but the action of the Ways and Means Committee a few weeks later virtually erased that aspect of the bill. The original version of H.R. 7 had included a large charitable deduction for taxpayers who do not itemize deductions, a provision that would have cost nearly $85 billion in lost federal revenue over ten years. These tax breaks were under the purview of the House Ways and Means Committee. In its markup of H.R. 7 on July 11, an amendment by Chairman Bill Thomas of California reduced the charitable incentives to only $6.4 billion, less than 10 percent of the original amount. Under the new language, deductions for those who do not itemize would start at $25 for individuals and $50 for couples in 2002, and would rise slowly to $100 and $200, respectively, by 2010. The huge scale-back was required, claimed its sponsor, because of lower than expected surpluses and the cost of the recently enacted tax reform law.[88]

Others speculated that Thomas preferred additional energy tax breaks over charitable-giving incentives.[89]

Democrats on the committee ridiculed the Republicans. "This is obviously just a press release bill," said Washington Democrat Jim McDermott. "It's going over to the Senate and into the trash can."[90] Representative Charles Rangel of New York mocked the size of the tax break: "I don't know how you could possibly think this could be an incentive that would warrant the further complicating of our tax code," he said. At the same time, he and other committee Democrats said they would oppose the bill if even these relatively minor tax breaks were not completely offset by other revenue increases.

The Ways and Means markup took place during the first few days of an explosive controversy that would cloud the last ten days of H.R. 7 in the House. The *Washington Post* reported on July 10 that lobbyists for the Salvation Army had apparently agreed to lobby Congress in favor of H.R. 7 in exchange for a Bush administration commitment to preempt any state and local gay-rights statutes that required them to pay domestic partner benefits in employee fringe-benefit packages.[91] While the Salvation Army does not discriminate according to sexual orientation in its hiring, it does oppose paying domestic partner benefits for those it hires. The news story, based on an early May memo to Salvation Army officials from a lobbyist working for the organization, appeared to imply a quid pro quo between the Salvation Army and the White House (see focal point 5.1, "The Salvation Army 'Memo'," in chapter 5). The White House quickly denied any such deal, and later interviews support the administration's claim that it never intended to take unilateral action on behalf of the Salvation Army. The Salvation Army also played down the news story, stating that the memo was the work of an overzealous contract employee and not a description of Salvation Army policy or its expectations from the Bush administration.[92]

Whatever the facts, the Salvation Army story was perfectly timed to do the most damage to the faith-based bill in the House. Several sources later identified the controversy as the chief lens through which the entire House bill was seen, since it seemed to provide a real-life example of how the Bush administration was encouraging discriminatory employment practices under the guise of religious freedom. Follow-up news stories over the next few days provided various versions of the facts from different White House staff, making it seem the administration was covering up and backtracking.[93] These later stories added more fuel to the controversy as House floor consideration of H.R. 7 drew near. Associating H.R. 7 with antigay attitudes that the Salvation Army allegedly held gave many Democrats one more reason to oppose a bill already in trouble. Representative Nadler summed up the opponents' position at a July 11 news conference with colleagues Bobby Scott and Barney Frank that was intended to highlight the *Post* story. Nadler told the press: "The only real purpose of this bill is to allow religious groups to discriminate on the basis of religion or sexual orientation or whatever else."[94]

The Salvation Army stories also made several moderate Republicans hesitant to support the bill, requiring H.R. 7's sponsors to look to the Democratic side of the aisle to make up for Republican votes that might be lost. Just days before the full House vote, several moderate Republicans said they still did not have enough information about the bill to make up their minds on how they would vote, a signal to the Republican leadership that passage was in trouble. H.R. 7 was scheduled to go to the House floor during the week of July 16, but by that time it had been hit with three damaging "bullets": one shooting down purist conservative supporters with its addition of the secondary opt-out; a second limiting the bill's tax-cutting appeal; and a third charging that the remainder of the original bill essentially created "government-funded discrimination."[95] Facing a far closer vote than they had thought only a few days before, supporters began to press hard. Even President Bush joined the effort, coming to a House Republican meeting in the Capitol on July 11 to personally plead for the bill.

July 17 to 19, 2001: Floor Debate and Passage

Confident it could convince a majority of the House to vote for the bill, the Republican leadership moved ahead with H.R. 7 during the week of July 16. Virtually all supporters wanted quick action—pessimists, in order to end the debate before another round of disastrous press reports; optimists, to claim another presidential legislative victory.[96]

Bills on the House floor are usually debated in two steps. First, a "rule" for consideration is debated, which details the time limits and allowed amendments to a bill. Then, if the rule passes, the bill itself is debated under the provisions of the rule. If the rule fails, often the bill to which it refers never comes up for debate. The House debated the rule for H.R. 7 on the evening of Tuesday, July 17. During that debate it became clear that the bill itself was in trouble. Most Democrats would vote against the bill, but sponsors had identified more than twenty Democrats they thought might vote for H.R. 7. During debate on the rule, however, several Democrats on this list announced their opposition to H.R. 7, nearly all of them referring to the hiring discretion controversy. The hiring issue had also affected the Republican side sufficiently to indicate that a dozen or so Republicans would vote against either the rule or the bill, or both. Hoping to force just such a vote against the bill, the bill's major opponents were devising a motion to recommit the bill to committee, instructing the committee to add a strong anti–hiring discrimination amendment. The addition of such an amendment to the bill would have been a substantive and procedural embarrassment for the bill's sponsors and for the White House, setting back the legislation for at least several weeks if not killing it outright. The morning of July 18, the day supporters were anticipating a final vote on H.R. 7, House leaders were still scrambling to put together a deal to win the vote on the rule. Late that day they finally agreed that the next day there would be a scripted floor discussion, or colloquy, between Representative Watts and a moderate Republican on the hiring discretion issue, during which Watts would pledge to remedy the matter to the wavering moderates' satisfaction in any House-Senate conference on H.R. 7.[97] On July 19, nearly two days later than scheduled, the House finally approved the rule for H.R. 7 by a vote of 233 to 194. After the colloquy between Watts and Representative Mark Kirk of Illinois, the House approved the bill 233 to 198.[98] Fourteen Democrats supported the rule, fifteen the bill—far fewer than had supported any previous version of charitable choice legislation. Only four Republicans, however, broke ranks with their party colleagues, most mollified by Watts's promise to fix the hiring discretion problem later in the legislative process.

The Partisan Push

Measuring by minimal legislative standards, the House journey of the president's faith-based initiative was a success.[99] A bill with much of what the president wanted made it through the House before the August 2001 recess. H.R. 7 expanded charitable choice into many new programs, something the Bush administration did not want right away but would have requested later. The tax provisions were small, but because they were whittled down with the administration's acquiescence they could hardly be chalked up as a "loss" for President Bush. H.R. 7 did not have a significant compassion capital fund, an item that was strongly supported by White House faith-based workers, but apparently by few others inside or outside the administration. (Late in 2001, Congress would pass a small appropriation for a technical assistance and research compassion capital fund that would eventually get spent in 2002.)

Measured by broader standards, however, the partisan push of H.R. 7 through the House cannot be seen as a success. The troubled legislative path of H.R. 7 was devised and implemented by House Republicans over the objections of an inexperienced and understaffed White House Office of Faith-Based and Community Initiatives that, in retrospect, probably had better instincts about what was legislatively wise. As one critic of DiIulio later put it: "John really thought he could pull off a victory using a 'left' strategy. I don't think he fully grasped what the right could pull, that the base could crumble."[100]

Relations among the WHOFBCI, House Republicans, other White House offices, and generally sympathetic interest groups worsened as the bill marched down the partisan path. The White House officials most intimate with the initiative's details—those in the WHOFBCI—lost control to groups that had less interest in enacting safely constitutional legislation. The purist interest groups seemed more concerned with staking out a larger parcel of religious ground in the public square than with passing a constitutionally secure bill; the faith-based debate seemed for them, win or lose, only a means to larger ends. It mattered less to them whether a bill passed by the House would then pass the Senate and, ultimately, be upheld in the federal courts.

The lack of coordination among the WHOFBCI and other White House offices significantly damaged efforts to promote faith-based policies inside and outside the government. The main White House offices, such as legislative affairs and public relations, needed to promote the whole Bush agenda, which required them to make trade-offs within and among even the top priorities. Because these key White House decision makers and their outside advisors had apparently little knowledge of the faith-based package and how each of its parts worked together, they traded away pieces of it, like the compassion capital fund—trades that would not have been made by those most knowledgeable about the various pieces and committed to their combined goal: better meeting human needs by "rallying the armies of compassion."

House Republicans wanted to get a strong bill quickly through the House. To them, a partisan and purist strategy seemed necessary to get there. Given the hangover of mistrust from the 2000 elections, a slower pace and the broader-based provisions that the pragmatists favored might have done nothing to attract Democratic support and ease Senate consideration. One White House staff person saw it this way: "Democrats on the Hill saw this as a perfect issue to put a stick in the wheels. [They were thinking], we want to give [the president] a defeat, and we don't want this to aid him with blacks and Hispanics."[101]

On the other hand, some believed that a more pragmatic bill might have given faith-based a better chance all around. One White House faith-based staff person later asserted that the House strategy was entirely avoidable, making it "one of the saddest things" about the initiative's first two years: "The White House [faith-based office] tried to stop them. The Speaker's office and J. C. Watts thought, 'Our side won, so let's stick it in their eye'—a bit like a wedge issue."[102] Another WHOFBCI official claimed that the fault was with the purist interests: "Orthodox sectarians on the Republican fringe right drove [H.R. 7] into the ground and into a ditch. There was never any possibility that it would pass in that form or see the light of day in the Senate."[103]

How faith-based played in the Senate or with the public was not a large concern of House Republicans. But Democrat activist and observer Will Marshall put the responsibility for the alienation H.R. 7 caused on the White House rather than on House Republicans: "The White House allowed the House Republicans to write a bill to alienate Democrats and not attract them. . . . The White House should have collaborated with the Democrats and the House Republicans, but that was not the path they chose."[104]

J. C. Watts's April 25 summit for African American clergy seemed to be the lynchpin event in how the faith-based efforts were portrayed. The summit "framed and shaped the debate," as one Democratic staff person put it, and to the Democrats it framed H.R. 7 as symbolic politics targeted at the most susceptible slice of minority voters.[105] Many opponents of the president point to the summit and the partisan push for faith-based initiatives to reinforce arguments that the president was at worst intolerant and at best clumsy in appealing to racial and ethnic minorities. Unfortunately for faith-based proponents, the disputes between the purist and pragmatic conservatives provided ample ammunition for those wanting to bolster such impressions.

Amendments to the legislation shrank rather than expanded faith-based support. The decision in the Judiciary Committee to add broader voucher language in exchange for a secondary opt-out was at best a "draw" for purist conservatives. Dropping tax cuts from the omnibus tax reform bill and scaling them down severely in H.R. 7 depressed potential support from a host of influential lobbying groups seeking tax benefits for non-profits. The very limited compassion capital funds, and the general belt-tightening of Republican budgets and deficit politics, caused already funded groups to see H.R. 7 as re-cutting a shrinking pie, not truly doing more to help the poor.

The attempt to use H.R. 7 to appeal to African Americans did not go well. Beyond their successful attacks on the summit, opponents easily portrayed the decision to drop compassion capital funds as further proof of Republican insincerity. The decision to eliminate large charity tax breaks hurt, and the Salvation Army story was the final blow. It looked to many African Americans as if they were being played the fool by Republicans, or at least their traditional Democratic allies could make that case to them.

No new broad and powerful interest group coalitions for the faith-based initiative were formed during the course of the legislation. As one observer noted: "The framework was the old interest groups and the old terms," and the opportunity for a new "coalition of care" was lost.[106] To the core members of these old interests, H.R. 7 was not a top priority. According to one White House source, the Republicans behind H.R. 7 "used this to appease people who were not interested in charitable choice" at all, but rather in furthering a broadly conservative agenda and more explicit protections for traditional Christianity in the public square.[107]

The faith-based initiative did not turn out to be the bipartisan rallying cry for the armies of compassion that Bush said he wanted it to be; rather, it became a throwback to partisan blitzkriegs of the Newt Gingrich era. Perhaps, given the political atmosphere after Florida in 2000, the legislative path of H.R. 7 could not have proceeded in any other way. But with control of the Senate held by Democrats, perhaps supporters earnestly seeking legislative success should have tried a different way.

Four

Who CAREs?

Faith-Based in a Divided Senate

> Very few people in the White House made [faith-based legislation] a priority. . . . Presidential phone calls did not happen. Deals were not made.
>
> *Senate staff person involved in faith-based efforts*

> There is a conservative base for CARE, but it is not at the top of their agendas. . . . They are passionate about specific issues, and this is not on their list.
>
> *Lobbyist for the Senate CARE Act*

February 7, 2002, seemed to be a new and more promising day for Senate faith-based legislation after a year of inaction caused by the partisanship of H.R. 7 and the distractions of September 11 and its aftermath. President Bush had just appointed Jim Towey to fill the six-month vacancy at the top of a reorganized White House faith-based office. In his State of the Union speech in late January, the president had recast faith-based in the uncontroversial context of encouraging volunteerism. He mentioned faith-based once in issuing a vague call for Congress to find "ways to encourage the good work of charities and faith-based groups." The White House was greatly scaling back its legislative expectations. The president wanted a bill, any bill, out of the Senate that could legitimately be called faith-based.

On February 7, it seemed likely he would get it. That day, Bush invited the key Senate faith-based proponents, Rick Santorum and Joseph Lieberman, to the White House to announce a bipartisan legislative agreement. Joining Lieberman and Santorum were three other Democratic senators—Evan Bayh, Hillary Clinton, and Bill Nelson—and three other Republicans—Sam Brownback, Charles Grassley, and Orrin Hatch.

Later that same day, Lieberman and Santorum would introduce a "consensus" bill—the Charity Aid, Recovery, and Empowerment (CARE) Act—that had the president's official blessing and support. CARE had new tax incentives: most importantly a large charitable deduction for nonitemizers and new provisions to encourage contributions from individual retirement accounts. It also included a large increase in social service block grants, expanded individual development accounts, compassion capital funds, and a few narrowly tailored "religious freedom" provisions.

Senators Santorum and Lieberman make something of a legislative odd couple. Young, hyperactive, black-haired Santorum is a physical contrast to the older, graying Lieberman. Santorum is a uniformly conservative voter, often achieving 100 percent approval ratings from the American Conservative Union and the Chamber of Commerce, and zeros from Americans for Democratic Action. One of the youngest members of the Senate, he has a blunt speaking manner, unusual among senators, and impatience that some interpret as arrogance. He defends his positions and style as "principled" and "doing what I was elected to do." Voting consistently for budget cuts, Santorum aggressively pursues federal funds for his state. He works hard to stay in touch with Pennsylvanians, visiting each of the state's sixty-seven counties every year.[1]

His style and substance help Santorum win elections. He won a narrow victory in his first House election in 1990, then won a tough race in a Democrat-leaning redistricted seat in 1992. Running for the Senate in 1994, he prevailed in a squeaker over incumbent Harris Wofford. His House career was marked by membership in the "Gang of Seven," a group of hard-charging junior Republicans who highlighted the congressional scandals of the early 1990s in order to indict the House's Democratic majority.

Departing the House in 1994, Santorum never left behind his combative "Gang of Seven" style. In Santorum's first month in the Senate, that body was debating a balanced budget constitutional amendment just approved by the House as the Republicans' fulfillment of the Contract with America commitment. Senior Republican senator Mark Hatfield was the only Republican to cast a vote against the amendment, and because of that vote the amendment failed to achieve the two-thirds support needed for approval. Santorum called on his Republican colleagues to discipline Hatfield by removing him from his Appropriations Committee chairmanship. Senator Hatfield was not removed, but Senate Republicans did change their caucus rules to improve party discipline. Santorum had made a point, if few friends, in the battle.[2]

Senator Lieberman, according to a popular research source on Congress, had carved out a "niche role as a sometimes lonely, moral crusader against Hollywood, 'Gangsta' rappers, and even his own Democratic White House" during the Clinton years.[3] He sometimes supported school vouchers, growth-encouraging tax incentives, privatization of social security, more military spending, and more aggressive foreign policy. Responding to President Clinton's problems with Monica Lewinsky, Lieberman was one of the first Democrats to condemn the president's behavior as "immoral." But he never called for the president's resignation, nor even advocated for senatorial censure. Lieberman's actions vis-à-vis Clinton raised the senator's stature outside the party. Lieberman's condemnation of the president without recommending removal may have helped Clinton stay in office.[4]

Some internal party critics do not like what they view as the senator's moralism, but such criticisms seem to carry little weight. Lieberman's voting record is characterized by solid allegiance to party values; his dissentions are infrequent and tend to arise only on a few high-profile issues. His vice presidential candidacy in 2000 added interesting twists to his independent image. During the campaign, Lieberman was accused of bowing to liberal interest group pressure, backing away from moderate positions, and tarnishing his profile as a principled centrist. The Florida recount underlined his party loyalty: he pressed hard to carry the recount fight into the Florida courts.[5]

Both highly skilled in the art of partisan combat, senators Santorum and Lieberman seem unlikely allies on any issue. They have other commonalities, though, that make their partnership on faith-based initiatives less surprising. Both are intensely religious; Santorum is an active Catholic, while Lieberman is dedicated to his Orthodox Jewish faith and practice. Each deeply believes in the effectiveness of social services delivered by religious groups. Both were early members and later cochairs of the Congressional Empowerment Caucus (CEC), a bipartisan group of legislators who seek innovative ways to coordinate government, business, and nonprofit efforts to combat poverty and address social needs. And for all their partisanship, each senator has been willing to break with his respective party on selected issues. Lieberman's differences with the Democrats are mirrored by Santorum's willingness to buck Republican orthodoxy and vote with labor unions on issues such as the minimum wage or unemployment benefits.

By early 2002, Santorum and Lieberman knew each other well. They had worked together for several years on creative legislative approaches to domestic social needs, jointly sponsoring a community renewal bill in 2000, portions of which became law in one of the last acts of the Clinton administration. They had also sponsored the two major Senate faith-based bills introduced in 2001—a tax bill for individuals, and another for foundations and corporations. Together they had suffered through the previous year's descent of the faith-based debate into the abyss of bitterness, a lesson for them in the failures of partisanship.

The only downside to their continued partnership was another of their commonalities. Santorum's aggressive brashness and Lieberman's studied independence placed each of them, at best, on the fringes of the Senate's inner circle where personal relationships and reciprocal courtesies still affect the legislative process.

On that early February day, CARE supporters anticipated that the new bill would have quick and smooth sailing after a year of frustration for faith-based initiatives. The *Washington Post* described the bill as "an important accomplishment for Bush as he seeks to post some legislative victories," its provisions "likely resolving an issue that has bedeviled the administration for the past year."[6] Lieberman described the act as a "balanced, bipartisan" piece of legislation that avoided the controversies of earlier faith-based proposals. The Connecticut senator recalled for the president the Fishing School event of a year before to remind him about what could, and did, go wrong with H.R. 7: "And I said then, because we were talking in general terms, that the devil—if I may use that term advisedly—would be in the details. Along the way, Congress, being what it is, turned out to be quite devilish. But in the end here today, I think we've put the good Lord right into the details." President Bush was equally effusive: "This legislation will not only provide a way for government to encourage faith-based programs to exist without breaching the separation of church and state, it will also encourage charitable giving." Senator Santorum chimed in with his view: "This compromise represents a critical step forward in empowering those small faith and community-based groups who give so much to care for so many."[7]

Within days key interest groups jumped onboard. Five large social service groups that receive federal funding—Catholic Charities, Volunteers of America, Lutheran Services in America, The Salvation Army, and United Jewish Communities—within days issued a joint letter supporting CARE. Key House leaders also were pleased. "While the bill may now be only half a loaf, it's the better half," said Representative Tony Hall of Ohio, the House Democratic sponsor of H.R. 7.[8] Representative J. C. Watts was encouraged, and even the conservative Family Research Council appeared to be onboard. Its leadership thought Senate passage of CARE was a good idea, although it expressed hope that charitable choice might be added in a House-Senate conference.

Dissenters seemed an isolated minority. Americans United leader Barry Lynn thought CARE gave "special treatment to religious groups"; he particularly objected to the religious protection provision that allowed faith-based organizations to keep their religious symbols on display: "It is simply wrong for a publicly funded job training facility to post a banner that reads, 'Only Jesus Saves.'"[9] Beyond Lynn, however, it was difficult to detect dissent. Maybe the faith-based legislative train was finally on track.

February 2002 was to be the first, and best, month for CARE. In the months to follow, CARE's support would widen slightly but not deepen significantly. While the bill frequently came close to floor action, it ultimately failed even to be debated directly. Thus, President Bush's faith-based legislative initiatives yielded virtually nothing in his first two years in office. To see why CARE failed requires a review of legislative events dating back before the 2000 election.

Santorum and Lieberman had supported charitable choice even before their involvement with the CARE Act. In the previous 106th Congress of 1999–2000, the two senators had been the main sponsors of the Senate version of a "New Markets" initiative. New Markets, one of President Clinton's domestic priorities in the latter part of his second term, was designed to spur economic activity in poor communities by encouraging innovative, market-based community development. The House of Representatives gave the initiative a great deal of attention, and Santorum and Lieberman introduced a Senate version of New Markets in June 2000.

That bill contained charitable choice language covering a broad range of programs, provisions virtually as extensive as those that would appear in H.R. 7 during the 107th Congress.

Of the two senators, Santorum seemed to believe more firmly in charitable choice, talking about it more frequently and using it as the centerpiece of his own approach to social service policy reform. Democrat Lieberman's support was more measured, a condition of the Clinton administration's view that, by law, pervasively sectarian social service providers were to be kept from the bidding process. The broad charitable choice expansion in New Markets drew a fair amount of interest group opposition through the summer and fall of 2000, presaging much of the debate to come in the Bush administration.

Early 2001: Developing a Senate Strategy

The Briefest of Honeymoons
Then, in the election of 2000, Lieberman simultaneously ran for the vice presidency and for his Connecticut Senate seat. Reelected in Connecticut, Lieberman seemed willing to set aside the Florida controversy over the presidential vote and help the new Republican president on faith-based initiatives. A few days after taking office and one day after signing executive orders to create a White House faith-based office and five agency satellites, President Bush invited key members of the House and Senate to the Fishing School—a religion-based social service agency in Washington, D.C.—to announce the launching of his faith-based plan. Lieberman and Santorum joined President Bush and Representatives Hall and Souder at the school on January 30, 2001, for a short visit and photo opportunity.

No legislative language was unveiled at that time, but Bush stated a few principles that included a compassion capital fund and recommended a few pilot programs, such as one for mentoring children of prisoners. The president did not explicitly endorse existing or expanded charitable choice laws. Press reports suggested that the first round of presidential initiatives would not expand charitable choice; one unnamed Bush advisor at the Fishing School event asserted that charitable choice "will be discussed today but not included in the first wave of legislation."[10]

Lieberman's presence at the Fishing School suggested that faith-based would take a moderate early course, one that would please the extremes on neither side but might in time develop a large centrist following. The president and the senator, Lieberman stated that day, were "of like minds" when it came to the initiative's goals.[11] Lieberman seemed committed to working with Bush and Santorum on an early Senate faith-based bill, partly in response to several White House steps that Lieberman supported, including John DiIulio's appointment as the faith-based director. The senator had already organized a group of nearly a dozen Democratic senators who seemed willing to endorse a faith-based package, even one that included a modest version of charitable choice, provided they could work out an agreement with the White House and other Republicans.[12]

Though Lieberman seemed steadfast in his support for a still-ambiguous initiative, a growing share of Democrats and their key interest group supporters, looking at faith-based developments in the House, were expressing concerns about both the substance and the style of the effort.[13] Taking up these concerns with the White House, Lieberman urged it to be specific about its legislative requests in order to assuage growing concern among his circle of contacts.[14] Meanwhile, the initially quiet center of the interest group community seemed to be moving toward skepticism. The bitterness of the 2000 election battle was leaching into this issue. Groups traditionally connected to each major party—racial minorities and civil libertarians for the Democrats, and politically conservative and religiously orthodox groups for the Republicans—were coalescing behind their respective sides.

Tensions were also rising among Republicans and conservatives inside the faith-based negotiations. As we noted in chapter 3, relations were strained between the Bush faith-based offices on the one hand and House GOP leaders and purist conservative interest groups on the other. Differences were cropping up within the White House Office of Faith-Based and Community Initiatives (WHOFBCI), and between it and other White House offices. As it became clear that purists were winning the negotiations over the House bill, Lieberman began to move away from charitable choice and, it seemed to some, from helping the Republican president on any part of the faith-based initiatives. By the second week of March 2001, Lieberman was starting to echo faith-based critics, expressing a range of concerns about how the legislation was developing in the House, and particularly about how it might affect hiring discretion.[15] In six short weeks the honeymoon was over.

Tax Provisions First

Lieberman and Santorum announced on March 13, 2001, that they would introduce to the Senate a faith-based bill the following week that would not include charitable choice. Santorum was now suggesting that charitable choice provisions in current law be fully implemented before being expanded to other programs. Lieberman also wanted to pursue a less controversial bill without charitable choice, arguing it made sense to not "rush to test the most difficult and complicated questions." Thus, their joint bill was mostly a tax bill, reflecting a go-slow approach that Lieberman stated had been checked out with DiIulio and had received his blessing.[16] A Santorum aide later confirmed that the incremental strategy signaled by the bill was "absolutely" worked out with the White House.[17]

Lieberman and Santorum's Savings Opportunity and Charitable Giving Act included four main tax incentives to increase charitable donations. The keystone of the bill was a provision to phase in a large charitable tax deduction for non-itemizing tax payers—up to a $500 deduction for individuals and a $1,000 deduction for joint filers. The bill also expanded individual development accounts (IDAs), in which the government subsidized banks to set up matching-funds savings accounts for low-income individuals who would use the funds in those accounts to later purchase a home, pay college tuition, or start up a small business. Other parts of the bill provided new incentives for charitable contributions from individual retirement accounts (IRAs) and in-kind contributions from businesses. Overall, the bill was estimated to cost $14 billion in lost revenue over five years.

The bill left out almost all controversial elements, and its sponsors hoped it would move through Congress quickly.[18] Legislative prospects initially looked good. As a tax bill, it faced a pragmatic Senate Finance Committee that was primed to reduce taxes in early 2001. But the bill still faced obstacles. The president was pushing a major tax reform bill in the House and Senate, and there were many organized and powerful constituencies lobbying for costly tax breaks in that bill, leaving less money available for charitable tax deductions like those in the Santorum-Lieberman bill.

Although Lieberman and Santorum were optimistic, other participants in the faith-based debate were not as sanguine. Many Christian conservative groups, against an incremental approach, opposed the Senate bill because it did not include charitable choice. Dividing the tax and charitable choice issues into separate bills harmed the prospects for what they thought was the more important portion of faith-based. Civil libertarians and others on the left of the political spectrum had few substantive objections to the Santorum-Lieberman bill, but did not want any bill to pass the Senate that might then go to a House-Senate conference with the "radical" House bill.[19]

House Bill Goes Right

Representatives Watts, Hall, and Hastert introduced H.R. 7 on March 28, one week after Santorum and Lieberman had introduced their bill. The main difference between H.R. 7 and the Senate bill was charitable choice. According to several sources interviewed later, already in March 2001 Senate faith-based supporters were worried that the House was "poisoning the well" for faith-based bills in the Senate. The Senate was going its own way substantively and strategically, partly to separate its work from the sharp partisanship of the House. The April 2001 black clergy summit organized by Watts and cohosted by Santorum cemented the view among Democrats that faith-based was a partisan strategy to steal a slice of the deeply religious black vote for the GOP. While the summit was officially separate from any legislation, for many observers the summit, the faith-based bill, Watts's black Republican strategy, and Bush's public religious language had merged into a single political movement that Democrats would fight every step of the way.[20]

The summit unified almost all House Democrats against Bush and all parts of the faith-based initiative. While they could do little about the House debate or eventual outcome, they could talk to their more powerful Senate colleagues. Representatives Scott, Edwards, and others went to work on the Senate during the House's earliest deliberations on H.R. 7.[21] The slim Republican majority that then held the Senate would still need about ten Democratic votes for a faith-based bill. Scott and Edwards were trying to make sure that would not happen. The tone of the House faith-based debate was a great help to Scott and Edwards; by early May, White House political operatives were aware that the overall effort was in trouble.

Some more-pragmatic friends of the faith-based initiative saw positive aspects to the Senate's path. For example, DiIulio could argue that a wider community-based, results-oriented initiative developed in a bipartisan manner—so different from the House strategy—was the only bill likely to get out of an evenly divided Senate. In fact, DiIulio's public disputes with purist conservatives helped keep Lieberman in dialogue with the White House and onboard with a Senate alternative.[22]

Senate Switches Parties

Things soon worsened, however, for faith-based legislative proponents. On May 24, while President Bush was on a promotional tour for his faith-based initiative, Vermont senator Jim Jeffords announced he would switch from Republican to Independent and caucus with Senate Democrats. This effectively shifted partisan control of the Senate. There now were fifty Democrats and one sympathetic Independent against forty-nine Republicans. Senator Tom Daschle of South Dakota became the majority leader and all committees had new Democratic chairpersons. The legislative calculus changed from a Republican majority needing about ten moderate Democrats to move bills, to a Democratic majority able to block virtually all of President Bush's initiatives except those that enjoyed the broadest bipartisan support.

Rethinking Senate Strategy

Overnight, the scenario for faith-based legislation had become far more difficult. No longer was it possible for a Republican Senate majority to troll for a handful of Democratic votes on a faith-based bill they were ready to schedule at any time—which, in itself, would have been a modestly difficult feat in a closely divided Senate. Under that scenario, some kind of faith-based bill would very likely have passed the Senate and moved to a House-Senate conference where the president could mold the details. Now, nearly all the Senate Democratic caucus would need to support a faith-based bill for it to see the light of day.

There would be plenty of space in the Senate for faith-based opponents, but little for those who liked the bill. Hearings would focus on its points of controversy, not consensus. A faith-based bill would get a Senate floor vote on the Democrats' timeline and only if the Democratic leadership saw it to be in the party's interest. The House's partisan path became more consequential than ever. Senate Democrats would need strong assurances that little or nothing from the Republican House bill would be picked up in any House-Senate conference on faith-based legislation. The whole faith-based strategy would have to change.

Senate Charitable Choice Hearing

Santorum and Lieberman's faith-based tax bill lay dormant in Senate Finance. But many other faith-based bills had been introduced by other senators. One, the Drug Abuse Education, Prevention, and Treatment Act of 2001, had been sponsored by Republican senator Orrin Hatch of Utah. The bill included a charitable choice provision that would allow intensely and vocally religious ministries to bid for drug treatment funds. Hatch had scheduled a June 6 hearing on the bill before the Senate Judiciary Committee, which he had chaired until the switch in the Senate majority. The committee's new Democratic chair, Pat Leahy of Vermont, agreed to go forward with the hearing as a courtesy to President Bush and Hatch, now the committee's ranking member.[23]

The hearing—four separate panels consisting of members of Congress, administration officials, practitioners, and legal experts—lasted most of the day and turned out to be the only Senate hearing in the 107th Congress on charitable choice. It was clear from the start that Senate faith-based bills were in trouble. Leahy opened the hearing by listing his concerns with the faith-based initiative, including charitable choice language and more. He worried about the loss of religious freedom of groups working with government, reporting that nearly one thousand religious leaders organized by the Interfaith Alliance interest group had announced opposition to faith-based legislation on those grounds.[24]

Other witnesses at the hearing raised a wide range of possible problems with charitable choice. Representative Bobby Scott came over from the House side to voice his concerns with H.R. 7. Democratic Senator Russ Feingold of Wisconsin, after the usual nod to the good work of faith-based organizations, expressed his concern that these organizations could take federal money and still hire on religious criteria, potentially discriminating in objectionable ways under the guise of religion. Other opponents defended the current relationship between government and religious groups, claiming that charitable choice was an unneeded solution to a nonexistent problem. On their view, religious organizations with strongly religious messages already successfully delivered social services with private funds and thus did not need federal funds. Other religious organizations that had eliminated religious messages from their programs, and thereby received federal funds, did a good job with them. There was no need for change. While the hearing aired nearly every common objection to charitable choice, opponents were increasingly focusing on the hiring discretion issue and calling it hiring discrimination.

Charitable choice's chief defender at the hearing was Carl Esbeck, then serving in John Ashcroft's Department of Justice as senior counsel to the deputy attorney general and as head of the department's faith-based office. Esbeck tried to turn the discrimination argument on its head. He asserted that "charitable choice provisions don't rescind civil rights protection. [Rather,] they strip away government funding discrimination toward groups with a 'high religiosity' or that are 'pervasively sectarian.' "[25] He argued for the civil right of religious groups to remain religious after they received federal funds, and dismissed problems of objectionable hiring discrimination as highly unlikely. On another issue, using government funds for religious purposes, Senator Santorum signaled that he and the Bush administration were already willing to ensure better firewalls between secular and religious funds and program elements, implying support for language requiring program separation and a secondary opt-out clause.[26] While both sides of the arguments were aired, it was obvious from the tone and proportion of witnesses at the hearing that under the new Senate regime charitable choice bills were not going to get out of committee, much less be debated on the floor.

White House Worries

The motivation for the Judiciary hearing under the Democrats was far different from what it would have been under the Republicans. Democrats used the hearing to publicize and test a variety of objections to the faith-based initiative, regardless of which particular provisions were to be actively considered by the Senate. The reaction of the White House to the new Senate environment was to push for faster consideration of the House bill—but different White House offices were pushing for different reasons. The political offices involved in legislative affairs and in contact with core Republican constituencies thought that a quick House faith-based victory would indicate momentum for the initiative that could be transferred to the Senate. Most staff persons in the faith-based offices, on the other hand, wanted the House to finish quickly so that partisan tensions could sooner dissipate. The earlier the House was done, they thought, the more time there would be for partisanship to cool and for the Senate to approve a far different bill.

Seeking Common Ground

Into the mess stepped Senator Santorum and an intriguing new ally. The Pennsylvania senator announced on June 19 that he was endorsing the formation of a working group of thirty-three prominent interest group leaders gathered to seek broad agreement on faith-based issues. The group would be sponsored by Search for Common Ground and chaired by former Pennsylvania senator Harris Wofford, the man Santorum had defeated in 1994. This new Working Group on Human Needs and Faith-Based and Community Initiatives was comprised of members ranging from representatives of the ACLU, Americans United, and People for the American Way (strongly opposing faith-based), to those representing the likes of Teen Challenge, the National Center for Neighborhood Enterprise, and Evangelicals for Social Action (in strong support). The thirty-three civil libertarians, clergy, lawyers, theologians, and leaders of social service programs were to discuss and develop whatever consensus they could around faith-based issues. The hope was that their "common ground" could be the basis of a new Senate legislative proposal that would complement the tax provisions in the uncontroversial but dormant Santorum-Lieberman faith-based tax bill.

FOCAL POINT 4.1

The Birth of an Issue Network

[T]he role of religion in public life is no longer an underlying discussion. It is the discussion.

Press release announcing creation of the Pew Forum
on Religion and Public Life

Public policy texts mention "iron triangles," "policy whirlpools," or "issue networks"—different names for the set of private interests and government officials who together make policy. Issue networks explain an issue to the public, define the important questions for political debate, and, most important, decide which groups and views get to resolve the issue. Networks often have several centers of activity around which a number of similar-thinking interest groups cluster. These clusters interact, framing the ensuing debate.

For most of the policy world and the media in early 2001, the faith-based initiative was new. Several groups started to form the issue network in which the issue became defined: a small group of those involved in the debate since its beginning, a forum for public intellectuals interested in questions of religion and public life, a set of conservative interest groups, and a diverse handpicked group charged with seeking common ground on faith-based initiatives.

The faith-based debate began in obscurity, and no large issue network emerged for several years. This began to change during the 2000 campaign with the major candidates' interest in faith-based issues. That same year, the Pew Charitable Trusts funded a gathering of representatives from several interest groups, which in February 2001 released *In Good Faith: A Dialogue on Government Funding of Faith-Based Social Services*, an early outline of the areas of agreement and disagreement. Strong faith-based supporters who helped write the report included the Center for Public Justice and the National Association of Evangelicals. Among the opponents were the Baptist Joint Committee and Americans United for Separation of Church and State. All were familiar names to those few who had followed early charitable choice debates.

George W. Bush's presidency assured the policy world that faith-based initiatives would be an important policy issue worth organizing around. On March 1, 2001, the Pew Forum on Religion and Public Life staked its claim as a center for discussion. Senator Lieberman gave the forum's opening address. "The challenge ahead of us now," he said, "is as much political as it is legal. Those of us who are seeking a suitable space for faith must engage those who feel threatened in a broad and open conversation. . . . This is a conversation begging for facilitation, for an honest broker."

The Pew Forum is cochaired by respected public intellectuals E. J. Dionne and Jean Bethke Elshtain and managed by Melissa Rogers, formerly of the Baptist Joint Committee. Described by Dionne as a "living op-ed page," the forum regularly hosts discussions about issues of religion and public policy, acts as a clearinghouse for materials on faith and public life, and initiates, commissions, and publishes scholarship in the area. Whereas some conservatives were skeptical of its impartiality, the Pew Forum carries great credibility in the D.C. policy community.

As the forum began its work, purist conservatives organized. One such group is the Capital Research Center (CRC). Established in 1984 to critically analyze "organizations that promote the growth of the welfare state" and to identify "viable private alternatives to government welfare programs," the CRC early in 2001 gathered conservative groups around more purist arguments about faith-based initiatives and sought to get congressional Republicans onboard.

As the House version of faith-based legislation foundered, Senators Santorum and Lieberman gambled that a new group of diverse interests could help reposition the issue nearer the center. They asked Search for Common Ground USA to form a Working Group on Human Needs and Faith-Based and Community Initiatives to find areas of agreement. The group's meetings started in the summer of 2001, and included representatives from thirty-three organizations across virtually the entire range of opinion—from Teen Challenge and Evangelicals for Social Action, on one side, to the NAACP, Americans United for Separation of Church and State, and the ACLU on the other. In early 2002, the Search for Common Ground working group issued recommendations largely consistent with the CARE Act proposal that senators Santorum and Lieberman unveiled a few weeks later.

The early issue network quickly defined the major concerns over faith-based initiatives. The number-one question was whether intense and vocal religion could safely operate in the public square and work closely with the machinery of government. Could religion be trusted to play by the rules under which everyone else played, or could it not?

—Melissa Fritsch

Sources

Horowitz, Michael, and Marvin Olasky. "Statement of Principles: Government Financing of Faith-Based Institutions." In *Mandate for Charity: Policy Proposals for the Bush Administration*, edited by Robert M. Huberty and Christopher Yablonski, 23–26. Washington, D.C.: Capital Research Center, 2001.

Huberty, Robert M., and Christopher Yablonski, eds. *Mandate for Charity: Policy Proposals for the Bush Administration*. Washington, D.C.: Capital Research Center, 2001.

Pew Forum on Religion and Public Life. "About the Forum." http://pewforum.org/
about/ (accessed 10 April 2003).
———. "In Good Faith: A Dialogue on Government Funding of Faith-Based Social
Services." http://pewforum.org/publications/reports/ingoodfaith.pdf (accessed
10 April 2003).
Search for Common Ground. *Finding Common Ground: Twenty-Nine
Recommendations of the Working Group on Human Needs and Faith-Based and
Community Initiatives.* Washington, D.C.: Search for Common Ground, 2001.

Despite their past history as election foes, Santorum and Wofford shared a belief in the need to "find common ground for trying to help some of our fellow Americans in greatest need, by strengthening the work of this country's many faith-based and other community organizations."[27] Wofford had worked with and for volunteer and community service groups, serving in the early years of the Peace Corps under President Kennedy and as the head of AmeriCorps, the national volunteer coordinating agency begun in 1993 under President Clinton. Santorum hoped that the new working group would keep the faith-based legislative track alive, lower partisan tensions, and illustrate that there could be areas of agreement. A few other pro-faith-based legislators thought the group could help the cause. Some others worried, and still others hoped, that forming the large and potentially unwieldy group would ensure that Senate faith-based legislation would be delayed many months or even die for the 107th Congress.

Baby Steps

After the House narrowly passed H.R. 7 in mid-July 2001, full attention moved to the Senate. With hopes of quick passage dashed weeks before, the White House began to realize that it would be lucky if the Senate considered any bill that contained any faith-based element. One of the few hopes for faith-based was continuing concern by centrist Democrats about how their party appeared to people with strong religious beliefs. In the middle of the Salvation Army scandal and the House floor debate on H.R. 7, the Democratic Leadership Council held its summer meetings, which centered on a discussion of values and how Democrats could regain the trust of more voters on cultural issues. A key point of discussion was, as Senator Evan Bayh of Indiana put it at the meetings, how to deal with "the seven out of every ten people who go to church every Sunday

[who] don't feel comfortable with the Democratic Party." Lieberman, also speaking at the conference, believed that Democratic officials had "too often dismissed and disparaged the importance of faith in American life." He still argued that Democrats needed to support faith-based ideas, implying that he would continue pushing faith-based legislation despite the apparent capture of the issue by purist conservatives.[28]

On July 22, three days after the House passed H.R. 7, Lieberman announced that he would draft his own comprehensive faith-based bill. Unlike the House bill, the senator's bill would not include any charitable choice language or other provisions that preempted state and local antidiscrimination laws. That same day, Senate majority leader Tom Daschle announced on a national news program that he would allow a faith-based bill on the Senate floor sometime in the 107th Congress. "I don't want to be tied to a specific time frame," Daschle stated, "but I clearly will give the president his opportunity, his day in court."[29]

In response, President Bush gave the go-ahead for his staff to cooperate with Lieberman on a new faith-based bill. Bush seemed willing to forgo federal preemption of state and local antidiscrimination hiring statutes, the main sticking point in the House bill, centered in the Salvation Army media frenzy. We are "willing to work with [Lieberman] without compromising on principle," the president stated. "One of our principles is that we should never undermine the civil rights laws of the United States."[30] In reality, the president was potentially abandoning all the contentious elements of H.R. 7—the very elements that many purists had demanded in the House—to get a bill through the Senate. Senate consideration of a comprehensive faith-based bill in late 2001 or early 2002 seemed possible.

At the same time, however, differences between Santorum and Lieberman on strategic questions began to show through the agreeable surface.[31] Santorum, wanting to compromise far less than the president seemed willing to, thought that dropping the state and local hiring preemption of the House bill would be sufficient. Lieberman, however, suggested it would be more "constructive" to begin "building from the ground up again," citing concerns about H.R. 7's costs, vouchers, and discrimination in service provision.[32] Lieberman planned to write a bill with other Democrats and White House faith-based staff, and then negotiate that text with Santorum. With DiIulio still head of the WHOFBCI in early August, that scenario seemed plausible and not a little troubling to conservatives.

Lieberman and Santorum were simultaneously putting the finishing touches on another set of tax incentives to help faith-based groups, continuing their incremental approach. This new package, called the Foundational and Corporate Charitable Giving Incentives Act, was introduced on August 3. The bill offered tax incentives to corporations and foundations to encourage philanthropic giving by "repealing the excise tax on net investment income for private foundations, raising the corporate giving cap from 10 to 25 percent, and including charitable donation incentives" for smaller corporations.[33] This new foundation and corporate tax bill complemented the individual tax bill that Lieberman and Santorum had introduced in March. By continuing their incremental approach with this second bill and committing to a third bill that addressed other elements of the faith-based initiative, Lieberman and Santorum kept momentum behind faith-based ideas. Still, by August 2001, the senators' plans were the only ones by which faith-based ideas were being advanced in the legislative process.

Mid-August 2001: *Unlevel Playing Field* and DiIulio's Departure

Two days in mid-August brought two events that defined the future of Senate deliberations. On August 16, the White House faith-based office issued its *Unlevel Playing Field* report (detailed in chapter 5).[34] One implication of the report was that the House and Senate were being bypassed, at least temporarily, to advance faith-based ideas administratively. The Bush administration wanted, and would eventually need, legislation. But the administration's faith-based offices were operating as if legislation might be far off or never coming.[35]

The next day, August 17, brought more big news: John DiIulio announced he would soon leave his job.[36] The media seemed unclear about what his leaving meant to the legislation. The *Washington Post* reported the move as a blow to the faith-based initiative, interpreting DiIulio's exit as a White House accommodation to white evangelicals and political conservatives—the purists who had taken control. Barry Lynn of Americans United chimed in with his confirmation, asserting that DiIulio "was left out of the loop in recent weeks as Bush operatives manipulated the faith-based initiative to make the plan more palatable to the religious right."[37] Lynn did not blame DiIulio for leaving, but warned that "it is a dangerous time to put a more hard-right person in the job." This, in Lynn's view, seemed a virtual certainty.[38]

Other leaders of key constituencies expressed their own views about what DiIulio's departure meant. Some prominent African American pastors, such as the Reverend Eugene Rivers, also thought it signaled a move to the right. Rivers warned that the departure of DiIulio "sends a signal that the faith-based offices will just be a financial watering hole for the right-wing white evangelicals." Purist conservatives were pleased DiIulio was gone, thinking and hoping that they now actually were in control of the White House office. Marvin Olasky responded that "students will benefit from having [DiIulio] back in the classroom," and Michael Horowitz of the Hudson Institute gave DiIulio good riddance, calling him "the most strategically disastrous appointee to a senior government position in the twenty-plus years I've been in Washington."[39]

The actual consequences for Senate deliberations were much more complex. DiIulio had been the White House's strongest tie to Lieberman, the director having eased President Bush's early working relationship with Lieberman. DiIulio's departure actually did little to disrupt the pace or to change the content of faith-based legislation. Most of the White House faith-based office staff working on legislative matters was staying on. The finished *Unlevel Playing Field* report gave new direction to the staff for its work in the agencies. John Bridgeland of the Domestic Policy Council took more formal control of day-to-day operations, but he had been keeping close tabs on the office for several months. The Search for Common Ground working group, serving as a testing ground for compromises and consensus, was holding monthly meetings and communicating closely with Santorum and Lieberman. DiIulio was not the central player in any of these activities, and in many of them he had no involvement.

September 11: Hindrance and Help

The horrors of September 11, 2001, suspended the normal activities of Washington, D.C. Overnight, national politics refocused on internal security, foreign diplomacy, and military operations. Further, in the weeks that followed, anthrax contamination incidents on Capitol Hill and in other locations in Washington required the temporary closing of House and Senate offices.

The faith-based bill became secondary, like much other legislation not directly responsive to the terrorist attacks. This seemed at first to reduce the likelihood of Senate passage. On October 9, Santorum openly speculated that the Senate was unlikely to pass a faith-based bill in 2001: "It's always difficult to pass something, and this year there is especially heavy competition." A Lieberman spokesman agreed: "We need a little more time and it will in all likelihood have to wait until next year. It is a complicated issue, and since September 11, many people's attention has been focused elsewhere."[40]

Other events, however, suggested this might be a good time for a faith-based legislative effort. In the wake of September 11, church attendance and attack-related charitable activities by churches increased; there was, in the American public, an extended rise in proreligious behaviors and attitudes.[41] Donations to September 11–related causes skyrocketed while other charitable giving dried up. In response to the near crisis among charities not directly related to September 11, the White House approached Lieberman in late September about broadening the focus of the newly started faith-based negotiations on a bill to jumpstart general charitable giving. David Kuo, DiIulio's prime WHOFBCI assistant and a legislative pragmatist, was directed to handle most of the negotiations with Lieberman's office. By late October, negotiations among Kuo, Lieberman, and Santorum were bearing fruit. Senators Max Baucus and Charles Grassley were brought in on tax provisions, since the lost revenue of the tax provisions seemed to be a major sticking point as reported federal deficits were rising. Soon a bipartisan outline developed with tax incentives reportedly in the range of $54 billion over five years, compassion capital funds of around $100 million, relatively minor "clarifications" of the status of religious groups seeking federal grants and contracts, and additional money for social services block grants. All charitable choice provisions and language on state and local hiring preemptions were dropped.

News agencies were reporting new life for faith-based, suggesting it could be folded into an economic stimulus plan that Congress was expected to pass by the end of the year.[42] The reported success of the closed Senate–White House negotiations started to attract outside attention. On November 7, President Bush wrote to senators Daschle and Lott, urging the Senate to act on a faith-based charitable giving bill by the end of the year. The presidential letter was notable in that it omitted any reference to charitable choice, signaling that its supporters were not going to try to add it in Senate floor debate.[43] Faith-based opponents, however, were still alarmed. One day later, the Interfaith Alliance asked Bush to hold off on the "divisive" issue, arguing that the president was using the September 11 events to pursue a "special interest project" contrary to the common good.[44] A few days later, Lieberman and Santorum appeared to have wrapped up every area of concern and to be merely waiting for White House and congressional leaders to fill in the size of the tax breaks.[45] A full draft of the reported agreement started circulating the week of November 19 with approximately $100 million in compassionate capital and about $28 billion in tax breaks over ten years. For the two weeks surrounding Thanksgiving Day 2001, the possibility of a bill from the Senate by the end of the year seemed quite good.

End of Year Possibilities

Through late November and early December, key senators and White House staff persons were daily tweaking the draft bill to make it palatable enough to pass the Senate quickly. The main substantive sticking point seemed to be the size of the tax incentives. The reported number, only about half an earlier estimate of $54 billion, was still too large for some. Tax increases to partially offset costs were being discussed, and other senators were withholding their support to gain special consideration for unrelated tax items. The most resistant interest groups were working to ensure that the hiring discretion issue would still be debated on the floor, even though the bill had no charitable choice language.

Momentum stalled again in early December. According to one source close to these negotiations, the "Democrats didn't need it; not many Republicans really wanted it, the president didn't push it, and [Republican sponsors in] the House didn't help."[46] According to this report, Republicans in Congress and the White House were of two minds. Some wanted a legislative victory for the president and pushed hard for passage. Others thought that faith-based failure in the Senate could be an effective campaign message the following year, allowing Republicans to argue to the voting public that the Democrats were fundamentally hostile to religion. These mixed motivations and the press of other legislation made it impossible to close a faith-based deal before the end of the year. Late November optimism faded fast, and the Senate adjourned five days before Christmas 2001 without taking action.

Early 2002: Seeking Common Ground and Getting a Consensus Text

It was easy to imagine that Senate faith-based efforts might never restart in 2002. The heightened religious sympathies brought by September 11 were fast dissipating. The dawn of an election year suggested that no stimulus plan, the likely vehicle for a faith-based bill, would get through the Senate: Democrats liked the idea of running in the fall with a chance to accuse Republicans of doing little about a faltering economy. The religious hiring issue, on which neither side was willing to compromise, was becoming the centerpiece of the debate. Faith-based proponents were demanding unrestricted hiring freedoms as essential to any bill they would support; opponents had made enough progress with their argument about charitable choice inviting discrimination that several Democratic senators were willing to hold up a faith-based bill until a long floor debate on the issue was guaranteed.

Somewhat ironically, the Search for Common Ground working group helped keep hope alive. Many interest group representatives in the Search group who opposed faith-based had agreed to join the effort the previous June in a thinly disguised effort to delay and dilute a faith-based legislative product that, at the time, seemed likely. The extended discussions in the Search group, they reasoned, might slow the initiative's momentum, gain some legislative compromises, and provide time and a forum to develop and test opposition arguments. They could support faith-based groups in ways other than the direct financing of charitable choice. Thinking that President Bush and other Republicans would not budge on that issue, they could voice general support for faith-based legislation in the Search process but still slow or even derail the major bills in play.

By early fall 2001, the Search group had produced agreements on some noncontroversial matters, and had agreed to issue a final report near the end of the year. At the same time, the White House's new strategy to find a "minimalist" Senate bill was slowly building momentum. The simple fact of the Search group's existence—a coalition of widely divergent voices—helped to cool the passions that rose in the House. Interim Search agreements were fed to those negotiating the developing

Senate text. Because few thought the White House would stick with a minimalist strategy after the Senate delivered a bill, it seemed a good idea to opponents to support doing something about faith-based while resisting what they thought would be the essential elements of any final deal acceptable to Bush.

On January 15, 2002, the Search group released its recommendations. Its report, *Finding Common Ground: Twenty-Nine Recommendations of the Working Group on Human Needs and Faith-Based and Community Initiatives*, came after seven months of difficult negotiations. Its tax recommendations were largely consistent with the basic elements of the previous two Santorum-Lieberman faith-based tax bills, encouraging new charity-oriented tax breaks for individuals and corporations. Another cluster of ideas tracked many of the White House's *Unlevel Playing Field* recommendations that were targeted to help all community-based social service groups, not only religious ones, seeking to cooperate with government agencies. The main difference from the Bush administration in this cluster of ideas was that the Search group essentially urged that current agency protocols for church-state relations should only be clarified—rather than revised, as the administration wished. A third set of Search recommendations suggested ways to make it easier and cheaper for deeply religious groups like churches to separate their social service work from the sponsoring religious organization. The Search group avoided charitable choice and only dipped its toe into the hiring rights controversy, supporting an explicit bar to race-based hiring discrimination by all groups.[47]

Members of the working group disagreed among themselves about the best legislative use of their report. Members of liberal and moderate interest groups thought that any new Senate legislation should not be more ambitious than the consensus Search package. Eliot Mincberg of People for the American Way argued: "You can do so much good without ever getting to" nonconsensus items.[48] Search participants from conservative groups thought additional provisions supported by the president could be added to the Search consensus. Ron Sider of Evangelicals for Social Action wrote in *Christianity Today* that the "recommendations represent the minimum, not the maximum, that is politically possible. . . . It is simply nonsense to suggest that the minimal, unanimous recommendations of this exceedingly diverse group represent all that Senators Santorum and Lieberman can persuade a majority of the Senate to pass."[49] Another

observer thought that the Search report left "affirmative faith-based behind; it is no longer an expansion of charitable choice" and as such would
lose an important part of the base support.[50]

Santorum and Lieberman endorsed the Search report as a foundation
for a new faith-based legislative proposal that they hoped would be introduced soon thereafter. Through a spokesman, Lieberman said that the
"report should serve as a good starting point for the president's plan this
year." Santorum thought that the Search report would "move the ball
forward" for Senate action on some sort of faith-based bill. More surprising, the White House seemed almost completely supportive. A presidential spokesperson called the report "further impetus for the Senate to
act quickly."[51]

The president's implied support for the Search report was one indicator
that he wanted any kind of faith-based legislative success. Another indicator came in the State of the Union address a few weeks later when Bush
omitted any reference to charitable choice and barely mentioned the faith-
based initiative. The "consensus" CARE bill that Bush announced with
Santorum and Lieberman at the White House on February 7, 2002, was
much like the draft circulated the previous November. Almost all of the
bill was tax incentives; of its eighty-two pages, fewer than five dealt with
religious groups contracting with government. In CARE, the faith-based
initiative had become essentially a package of individual and corporate
tax provisions channeling private money to charitable organizations and
smaller providers, whether based in religious faith or not—a modified
combination of the two tax bills previously introduced by Santorum and
Lieberman. Its major tax provision was an $800 charitable tax deduction
for married couples or $400 for single filers. To reduce the "sticker cost"
of these deductions, they were allowed for only two years, cutting the
official cost of the bill to about $11 billion. The bill also included compas-
sion capital funds, an increase in the social services block grant, and a
few minor provisions suggested by the Search group.

Title III of CARE, dealing with the qualifications of religious groups
applying for federal funds, was the key item of debate. In shorthand
description, it prohibited unequal treatment of programs merely because
of the religiosity of the sponsoring group or its location. More specifically,
the title stipulated that an applicant may not be disqualified from competing for government grants and contracts simply because the applicant

imposes religious criteria for membership on its governing board, because the applicant's chartering provisions contain religious language, because the applicant has a religious name, or because the applicant uses facilities containing religious art, icons, scriptures, or other symbols. This section of the bill also made clear that these protections did not exempt any applicant from meeting other grant criteria an agency might set, nor did they preempt state and local civil rights laws. The bill did not specifically address the issue of hiring discretion of faith-based groups receiving federal funds.[52]

This title clarified that the religious characteristics of a provider—such as the name, location, or composition of a board of directors—were not relevant to funding eligibility, provided these characteristics had no influence on program content. By implication, though, the content of the program was still critical to eligibility. The bill did not raise many concerns, but more surprisingly, it also failed to appeal to powerful groups that might help push it through Congress. Conservatives wanted more sweeping legislation that would clarify their right to incorporate religious teachings in funded programs and retain the right to hire whomever they wished. Michael Horowitz at the Hudson Institute called the measure "profoundly dangerous and constitutionally inappropriate" because it did not go far enough.[53] Liberals still argued that the bill gave preferences to religious groups and still opposed its silence on hiring discretion. Representative Scott worried that "anything that passes anywhere close [to what was in title III of CARE] will give the administration moral authority to go ahead and start discriminating."[54]

The large middle of the spectrum of political interests seemed mostly appeased. Senate Democrats were firm that they were not interested in getting into a conference with the House bill, but expressed support of CARE. "I don't think we are willing to go much further than this bill" to protect the religious identity of funded groups, stated a spokesperson for Senator Lieberman. Even majority leader Daschle wrote a newspaper column committing himself to "get[ting] this proposal signed into law." The White House appeared ready to ask the House to accept the Senate version, if and when the upper body acted on the bill. Representative Watts, the chief House sponsor of H.R. 7, was reasonably enthusiastic about CARE, although he implied that he would push for some accommodation with the House's faith-based bill. "Once the Senate finally passes a bill," Watts argued, "we can work out our differences and put the armies of compassion in the field."[55]

Interest group reaction was mixed, but the coalition uniting behind CARE seemed large and influential. The Salvation Army was onboard despite the silence on hiring discretion. Catholic Charities was firmly supportive. Bob Edgar of the National Council of Churches, a group that had strongly opposed H.R. 7, endorsed the Senate bill.[56]

Conservatives were split. The most pure conservatives did not want to drop their fights on charitable choice and hiring freedoms. *Christianity Today*, the flagship publication for political and religiously orthodox Christians, editorialized in its March 7 edition against a bill it thought too weak. A spokesperson for the Family Research Council said that the group was disappointed there was no clear protection of hiring rights. But other orthodox believers were happy with CARE. Somewhat surprisingly, Charles Colson of Prison Fellowship Ministries praised the compromise: "I am greatly encouraged that a bipartisan coalition in the Senate supports this new bill. While not containing everything we would like to see, this legislation is a major step forward. . . . This is a time for right-thinking Americans to get behind this bill."[57]

Doesn't Anyone Care about CARE?
February–May 2002

After introduction, CARE lay dormant while faith-based offices in the executive branch moved ahead with rules changes recommended by the *Unlevel Playing Field* report. In March the Department of Housing and Urban Development came out with rule revisions that encouraged religious groups to offer services for public housing residents, and in April the Department of Labor announced a new program to help ministry groups provide job training and counseling for the needy.[58] These announcements drew criticism from the most fiercely opposed interest groups but generated no sustained controversy. It seemed that antifaith-based rhetoric was dying down.

But still the Senate was slow. One problem was a disagreement between the House and Senate faith-based leaders. Representative Watts was still anticipating a House-Senate conference between H.R. 7 and CARE; Lieberman made clear that a conference and its inevitable compromise would doom any chance for Senate faith-based action. President Bush continued his campaign for CARE's passage, issuing intermittent calls for the Senate to act on CARE, while at the same time refusing to disavow completely the House bill. The biggest obstacle appeared to be the cost of the non-itemizer's charitable deduction. Its official cost was about $10 billion, but this was artificially low because the break was rather disingenuously limited to only two years. It would cost far more to extend the deduction beyond two years, which Congress would certainly be pressured to do.

The groups with the strongest interest in the bill now were the non-profit and educational lobbies, far afield from the original faith-based core. CARE provided, among other tax breaks, a provision to people who make donations to nonprofit institutions from retirement accounts, a $2.9 billion idea that college and university lobbyists had been promoting for more than five years. As a result, college and university groups started to take the lead in lobbying for the bill.

CARE Advocacy Day
Santorum, Lieberman, and a growing CARE network tried to generate grassroots pressure. They designated May 2 as CARE Advocacy Day, a rally day for the CARE Act, when representatives from scores of interest groups and their local affiliates would visit Senate offices urging senators to support the bill, and especially to hasten Finance Committee approval.[59] The day was organized by Americans for Community and Faith-Centered Enterprise (ACFE), a small office founded about one year earlier by conservative philanthropist and activist Michael Joyce. The day brought an estimated six hundred activists from twenty states to the capital.[60] ACFE deserves some credit for the rally's size, but Joyce's strong identification with politically conservative causes limited ACFE's influence outside a coterie of conservative groups.[61] The most powerful of the 1,600 groups that senators Santorum and Lieberman claimed supported CARE were large nonprofit charities and educational institutions attracted to the big tax breaks. CARE was a top priority for only a fraction of the 1,600, and for almost no religious groups, the early claimed beneficiaries of faith-based initiatives.

Indifference in the Finance Committee
The Senate Finance Committee leadership seemed willing to approve CARE if plausible revenue offsets for its tax breaks could be found and

if enough members seemed supportive.[62] Because Finance dealt exclusively with the bill's tax matters, the parts of the bill dealing with religious organizations were separated from the bill given to Finance; these would be reattached when the bill came to the Senate floor.

On May 22, Max Baucus, chairman of the Senate Finance Committee, announced that in June he would take up the tax portions of CARE. Behind the scenes at Senate Finance, CARE was much less of a sure thing. On June 4, committee members met privately to review the upcoming schedule. No committee member strongly advocated for CARE, and it seemed possible that the committee might not even bring it up. CARE's costs had to be offset by tax increases elsewhere, and there were only so many politically appealing revenue-raising options available. Worried about the lack of enthusiasm, the tax coalition supporting CARE held an emergency conference call on June 6 to plan strategy. They agreed that CARE's sponsors would circulate a letter in the Senate for colleagues to sign, urging Baucus and ranking committee Republican Charles Grassley to approve CARE. The next day, a Capitol Hill daily newsletter announced that Santorum and Lieberman had obtained the signatures of twenty senators on such a letter.[63]

The little extra pressure seemed to work: CARE was formally put on the Finance Committee's markup schedule for June 13. Senators Baucus and Grassley had agreed to offset the costs of CARE with revenue-raising "loophole" closers that discouraged U.S. companies from relocating their corporate headquarters in overseas tax havens, shut down "abusive" tax shelters, and extended Customs Service user fees. The markup bogged down, however, when it was discovered that the Customs Service fee increase had been used to offset other revenue losses in two bills already approved by the committee. Some members characterized the proposed triple-counting of Customs income as dishonest and balked at the idea. The markup quickly deteriorated into near chaos, forcing chairman Baucus to adjourn.[64]

Five days later the committee came back to the bill, however, and finally approved it by voice vote. Though it had crossed a major hurdle, CARE's support was still as shallow as ever. Some Republicans opposed the bill's individual development accounts; a few members of each party were concerned that revenue offsets were illusory. Others had qualms with the nonitemizer charitable deduction itself.[65] The large nonprofit and educational lobbies seemed to be pulling the most weight in the bill's favor. After CARE passed the committee, a government relations executive for university development and alumni offices said: "I'd like to think we had quite a bit of influence" on the bill. That pressure did seem to have moved a few senators. John Kerry of Massachusetts, for example, said that while he opposed the expanded nonitemizer deduction he supported the total package because educational institutions in his state would benefit from other breaks.[66]

Preparing for Floor: Late June to September 19, 2002

It seemed likely that CARE would be scheduled for floor action in the summer of 2002. The tax provisions had been worked out to the satisfaction of most critics. Santorum and Lieberman planned to add the non-tax provisions, such as the religious equal treatment language and the additional funds for block grants, as a manager's amendment to the bill at the onset of floor debate. The only potential challenge seemed to be from Republican senators seeking to advance the purists' cause by adding charitable choice language, but that problem seemed solvable if the White House would pressure those Republicans to stand with Santorum, at least at this stage.

Behind the scenes, however, faith-based critics were making inroads into CARE's support. The House duo of Edwards and Scott were intensely lobbying their Senate counterparts to demand floor debate on the controversies raised by H.R. 7 even though they were not part of the Senate bill. As a measure of their success, some Democrats were demanding amendments that explicitly prohibited hiring discrimination by any religious group using federal funds, prohibited any religious uses of any federal funds, and forbade the preemption of state and local civil rights laws, among other items, as the price for floor consideration. Conversely, religious conservatives were demanding stronger religious rights language in the bill and wanted a floor fight on those provisions.[67]

The president pushed publicly for a bill. In a Milwaukee speech on July 2, Bush called for the Senate to pass CARE quickly. In response, a spokesperson for Daschle said that the majority leader would like to do so but that there were a lot of "competing priorities" for the rest of the year, hinting both that floor debate might be time-consuming and that Democrats wanted some space for their own legislative priorities.[68] On the whole, however, things seemed slowly to be working out. On August 1, Santorum took to the Senate floor to describe the parameters of a yet-hoped-for unanimous consent agreement that would bring CARE up for consideration under explicit rules allowing a fixed number of amendments and time for their debate. That day it seemed a firm unanimous consent agreement was a long way off; Democrats objected to any time or numerical limitations on amendments.

Work continued sporadically through the August 2002 recess. An early September e-mail from the Santorum office to CARE supporters indicated that an agreement was possible within a week's time, although it might take another month to actually have the floor debate. CARE looked alive, but "closing the deal" on a unanimous consent agreement involving one hundred legislators is exceedingly difficult under the best of circumstances. Daschle and Lott both seemed to be working in good faith to urge their respective party colleagues to allow CARE to be debated, although some doubted their support was complete. While Daschle had repeated his commitment to a Senate debate on faith-based initiatives, he seemed to be suffering little from not setting a firm date. Lott certainly wanted floor debate, but for political and substantive reasons many in his party preferred no faith-based bill at all.

A handful of Democratic senators fully resisted the bill, among them Mary Landrieu of Louisiana, Blanche Lincoln of Arkansas, Jack Reed of Rhode Island, Edward Kennedy of Massachusetts, and Dick Durbin of Illinois. Some of these senators seemed to be treating the CARE Act as a likely-to-pass initiative to which they wanted to add their pet proposals. Lincoln, for example, was reported on September 13 to be seeking to add a tax provision to CARE that would benefit only the Wal-Mart Corporation, headquartered in her state.[69] Others appeared intent on stopping the bill by demanding time for amendments that would engender long debate. Rhode Island senator Reed insisted on a full debate on amendments about hiring and other matters.[70] Nevertheless, supporters pressed on. On September 19, Santorum announced to his colleagues a provisional agreement he thought was close to completion. The deal provided for an omnibus Republican amendment that addressed the tax-related concerns of members, a Santorum-Lieberman amendment to add the religion provisions, and a Democratic consensus amendment offered by Senator Reed to calm the concerns of faith-based opponents.[71]

The First Endgame: September 23–October 18, 2002

Still, not every senator seemed willing to go along. Throughout late September, Senator Reed continued to demand a floor debate in which several different, separable amendments would be debated without significant time restrictions. The bill's proponents grew increasingly frustrated; one source identified People for the American Way as the interest group responsible for blocking floor action.[72] Majority leader Daschle juggled his commitment to bring faith-based to the floor with his desire to accommodate every senator's concerns. House Democratic opponents persisted in pressing their case with senators to demand extended debate and, if necessary, to defeat the bill if that request was not granted.[73]

On September 24, Santorum tried to move the bill without a firm agreement from all parties. His attempt was blocked by a handful of senators, with assistant Democratic leader Harry Reid of Nevada apparently taking the fall for several of his party colleagues by objecting on their behalf.[74] Daschle and his staff kept working the Democratic caucus, but the lack of progress led Republicans to doubt the Democratic leader's sincerity. House Democrats Edwards and Scott, who had been lobbying the Senate for over a year, saw the first public notice of their efforts in two press reports of September 25. In one, they were given almost full credit for stalling the Senate bill.[75] In the other, the *Boston Globe* noted that others besides Scott and Edwards were working against CARE, including Massachusetts representative Barney Frank, who was said to have engaged in "unusually personal" lobbying against CARE on the basis of gay rights. Frank claimed that CARE would advance bigotry against minority races and sexual preferences, contending that religious groups would hire only those from their predominant racial group, while "fundamentalists won't hire gays or lesbians."[76]

The elusive search for a debating agreement continued but kept failing. Even Lieberman was getting frustrated with his Democratic colleagues. "For reasons that are sometimes clear and sometimes not so clear, some of our colleagues are holding up action," he complained.[77] Reed insisted that he did not want to kill the bill, only to ensure a full debate on a range of important issues related to federal funding of religious service agencies. Lieberman countered that the proposed Reed amendments were not even relevant to CARE. Whatever the substance of the argument, Reed's position reflected the highly successful House argument that faith-based opened the door to discrimination under the guise of religion.

One major roadblock seemed to fall on October 14 when Representative Watts announced that he would support CARE as-is, officially dropping his earlier demand for a conference and negotiation between CARE and H.R. 7.[78] Some thought that Watts's announcement would finally clear the way for CARE. A news article the next day stated that floor action was close, with Reed apparently agreeing to consider the bill if he was granted a time-limited debate on four separate amendments.[79]

Now Santorum and Lieberman held back. They wanted time to survey the entire Senate to make sure that the Reed amendments would fail. Watts's announcement had come too late.[80] The Senate adjourned on October 18 for the November elections. At a research forum on faith-based issues sponsored by the Roundtable on Religion and Social Welfare Policy a few days later, WHOFBCI director Jim Towey singled out Reed as the chief cause of CARE's apparent demise. Not wanting to take complete responsibility for killing the bill, Reed later replied that he would be happy to see the bill on the floor sometime during the Senate lame-duck session following the elections, if he was allowed all his amendments and enough time to debate them.[81]

FOCAL POINT 4.2

The Issue Network Expands

As the 107th Congress progressed, an increasing share of the Washington interest group community lined up for and against faith-based legislation. A large coalition formed to support the Senate CARE Act, with nonprofit groups the major force behind the bill because of its large tax credits. CARE also drew the support of most religious social service providers, both long-standing federal aid recipients like Catholic Charities and potential new beneficiaries like Prison Fellowship. Additional faith-based foes like public employee unions and civil rights groups joined earlier opponents such as Americans United and the ACLU.

Groups less involved in direct lobbying focused on the important policy questions that faith-based raised—the effectiveness and efficiency of faith-based social services and the suitability of deeply religious voices in the public square. The Pew Charitable Trusts, headquartered in Philadelphia, played a huge role in funding three new projects in addition to the Pew Forum on Religion and Public Life. In June 2001, the Pew Charitable Trusts granted $2.6 million to the University of Pennsylvania's Center for Research on Religion and Urban Civil Society, to "serve as a hub for scholarly research and teaching [on] the impact of faith-based initiatives on urban problems." The Pew Charitable Trusts website stated: "The Center's research will begin to fill the large gap in knowledge of the extent and efficacy of faith-based social services."

Six months later, the Trusts provided $6.3 million to a new Roundtable on Religion and Social Welfare Policy to "rigorously assess existing studies, produce first-rate, nonpartisan research to fill the gaps in knowledge, and engage policymakers, the media and religious and civic leaders in a sustained discussion of the findings." And in March 2002 the Trusts provided $6.2 million to the National Crime Prevention Institute to "gather information on the best practices in faith-based social services and to provide educational and training programs targeted at practitioners. The Faith and Service Technical Education Network . . . will do in-depth studies of exemplary practices in faith-based social service delivery, including how religious organizations work with other partners in addressing community problems."

The Roundtable, headquartered at the Nelson Rockefeller Institute at the State University of New York at Albany, soon played a major role in defining the legitimate social science and legal questions that surrounded faith-based as it sought to develop a comprehensive database of relevant social science research and centralize the tracking of legal and policy developments in the area.

Research collection and dissemination are coordinated by the Rockefeller Institute in upstate New York, but many of the Roundtable's public activities are in Washington, D.C. It has a schedule of spring and fall conferences each year to gather policymakers and scholars together to share information about faith-based programs.

The law school at George Washington University has partnered with the Rockefeller Institute and the Roundtable in investigating legal questions. The regular meetings address interested parties in the Washington policy and media communities and play a major role in defining legitimate points of controversy and consensus.

The Roundtable has also used some of the Pew Trusts' funds to support a second round of meetings by the Search for Common Ground Working Group on Human Needs and Faith-Based and Community Initiatives. The working group's first report, issued in early 2002, was well received, and it seemed possible for a similar group to influence later faith-based discussion. The second working group issued its report *Harnessing Civic and Faith-Based Power to Fight Poverty* in April 2003. This report included thirty-eight specific recommendations that fell into five categories: increased resources to meet human needs, government agency responsibilities, responsibilities of faith-based organizations, community empowerment, and closing knowledge gaps. The report broke little new ground, but it did illustrate what policy issues might make some headway and what issues would stall out from controversy.

By early 2003, the faith-based issue had become a fixture in the Washington policy community. A new issue network had arisen to raise and shape related problems and the possible solutions to them. Issue networks define which solutions are possible and which are not possible, and help implement favored solutions and reject unpopular ones. Issue networks also often encourage the continued political relevance of issues, because interest groups, the media, government officials, and others have incentives to keep alive the topic that first brought them together. That certainly seems to be the case with faith-based initiatives.

—Melissa Fritsch

Sources

Pew Charitable Trusts website. www.pewtrusts.com.
Roundtable on Religion and Social Welfare Policy. "About Us."
    www.religionandsocialpolicy.org/about_us/index.cfm (accessed 11 April
    2003).
————. "Partners." www.religionandsocialpolicy.org/about_us/partners.cfm
    (accessed 11 April 2003).

Working Group on Human Needs and Faith-Based and Community Initiatives. *Harnessing Civic and Faith-Based Power to Fight Poverty.* April 2003. www.workinggroup.org/Documents/SFCGbook2003Final.pdf (accessed 11 April 2003).

Election Surprises

Surprisingly, the 2002 elections moved control of the Senate back to Republican hands. The numerical shift would actually take place before the 108th Congress was seated, when Missouri Republican Jim Talent was sworn in to replace Democrat Jean Carnahan immediately following the verification of election results. Thus, just days after the election Republicans had majority voting power, although full reorganization would not come until the following January. Some faith-based supporters saw in the numbers a final opportunity for CARE to pass during the 107th Congress, discounting the fact that the majority, if newly favorable, was slim.

On November 14, Senator Santorum made what turned out to be the final attempt to debate CARE on the floor. The debating agreement he proposed allowed one Republican amendment to be offered by Senator Phil Gramm of Texas concerning the scope of a narrow charity tax provision in the bill. Democrats would be allowed four amendments to the religious treatment provisions, all to be offered by Senator Reed.[82] The four amendments would prohibit proselytization with government funds, hiring discrimination by any religious group receiving government funds, direct government funding of religion, and preemption of state and local antidiscrimination rules.[83] All amendments would be allowed one hour of debate.

Santorum acknowledged in his statement that if the Senate proceeded and if any of the Democratic amendments were successful, CARE would be dead for the year. Santorum also took this last opportunity to describe the bill and why the Reed amendments should be defeated. He contended that all the provisions in the bill, by themselves, were uncontroversial, even the religious rights language. Lieberman, taking the Senate floor right after Santorum, extended the argument, claiming that the opponents to floor debate did not really object to the contents of CARE, but rather to other laws, "particularly language in Title VII of the Civil Rights Act that allows faith-based groups to hire people only of the faith of the group. That is an issue on which we can all agree or disagree," Lieberman continued. "But I plead with my colleagues, it is an issue for another day."[84]

Lieberman's Democratic colleagues were not much moved. Senator Carl Levin of Michigan stated that he would object to considering CARE because he could not offer amendments about unemployment benefits, stock options, and the Securities and Exchange Commission. Senator Dick Durbin of Illinois was ready to object because he did not want any time limits on the Reed amendments. After much back-and-forth among the key senators, Durbin formally objected to Santorum's request. With Senator Durbin's objection, the CARE Act finally died for the 107th Congress.

Aftermath: Recriminations and the Bush Executive Order

An article in the next day's *Washington Times* blamed five Democratic senators—Durbin, Reed, Levin, Sarbanes, and Clinton—for CARE's failure. The floor record is murky enough and eyewitness interpretations contradictory enough, however, that only Reed and Durbin can, with certainty, be identified as responsible for that failure.[85] Many others played a role in the ponderous legislative process and could be charged with allowing CARE to die. Senator Daschle is one suspect fingered by some Republicans, but probably unfairly so. Daschle tried to bring CARE to the floor, although he seemed nonplussed that his pledge for floor action went unfulfilled.[86] One could point to House Republicans for the acrimonious tone of the 2001 House debate. Some insiders place the blame on the White House, especially the legislative affairs staff, which did not aggressively court senators at key moments in the legislative dance. One observer sympathetic to the initiative said that the White House legislative affairs staff "didn't advance on that front with any strenuousness."[87]

Others put forth ideological reasons for CARE's failure. Marvin Olasky, speaking for many religious conservatives, said that because Republicans allowed the bill to be so weakened, "conservative Christian groups did not fight to keep it alive." Olasky blamed DiIulio for a White House that in its Senate legislative strategy "departed from its usual procedure of securing the base and then casting about for allies."[88] Supporters of full debate on the Reed amendments contended that they would have supported CARE if their amendments had been added, looking past arguments that those amendments would have undone more of the cooperation between government and religious groups than other CARE provisions would have fostered.

The day after CARE failed, the White House signaled its next step. WHOFBCI director Jim Towey announced that the president would move ahead with faith-based ideas administratively: "We're now going to leave the exploration stage [of identifying barriers to faith-based groups] and start the implementation phase."[89] Less than one month later, on December 12, 2002, the president issued his executive order, essentially implementing by presidential fiat the religious protection provisions in CARE. The next chapter outlines the path the executive branch took to this decision.

Five

Rocky Roads

Faith-Based Efforts in the Executive Branch

> One of the great goals of my administration is to rally America's armies of compassion and restore a spirit of caring, citizenship, and community. One of the things that makes America unique is the loving spirit of the many people in our great country who want to help those in need. Government should encourage them, and if these good people are acting on the calling of their faith, we should respect and welcome them, and never stand in their way.
>
> *President George W. Bush, July 19, 2001,*
> *Speech commending House passage of H.R. 7, the Community Solutions Act*

When George W. Bush announced his first two executive orders, he created six offices devoted to faith-based initiatives: the White House Office of Faith-Based and Community Initiatives, an independent office within the Executive Office of the President to focus on this policy goal, and five satellite centers located in cabinet-level departments to encourage faith-based cooperation in the executive branch. Standing at the new president's side was a burly man whom he introduced as Dr. John J. DiIulio, Jr., the person who would lead the White House faith-based efforts and report directly to the president.

DiIulio was well-known in academic circles for his work on social policy. A professor and researcher at the University of Pennsylvania, senior fellow at the Brookings Institution and Manhattan Institute, and coauthor of one of the best-selling American government textbooks, he was both a respected academic and an outspoken and determined advocate for the poor. Described by one journalist as "Joe Pesci with a Ph.D.,"[1] DiIulio was raised in working-class South Philadelphia and was the first in his family to attend college. After earning his Ph.D. in government from Harvard, he joined the Princeton faculty, earning tenure in only two years.

Often described as a bull in a china shop, DiIulio's direct style and willingness to speak his mind sometimes created problems. As his friend and fellow academic Bill Galston noted: "Diplomacy is not among his many virtues."[2] A registered Democrat who has published in both liberal and conservative publications, DiIulio wrote an editorial just weeks before his appointment that criticized the Supreme Court's decision in *Bush v. Gore*, the case that ended the 2000 presidential battle in favor of George W. Bush. A few months after his appointment, *The New Republic* described DiIulio as first on its list of "the Bush appointees least likely to keep their jobs," commenting that "[a]lmost everything about the rumpled, combative social scientist contrasts with the 'organization man' ethos of the administration he serves."[3]

Why was this Democrat standing next to the president, accepting a job in a high-profile new office of a Republican administration? Although he was most known for his academic writing, DiIulio was far more than an ivory tower researcher who studied social policy. DiIulio's academic interest in faith-based organizations grew out of his research on crime and prison policy as he discovered the success of religion in combating crime. In many ways, his research became a life mission. A self-described "born-again Catholic," he speaks of a transforming religious experience on Palm Sunday 1996, when he discovered his calling to work with the people of the inner city. Guided by his faith, he was determined to use the tools of social policy to make a real difference in the lives of the disadvantaged. When he met then-Governor Bush, the two men discovered that they had much in common and found a bond in their committed Christian faith and desire to serve the poor.

John DiIulio has recounted his first meeting with George W. Bush, when Karl Rove, chief strategist for the presidential campaign, invited him to Texas to meet with the governor and a gathering of advisers to discuss social policy. Although the two men had never met, DiIulio recalls that Bush embraced him warmly. Later, as they sat through a meeting that DiIulio remembers as something of a "boring conversation," Bush told the assembled group that he was looking for some new ideas and asked specifically for DiIulio's input. Having the floor for the first time in the meeting, DiIulio described his concept of government partnership with faith-based organizations and offered a concrete proposal: Why not help one of the most at-risk populations in the country, the children of prisoners? Government, in cooperation with an organization like Big Brothers/Big Sisters, could train mentors and match them with boys and girls who had an incarcerated parent, providing them much-needed guidance and direction. Bush's response was immediate and positive—he embraced DiIulio's proposal with the same enthusiasm with which he had earlier embraced the man. Throughout the campaign and into his presidency, Bush's commitment to mentoring programs for the children of prisoners remained steadfast.

After that first meeting in Texas, DiIulio agreed to advise the Bush campaign and, for a matter of months, he reviewed their domestic and social policy proposals, including a few faith-based ideas. As the volume of faxes from the campaign increased, DiIulio ended his direct involvement with the campaign and focused his attention on his research and teaching. Called on occasion to assist with key speeches, DiIulio recounts among his most important work assisting with the "Duty of Hope" speech in Indianapolis, the first major policy speech of the campaign and the one in which Bush introduced his faith-based proposals. DiIulio provided examples and details, reviewed and edited a series of drafts, and helped craft phrases including the reminder, "It is not enough to call for volunteerism. Without more support—both public and private . . ." that spoke against the libertarian view that the private sector alone can solve social problems. The day of the speech, then-Governor Bush called DiIulio to thank him for his assistance with the drafting.

On June 9, 2000, Bush was giving a speech in Philadelphia. The campaign called DiIulio to invite him to the event and to extend a personal invitation from the governor to stay after the speech and talk with him. DiIulio vividly recounted the day: It was an incredibly hot summer day, he was exhausted, and he was kept waiting for so long he almost left. When Bush finally was free to speak to DiIulio, he invited him to lunch and ushered him through the crowds towards the motorcade. A C-SPAN camera caught the two as they were leaving. Bush turned to Pennsylvania governor Tom Ridge and said: "Do you know John?" He then gestured towards DiIulio and exclaimed: "This man's a genius."

DiIulio and Bush then met alone for the better part of an hour "discussing how government might partner with faith-based organizations, especially urban ministries, and how to make faith-based initiatives really work on behalf of needy children and families."[4] Joined later by Governor Ridge and Indianapolis mayor Steve Goldsmith, DiIulio and Bush continued their discussion of the policy. DiIulio summed up his meeting with the future president, observing: "This guy's for real. He really believes. He had no reason in the world to spend one hour and fifteen minutes with me. He gets it, and he knows it's not going to be easy."[5]

Promises, Promises:
From the Campaign Trail to the Administration

As detailed in chapter 2, the faith-based issue was front and center in the George W. Bush campaign. Although both Bush and Gore advocated greater partnerships between the government and religious organizations, candidate Bush raised the issue repeatedly in campaign visits across the country. Among the many promises made on this issue, Bush said his administration would look to religious groups in all decisions to see how they could cooperate to do good works. To accomplish his purposes, he promised to create a separate "Office of Faith-Based Action" within the White House with the goal of facilitating the work of faith-based groups and eliminating obstacles to their partnerships with the government.

Despite the clear support Bush received on the campaign trail when he promised to work with and assist faith-based organizations, the issue was also beginning to stir opposition. As one commentator explained: "No one has found a way to harness the power of faith without letting religious believers share their faith, including the messy details. In other words, it's hard to use government funds to light revival fires in human hearts without giving other people heartburn."[6] Once Bush was named the winner of the 2000 election, advocates of strict separation of church and state and other opponents of faith-based initiatives organized in earnest.

By the time of Bush's inauguration, most of the signs of bipartisan agreement on the faith-based issue in the campaign had dissolved. With Democrats angry over the thirty-six-day battle that ended in Bush's narrow electoral college win, and facing an evenly divided Senate and narrow margins in the House, party leaders set their sights on 2002 and the opportunity for Democrats to take firm control of Congress. Democrats did not want the new president to win many policy victories, and they wanted to fuel partisan fires for the next election. In this highly charged environment, the hope of bipartisan cooperation was slim. George W. Bush had managed to win the presidency, but he had accumulated very little political capital to promote his domestic agenda.

In the midst of this difficult political climate, President Bush announced his foremost legislative priorities for his first year: tax cuts, education reform, and promoting faith-based initiatives. The week after the inauguration (the third week in January), White House publicity efforts centered on education. The faith-based issue received top billing the second week, as Bush announced the creation of the White House Office of Faith-Based and Community Initiatives (WHOFBCI) and its cabinet agency satellites. The second week of February, the administration turned its focus to a third domestic issue from the campaign, tax policy. With the Republican-controlled Congress poised to act rapidly on economic issues, the White House devoted significant time and resources to promoting the Bush tax plan.

By the end of Bush's first year in office, two of the president's three priorities had become law. Bush signed the House and Senate compromise tax bill, the Economic Growth and Tax Relief Reconciliation Act, on June 7, 2001, less than six months into his term. Although Bush's education plan stalled for several months in conference committee, he signed the No Child Left Behind Act on January 8, 2002. Congressional action modified both of these bills, but the new laws retained most of the central elements of Bush's original proposals and represented key legislative victories for the president.

Despite the policy successes on other high-profile presidential priorities, President Bush's faith-based program was not a major policy triumph. As chronicled in the previous two chapters, Bush's faith-based legislative agenda was only a minimal success in the 107th Congress, with the Senate unable to pass even a significantly weakened and seemingly uncontroversial bill.

But the legislative story is only one part of the larger battle to promote faith-based initiatives. In this chapter, we will examine the Bush administration's work on behalf of faith-based proposals across the executive branch, considering how strategic choices and political decisions affected an issue of central importance to the president. After examining the creation and work of the WHOFBCI and its satellites, we will chronicle the White House's promotion of the faith-based legislation, identifying some of the larger roadblocks encountered along the way. In addition, we will examine and evaluate the administration's efforts within the executive branch to promote partnerships between religious organizations and the federal government.

The White House Office of Faith-Based and Community Initiatives

At the very beginning of his administration, George W. Bush signaled that his faith-based initiative was a high priority. In one of his earliest actions as president, Bush announced his first two executive orders on January 29, 2001. The first order created a new office in the Executive Office of the President, the White House Office of Faith-Based and Community Initiatives, which was assigned the purpose of taking the "lead responsibility in the executive branch to establish policies, priorities, and objectives, for the government's efforts to enlist, expand, equip, empower, and enable the work of faith-based and community groups."[7] According to the founding executive order, this White House office was to carry out eleven stated functions, including coordinating public education activities, showcasing innovation, and monitoring implementation of these new initiatives.

The second executive order created faith-based centers in five cabinet-level departments: Health and Human Services, Housing and Urban Development, Education, Labor, and Justice. Besides working to remove obstacles that inhibit faith-based and community organizations from providing government social services, these centers were charged with the duty of conducting "a department-wide audit to identify all existing barriers to the participation of faith-based and other community organizations in the delivery of social services."[8] Each cabinet center submitted audit reports to the WHOFBCI, which then compiled the data into *Unlevel Playing Field*, a report released in August 2001 that detailed the various barriers to government cooperation with faith-based and community groups.[9]

Designing the Office during the Transition

As the nation waited for court decisions to determine the winner of the 2000 presidential election, Clay Johnson directed a skeletal Bush transition team working in an office building in McLean, Virginia. Harried, understaffed, and permeated by a mood of uncertainty, advisers for the transition began to plan what they hoped would be an incoming Bush administration. Until the battle over Florida's electoral votes ended, neither Bush nor Gore could begin the full-scale transition effort so crucial to establishing a new presidential administration. While the Bush team waited for the final verdict, many issues and campaign proposals, including the faith-based initiative, were virtually on hold.

The transition team did not begin focused, detailed work on the faith-based initiative until the December 26 arrival of Don Willett, a young attorney who worked in then-Governor Bush's policy office in Austin handling a wide range of issues including faith-based initiatives. Stuart Bowen, who served as assistant general counsel to Governor Bush and later as deputy staff secretary in the White House, described Willett's role in Texas, lauding him for his pivotal work on the faith-based issue there: "Don Willett did a fantastic job in shaping the [faith-based] task force, prepared a great report, and advanced the governor's agenda to success. He deserves credit. In Texas, he was the star."[10] It seemed a natural fit to bring Willett to Washington to begin shaping and planning the faith-based agenda for the new administration. Willett enlisted the help of Don Eberly, a former Reagan official and activist in the civil society movement, who had volunteered to assist Willett with the transition work on faith-based policies. Recounting the work of the transition team, John DiIulio described Eberly as someone who "has lots of friends [in Washington]; he's respected on the religious right, respected for his fatherhood stuff."[11]

With little direction from political advisers, Willett and Eberly, affectionately dubbed "the Dons" by many who knew them, began to design the structure and duties of the White House office Bush had promised on the campaign trail. Willett recalled these stressful days: "Roughly half the normal transition time was robbed by the recount wars, so things were incredibly crunched and compressed, especially for senior staff. To say they were drinking from a fire hose really understates things. They were juggling innumerable balls and each one was critically important, so the daunting task of recommending the design of this culturally consequential office, from a blank sheet of paper and with only the vaguest of campaign descriptions, fell to me and a volunteer colleague, Don Eberly, a civil society guru who'd also worked in the Reagan White House."[12]

What would have been a daunting task for two people under the best of circumstances was nearly impossible for Willett and Eberly under such time pressures. Top political advisers had many priorities and mountains of work; two people trying to create a faith-based office had great difficulty attracting and keeping the attention of key White House staff.

As top political advisers made plans for the beginning months of the new administration, they decided to spotlight one major issue priority each week. Bush would unveil a central piece of his policy agenda each week, and the White House would create a week's worth of events and pronouncements to frame the issue for the media. Originally, officials planned to introduce education the first week, taxes the second week, and faith-based initiatives the following week. When Karl Rove, by then senior adviser to the president, determined that the tax announcements would not be ready on schedule, he decided to make the faith-based announcements a week early. Don Willett and Don Eberly both recall learning on a Tuesday that they had to be ready for an official announcement by the following Monday. In other words, they needed to design the structure for faith-based offices in the White House and executive branch, write executive orders, and fill high-profile staff positions, all in a matter of days.

The faith-based team did create the separate White House office Bush had promised in the campaign as well as centers in cabinet-level agencies that they deemed the most appropriate places to ease regulatory burdens. But they did not have sufficient time to research options and consider their implications. A director of one cabinet center described some of the problems that arose from the lack of time and attention to detail: "Because it happened so quickly, there was no clearly defined relationship between the center, the director, and the secretary and the WHOFBCI."[13] The newly appointed cabinet secretaries were, in essence, given faith-based offices in their agencies, complete with directors, and told to begin their work.

The Original Structure of the Office

Told in late January 2001 to have an office up and running by February 15, Don Willett and Don Eberly scrambled to get the office open. Without the benefit of time to learn the external and internal political landscapes, the WHOFBCI staff were often harried and disorganized. The office moved into its original suite in the Eisenhower Executive Office Building by the February deadline, but it would be many more weeks before the staff even had business cards.

Rumors about the new religious office in the White House circulated quickly inside the Beltway, with reports claiming that as many as a hundred people would staff the new office. In reality, the office built to a staff of seven, likely the maximum number possible given the finite number of political appointees to be distributed across the White House. Although Bush had promised on the campaign trail to create an "Office of Faith-Based Action," advisers decided to change the name to the more benign sounding "Office of Faith-Based and Community Initiatives."[14] Right before Bush unveiled the executive orders creating the new office, political advisers tried to reverse the terms in the name to the more innocuous "Office of Community and Faith-Based Initiatives." Insiders working on the faith-based issue were angry about the proposed name change, and John DiIulio reportedly refused to head the office unless he was guaranteed that "faith" would appear first in the title.

Before the president and his advisers had selected DiIulio to direct the office, the transition team had already assembled most of the staff. The faith-based issue was still quite new, and only a handful of people truly understood charitable choice and its implications. Transition volunteer Don Eberly, a conservative evangelical Christian who was well-respected for his work with the Fatherhood Initiative, was named the deputy director of the office. Don Willett was appointed director of law and policy, and Stanley Carlson-Thies, a researcher from the Center for Public Justice who had written extensively on charitable choice, was named the assistant director for law and policy under Willett. Support staff included Catharine Ryun, daughter of a conservative Republican congressman from Kansas. Although the senior staff were well-respected and knowledgeable experts in other areas, none had recent experience on Capitol Hill, and many were Washington neophytes. Researcher Kathryn Dunn Tenpas described the situation this way: "Understaffed, underfunded, and without a firm grasp of their responsibilities, the White House OFBCI forged ahead in what would soon become very rough waters."[15]

The DiIulio Selection

In addition to the short timetable for the creation of the WHOFBCI and the administration's faith-based policies, President Bush waited until almost the last minute to name the office's director. Officials close to the development say it was widely assumed that former Indianapolis mayor Steve Goldsmith would get the job. Goldsmith had served as the chief domestic policy adviser to the Bush campaign and was well-recognized for his innovative work with public-private partnerships in Indianapolis. As the time for the announcement drew near, however, insiders say it appeared someone in the White House had decided against offering Goldsmith the post. A matter of days before the official announcement, Bush offered the director's job to John J. DiIulio, Jr., the university professor, sometime campaign adviser, and self-identified Democrat. Goldsmith was asked to chair the board of the Corporation for National Service and serve as special adviser on domestic policy and philanthropy. Bush announced the Goldsmith and DiIulio appointments at the same news conference.

John DiIulio did not seek the position, and he likely agreed to serve only because of his own personal commitment to the issue and his respect for the president. He clearly preferred that the president choose someone else. When he did agree to serve, he placed conditions on his acceptance. Among the stipulations, he said that he would only serve six months, that he intended to commute from Philadelphia so he would not have to uproot his family, and that he would not attend senior policy meetings.

By the time DiIulio had agreed to take the job, most of the staff was in place, creating the awkward situation of someone directing a staff he did not hire and who were not directly loyal to him. Eventually he was able to bring in Rev. Mark Scott as the associate director for outreach and Lisa Trevino Cummins as the associate director for special projects— both of whom, among other things, helped with outreach to African Americans and Latinos. As the legislative battle in the House of Representatives intensified, DiIulio asked David Kuo, former policy director for Senator Ashcroft, to join the office. Kuo remembers meeting with DiIulio at the Old Ebbitt Grill in the spring of 2001. Although reluctant to return to politics, he arrived on June 4, agreeing to volunteer for two months to help with House passage of H.R. 7. John Bridgeland later asked him to join the staff, which he did, in effect running the office for months after DiIulio's departure.[16]

On many levels, the DiIulio appointment was a wise choice. First and foremost, DiIulio and the president shared both a personal connection and a vision for serving the poor. In addition, many observers applauded Bush reaching out to a Democrat to head the office, interpreting the selection as a sign of the administration's willingness to work across party lines. As one congressional aide explained: "Bush connects at a heartfelt level with John DiIulio, and politically it makes sense. The reality of that announcement—we said, 'Wow, this is a big deal.'"[17] DiIulio's background as a social scientist with a passion for faith-based programs also provided a depth of understanding of the issue and a perspective very different from more traditional political appointees. In an editorial after DiIulio announced his departure, the *Washington Post* praised the director: "DiIulio knew that the plural of anecdote is not data. He was cautious about suggesting that faith-based programs might be superior, because no social science demonstrates that contention. . . . He was an honest body slammer rather than a charming fraud."[18]

The same qualities that appeared to be DiIulio's greatest strengths to some were also his greatest liabilities with other constituencies. Unlike the *Post*, which lavished praise on DiIulio as he left the White House, Jerry Falwell bade him good riddance: "John DiIulio got into trouble the first day in office because he didn't know the clientele. I would hope President Bush gets someone who knows the faith-based community and doesn't leave anyone out of it. Anyone would be an improvement on John DiIulio."[19] Of course, Falwell's critique was not that DiIulio did not understand faith-based organizations; it was that the director was not sufficiently connected with and beholden to a particular segment of the faith community—in this instance, conservative white evangelicals. While many Democrats had praised the apparent bipartisan strategy behind the choice of DiIulio, many conservative Republicans had seen danger in this moderate move. DiIulio advocated a slow and deliberate approach to implementing existing charitable choice law, and he specifically reached out to Democrats. Kathryn Dunn Tenpas, the first researcher to systematically study the WHOFBCI, has written: "His consensus-building approach to the issue set him apart from his White House and Capitol Hill allies, who preferred a 'move it or lose it' approach."[20] DiIulio wanted time to build stronger support for a faith-based program; conservatives wanted immediate legislative action and tightened language to protect churches from what they perceived as threats. As one reporter summarized: "Mr. DiIulio, an academic, opposed the White House's initial strategy and often sparred with conservative Republicans over the details of the faith-based initiative."[21]

Perhaps nothing captures the reaction to DiIulio more succinctly than the aftermath of his speech before the National Association of Evangelicals (NAE) on March 7, 2001. In a long and detailed address, he described the administration's faith-based initiative, explained and defended the need for charitable choice, and offered detailed, Scripture-laden defenses of common critiques of the Bush plan. Although the speech was lengthy and rich in detail, reporters and conservative critics immediately latched onto DiIulio's most critical comments directed at "white ex-urban evangelicals." In one section, he reminded those conservative leaders who contend that government funding inevitably leads to secularization that they need not apply for such funds. Not stopping at that point, he argued that many churches want and need public support:

> In particular, compared to predominately ex-urban white evangelical churches, urban African-American and Latino faith communities have benevolent traditions and histories that make them generally more dedicated to community-serving missions, and generally more confident about engaging public and secular partners in achieving those missions without enervating their spiritual identities or religious characters.... [T]he 'hijacked faith' fears expressed by some are less pointed and less prevalent in urban America.[22]

Referencing academic studies and practical examples of urban ministries wanting to partner with the government, DiIulio cited I John 3:17, called his audience to "truth in action," and then continued:

> In all truth and grace, and speaking now only for myself and as a fellow Christian, I would call upon the National Association of Evangelicals to (as we say on the inner-city streets) get real—and get affiliated church leaders and their congregations to get real—about helping the poor, the sick, the imprisoned, and others among "the least of these." We all have ears to hear and a heart to listen—and act. It's fine to fret about "hijacked faith," but ... such frets would persuade more and rankle less if they were backed by real human and financial help.[23]

Although these comments represented a small fraction of DiIulio's remarks that day, most media accounts the following day framed the story as DiIulio attacking religious conservatives in white suburban churches. Thomas Edsall and Dana Milbank of the *Washington Post*, reporters who followed reactions to the faith-based initiative in numerous stories, led their story of the NAE speech with the paragraph: "White House official John J. DiIulio, Jr. yesterday lashed out at critics on the religious right who oppose President Bush's plan to provide government funds to religious charities, deepening a rare rift between the new administration and once-loyal social conservatives."[24] The *National Review* highlighted the offending remarks and offered commentary: "Support for the president's faith-based initiative—at least the part of it that requires discretionary grants to religious charities, as opposed to its indirect tax credits and deregulation—is waning on the Right. DiIulio's speech yesterday will not do anything to stop it from waning."[25] Already skeptical of this Democratic outsider, conservatives who were outraged by the speech wasted no time expressing their ire. David Horowitz of the Hudson Institute, for example, "dashed off an e-mail message to [conservative Marvin] Olasky and others (subject: 'DiIulio is at it again'), warning that 'the federal government will seek to radically secularize' faith-based programs under DiIulio's plan."[26]

As the example of the NAE speech demonstrates, John DiIulio's relationship with the religious right was rocky at best. With the benefit of hindsight, it is easy to conclude that DiIulio was not the right person for the job. Given the way the House legislative battle unfolded, it might indeed have been better to head the office with someone trusted by leaders of the Christian right. But DiIulio brought important qualities and talents to the job that, given a different political environment, could have spurred significant policy changes and built momentum for more moderate legislation. Democratic supporters who wanted to partner on some form of faith-based legislation would have openly embraced a more moderate approach, and President Bush might have signed a bill into law. For advocates on the political right, however, such an outcome would have been disastrous. As one Republican staff member explained, no legislation at all would be far better than the wrong legislation that did not provide full protection for religious organizations.

The WHOFBCI and its controversial director received much media attention in the early days of the Bush administration. Although this office was clearly at the center of the development of faith-based proposals, it was not the only place for promoting faith-based activity in the executive branch. While most reporters focused on what the WHOFBCI was or was not accomplishing, five other faith-based offices were quietly at work rewriting regulations and removing government barriers to partnerships with religious organizations.

The Work of the Satellite Offices

The second executive order issued on January 29, 2001, created a separate office inside each of five cabinet-level departments—Education, Health and Human Services, Housing and Urban Development, Labor, and Justice.[27] Although not without its challenges, the work of these centers was one of the greatest successes of the first two years of the faith-based initiative. The August 2001 *Unlevel Playing Field* report documented continued regulatory and procedural barriers to faith-based partnership with government, a step that laid the groundwork for future efforts to change bureaucratic patterns. In addition, the centers created outreach, technical assistance, and grant programs to facilitate greater interaction between their departments and faith-based and community organizations.

Staff in the satellite offices report to both the WHOFBCI and their respective cabinet secretaries. The nature of the relationship between the staff of each of these satellite offices, the cabinet secretary (or the attorney general, in the case of the Department of Justice), and the White House has varied across agencies and over time as each key player learns to negotiate the complexities in the structure of the offices. All of the center directors keep in regular contact with the WHOFBCI, just as they also report to their secretaries to achieve the goals and expectations of their agency.

Although housed in different executive branch agencies, the faith-based centers are, at their core, a creation of the White House. The secretaries had no choice but to accept these centers, and the directors selected by the White House, within their agencies. Former WHOFBCI staff member Stanley Carlson-Thies, who served as the liaison to the cabinet centers for part of his time at the White House, described the tension facing staff in the satellite offices: "To use Biblical imagery, you have to be in the world but not of it—you have to be in the departments but not of them. If you are too much tied to the White House, you are alienated. You have to find a way to become a part and be trusted. It's a continual back-and-forth, strategizing how you find the right balance."[28] Reports differ about the specific tensions within each department, but one thing is certain: the original cabinet center directors did not stay long. *The Federal Paper* described the turnover: "The team originally in charge of the initiative has been almost entirely replaced. At the agencies, two directors were fired, one transferred, and two others left voluntarily."[29] Although the White House maintains strict oversight of the cabinet centers, evidence so far suggests that the second wave of directors placed at the satellite offices learned to negotiate the tensions of serving two masters: a cabinet secretary and the White House.

Each satellite office faces challenges unique to its agency, so the work varies somewhat from center to center. The Department of Health and Human Services, for example, spends almost half a trillion dollars to provide a wide range of services. Center director Bobby Polito has focused much of his time and effort on identifying which departments within Health and Human Services are a natural fit for faith-based organizations and which are not: "I categorize various departments sort of like a stop-light. Green means 'go' for faith-based organizations, yellow is 'caution', and red is 'stop'."[30] Some areas, he explains, are not a natural fit for faith-based groups because they require particular expertise or credentials; thus, the Food and Drug Administration is a "red" program, as is the Agency for Health Care Research and Quality, which funds academic studies. Many Department of Housing and Urban Development regulations preclude partnership with religious organizations. In the Department of Labor, the cabinet center has discovered sharp disconnects between federal, state, and local officials. As center director Brent Orrell described it: "In the federal and state bureaucracy level of senior management we see opposition. But at local levels, they really want to do this and are always looking for new partners. We see lots of support and lots less prejudice against faith-based organizations."[31]

The Barriers Report
Although each office has some flexibility in identifying and confronting the unique challenges of its host department, all share in the same charge to conduct an annual audit of department cooperation with faith-based groups. President Bush described this reporting process:

Each Center for Faith-Based and Community Initiatives will, within 180 days, and then annually thereafter, report to the White House Office on barriers it has identified to the participation of faith-based and community groups in the delivery of social services and on the solutions it has identified; provide a summary of technical assistance and other information that is offered to faith-based and community organizations that desire to work with the Department; and develop and issue a set of performance indicators and measurable objectives for the reform of the Department's policies and practices.[32]

Regulatory barriers and administrative hurdles block religious organizations from participation in many government programs, so these annual audits are an important tool for advancing the faith-based initiative in the executive branch. Describing the program audits, then-Director John DiIulio explained: "This is easily the most crucial, but least well-understood, part of our mission. It's about paving the path to civic results through greater government solicitude for faith-based and community organizations."[33]

The WHOFBCI released its first five-department audit, *Unlevel Playing Field: Barriers to Participation by Faith-Based and Community Organizations in Federal Social Service Programs*, on August 16, 2001. Compiling data received from all five cabinet centers, the report attempts to measure the amount of federal funding that currently goes to faith-based and community organizations. It includes a section that describes "a federal system inhospitable to faith-based and community organizations," discussing how the current grant system allows current grantees to receive funding each year without demonstrating their effectiveness and essentially shuts out new organizations from receiving grant money. Additional sections list six barriers specifically facing faith-based organizations that would want federal money to provide services, and seven additional barriers that affect community-based organizations. The report notes numerous discontinuities between what is written in the law and what is allowed by agency practice. It concludes:

The Federal Grants process, despite a few exceptions and a growing sensitivity to and openness towards both faith-based and community groups, does more to discourage than to welcome the participation of faith-based and community groups. . . . Too much is done that discourages or actually excludes good organizations that simply appear "too religious"; too little is done to include groups that meet local needs with vigor and creativity but are not as large, established, or bureaucratic as the traditional partners of Federal Government.[34]

The release of this report was an important milestone for the WHOFBCI, as it documented barriers to participation and provided a blueprint for potential executive branch action.

The Cabinet Centers at Work

As the legislative battle intensified on Capitol Hill, the cabinet centers continued their work, typically off the "radar screen" of the major media outlets. Communicating regularly with the staff of the WHOFBCI, each office had a good measure of autonomy as staff worked to facilitate partnerships with faith-based and community organizations. Elizabeth Seale, the original director of the Health and Human Services office, praised the WHOFBCI staff for "[allowing] us to carry out the terms of the executive order within the environment of each department."[35] To accomplish their goals, cabinet center staff designed and implemented outreach efforts, created new grant programs targeting new partnerships, and began the slow but influential process of rewriting regulations to assist in "leveling the playing field."

Cabinet center staff, speaking off the record, disagree about the impact of the high-profile and emotionally charged debate over H.R. 7. Whereas some found that the increased attention and controversy complicated the work of their offices, others argued that the House debate in some ways freed them. The House appeared to be the center of the attention, debate, and hostilities on faith-based issues, so cabinet center work received little public notice or scrutiny. Whether impeded or freed, all parties do seem to agree that the cabinet centers made significant contributions in the first two years of the administration. Clearly, changing regulations and decreasing barriers are an influential and significant piece of the faith-based initiative.

The WHOFBCI in Action: Benefits and Challenges

When President Bush announced his faith-based initiative, he did not need to create a separate office within the Executive Office of the President, and he did not need to name director John DiIulio an assistant to the president—the highest-ranking title granted to White House staff, signifying a position that reports directly to the president. Were these decisions prudent politics? What are the strengths and weaknesses of the structure of the White House Office of Faith-Based and Community Initiatives?

The Anomaly of a Separate Office

The plan for a separate office began in the campaign. As then-Governor Bush trumpeted his faith-based proposals across the country, he often mentioned his goal of establishing a separate office in the White House, as if to emphasize the issue's importance and the depth of his commitment to it. Pondering the reasons for the separate office, researcher Kathryn Dunn Tenpas noted: "The motives for establishing a specialized White House Office are many—an attempt to gain national recognition for a pet issue, the pursuit of support from an important constituency or an effort to create a legacy. In this case, it was primarily the result of a campaign promise coupled with a president deeply devoted to the concept of faith-based initiatives."[36]

In addition to raising the profile of the proposal, the creation of a separate office by executive order forces future presidents to address the issue. As then–White House deputy communications director Jim Wilkinson explained: "The separate faith-based office is a good thing because they are always on their issue. Future presidents will have to have a faith-based office or abolish it. It was created by executive order. It is forcing future presidents to take these issues seriously."[37] A subsequent president who does not share Bush's passion for this issue will have few options: make a media splash by abolishing the faith-based office, or maintain the office while limiting or changing the focus of its work.

On the other hand, the design of a separate office places it outside the traditional structure of the White House apparatus, comprised of eighteen specifically defined units. Under the best of circumstances, the White House is a complex organization with many functions to coordinate. Bradley Patterson described it in his definitive work on the White House staff: "Across the whole White House is a demand that overrides any and all individual preoccupations: the necessity for cooperation. The eighteen units of the White House staff must be as precisely interlinked and sequenced as the pistons of an engine."[38] Occasionally, presidents create new offices within their administrations that are not a part of the accepted eighteen units, such as the Office of Drug Control Policy. Although these separate offices are technically part of the White House operation, many D.C. insiders view them as "step-children" that are not part of the original family. In the same way, the WHOFBCI was a new, separate office that did not fit within the understood bureaucratic structure of the White House. One former WHOFBCI official described the confusion that resulted: "What was clear to me—it was a rocky relationship with the rest of the White House. I am not a scholar of administrations at all, but we were experiencing: 'Are we on the same team? Why is this happening?' We were kind of an anomaly, so it became very problematic."[39] Another former WHOFBCI staff member expressed frustration with the location of the office outside the traditional structure of the administration this way: "White House offices don't fit. They are viruses that enter the blood stream."[40]

When asked his perspective on the structure of the WHOFBCI, DiIulio's successor Jim Towey made his point emphatically: "It doesn't matter how you organize it—it would raise the same issues. The separate office isn't an issue at all. I work for the president, and this is an issue that is close to his heart. You could put this office on the planet Pluto and it would still be effective because the president is committed to making it work."[41]

Although it is unclear how much the location of the office outside the communication loop affected coordination efforts, by almost all accounts the WHOFBCI encountered problems synchronizing its efforts with the West Wing. Expressing his frustration with the lack of coordination, Stanley Carlson-Thies recounted last-minute requests for help that came too late: "Often we would get called in at the last minute. 'We're talking to the Senate in thirty minutes, what should I say?' They're walking down the hall on a cell phone—not the best way to prepare someone on such complicated issues."[42] One particularly egregious coordination error could have compromised faith-based legislation in the House. On the afternoon that the House Judiciary Committee held the markup of H.R. 7, a group of House Republicans (including a handful of members of the committee) were scheduled to meet with President Bush to discuss pending legislation on medical patients' rights. Caught in the conflict of attending a meeting with the president at the same time they needed to be present in the committee to secure sufficient Republican votes to save his faith-based legislation, the legislators scrambled to juggle the two demands. When asked for a potential explanation for this scheduling error, a high-ranking administration official guessed that such mix-ups are not that infrequent, noting that congressional committees rarely provide much advance notice of their schedules.[43]

Our research leads us to conclude that the decision not to enfold faith-based into the existing White House structure was a political mistake. The WHOFBCI was too weak and too disconnected from key White House staff to provide the support, expertise, and political muscle needed to champion the faith-based initiative. Although staffed with experts who understood the complexities of faith-based proposals, the original WHOFBCI lacked personnel with recent experience on Capitol Hill and expertise in building communications strategy. The permanent White House structure includes offices of Legislative Affairs, Communications, Public Liaison, Domestic Policy Council, and others that could have helped guide a successful faith-based initiative, but these departments did not appear to work effectively with the WHOFBCI. This lack of coordination significantly harmed efforts to promote faith-based policies inside and outside the administration. One congressional aide described White House efforts from the vantage point of many on Capitol Hill: "The White House was very disorganized. They needed a full-fledged lobby effort on the Hill. The WHOFBCI did not seem to know the details; they needed a more broad effort. They had good people but not the right people."[44]

Early Efforts to Promote the Faith-Based Initiative

When President Bush first announced the establishment of a White House Office of Faith-Based and Community Initiatives, interest was high; journalists, interest group leaders, members of Congress, and the American public waited to see what this new office would do. Hastily created behind the scenes and cloaked in uncertainty, the WHOFBCI nonetheless opened with much public fanfare. Bush kept his campaign promise to create an office, and the quick and bold move suggested that the faith-based initiative would be a centerpiece of the new Bush administration.

Although the short time frame significantly complicated the work of the new office, the pressure from political advisers to get the office up and running so quickly was strong evidence that faith-based initiatives would be a high priority in the administration. And in the first month, this was indeed the case.

But the intense White House focus on faith-based initiatives was short-lived. The WHOFBCI was always "on issue," but many of the other arms of the administration turned to other policy priorities. Although some officials interviewed for this project insist that faith-based was always an important administration priority, much evidence suggests this was not the case. One staff member whose boss was a vocal supporter of H.R. 7 assessed the situation: "Legislative Affairs, Domestic Policy Council, OMB—they didn't care about this. Point blank, it wasn't a priority for them. They weren't trying to kill the bill; it just wasn't important."[45]

Though members of the White House staff varied in their levels of interest and support for faith-based proposals, one person never wavered: the president himself. Rooted in his faith commitment and his personal experience overcoming a drinking problem, Bush believes wholeheartedly that faith-based organizations can meet needs in ways that traditional government programs often cannot. Elizabeth Seale, who began working with Bush on the faith-based issue back in Texas, described the president's commitment as heartfelt: "The story in Texas speaks volumes. . . . What I've seen in him—he has a tender heart for people in need. . . . He engages one-on-one and he connects with people. It causes him pain to experience people's needs and at the same time to feel like there are barriers in place that keep the needs from being met. Our problems aren't cut and dried; religion can do what policy cannot."[46]

Although some observers argue that key White House officials disliked the issue and therefore avoided it, a more accurate assessment is probably that the issue suffered from neglect. With so many issues competing for scarce time and resources, the White House cannot concentrate full attention on every proposal. Advisers fight for even a few minutes of the president's time, as they try to move forward programs they believe are most important. John DiIulio readily admits that he should have been more aggressive in demanding time on the president's schedule. The president himself even raised the issue with DiIulio. As the former director recounts: "When the president called me, each time, he would say, 'How come you're not getting on my dance card?' "[47]

To someone unfamiliar with the complexity of the issue, faith-based appeared reasonably simple and relatively noncontroversial. In all likelihood, most of the key policy advisers in the West Wing were completely unprepared for the faith-based firestorm that was brewing. Awakened to the building controversy in the House when it became apparent that H.R. 7 would not be a quick and easy victory, the administration did, belatedly, turn its attention to the faith-based issue. Vice President Cheney and White House Chief of Staff Andy Card met with Judiciary Chairman Sensenbrenner to negotiate new language and save the bill in committee,[48] and Cheney aggressively worked the phones to build support for the bill on the House floor.

Effects of Internal and External Pressures: A Chronology

The haphazard nature of the creation of the WHOFBCI had many spill-over effects. With almost no time to evaluate and develop different proposals for structuring the office, its staff, and its mission, DiIulio and his team spent most of their time in the first year reacting to external events and internal office problems. Although a comprehensive assessment of the work of the WHOFBCI is beyond the scope of this chapter, the following sections will consider several key events and decisions that moved the WHOFBCI into the spotlight and demanded its response.

Spring and Summer 2001:
Disagreement over Legislative Strategy

Throughout the campaign and during his first weeks in office, President Bush made clear his expectation that his administration would promote the faith-based agenda. Although Bush had provided a broad general outline for the initiative, leaders in the administration and in Congress now had to work out the details. The general goal of helping faith-based and community organizations had broad, diverse support, but points of agreement quickly disappeared as the WHOFBCI and congressional staff began to hammer out the details of how and when they would implement the president's goals.

Interviews with administration officials and congressional aides indicate significant disagreement among White House advisers, the staff of the WHOFBCI and the House Republicans over what strategy would be most effective for advancing the president's goals. Staff for key House

Republicans wanted quick and decisive legislative action, whereas John DiIulio and some of his team in the WHOFBCI advocated a slower approach. Former staff member Stanley Carlson-Thies remembers some of the internal discussions on strategy: "One view was: We need a measured approach; we should take more evidence and build a case for expansion. The other view was: We already made a case for this; charitable choice has already passed, which shows there is no need [for building a case]."[49] DiIulio and others emphasized the importance of identifying the most significant problems confronting faith-based organizations while simultaneously building support for and an understanding of the need for new law and regulations. By most accounts, key staff disagreed on strategy and fundamental goals. For most of the first few months, policy advisers weighed the options and debated what would be the best way to promote the president's faith-based goals.

While those within the administration were weighing their options, House Republicans were ready to push legislation. Concerned that the White House was too slow in suggesting legislative language, House Republican staff members began the process on their own: "We decided we needed to get the ball rolling, so we wrote our own bill."[50] Aware that they had the votes for passage and apparently unconcerned about the broader effects of a party-line vote, House Republicans moved forward with a conservative bill. One congressional aide described the improvements in the House bill: "The charitable choice language was tighter and better than the 1996 language. We included a trap door that was constitutionally sound so clients could leave the program if they objected to it. It was a better set of language."[51]

What House Republicans saw as legislation that would significantly help religious organizations, some in the White House saw as potentially threatening the success of the entire initiative. One former official described the situation this way: "We lost control in the House. There is no question that House Republicans looked at this through a different prism. Members and key staff had no clue of the changing dynamics, they were so confident of a majority without regard for caution. It was as if you could still feel the effects of the Gingrich era, the blitzkrieg era. There was no concern about this being bipartisan; they wanted to seize the high road.... They said they knew their chamber, so they dictated the terms of the legislative package."[52]

Democratic observer Will Marshall argued: "The White House allowed the House Republicans to write a bill to alienate Democrats and not attract them. . . . They hadn't worked hard for bipartisanship, and the scare campaign from civil libertarians worked. The White House should have collaborated with the Democrats and the House Republicans, but that was not the path they chose."[53] The *Washington Post* described some of the various camps and their responses to the House bill: "Several Republican lawmakers have warned the administration that the faith-based legislation introduced in the House is unacceptable to Democrats and has no chance in the Senate. Some White House officials say House conservatives overreached when they were writing the bill, giving too much leeway to churches. Some congressional negotiators retort that the president invited trouble by sketching his plan too vaguely."[54] Although key participants offered slightly conflicting views of who had control of the political agenda, almost everyone involved in the debate agreed that the House Republicans' conservative strategy alienated most Democrats and complicated the prospects for faith-based legislation in the less conservative Senate.

Once faith-based policy had moved from general prescriptions to an actual bill, H.R. 7, interest groups began to react and mobilize in response to this concrete proposal. As one former White House official explained: "The moment it was filed, it would polarize debate. Instantly, people would retreat to their bunkers and lob rhetorical missiles back and forth."[55] Even though the WHOFBCI did not have a significant role in drafting H.R. 7, it was seen as the president's bill, and so its staff had the charge of defending the bill publicly. Critics on the left, right, and center found problems with the legislative proposal: "Bush's plan has critics across the political spectrum. Conservative Christians have said they fear government involvement in church programs could lead to corruption and waste. Civil rights groups worry that government money could go to groups that discriminate in their employment and that the plan will lead to cuts in government programs. Americans United for Separation of Church and State calls the plan 'unconstitutional, unnecessary and unworkable.' "[56] Opposition to faith-based in general was building, and opponents now had a high-profile bill to attack. Staff in the WHOFBCI found themselves in a difficult position: they needed to build support for a faith-based initiative larger than H.R. 7 in a context that was becoming narrowly defined and polarized by the controversial House bill.

As we have noted in earlier chapters, liberal opponents of the bill found an argument that resonated well with the media and their constituencies. Supplanting older separation of church and state arguments, opponents described the president's initiative as "government-sponsored discrimination." The cries of discrimination quickly framed the argument and forced the bill's supporters, including the WHOFBCI, to play defense against formidable foes.

Some groups feared that the faith-based initiative would take money from existing social welfare programs. Although the president had promised a compassion capital fund to provide money for technical assistance, the House bill, as written, did not provide new funds to help religious organizations learn how to apply for and win grants. Unsure the caucus would support a bill that increased government spending, House Republicans did not include this White House prescription.[57] This absence of additional spending discouraged many moderates. As Meg Riley of the Unitarian Univeralists explained: "'No new money' resonates with practical people, especially as we move into a war economy. What are we going to cut? What will you get rid of?"[58]

As House Republicans moved to the political right of the White House's original intentions, party competition intensified. The *Congressional Quarterly* summarized the effects of the rightward move: "Republicans ended up with a bill that is defined as much by concerns about religious bias and the possibility of discrimination against gays and lesbians as by its intended mission of helping faith-based groups fight poverty and ease social problems."[59] Many moderate Republicans began to waver in their support.

Even though the bill was written to allay many conservatives' fears, groups from the political right raised significant concerns about the direction in which faith-based politics was moving. According to one former member of the WHOFBCI staff, many conservatives opposed the faith-based initiative because they feared the implications of government partnership with churches. Other conservative groups opposed government-sponsored welfare altogether. Offering a specific example, one former WHOFBCI staffer noted: "The Christian Coalition wanted welfare nondependency. They would not pay attention because they wanted to abolish welfare, not invite faith-based organizations to participate."[60] Characterizing members of a coalition of conservative family values groups, one legislative staffer explained: "They are scared of the federal government, see it as risky, and worry that faith-based won't have an impact on the kind of groups we want it to have an impact on."⁶¹ Perhaps lobbyist Ralph Benko described the potential for conservative backlash most succinctly: "John [DiIulio] was walking on a tightrope; and I don't think he fully grasped what the right could pull, that the base could crumble. It could cripple the bill and embarrass the president."⁶² The irony of the situation did not go unnoticed. As two journalists observed: "A program designed to appeal to evangelicals is instead deeply offending them."⁶³

As H.R. 7 moved through the House of Representatives, opposition to the larger faith-based initiative was growing from both the right and the left. The legislative battle forcefully moved the issue into the public eye, created an arena for media and interest groups to frame the debate, and opened the policy to criticism from the right and the left.

July 10, 2001:
Dana Milbank and the Salvation Army "Memo"

In the midst of the heated debate over faith-based legislation in the House, *Washington Post* reporter Dana Milbank broke a front-page story leaking information from an internal Salvation Army memo that reportedly showed the White House colluding with the Salvation Army to gain the organization's support for H.R. 7. Milbank's article reported a secret White House agreement with the Army guaranteeing to shield religious organizations from local ordinances that prohibit discrimination against gays in return for the Army's political support.⁶⁴

FOCAL POINT 5.1

The Salvation Army "Memo"

When one lists charities helping the poor and the homeless, the Salvation Army often comes first. The red kettles collecting change every December raise a small percentage of the Army's annual $2.3 billion budget. Shelters, rehab clinics, Boys and Girls Clubs, disaster relief, and the world-famous soup kitchens are just a few of the organization's services in America and abroad.

The Salvation Army is not primarily a charity organization. It is a church, with doctrine, Sunday services, and a defined mission. The organization's mission statement reads: "[The Salvation Army's] mission is to preach the gospel of Jesus Christ and to meet human needs in His name without discrimination."

According to the Army's 2001 annual report, 13 percent, or $300 million, of its operating income came from government contracts to build facilities or offer a range of community services. The Army supported faith-based legislation very early, believing such policy would help the organization expand services to the needy. Then, in July 2001, Dana Milbank of the *Washington Post* wrote a front-page story on a "secret memo." Leading with the statement, "The Bush administration is working with the nation's largest charity, the Salvation Army, to make it easier for government-funded religious groups to practice hiring discrimination against gay people, according to an internal Salvation Army document," Milbank reported that the memo revealed a quid pro quo: the Salvation Army would support the legislation in exchange for exemption from antidiscrimination laws.

Both sides quickly denied any political deal. The White House immediately issued a short statement reaffirming the administration's commitment to "current civil rights protections under Charitable Choice" and stating that it would not pursue the Army's request. The Salvation Army issued a statement declaring that the memo was *not* generated by the Army and that the organization's hiring policies complied with federal employment laws. The organization's national commander, John A. Busby, also wrote an open letter to clarify that it "has not and does not show bias in its employment practices." The Army expects sexual purity that would forbid homosexual behavior among all ministers and workers directly involved in ministry, but it does not inquire into the sexual orientation of its other employees. Because federal civil rights laws do not currently protect sexual orientation, it is impossible to not be in compliance on that point.

What really happened? Had a sophisticated and respected charity made a huge blunder? Was the White House making covert deals? As in many cases, the whole story was not told in the first news article. The Salvation Army did not write the memo; nor did they request a quid pro quo from the administration. In fact, the issue in the memo had its roots in events that occurred years before. In 1997, the city of San Francisco passed a landmark domestic partners law that required all employers who contract with the city and who provide health insurance to workers' spouses to also provide that insurance for gay, lesbian, and unmarried domestic partners. Groups like Catholic Charities and the Salvation Army fought the law for a time. Catholic Charities decided to extend insurance to anyone living with an employee, but the Salvation Army chose a different option, announcing in June 1998 that it would no longer accept nor compete for San Francisco's contracts. The services provided by those funds would be transferred to other organizations or funded from other sources.

Seeing similar legislation developing across the country, the Salvation Army's Western Territory legal counsel hired the law firm of Loeb and Loeb to research the implications of local antidiscrimination ordinances. After its study, Loeb and Loeb approached Salvation Army national headquarters to outline the situation, and the headquarters requested that the firm submit a proposal to expand its work. The subsequent seventy-nine-page document from Loeb and Loeb presented an action plan that included suggestions for lobbying, communications, and further monitoring of new ordinances, with a price tag of almost $1 million. One idea offered in the proposal was to seek an Office of Management and Budget regulation change. This is the memo on which Dana Milbank based his story, and this explains why, as he noted, the memo is addressed *to* Salvation Army commanders and not *from* them.

The Milbank story created strong reverberations inside the Beltway, but drew less attention elsewhere. Research conducted later by the Salvation Army suggested that the American public largely ignored the story. The media and involved groups inside the Beltway gave the issue great attention, however, creating a lasting impression, fair or not, about one of the primary motivations of faith-based proponents.

—*Kristin Brostrom*

Sources

Busby, John A. "Open Letter from National Commander." *Salvation Army*, 13 July 2001.

Fernandez, Manny, and April Lynch. "Salvation Army Cuts S.F. Programs; Charity Spurns City's Domestic Partner Law." *San Francisco Chronicle*, 4 June 1998.

Fleischer, Ari. "Statement by the Press Secretary on the Request by the Salvation Army for an OMB Circular." Office of the Press Secretary, 10 July 2001. www.whitehouse.gov/news/releases/2001/07/20010710-12.html.

Interview with Major George Hood, Public Affairs Director, National Headquarters, Salvation Army, 23 September 2002.

Milbank, Dana. "Charity Cites Bush Help in Fight against Hiring Gays: Salvation Army Wants Exemption from Laws." *Washington Post*, 10 July 2001, A1.

Salvation Army. Statement issued 10 July 2001.

Salvation Army America website: www.salvationarmyusa.org/www_usn.nsf (10 September 2001).

The original story and those that followed on subsequent days directly connected Bush's faith-based initiative with hiring discrimination and served to rally civil rights groups in opposition to the bill. One Democratic congressional aide asserted: "Dana Milbank wanted to torpedo the initiative. He wrote the story hard."[65] A former administration official blasted the article, saying: "This was a quid pro quo in the mind of one person, Dana Milbank—his wild and fanciful thought. No one in the Salvation Army saw it as a quid pro quo."[66] Although outsiders can only speculate on the journalist's motivations, key actors involved on both sides of the faith-based debate agree that the story significantly harmed faith-based proposals far beyond H.R. 7. Directly connecting the administration's policy to discrimination against gays and lesbians, the Salvation Army story provided fuel for the "religious discrimination" argument and energized civil rights groups uniting in opposition to faith-based proposals.

August 17, 2001: DiIulio's Departure

On August 17, 2001, the day after the WHOFBCI released the *Unlevel Playing Field* report, John DiIulio announced he would be stepping down as director of the office, citing personal and health reasons. The eighteen-hour days with a daily commute from Philadelphia had taken their toll, and DiIulio was ready to spend more time with his family. The *Washington Post* reported on the official White House reaction to the news: "Ari Fleischer, Bush's press secretary, said DiIulio's departure was expected. 'It was a six-month stint,' he said. 'John DiIulio has done a wonderful job.' Fleischer said the faith plan 'will continue to live after John goes back to Philadelphia.' Fleischer echoed another White House official's view that DiIulio is 'a sage and a saint.' "[67]

Although White House insiders knew, and a few early media reports acknowledged, that DiIulio had only agreed to serve six months, the announcement still managed to send shockwaves across Washington. The first departure of a high-ranking member of the Bush administration was sure to draw media attention, and the exit of a Democrat in a Republican administration added to the drama. Speaking to a reporter after the announcement, DiIulio explained: "I've always said that I agreed to stay for six months, to help launch the initiative, help mobilize people who would not be traditional friends and allies. I feel I have run this race."[68]

Clearly, DiIulio's preference for a moderate strategy had created tensions between the outspoken director and conservative supporters of the administration. Many on the religious right distrusted a Democrat in the WHOFBCI; DiIulio's critique of white ex-urban churches in his March address to the National Association of Evangelicals had served to confirm their fears. DiIulio was not without critics even in his own office. Reports from within the WHOFBCI hinted at tensions among the staff. One administration official, speaking off the record to reporters from *The New Republic*, wasted no time criticizing the departing director: "The sort of people who are good about thinking up ideas are not necessarily the sort of people who are good at getting them done."[69]

Although DiIulio's departure followed the timeline he had announced in advance, frustrations with internal and external politics surrounding the faith-based issue likely contributed to his resignation. Having spearheaded the office during the rancorous debate over a House bill he could not fully support, DiIulio was physically and emotionally exhausted. The outlook for successful faith-based legislation in the Senate was bleak. Perhaps most importantly, however, he and his staff had completed the *Unlevel Playing Field* report, a document DiIulio believed crucial for identifying the barriers facing faith-based and community organizations and laying the groundwork for future executive branch action. Having completed this important project, it was a good time to leave.

The resignation of such a high-profile official was a setback to the office and its work. The loss of a spokesman, even a controversial one like DiIulio, left a void. DiIulio's critics lost no time in praising the announcement. Marvin Olasky called it "a merciful resignation" and the Hudson Institute's Michael Horowitz disparaged DiIulio as "the most strategically disastrous appointee to a senior government position in the 20-plus years I've been in Washington. He has taken what could have been a triumphant issue and marched it smack into quicksand."[70] While conservatives used the opportunity to highlight their dislike of the out-going director, many on the left used the occasion to praise DiIulio and remind the president to maintain a moderate position. Although his organization vehemently opposed the faith-based initiative, Rabbi David Saperstein, Director of the Religious Action Center of Reform Judaism, commended DiIulio for his work and called on Bush to replace DiIulio with another moderate:

> John's resignation marks a crossroads for the president. In filling this position, the president must decide if he wants to forge a consensus around aspects of his plan which can unite Americans—such as helping non-profit organizations, including religiously affiliated organizations, better serve those in need—or if he wants to push ahead with those aspects of the plan—such as direct government funding for churches and synagogues—which will divide Americans along religious lines. President Bush campaigned, famously, as "a uniter not a divider." In filling this important position he has an opportunity to live up to that promise.[71]

Observers on the left and the right awaited the Bush administration's next move to see if the incoming director would steer the office in a new direction or attempt to stay the course.

September 11, 2001:
From Domestic Policy to Domestic Consequences

No single event affected the work of the WHOFBCI and the direction of faith-based initiatives more profoundly than the tragedy of September 11, 2001. Stunned by the events of that day, the direction of the adminis-tration changed. John Bridgeland, who was the head of the Domestic Policy Council at that time, describes the impact of that day: "Then September 11 hits. For all of us at the Domestic Policy Council we went from domestic policy to domestic consequences. It totally changed our lives."[72] No longer free to reflect and build a policy agenda, the White House staff needed "all hands on deck" to assess the potential threat and take any action possible to secure the nation. Foreign policy took front and center stage; domestic proposals not directly related to homeland security slid into the background. White House officials who could have helped the staff of the WHOFBCI found themselves consumed with the work of national security. Hence, an issue of highest priority on September 10 might seem near to irrelevant on September 12.

Ironically, while the events of September 11 captured the attention of domestic policy staff, they also created a more hospitable political environment for discussion of faith and community service. Confused, stunned, and grieving, Americans flocked to religious services. Organized prayer vigils across the country memorialized the victims, and Americans expressed a renewed interest in faith and spirituality. Political scientist Robert Putnam described the environment: "A window of opportunity has opened for a civic renewal that occurs only once or twice a century."[73]

Reflecting this new political environment, the focus of the faith-based initiative shifted. Michael Gerson, Bush's director of speechwriting, described the new focus: "In the aftermath of 9/11, we have focused on broader themes of civic engagement and citizenship. . . . This was very much driven by policy and the call to civic engagement—that's the policy we announced in the State of the Union, so that was the focus of the speech."[74] Already in the works before September 11, reform and expansion of national service programs became a higher priority in the wake of the tragedy. A House staff member working on the AmeriCorps reauthorization described community service as the president's number-one agenda item following his State of the Union address. Although the Corporation for National Service played the most substantial role in supporting the legislative effort, the WHOFBCI also helped with the issue.[75]

In the immediate aftermath of September 11, direct efforts to promote the faith-based initiative made very little progress. John DiIulio was gone. David Kuo took over the day-to-day operations of the office, trying to manage the legislative battle in the Senate and hold the staff together until the president appointed a new director. The White House and members of Congress were preoccupied with the war on terrorism. Faith-based would have to wait.

February 1, 2002:
Arrival of Jim Towey and Restructuring of the WHOFBCI
Almost exactly one year after his executive order creating the WHOFBCI, President Bush made a new announcement—this time welcoming a new director, Jim Towey. Recommended for the job by the president's brother,

Florida governor Jeb Bush, Towey had an impressive background. A committed Catholic with a bipartisan resume, Towey's experience varied widely. He served as Republican senator Mark Hatfield's legislative director, headed the Department of Health and Rehabilitation Services under Democratic Florida governor Lawton Chiles, founded and ran the non-profit group Aging with Dignity, and served as legal counsel to Mother Teresa for twelve years. A small, soft-spoken, and gentle-mannered man, Towey had a very different style than his predecessor.

In remarks introducing his choice to direct the faith-based office, President Bush praised Towey's years of public service:

> He has served a Republican senator and a Democratic governor. He understands there are things more important than political parties. And one of those things more important than political parties is to help heal the nation's soul. He's run a statewide Department of Health—in other words, he's an administrator. He also worked with Mother Teresa for more than a year—for more than a decade. He brings to the job managerial skills and a servant's heart. He will be a great director, and I look forward to working with him to advance a bold initiative.[76]

Conservative organizations responded positively to Towey's appointment, and most opponents of the faith-based initiative did not publicly criticize the selection. Given the intensity of the rhetoric on both sides of the debate, this lack of controversy suggested that Bush had made a wise political choice.

The same week that Bush announced his selection of Jim Towey, he also reorganized the WHOFBCI. Unlike the previous director, John DiIulio, who had reported directly to the president, the new director was named deputy assistant to the president. Instead of reporting directly to Bush, Towey would report to John Bridgeland, who had been newly promoted to assistant to the president and selected to head the USA Freedom Corps. The change gave Towey less authority than DiIulio had exercised.

When Towey began his work at the White House, he made many changes. Although he retained a few of the first year's staff, the new director chose to build a team of his own for the WHOFBCI and inspired "house cleaning" at the satellite offices. As Towey himself said: "A lot of the secretaries didn't have people of their choosing—people have since been fired or moved. I met with the secretaries and the attorney general in the first week I was here and said to put whomever they want in the offices as long as they will work in a way coordinated by the WHOFBCI."[77]

While continuing to promote a legislative agenda and regulatory reforms, under Towey the WHOFBCI began conducting outreach programs designed to reach thousands of organizations nationwide. Beginning in late 2002, the WHOFBCI planned a series of regional conferences, each sponsored by one of the cabinet centers. At these gatherings, the White House office networked with religious and community leaders to educate them about the federal grant process and encourage partnerships where appropriate. The *Washington Post* described the conferences this way: "The administration also plans to stage seminars around the country over the next seven months to teach more than 5,000 religious groups how to use current law to win federally funded contracts. Although critics contend that Bush's faith-based measure will blur the separation of church and state, his aides said that it remains one of his most important goals."[78]

FOCAL POINT 5.2

Spotlight on San Diego

Faith-Based Regional Conferences

One of the stated goals of the White House Office of Faith-Based and Community Initiatives is outreach—educating potential grantees about the process for applying for federal funds, and networking with faith-based and community organizations. As a vehicle for such outreach, the White House and cabinet center faith-based offices sponsored a series of free one-day regional conferences across the country, beginning in Atlanta, Philadelphia, Denver, San Diego, and Chicago.

The San Diego conference, for example, hosted approximately 1,500 leaders and volunteers from nonprofits and religious congregations who expressed an interest in learning more about collaborating with government. Some attendees represented groups that already receive government funds; others came to satisfy their sense of curiosity about the White House's purposes.

After waiting outside for as much as an hour in a long, twisting line to clear security, participants filled a cavernous ballroom packed with 140 circular tables. Late arrivals found seating in a balcony that offered a view of the spectacle below—two giant jumbotron screens with the red, white, and blue logo "White House Faith-Based and Community Initiatives," and a podium in front of a blue and red curtain. A wide white banner announcing the "White House Confer- ence" stretched across the curtain.

Each participant received a slick white binder including five de- tailed red, white, and blue brochures with facts about the White House office and cabinet centers as well as resource materials for grant writing. The inside faces of the booklet's cover included words of George W. Bush, with bright white print imposed on a blue background. The front cover, for example, quotes the president exalting the work of faith-based groups: "The indispensable and transforming work of faith-based and other charitable groups must be encouraged. Government cannot be replaced by charities, but it can and should welcome them as partners. We must heed the growing consensus across America that successful government social programs work in fruitful partnership with community-serving and faith-based organizations."

Addressing the racially diverse audience, Rebecca Beynon of the WHOFBCI introduced the day's events, saying that the goal of the conference was to "take the mystery out of partnering with the federal government." Each of these regional conferences typically highlights a few WHOFBCI staff and features a guest speaker from the administration. Attorney General John Ashcroft addressed the crowd in Denver; Agriculture Secretary Ann Veneman spoke to the conference in San Diego; and the president himself appeared at the Philadelphia conference to announce two new executive orders expanding faith-based efforts in the executive branch. At all the conferences, a short video greeting from the president begins the day's events.

The San Diego conference featured a slightly altered array of speakers, as a blizzard across the northeast had closed Washington,

D.C.–area airports for most of three days. High-ranking Washington staff scheduled to appear at the conference were homebound, so the lower-level staff sent earlier to prepare for the conference suddenly found themselves in more prominent roles. They huddled near the registration booths talking furiously into cellphones as they reshuffled plans. Catharine Ryun, Jim Towey's assistant, introduced her boss to the crowd, pointing them to the large screens for a video-conference address hastily taped early that morning. Despite his inability to address the crowd live, Towey elicited laughter and cheers from the audience, beginning his address with the quote, "If you want to make God laugh, show Him your plans." Towey noted that God was laughing in abundance that day, as their best-laid plans fell to the wayside in the wake of the blizzard. Recalling stories of his work with the poor in Tijuana and with Mother Teresa in India, Towey exhorted the participants to serve the needy, and pledged the support of his office and the conference to help them learn more about partnering with the government.

By the end of the day's events, participants had been introduced to the federal grant process, had heard from faith-based practitioners already receiving government funding, and had been walked through a sample grant application. Organizers attempted to provide opportunities for questions and answers, but the size of the conference precluded much individual interaction. Even smaller breakout sessions were attended by as many as 800 people. Throughout the day, officials from the faith-based cabinet centers and government agencies staffed tables and distributed literature. Attendees scrambled from table to table, scooping up brochures and stuffing them into plastic shopping bags provided by the USDA. One participant, citing information overload, clutched her binder, noted "everything that I really need is in here," and left the meeting for an afternoon in the San Diego sun.

—Amy Black

Under Towey's watch, the WHOFBCI took more direct control of the satellite offices. As the new director explained: "We want to know what they're up to so we can make sure that the left hand and the right hand are in sync. . . . It's the president's initiative first and foremost."[79] The new structure required cabinet center directors to meet biweekly with Rebecca Beynon of the WHOFBCI; most reported talking with her daily, if not more often. Beynon was directed to keep tight reins on the satellite offices, for "in Towey's tightly-controlled shop, Beynon must sign off on all proposed changes—and all statements to the media."[80] Under Towey's restructuring, the faith-based offices began working together in a more coordinated and directed fashion.

December 12, 2002:
Moving Forward with Executive Branch Action

As the end of the 107th Congress drew near, faith-based legislation had stalled in the Senate. Perhaps recalling the effectiveness of regulatory reforms in Texas, President Bush renewed his effort to promote faith-based policies using executive power to accomplish what had not succeeded in Congress. Legislation was only one piece of the larger faith-based initiative; many of the barriers impeding government partnerships with faith-based organizations were embedded in government regulations and therefore subject to the president's control.

Speaking before the attendees of the WHOFBCI regional conference in Philadelphia, President Bush announced two new executive orders. One added cabinet centers at the Department of Agriculture and the United States Agency for International Development, thus extending the scope and sphere of influence for further executive branch reforms. The other executive order, titled "Equal Protection of the Laws for Faith-Based and Community Organizations," removed many barriers that had prevented faith-based organizations from partnering with government social service programs.[81] As the Pew Center for Religion and Public Life summarized: "The president's order effectively applies charitable choice principles through administrative regulation rather than legislation."[82] Unwilling to wait for Congress to act, and aware of ways to achieve some of the same goals, the administration found a way to move forward with the faith-based initiative without legislation.

Looking Ahead: Faith-Based beyond the 107th Congress

Although faith-based legislation failed to become law during the 107th Congress, the initiative was not the complete failure many commentators named it. Most media attention on the issue focused on the legislative piece of the program, but Bush furthered his faith-based initiative by implementing program changes by executive action. As the battle raged on Capitol Hill, staff in the WHOFBCI and at the original five (and now seven) cabinet centers were quietly beginning to change regulations, earmark money for faith-based organizations, and generally transform the relationship between the executive branch and religious groups. Although the implementation of the initiative in the executive branch faced some setbacks, the story of administrative reform, at least to this point, appears to be a qualified success.

The story of the faith-based initiative extends beyond the executive branch as well. As Congress debates legislation and bureaucrats rewrite regulations to remove barriers that faith-based and community organizations often confront, the third branch of American government is also at work transforming our understanding of religion and politics. It is to the judiciary, and the recent evolution of church-state law, that we now turn.

Six

Pervasive Confusion

The Federal Courts and Faith-Based Initiatives

Is the doctrine of pervasively sectarian institutions dead? If not, it's as close as possible to being dead. . . . There's no general bar . . . on financing organizations because of their sectarian character or degree. But government may not pay for religious activity, that is, activities that would make the government responsible for indoctrination, religious formation, or worship.

Robert Tuttle, George Washington University Law School

The life of Sandra Day O'Connor is one defined by achievement and influence. When women were a rarity in law schools, she graduated third in her Stanford Law School class, just behind classmate William Rehnquist. The realities of the 1950s—private law practice opportunities were off limits to her because of her gender—did not stop O'Connor from carving out a highly successful career in public service. Elected as a Republican to the Arizona State Senate, she became its first female majority leader. In 1981, she realized another, far greater, historical first: when President Ronald Reagan selected her as the first woman to sit on the United States Supreme Court.

On the Court, O'Connor has risen to the apex of influence. Her centrist position on a highly polarized and evenly divided Court gives O'Connor the decisive swing vote in case after case. Whether the issue is racial redistricting, abortion, affirmative action, or the limits of federalism, O'Connor's vote determines whether the majority will swing in a conservative or liberal direction. Lawyers appearing before the Court often write their briefs and shape their oral arguments with a singular objective in mind: winning Sandra Day O'Connor to their side. Her determinative influence on the great political and legal issues of the day has led some to describe American politics during her tenure as a government of one.

Nowhere is this more clearly illustrated than in the realm of church-state relations. The cautiousness and care that mark O'Connor's opinions account for the current constitutional divide over church and state. In *Zelman v. Simmons-Harris*, discussed below, she joined her conservative brethren in embracing the concept of neutrality as grounds for permitting school vouchers. Yet she has refused to support them in explicitly over-throwing the "pervasively sectarian" standard. The result is confusion as to whether that principle is still a barrier to government funding of religious institutions. In the end, the answers to the constitutional questions surrounding government's funding of religious service providers will almost certainly emanate from one person: Sandra Day O'Connor.

"Debating" the Faith-Based Initiative's Constitutionality in a Political Climate: Fact and Fiction

The war over publicly subsidized faith-based social service programs has been a multifront conflict, as the preceding chapters reveal. On the partisan front, both Democrats and Republicans sought to maximize their electoral appeal by co-opting the faith-based initiative during the 2000 presidential campaign. Once George W. Bush took office, the conflict greatly intensified as the faith-based initiative shifted to the legislative front, and as it met with varying degrees of success in the U.S. House and Senate. The White House was eventually able to focus its efforts on the administrative front, identifying and working within a handful of agencies where, even in the absence of new legislation, grant-making practices and regulations could be remolded to accommodate partnerships between faith-based organizations and the federal government.

In this chapter we turn to another front: the constitutionality of government's efforts to involve faith-based providers in publicly funded social service programs. The fascination of the faith-based story is that it engages every dimension of a policy idea: partisan politics, the legislative process, administrative authority, and the constitutional basis. The challenge in telling this story is that these elements play out over dramatically different spans of time and at differing paces. The key twists and turns in the partisan and policy sides of the story occur in a matter of months. The constitutional story unfolds at a glacial pace, stretching, as it does, over decades. Nevertheless, the Bush initiative was thrust into a constitutional arena that had undergone major changes in the past several years; indeed, the legal ground continued to shift even as the debate played out. Ultimately, the intense political environment undermined a more edifying or enlightened treatment of the complicated constitutional picture.

The Initial Outlook
As the White House headed into its first legislative term, the constitutional prospects for the faith-based initiative looked highly favorable. Both in the broader sweep of establishment clause interpretation and in more recent cases, decisions were moving in an accommodationist direction. The Bush plan appeared to have solid footing at least on the legal terrain.

In the larger context, establishment clause doctrine was gradually but inexorably growing more favorable to government/religious sector collaboration, at least in the realm of government financial aid to religious institutions.[1] Until the latter half of the twentieth century, the establishment clause had essentially been a dormant piece of the Constitution, at least with respect to state and local governmental action. With its 1947 *Everson* decision, the Supreme Court woke to the issue: its dominant focus on limiting public aid to Catholic parochial schools led to a highly separationist understanding of the establishment clause. From the 1940s through most of the 1970s, the Court was relatively stringent in barring the use of public funds to support educational enterprises in religious contexts. In so doing, it presumed religious schools to be pervasively sectarian institutions and thus disqualified from public aid.

Both before and during the modern era of establishment clause jurisprudence that began with *Everson*, religious organizations had a long and rich tradition of participation in government social programs. But that involvement came with certain limits: namely, that government money could not flow directly to pervasively sectarian organizations. As a condition of doing business with the funding agency, the provider had to separately incorporate and was expected to purge or scrub its services clean of any religious trappings. In short, religious activities, worship, and sacred artwork and imagery were thought to have no place in the delivery of services. The provider was expected to secularize those services for which it received public money.

By the late 1970s, the strict separation of government aid and religious education began to yield to a more permissive, accommodationist view. The Supreme Court decided in a string of cases to permit aid in various forms to flow to parochial schools. More significantly for charitable choice, the 1988 decision in *Bowen v. Kendrick* allowed government dollars to reach social service agencies, as the Court affirmed a federal statute that included religious service providers as grantees of a program aimed at preventing teen pregnancy.

As establishment clause jurisprudence grew more accommodationist, the doctrines historically relied upon to preclude public aid to religious schools were likewise diluted. The much-maligned *Lemon* test, while formally retained by the Court, was weakened as a bar to the funding of religious institutions.[2] Its twin prongs—that the "primary effect" of a program must not advance religion, and that the program must not "excessively entangle" government in the business of religion—were collapsed into a less rigorous single inquiry about whether or not a program served to promote religion. And while the Court still mouthed the language of pervasive sectarianism in determining what religious organizations might qualify for public monies, the starch behind the principle seemed to be eroding. In *Agostini v. Felton* (1997), the Court appeared to close the door on the era of strict separation by upholding a program that allowed public employees to provide remedial educational services on-site at sectarian schools. In so doing, it abandoned the presumption that public school employees would necessarily be pressured by the pervasively sectarian surroundings of the parochial school into advancing religious ends.

As the principle of strict separation was losing currency, an alternative constitutional paradigm of neutrality was gaining ground. The cases allowing aid to parochial schools emphasized that those programs were neutral: that is, they made no distinctions between religious and nonreligious private or public schools. Neutrality as a guiding principle likewise surfaced in a related bloc of cases that dealt with access to school space and resources for religious organizations.[3] In each of these cases, the Court extended to religious groups the same access to meeting space or institutional resources as was enjoyed by other, nonreligious groups. For the Supreme Court, neutrality of access to government resources increasingly trumped objections that the receipt of funds or use of resources for religious ends violated the establishment clause.[4]

More immediate signs were equally encouraging for fans of faith-based programs. The new Bush administration had to have been emboldened by prior charitable choice experiments. The charitable choice language attached to the welfare bill of 1996 put religious groups on equal footing with secular ones in seeking welfare funding, while explicitly protecting them in their religious expression and activities. Yet it became law without fanfare and with only the skimpiest of constitutional discussion. Even after its passage, charitable choice received little attention and generated only mild debate. The constitutional objections were muted, with the isolated dissenters confined to academic settings outside the public view.[5] While charitable choice did not exactly rock the world of social service delivery, neither did it do much to muddy the constitutional waters of church-state collaborations. Prior to the presidential campaign of 2000, charitable choice had not markedly altered the broader constitutional landscape of government partnerships with faith-based organizations. Moreover, the adding on of charitable choice language to three subsequent pieces of legislation suggested some momentum behind faith-based legislative proposals.

The soon-to-be-introduced faith-based initiative received one final boost with the *Mitchell v. Helms* decision rendered the summer of 2000. In *Mitchell*, the Court approved a federal statute that made funding to local educational agencies for library, media, and computer materials equally available to both public and private schools, including schools that were predominantly religious. *Mitchell* was the latest in a string of cases allowing public funds to go to religious schools, and was the strongest evidence yet that strict aid separation was withering and giving way to formal neutrality. A four-member plurality on the Court raised the principle of neutrality to new heights. It said that neutrality meant that programs had to be neutral in distributing funds to sectarian schools and other private and public schools, respectively; and aid could not be made contingent at all on the religious persuasion or beliefs of those receiving benefits from the program.

Mitchell was the most serious attack to date on the "pervasively sectarian" standard. Since the high tide of strict no-aid separationism, the Court had explicitly drawn the line of funding at those institutions that were pervasively sectarian. In *Mitchell*, however, the plurality launched an open attack on the standard, characterizing it as "born of bigotry" and calling for its abandonment. The plurality opinion revealed just how far four members of the Court would go in church-state matters. They were sure to be very permissive in allowing aid to religious institutions, and would almost certainly uphold charitable choice. Commentators sympathetic to faith-based programs trumpeted *Mitchell* as marking the end of pervasive sectarianism. In the wake of *Mitchell*, the Center for Public Justice concluded that the standard "has been essentially abandoned by the U.S. Supreme Court."[6] Carl Esbeck, a drafter of the original charitable choice bill, characterized O'Connor's *Mitchell* opinion as having "render[ed] the 'pervasively sectarian' test no longer relevant to the Court's analysis."[7]

FOCAL POINT 6.1

The Continuing Constitutional Clash

Justices Souter and Thomas

President George H. W. Bush successfully appointed two justices to the U.S. Supreme Court: David Souter and Clarence Thomas. While one might assume that justices Souter and Thomas would agree on most decisions, this is far from true. For over a decade, they have voted on opposite sides of establishment clause cases, including recent cases such as *Mitchell v. Helms*, *Good News Club v. Milford Central School*, and *Zelman v. Simmons-Harris*. Based on these precedents, these two would most likely disagree on charitable choice, should it ever reach the Supreme Court.

To understand the current makeup of the Court, it is useful to examine the circumstances of the elder Bush's appointments. Prior to Bush's choice of Souter, President Reagan had nominated Robert Bork to the Supreme Court. Concerned about his conservative ideology and judicial philosophy, Senate Democrats strongly opposed his nomination. The ensuing political battle led to Bork's defeat on the Senate floor by a vote of fifty-eight to forty-two and to the eventually successful nomination of Antonin Scalia. With the Bork controversy freshly in mind, in 1990 President George H. W. Bush wanted a less outspoken nominee to replace retiring justice William Brennan. His choice was David Hackett Souter, a well-respected judge from New Hampshire whose political views were largely unknown, even to the president. What Bush did know was Souter's reputation as an intellectual who made decisions based on precedent. Perhaps hoping to sneak a quiet conservative through the Democratic Senate, Bush nominated Souter. The Senate confirmed "stealth nominee" Souter with little controversy.

Bush's next Court nomination became a point of strong contention. In 1991, Justice Thurgood Marshall, the noted champion of civil rights, retired. To replace him, Bush selected Clarence Thomas, whose most notable public service was as chairman of the U.S. Equal Employment Opportunity Commission (EEOC) from 1982 to 1990. Unlike Justice Souter, however, Clarence Thomas was marked as a political conservative, with well-known positions against affirmative action and abortion. During the Senate's review of Thomas's appointment, Anita Hill, a former EEOC employee, recalled incidents of sexual harassment by Thomas at the commission. A media frenzy ensued in the Senate Judiciary Committee. Pitting Thomas's word against Hill's, the controversy nearly killed the nomination. In the end, however, the Senate confirmed Justice Thomas by a slim margin of fifty-two to forty-eight.

Justice Thomas has aligned himself with the conservative wing of the Court, as everyone expected. However, Justice Souter has proven more of a surprise, often siding with the more liberal justices. The fact that Souter's political opinions were largely unknown helped in his confirmation, but his liberalism on the Court has greatly disappointed conservatives, including the elder Bush. In contrast, Thomas's unashamed conservatism certainly sparked some of the controversy around his appointment, yet because his opinions were so public, his behavior on the bench has generally followed expectations.

Justices Souter and Thomas consistently disagree on First Amendment establishment clause cases. For Thomas, government aid to religious institutions is permissible for civic purposes, as long as funds are given to all types of religions evenhandedly and people have a viable secular alternative to the religious organization. Souter opposes government aid to religious institutions. The opinions of the two justices in *Mitchell v. Helms* exemplify their dissimilarity. Thomas wrote the Court's opinion in which a plurality agreed that government money could aid religiously affiliated schools in purchasing educational equipment and materials, while Souter penned the dissent. Writing for the majority, Thomas explained: "As a way of ensuring neutrality, we have repeatedly considered whether any governmental aid that goes to a religious institution does so 'only as a result of the genuinely independent and private choices of individuals.'" Because funds were neutrally distributed and private individuals made the spending choices, the aid was approved.

In his dissent, Souter denounced these standards, claiming that "the plurality's proposal would replace the principle of no aid with a formula for generous religious support," a position he thought was clearly unconstitutional.

The elder Bush's two Supreme Court nominees differ sharply on First Amendment interpretation, and in many other areas as well. Cases about funding intensely and vocally religious groups, the clash between hiring discretion and civil rights protections, and possibly a direct charitable choice challenge seem certain to make their way to the Supreme Court in upcoming terms. If a Court vacancy occurs during George W. Bush's presidency, his nominee may very well cast the determining vote on such issues. Should that opportunity come to the younger Bush, the political strategy of his father in choosing both Souter and Thomas, and their respective records once securely on the Court, will surely be on his mind.

—*Christopher Upham*

Sources

Cushman, Clare, ed. *The Supreme Court Justices: Illustrated Biographies.* 2d ed. Washington, D.C.: Congressional Quarterly, 1995.

Farber, Daniel, William Eskridge, and Philip Frickly, eds. *1996 Supplement to Cases and Materials on Constitutional Law: Themes for the Constitution's Third Century.* St. Paul, Minn.: West, 1996.

Hanks, Liza W. "Justice Souter: Defining Substantive Neutrality in an Age of Religious Politics." *Stanford Law Review* 48, no. 903 (April 1996).

Media Transparency. "Robert Bork." www.mediatransparency.org/people/robert_bork.htm (accessed 16 October 2002).

Mitchell v. Helms, 530 U.S. 793 (2000).

Urofsky, Melvin, ed. *The Supreme Court Justices: A Biographical Dictionary.* New York: Garland, 1994.

With *Mitchell*, the constitutional sands of church-state jurisprudence continued to shift, even as the presidential campaigns of Bush and Gore actively touted faith-based initiatives. From *Bowen* (1988) through the increasingly accommodationist cases of the 1990s and including *Mitchell* (2000), it was evident that the Court was growing more lenient in allowing the government to send funds in the direction of religious institutions. But if advocates of the initiative thought this meant a free pass on the constitutional front, they were sorely mistaken. The plurality in *Mitchell* had been unable to win a decisive fifth vote, either for their desired burial of pervasive sectarianism or for their broader application of formal neutrality. This gave a glimmer of hope to separationist opponents of faith-based initiatives. Justice O'Connor's more cautious concurring opinion in *Mitchell* (with Justice Breyer joining) refused to accept neutrality as the sole governing principle of aid to religious organizations. Even after *Mitchell*, five justices would still consider public funding of religious organizations according to some standard more demanding than simple neutrality. As O'Connor stated in her *Mitchell* concurrence: "No aid to religious mission remains the governing understanding of the establishment clause as applied to public benefits inuring to religious schools."

Both the *Bowen* and *Mitchell* decisions were tentative and divided enough in their renderings to allow foes of government/religious sector collaboration to argue that the law, as it currently stood, still disapproved of government funds for religious institutions. In other words, the ongoing lack of decisiveness and clarity in establishment clause jurisprudence ensured a lively and hard-fought, if not always enlightening, debate on the constitutionality of the faith-based initiative. That it was a piece of a much larger and highly public policy debate did not bode well for the thoughtfulness or substance of the constitutional debate.

The Constitutional Debate of 2000–2002

Most facets of President Bush's faith-based initiative were noncontroversial constitutionally. Tax incentive proposals to encourage giving to religious service providers generated little or no constitutional fuss, nor did offers of technical assistance for religious groups. The crux of the constitutional debate centered on several relatively simple questions, the answers to which would prove far more complicated. Could government financially aid religious social service organizations? What was the nature of those organizations that would qualify for aid? Finally, what conditions or restrictions would accompany the aid?

Charitable choice contemplated several distinct channels by which aid could flow to religious organizations. Money could go to agencies directly in the form of awarded grants or contracts; it could also reach the provider indirectly, with funds distributed via coupons or vouchers to program recipients, who in turn could use their coupons to select from a menu of providers. Complicating the picture was the Cleveland school voucher case pending before the Supreme Court. The outcome of that decision, all agreed, would have broad implications for the use of vouchers in the parallel social service context. Hence, as the storm gathered over the constitutionality of aid to religious social service providers, all awaited the decision in the *Zelman v. Simmons-Harris* school voucher case.

"Pervasive Sectarianism": Does It Still Matter?

At the heart of the constitutional debate over direct aid was the question of whether the limitation against aid to pervasively sectarian organizations was still viable. Despite the wishes of its drafters, the 1996 charitable choice bill and its progeny had failed to resolve this question. It did, however, along with subsequent court decisions, put *Bowen*'s pervasive sectarianism prohibition in serious peril. The inconsistencies between charitable choice and the "pervasively sectarian" limitations of *Bowen* led to a tug of war over which standard more accurately captured current Supreme Court church-state doctrine. That tug of war had surfaced at the time of the passage of the original charitable choice statute in 1996. John Ashcroft, its main sponsor in the Senate, argued that pervasively sectarian groups were now fully eligible on equal terms with wholly secular ones.[8] Ashcroft was joined in that view by groups like the Center for Public Justice and the Christian Legal Society. Even as they asserted that charitable choice only represented a codification of existing Supreme Court precedent, they proclaimed the death knell of pervasive sectarianism.[9]

In contrast, President Clinton, in signing the original welfare bill into law, interpreted charitable choice as subject to, and to be implemented consistent with, the "pervasively sectarian" standard. Separationist groups like Americans United for Separation of Church and State and the ACLU took the same position, arguing that charitable choice was unconstitutional to the degree it failed to adhere to the constraints of pervasive sectarianism. President Clinton maintained that stance as he signed later charitable choice provisions into law, explicitly construing them as "forbidding the funding of pervasively sectarian organizations."[10]

The debate over the Bush initiative echoed these arguments. Was the "pervasively sectarian" standard still good law? Or had it been displaced by an accommodationist standard that permitted public dollars to go to intensely religious organizations? This debate was largely attributable to the undeniable tensions, if not outright contradictions, in charitable choice itself. Boosters of charitable choice claimed that it only clarified ambiguity regarding the already existing rights of religious nonprofits. A more honest assessment was that the drafters of charitable choice were taking into account where the Court had moved since *Bowen* was rendered in 1988. In other words, charitable choice reflected a statutory redefinition of the bounds of church-state relations, but one that its framers thought would be accepted by a majority of the Supreme Court justices.

The "pervasively sectarian" standard dictated that funding to religious nonprofits be earmarked solely for their secular activities; it required that an organization's religious elements be partitioned off from the secular aims of the funded program, so that funds could not be applied to religious uses. Charitable choice did the opposite, offering explicit legal protection to the religious dimensions, practices, and expressions of funded groups. The statutory safeguards appeared to allow aid to go to groups for whom the spiritual and social service elements were part and parcel, and would not require them to alter their existing practices.

For example, charitable choice explicitly laid out those activities of recipient religious groups that were to be protected. These groups were free to make hiring decisions based on faith requirements and to openly display religious art and imagery; further, they did not have to form a separate corporate entity. These very same practices had previously been identified by the Court as indicative of a pervasive sectarianism that would *disqualify* an organization from public funding. Proximity to a sponsoring church, the presence of religious symbols and art, denominational control, hiring based upon religious criteria, the presence of religious services and activities—all were mentioned in *Bowen* as possible signs of a pervasive sectarianism.

In the end, neither the spirit nor the letter of charitable choice—and its protection of the right of religious nonprofits to fully practice or express their religious beliefs—could be squared with pervasive sectarianism. Charitable choice proponents hoped to ease what they saw as the "secularizing pressure" of funding programs, a pressure that forced non-profits to cleanse their social services of the religious aspects. Implicit in the statute was the notion that the secular and religious elements of intensely religious groups not only could not, but should not, be separated. Charitable choice suggested that it was the very attention to the spiritual, as bound up with other aspects of well-being, that allowed faith-based nonprofits to achieve better results. If anything, an undercurrent of charitable choice was the tacit acknowledgment of the transformative power of religion, and an acknowledgment that those religious values and messages would at some point be shared with a program beneficiary. Thus, charitable choice did more than merely codify existing First Amendment case law; it permitted funding to go to groups that would be labeled pervasively sectarian under *Bowen*. In so doing, it "pushe[d] the envelope of existing judicial interpretations of the establishment clause."[11]

The substance of the legal debate in 2000–2002 occurred at the intersection of these contradictions between charitable choice and the "pervasively sectarian" standard. The *Mitchell* decision, while bolstering the arguments of charitable choice proponents, did not definitively foreclose the arguments of the opponents. While the plurality opinion revealed the "pervasively sectarian" standard to be on its deathbed, Justice O'Connor's hedging left the door ajar.

Sorting Out the Voices

The voices weighing in on the constitutionality of aid to religious institutions were many and varied. With constitutionality hanging on the specific issue of the viability of pervasive sectarianism, the positions of those who publicly addressed faith-based policies tended to flow from, and reflect, their underlying preferences on the appropriate relationship between the church and the state.

This larger constitutional backdrop for the faith-based initiative was one of rival paradigms; with the principle of neutrality clearly gaining currency and separationist doctrine in decline, opponents of faith-based initiatives were relegated to waging a rearguard action.[12] At issue was just how much of the law of separation remained in the evolving realm of establishment clause doctrine.

On one side of the divide were those who would maintain as high and strong a metaphorical "wall of separation" between religion and government as possible. This traditionally has meant opposing any governmental aid whatsoever to parochial schools or other religious institutions. Advocacy groups like the American Civil Liberties Union and Americans United for Separation of Church and State represent the full-fledged secularist position. Unmoved by recent Supreme Court decisions, they maintain that the "pervasively sectarian" standard still stands, and that charitable choice fails to protect the religious liberty rights of beneficiaries.

Separationists vigorously opposed the Bush initiative on constitutional grounds. *Mitchell* notwithstanding, they contended that the government is precluded from funding intensely religious groups who will not or cannot separate the religious from the secular dimensions of their services. Public funding would inevitably promote and advance religion, in violation of the establishment clause. Moreover, the mode of financing is unimportant. Vouchers are as objectionable as direct aid. As long as public dollars end up in the coffers of religious institutions, separationists see the establishment clause as being violated.

Separationists who took this position on the Bush initiative were motivated by divergent philosophies. Some came from a purely secularist angle, strenuously opposing any material assistance whatsoever to religious organizations. They tended to be driven by their sense that religion is an undesirable presence in public life, one that causes division, narrow-mindedness, and conflict. Other separationists opposed the initiative out of a concern for religious entities and what might happen to them if they availed themselves of public dollars. Their worry was that government money inevitably brings pressures to alter a group's primary mission or focus. Their fear was the perversion of the religious group, and the loss of its prophetic voice calling the government or society to account.

Regardless of their motives, the separationists agreed on one thing: No direct public aid should flow to religious institutions for religious activities. Funding had to be limited to secular purposes alone. The maintaining of the "pervasively sectarian" standard was critical to this position. For secular separationists, if a recipient group was so sectarian that it could not partition off its religious activities, funding meant that the government would be unacceptably advancing religion. For religious separationists, funds to pervasively religious groups meant the intrusion of government into those groups' activities, a presence that was sure to entangle and interfere with the work of the church. They saw no need to revise or alter the long-standing practice of funding groups like Lutheran Social Services or Catholic Charities or the Salvation Army. Those organizations take care to create separate entities through which public funds are channeled, thus insulating their religious identity and mission.

Those in this camp read *Mitchell v. Helms* as maintaining the pervasive sectarianism restriction, albeit narrowly. An article in *Liberty* magazine reflected this position when it argued that, *Mitchell* notwithstanding, "if a religious institution cannot segregate its religious from its secular activities, then government aid to that institution is therefore unconstitutional."[13] Rabbi David Saperstein, director of the Religious Action Center of Reform Judaism, gave voice to the separationist position in his testimony on H.R. 7 before the House Constitution subcommittee. He asserted that the "constitutional prohibition against direct government funding of sectarian organizations" survived *Mitchell v. Helms*. In opposing the House version of the faith-based initiative, Saperstein stressed the "special concerns associated with the flow of government funds to pervasively religious organizations."[14] For separationists, even if the doctrine of pervasive sectarianism as a constitutional barrier were to fall, the policy concerns behind it would still deny public funds to religious entities.[15]

In contrast, neutrality reflects a far more accommodationist position. Promoters of this standard support government aid for religious activities and organizations, provided it is applied evenhandedly and without favoring a particular faith or denomination. For those who argued for neutrality with respect to faith-based initiatives, the "pervasively sectarian" standard was unacceptable. To them, banning intensely religious groups from public contracting offended the very ideas of evenhandedness and fairness. They acknowledged that public funding had to address a public problem or advance secular purposes. But provided this criterion was met, the extent of a provider group's religiosity was not pertinent to its qualifications to address a problem and receive public funds. Neutralists also felt that the Constitution allowed there to be incidental benefits to the religious side of the funded organizations as long as the secular ends were met. Unsurprisingly, those in this camp argued that *Mitchell* had put an end to the pervasive sectarian limits. The Institute for Public Affairs, representing the perspective of the orthodox Jewish community, declared definitively that the "doctrine [of pervasive sectarianism] has now lost all relevance" after *Mitchell*.[16]

As with the separationists, accommodationists vary widely in perspective. For example, Ron Sider of Evangelicals for Social Action, in supporting faith-based initiatives, argued for neutrality in government funding of religious and secular organizations, provided it is based on specified secular outcomes. He and others supported the right of faith-based organizations to express their faith freely; the religious liberty of recipients could be protected, they argued, by the use of vouchers or intermediary agencies.

For others, neutrality did not go far enough in paving the way for religious groups' entry into the public square. These voices, typically overtly Christian, were embodied in people like Pat Robertson and Jerry Falwell. They had two objections to neutrality. First, neutrality was unacceptable if it meant that religious groups would have to submit to the regulatory and oversight machinery of the government as the cost of admission to public programs. Religious providers, they asserted, ought to be able to participate in the benefits of public dollars without government meddling that might compromise the religious purity of the group. Second, they rejected a neutrality based on a vision of religious pluralism. They desired a public square open to Christian groups, but were openly distrustful of public funds flowing to religious groups like the Nation of Islam, the Church of Christian Science, and the Unification Church.

Constitutional Differences: Imagined and Real

The debate over the faith-based initiative polarized the divide between the neutralists and the separationists. Unfortunately, it captured little of the nuance and complexity of the actual state of the law. Instead, the media consistently sought out the most hyperbolic figures who were good for pithy sound bites, but did little to shine light on the actual constitutional questions surrounding the initiative. Barry Lynn of Americans United for Separation of Church and State is emblematic, accusing the president of believing that "government should use religion to solve all of the nation's social problems" and of wanting to "merge church and state into a single bureaucracy."[17] On the other end of the spectrum, Pat Robertson is viewed by many in the media as a prime spokesperson for the religious right. Hence, he caused a stir by labeling the faith-based initiative "appalling" because it would make "the Unification Church, the Hare Krishnas, and the Church of Scientology ... financial beneficiaries ... of government grants to religious charities."[18]

Though one would not know it from reading the exchanges in the press, the actual differences of opinion on the constitutionality of charitable choice–type provisions are relatively small among more objective, less partisan analysts. Serious constitutional scholars disagree primarily on the extent to which charitable choice captures or diverges from current Supreme Court sentiment. Scholars offer three differing views.

One view is represented by the opinion of David Ackerman, a legislative attorney analyzing charitable choice for the Congressional Research Service. In his analysis of the *Mitchell* case, Ackerman placed Justice O'Connor with the separationist bloc for deciding that religious providers be granted direct aid for secular use only. But he also concluded that O'Connor was with the four accommodationist/neutralist justices in holding that "whether a recipient institution is pervasively sectarian is no longer a constitutionally determinative factor." Finally, he suggested that the inconsistencies within charitable choice raise lingering questions of its constitutionality under the establishment clause. "The intent of charitable choice [appears to be] that the religious entities receiving direct public aid be able to employ their faiths in carrying out the subsidized programs; and to the extent they do so, a constitutional question seems to exist even under the Court's revised interpretation of the establishment clause."[19]

Ackerman and others who share his view read charitable choice legislation as allowing practices that are by no means clearly permissible under the establishment clause; these include explicitly permitting grant-receiving religious organizations to hire based on religion, to maintain overt religious displays in the workplace, and to practice their religious beliefs. Moreover, charitable choice tries to have it both ways, barring the funding of "sectarian worship, instruction, or proselytization" while simultaneously protecting the right of religious groups to fully practice and express their beliefs. These are not mutually exclusive categories. For many evangelical organizations, the sharing of faith—proselytization—is an essential component of their religious practice. Furthermore, the underlying spirit of charitable choice is at odds with the notion of nonestablishment. Subsidizing religious groups in social welfare programs is based on a tacit acknowledgment of the transformative power of religion, and the presumption that it will be shared or transmitted at some point in service delivery. The belief that religious groups have a special capacity to serve and address problems effectively suggests that they need to be able to share the tenets of their particular belief.[20] Thus, government dollars would be used to promote religion. Because charitable choice pushes the envelope of existing judicial interpretations of the establishment clause, it leaves "charitable choice programs vulnerable to the possibility of litigation."[21]

In what is the most exhaustive legal analysis of the faith-based initiative to date, George Washington University law professors Ira Lupu and Robert Tuttle see the matter somewhat differently. They characterize charitable choice as roughly "approximat[ing] the boundaries of the Constitution" and conclude that pervasive sectarianism is essentially a dead letter. No longer does the nature of the organization receiving funds matter constitutionally. Rather, the Supreme Court is likely to focus on the nature of the services provided. So while the religious characteristics of providers are constitutionally indistinguishable from those of secular providers, the Constitution nevertheless forbids direct aid to be put to religious uses.[22]

Based on this distinction, it is the nature of the program that becomes determinative. Charitable choice was largely unobjectionable, since its focus on welfare to work opportunities did not implicate or demand "any sort of religious commitment or conversion" on the part of the recipient. In stark contrast, Lupu and Tuttle see serious constitutional problems in the faith-based law that Bush implemented as governor in Texas. That law extended the partnership with faith-based groups beyond welfare and work to include programs addressing substance abuse, juvenile delinquency, and adult criminal recidivism. These faith-based programs were "transformative in the deepest sense," seeking to "change the fundamental beliefs and practices of participants in order to turn them away from destructive behavior and give them the strength to resist such behavior in the future." In the view of Lupu and Tuttle, the "project of awakening or deepening spiritual faith" that is presumed in these programs is simply beyond the competence of the state. While harnessing religious transformation may be the best means to combat personal and social pathologies, the authors see the Constitution as preventing government from using the instrument of religious transformation for the government's ends.[23]

According to this position, neutrality demands undifferentiated treatment of secular and religious groups, no matter how religious the latter might be, as long as the services provided are indistinguishable. Constitutional problems arise when religion lies at the very center of the services provided and not just at the margins. The White House itself appears to have adopted this view in its most recent executive action. In extending faith-based regulations to two more federal agencies, the president's executive orders essentially allow funds to go to intensely religious organizations as long as the government does not fund inherently religious activities. Rather, the religious activities are to be separated in time and place from the government-funded services.

Both Ackerman's view and the view put forth by Lupu and Tuttle hold that public money cannot go to inherently religious activities, even if there are secular benefits. "The government may not directly finance a job training program that uses Biblical materials to teach about good work habits, or a 12-step program, for recovery from substance addiction, that urges participants to have faith in a higher power."[24] A third view takes a more positive and permissible view of neutrality. It would allow public funds to be applied to explicitly religious activities, provided those religious activities further legitimate public goals or objectives and the programs are truly voluntary in nature. Steve Monsma, Ron Sider, and others argue that publicly funded programs are permissible even if they advance religion, as long as the religious benefits are incidental to the secular ones, and beneficiaries can choose from a range of other, secular alternatives to that program.[25] A Bible-based prison ministry run with government funding would be constitutional, as long as participation was voluntary and as long as functionally equivalent secular programs were offered.

The differences in these three positions, while real, are nothing like those suggested by the distorted and skewed public debate over the Bush plan. The key question of direct aid revolves around how government should balance the constitutional requirement to protect the religious character of intensely religious groups that receive funding, on the one hand, and the constitutional requirement not to fund religious activities themselves, on the other. The commentary on the constitutionality of faith-based programs has centered on what the Supreme Court might decide. Unfortunately, there simply is not a conclusive or authoritative answer to the question of how the Court would resolve a constitutional challenge to a publicly funded program that simultaneously advances a secular purpose and religious activities.[26] This is the inconsistency of charitable choice itself, and the question that remains for the future.

Zelman and the Indirect Funding of Faith-Based Social Services

Although the constitutional parameters of direct aid to religious groups remain unclear, the status of the constitutionality of indirect aid became much clearer in the summer of 2002 with the Supreme Court's much-anticipated school voucher decision in *Zelman v. Simmons-Harris*. *Zelman* marked a major development in one of the longest running and most controversial of establishment clause questions: the constitutionality of vouchers for private school tuition. Given the parallels between school vouchers and the use of similar indirect payment mechanisms for social welfare programs, the Supreme Court's vote to uphold the constitutionality of the Cleveland voucher program was a big victory for the backers of faith-based social services. Previously, opponents of faith-based social services had argued that the financing mechanism was unimportant; the determinative fact establishing a constitutional violation was the end result of public dollars in the coffers of religious institutions. Friend and foe of faith-based programs agreed that *Zelman* essentially debunked this position.

Zelman involved a challenge to the Ohio Pilot Project Scholarship Program, which provided school tuition vouchers for students in the Cleveland city schools. The vouchers, distributed on the basis of financial need, could be spent at any of a number of schools. On its face, the program made no distinctions between, and expressed no preference for or against, public or private schools. However, voucher recipients were limited to participating schools—those willing to accept the vouchers. While those included both public and private institutions, many public schools refused to participate. As a result, 96 percent of the students who received vouchers ultimately enrolled in religious schools.

The Court upheld the voucher scholarship program by a narrow five-to-four vote. The majority opinion rested squarely upon the principle of neutrality. As long as the voucher program was neutral with respect to religion, the Court said, it was not susceptible to an establishment clause challenge. Here aid went to religious schools only as the result of the independent decisions of individual parents, thus avoiding the danger of government endorsement of or support for religion. Assistance was available "to a broad class of citizens who, in turn, direct[ed] government aid to religious schools wholly as a result of their own genuine and independent private choice." Even though the vast majority of the tuition aid ended up with religious schools, the majority concluded that the parental choice insulated the voucher program from carrying government's endorsement or approval. The program was neutral on its face, providing no incentive or encouragement to use vouchers at religious rather than secular schools.

Most significant for Court watchers was Justice O'Connor's embrace of this reasoning. With four justices comfortably settled on either side of the neutrality/separation divide, any close establishment clause questions invariably come down to the ever-cautious Justice O'Connor.[27] Her critical vote in *Zelman* hinged on the "primary effect" prong of the *Lemon* test and the government's avoiding the appearance of religious "endorsement." The presence or absence of governmental endorsement depended on two questions: Was the aid administered in a neutral fashion, without consideration for the religious status of beneficiaries or service providers? And did beneficiaries have a genuine choice among religious and nonreligious organizations?

O'Connor determined that the Cleveland voucher program met both of these demands. Aid was available to families on the basis of financial need without regard to religious affiliation. Moreover, both religious and nonreligious schools were free to participate in the program, and the government provided no financial incentive for parents to select one over the other. Hence, the program satisfied O'Connor's nonendorsement criteria.

Zelman sent strong signals, both general and specific. On a broader level, it was the latest and most striking shift away from strict no-aid separationism toward neutrality. The separationist vision of neutrality— no funding that would aid or support religion, Jefferson's metaphorical wall of separation between things religious and governmental—is a thing of the past. A clear consensus from the *Zelman* opinions—conceded, if not approved of, even by the dissenters—is that neutrality today means something other than separation. It means governmental evenhandedness toward things religious and secular. The state should not favor religion;

neither should it subordinate it. Equal treatment—of religious entities vis-à-vis secular ones, and between competing or differing religious faiths and traditions—is what is required. The *Zelman* decision "opened the door for a wide range of relationships, once thought impermissible, between government and religious institutions."[28] What mattered, the decision said, was genuine private choice. Neither the degree of religious content of the program nor the religiosity of the provider had any constitutional significance, provided genuine private choice for the beneficiary existed. In other words, the pervasive sectarianism of the institution was irrelevant.

The specific implications of *Zelman* for voucher-based social service delivery programs were also clear. If vouchers were okay for schools, then "you can surely have vouchers for adults who need substance abuse treatment and want to get that treatment from a religious program."[29] Even voucher opponents conceded that flat constitutional objections to indirect aid would fail in the wake of *Zelman*. Charles Haynes of the anti-voucher Freedom Forum First Amendment Center foresaw that "voucher arrangements for government grants to religious groups for social services are now certainly going to be seen as not only possible, but constitutional. . . . [*Zelman* demonstrated that] the court does not any longer worry too much that government money may eventually end up with religious institutions."[30] Lupu and Tuttle concur that "as applied to social service programs, the voucher device would permit government to finance beneficiaries who choose to obtain services at faith-based providers, so long as secular providers were among the available choices." After *Zelman*, vouchers are "an important solution to the federal constitutional problems posed by government relationships with faith-intensive private entities."[31]

Consequently, social service voucher programs that include religious service providers appear to be constitutional, as long as they are appropriately (i.e., neutrally) constructed. Is the statute on its face neutral toward religious and secular social service providers? Are vouchers available to program recipients without reference to their religious preferences or beliefs, or lack thereof? Does the program offer real choices for beneficiaries, with a menu of both religious and nonreligious providers? If the answer to these questions is "yes," then a voucher program is likely constitutional.

Zelman does not absolutely guarantee that a majority of the Supreme Court would uphold a faith-based social service voucher program. The

Court's treatment of vouchers in the context of social welfare services might not necessarily mirror its treatment of them in the educational setting. However, aid to schools arguably raises greater establishment concerns, since it involves the instruction of elementary and secondary school children who are more impressionable and susceptible to religious indoctrination. By comparison, most welfare programs involve adult beneficiaries, who are less vulnerable to heavy-handed religious proselytizing or coercion. Moreover, religious instruction might well be more easily integrated into broader educational programs supported by school vouchers. Hence, the case for the constitutionality of vouchers in a faith-based social service program is likely to be at least as strong as the case for school vouchers.

Following *Zelman*, federal constitutional challenges to voucher-based social service programs will likely be limited primarily to questions of implementation. *Zelman* virtually assures that voucher-oriented programs will be at the center of attempts to bring religious providers into the sphere of social service provision. Especially when the state wishes to preserve the overt religious dimensions of services, vouchers are the preferred mechanism of funding. President Bush wasted no time in adopting this strategy, calling in his 2003 State of the Union address for $600 million in voucher-based drug treatment funding. As law professor Tuttle notes: "a voucher program is going to give you infinitely greater latitude in the [religious] content of the service provided."[32] For program administrators who want to avoid constitutional challenges while allowing faith-based organizations the freedom to maintain the religious dimension of their services, vouchers are the likely vehicle of choice.

State Constitutions:
The Next Frontier in Church-State Relations

Zelman does not necessarily close the door on the debate over vouchers, especially with regard to their implementation. Vouchers may not always be a practical or feasible choice. The paucity of secular providers in certain geographic locations may mean that genuine choice is impossible. Similarly, some services are dominated by religiously affiliated providers, rendering the requirement of nonreligious options difficult to satisfy. So despite the removal of constitutional barriers, the unworkability of voucher-based programs in some circumstances, in fact, means that the doubts surrounding direct aid programs are still highly relevant.

More significantly, the next frontier in church-state law has received virtually no public attention amid the furor surrounding the Bush faith-based initiative. Many state constitutions contain explicit provisions, generally known as Blaine amendments, which prohibit public funds from flowing to religious schools or other religious institutions.[33] While Blaine amendments vary widely from state to state, they typically are stricter and more explicit than the First Amendment of the U.S. Constitution in banning government money to religious organizations or instruction. Some states merely replicate the federal establishment clause, while others explicitly outlaw public funding of religious organizations or places of worship. Still others explicitly preclude funding of religious schools. Only now are the more sophisticated church-state scholars directing their attention to state constitutions as the next constitutional barrier to government-funded social services.

FOCAL POINT 6.2

Blaine Amendments in State Constitutions

In the wake of the U.S. Supreme Court decision approving of school vouchers (*Zelman v. Simmons-Harris*, 2002), many consider the so-called Blaine amendments the final constitutional firewall against greater church-state interaction in America. In 1875, James Blaine, a U.S. senator and three-time presidential candidate from the state of Maine, proposed an amendment to the U.S. Constitution that would bar the government from giving financial aid to any "sectarian institution." When Blaine's effort to amend the U.S. Constitution failed, he turned his attention to state constitutions, where he achieved much greater success. Blaine amendments in one form or another were incorporated into a majority of state constitutions. Presently, variations of the original Blaine amendment can be found in the constitutions of thirty-six states and the commonwealth of Puerto Rico.

Advocates on both sides of the church-state divide have trained their sights on the federal constitutionality of these state Blaine amendments as the next crucial establishment clause battleground. That fight is likely to be fought in the arena of school choice, dominated in recent years by the debate over the constitutionality of publicly funded vouchers that can be applied by families to pay for private parochial school tuition. The U.S. Supreme Court took a major step in resolving that debate in *Zelman*, when it narrowly upheld a school voucher program for students living in Cleveland, Ohio, finding that the program did not violate the establishment clause.

Rather than concede defeat, school voucher opponents began to search for the next line of defense. Blaine amendments go much further than the First Amendment of the U.S. Constitution in explicitly prohibiting any public funding of religious institutions. If taken at face value, the language of the Blaine amendments would appear to prevent public funds from flowing to private religious institutions, whether for education or to support social services. If these state amendments are found to trump the U.S. Constitution, they would likely stop the voucher movement in its tracks. Proponents of school vouchers are eager to litigate the Blaine amendments, despite the apparent clarity of the language banning public funding of sectarian organizations. They are relatively confident that the state constitutional provisions would be subordinated to the federal constitution.

That confidence stems in large part from the history of anti-Catholic bias underlying the original movement for Blaine amendments. The original push to add Blaine provisions to state constitutions occurred in the late 1880s as the United States experienced waves of Catholic immigration from European countries. That influx generated strong anti-Catholic sentiment in many parts of the nation. At the time, it was generally assumed that the public schools, known as "common" schools, would include religious instruction, but of the dominant Protestant persuasion. Catholic schools were typically referred to as "sectarian" schools, and would instruct their students in Catholicism. Since almost all Blaine amendments specifically bar aid to "sectarian" institutions, school choice advocates argue that the amendments are rooted in the anti-Catholic animus of the late 1800s. They contend that the amendments therefore violate the equal protection clause of the U.S. Constitution.

The constitutional battle is thus joined over the potential impact of the Blaine amendments and the extent to which their seemingly plain language might be qualified by the intent underlying their passage. The focus on Blaine amendments has effectively shifted the debate from the federal level of government to the state level. As of early 2004, the Supreme Court has heard oral arguments in *Locke v. Davey*, a Washington state case that hinges directly on the constitutionality of that state's Blaine amendment.

While future court rulings on Blaine amendments will determine the fate of educational vouchers, they could prove equally important for faith-based social programs. Many Blaine amendments apply specifically to education and sectarian schools; others, however, are more broadly drafted to bar public funds to any religious organization. For example, the Colorado constitution prohibits appropriations "for charitable . . . or benevolent purposes to any person, corporation or community not under the absolute control of the state, nor to any denominational or sectarian institution or association." The Florida version bars state revenues from being used to aid "any church, sect, or religious denomination or in aid of any sectarian institution." Blaine amendments differ broadly from state to state, and the legality of some faith-based aid programs may have to await litigation of Blaine provisions within individual states.

—*Jeremy Brieve*

Sources

Colorado constitution, article 5, section 34.

Florida constitution, article 1, section 3.

Kirkpatrick, David. "A Blaine Amendment Update." www.schoolreport.com/schoolreport/articles/blaine_7_00.htm (July 2000).

Komer, Richard, and Clint Bolick. "School Choice: The Next Step: The State Constitutional Challenge." www.ij.org/editorial/choice_next.shtml (1 July 2002).

Lardner, Lynford. "How Far Does the Constitution Separate Church and State?" *American Political Science Review* 45, no. 1 (March 1951): 121.

Where do state constitutions stand relative to the U.S. Constitution on aid to religious institutions? This question is likely to play out in the context of school vouchers, but with obvious repercussions in the faith-based social services realm. Some state legislatures will almost surely push school choice legislation on the heels of *Zelman*, thereby bringing Blaine amendments into the courts. Voucher foes and friends alike are eying litigation over whether stricter state prohibitions are viable in the face of *Zelman* as the next round in the fight. Voucher opponents are beginning to focus on state constitutional provisions as the last line of defense in preventing government aid to religious institutions. Prior to *Zelman*, there had been little motivation for separationists to seek additional protections or remedies under state constitutions. But as the Supreme Court has grown consistently more amenable to government funding of religious institutions, the obvious strategic choice is to argue that such actions run afoul of the applicable state constitution.

Those sympathetic to government/religious sector collaboration are also intent on focusing on state constitutions—and attacking what they see as the most significant remaining obstacle. The Institute for Justice, a pro-voucher legal advocacy group, has adopted a conscious strategy of bringing lawsuits in a handful of states to test the state constitutions there, either to resolve the suits consistent with *Zelman* or to create sufficient conflicts in the law that the Supreme Court will get involved.

Given the degree of variation in state constitutions on the question, it is impossible to generalize on likely legal outcomes. Even the most expert church-state analysts are wary of predicting how these state constitutional battles might go. The most interesting wrinkle is the extent to which courts would analyze the historical motives behind the funding limitations in state constitutions. Given that the impetus for the enactment of the Blaine amendments historically grew out of anti-Catholic animus, state constitutional barriers to funding of religious organizations might well be considered discriminatory by the courts. Blaine amendments also present a philosophical dilemma for the justices, given their natural orientations. Those more conservative justices who are inclined to support accommodationist establishment clause doctrine and thereby strike down state barriers are, at the same time, theoretically predisposed to defer to state judges responsible for interpreting state law. The opposite is true for the more liberal bloc of justices. In the end, the complexity and diversity of state constitutional provisions ensure that this next battle—for both parochial school and social service voucher-based programs—will be an arduous and multifaceted one.[34]

The Faith-Based Initiative's Third Rail: The Hiring Issue

With *Mitchell* and *Zelman* further weakening the constitutional case against the faith-based initiative, its opponents cast about for an issue that might slow the momentum of the legislation. As we have noted, they stumbled upon a winner in their challenge to the right of funded organizations to make hiring decisions based on religious belief. Stoking perceptions of publicly funded discrimination proved to be a more effective brake on the progress of the faith-based plan than they possibly could have realized. Nothing ultimately proved more damaging to the political popularity of faith-based initiatives than the objections to the hiring autonomy of publicly supported religious nonprofits.

For religious groups intent on preserving their character, the right to hire individuals whose beliefs are in accordance with their religious identity or mission is a central imperative. The Bush initiative recognized this, proposing the same kind of hiring protections that were originally set forth in the 1996 charitable choice statute. These charitable choice provisions specified that religious nonprofits would not have to forfeit their prerogatives to make personnel decisions based on the religious commitments of applicants.

Opponents of the faith-based initiative, sensing an issue with greater emotional appeal than the constitutionality of church-state separation, portrayed the protections as a guise for allowing overly zealous religious organizations to practice intolerance through discriminatory hiring practices.[35] This argument was to prove highly effective in undermining the proposal. The uproar that swirled around this issue caught the public's attention as no other aspect of the faith-based proposal had; in the end, it was a central factor in sinking the proposal's popularity.[36]

This issue personified the disconnect between the public rhetoric and the actual merits of the proposal. Nowhere was the gap between the crudeness of the public exchanges and the actual complexities of the law greater than in the exchanges over whether religious providers who receive funds could, constitutionally, exercise hiring preferences on the basis of religion. Democratic congressmen who opposed the plan characterized religiously based hiring rights as "government funded religious discrimination." One charged that "if Bob Jones University qualifies for charitable choice dollars, they can put up a sign that says 'no Catholics need apply here.' "[37] Representative Bobby Scott, one of the most ardent opponents of charitable choice, described it as "federally funded religious bigotry." Senate majority leader Tom Daschle conjectured that it would "be a guise for intolerance, because it permits faith-based organizations to hire only those job applicants who can agree with the religious basis of their programs."[38]

Interest groups chimed in. The Coalition Against Religious Discrimination decried the initiative as "turn[ing] back the clock on civil rights." Nancy Zirkin of the American Association of University Women claimed that it "would open women to all kinds of employment discrimination that is currently prohibited by federal law." Barry Lynn of Americans United for Separation of Church and State warned that the proposal "is intended to permit some fundamentalist organization to put a sign on the door saying, 'no Jews need apply.' "[39]

An eclectic array of voices weighed in on the other side. Jeffrey Rosen, writing in *The New Republic*, favored the right to hire based on religious beliefs, arguing that the same protection exists for any group, secular or religious. He offered the analogy of Planned Parenthood, which avails itself of public funds while retaining its freedom to hire based on its values and mission.[40] Carl Esbeck, a primary drafter of the original charitable choice language, asserted that religious organizations can "hardly be expected to sustain their religious vision without the ability to employ individuals who share the tenets of the faith."[41] The Center for Public Justice's Steve Lazarus similarly contended that "[a]ll should be free to hire staff that reflect their principled convictions, religious or secular."[42] For those of the neutralist persuasion, religious discrimination in hiring simply meant giving religious groups the same rights given to their secular counterparts to hire those whose beliefs were consistent with their mission or philosophy.

Once again, the constitutional merits of the issue were considerably more complicated and multifaceted than either side presented them to be. A pair of in-depth constitutional analyses of the hiring issue that were conducted following the imbroglio over the Bush initiative reached the same qualified conclusions: that the current state of constitutional doctrine probably protects religious providers' hiring autonomy, but that this is only the beginning of a very complicated legal analysis. Those studies, one conducted by John Orr and the other by Ira Lupu and Robert Tuttle, both concluded that religious service providers, under federal constitutional law, would likely enjoy the exception from general antidiscrimination civil rights statutes that has existed for religious groups generally.[43] Churches and other religious groups for decades have had exempt status under the Civil Rights Act, which permits them to take religious affiliation or conviction into account in their hiring and personnel decisions. That exception was validated in a unanimous decision by the Supreme Court in *Corporation of the Presiding Bishop v. Amos* (1987).

That exemption, contained in Title VII of the Civil Rights Act, does not specifically include *publicly funded* faith-based service providers, however. Initiative opponents responded to the *Amos* decision by arguing that public funding disqualifies religious groups from that special status. They see the extension of the religion-specific hiring exemption to situations involving federal contracts or grants as tantamount to governmental endorsement of discriminatory hiring. Indeed, they turn the neutrality argument back on its supporters: they contend that it is incongruous to treat a religious provider as a neutral dispenser of secular services for funding purposes, while simultaneously giving it special allowance to hire religiously compatible workers and employees on grounds that they are essential to carrying out its institutional mission.

Faith-based backers counter that the more the Court warms to formal neutrality, the more it is likely to extend hiring autonomy to publicly funded religious groups. They point to the publicly funded secular organizations that hire only those applicants who are aligned with their ideological or policy aims, and who can be counted on to carry them out. Faith-based supporters argue that if publicly funded religious charities were to lose their right to hire as they choose, it would represent a constraint on religious groups that is not imposed on secular organizations. The unequivocal message would be one of government bias against religious providers. Hence, neutrality demands that religious organizations' rights of freedom of association and religious free exercise outweigh the discrimination claims of individuals.

Both the Orr and the Tuttle/Lupu studies conclude that the Supreme Court likely would extend the holding in *Amos* to faith-based nonprofits involved in administering government-funded programs. First, the *Amos* case revealed an expansive approach in applying the Title VII exemption to faith-based groups. Orr additionally relies on the fact that the Civil Rights Act itself pointedly omitted religion from the listed forms of discrimination explicitly prohibited in federal contracts in Title VI. Had Congress intended to outlaw religion-based employment discrimination by faith-based organizations in federal contracts, it would have been explicit in saying so. "When Congress is silent about the matter, the Title VII exemption applies," Orr argues. Moreover, Orr found it significant that Congress invoked language from the Civil Rights Act in the original charitable choice law, suggesting that legislators wished the religious exemption to apply.[44]

To bolster his analysis, Orr provides a thorough review of the case law relevant to the hiring rights of publicly funded religious groups. He cites a litany of federal and state cases from the past two decades in which courts upheld the use of religion-based employment criteria by religious organizations, even when they were receiving public financial assistance. Based upon these cases, he posits that the courts would likely extend to publicly funded religious groups the freedom to hire whom they please when providing social services. Even when federal assistance is present, courts have consistently allowed "the use of religion-based employment criteria when the theological grounds for their use are clearly documented in the organizations' creeds, charters, or by-laws and when federally-funded positions are not used to advance religion."[45]

Law professors Ira Lupu and Robert Tuttle carefully hedge their conclusions on the hiring issue.[46] They suggest that the U.S. Constitution is not determinative on whether funded religious groups retain the exemption for religious hiring; the decisive factor, they argue, is whether the statute creating the funding stream is explicit in granting hiring protections to funded groups. Since charitable choice provisions explicitly contain that exemption, groups receiving funds pursuant to those programs are presumably safe in hiring only coreligionists. Many other federal programs, however, have no such protections.

The picture is further convoluted by complex and varied state and local laws that pertain to employment discrimination. A survey of state laws undertaken by Lupu and Tuttle reveals that many states have employment discrimination provisions that simultaneously grant exemptions from these provisions for religious groups. In some of those states, however, groups lose the exemption when they accept contracts from the state. In addition, many major and midsized cities have antidiscrimination laws with no built-in exemption for religious employers. This raises important questions as to whether and when the U.S. Constitution or federal statutes would preempt these state and local laws. An explicit statutory exemption from the federal civil rights hiring protections does not automatically override state and local antidiscrimination laws. Congress may explicitly exempt a program from state laws, but has not done so in the charitable choice laws.

In short, the issue of hiring autonomy for religious service providers under state and local laws is an intricate and complicated one. The questions it raises are thorny, even for the supposed experts in the field. Nor can this complexity be easily simplified for public consumption, making the issue susceptible to demagoguery. That opponents of the faith-based initiative have used the discrimination argument to wide success assures that it will be front and center in any future legislative or public debate.[47] Hence, the status of federally funded religious groups' rights relative to antidiscrimination hiring laws will be central to the future of any faith-based programs.

The Litigation Front:
Faith-Based Initiatives in the Lower Courts

Another legal development unfolding below the public's radar screen is the resort to litigation as a tool for challenging faith-based programs. At least half a dozen lawsuits involving state-subsidized religious social agencies are at various stages in the lower courts, and that number is steadily rising. While none of these suits directly challenges the 1996 charitable choice law, as a body they loom large in shifting the constitutional debate from the abstract to the actual context of faith-based programs.

These factual contexts are likely to prove critical in resolving questions of constitutionality. If the Supreme Court follows the pattern set in the 1988 *Bowen* decision, it is unlikely to sweep aside charitable choice or other faith-based programs created by law. The *Bowen* Court upheld a statute on its face that included religious organizations in a larger pool of potential recipients of federal funds. In returning the case to the trial court, the justices stressed the importance of scrutinizing programs as they were implemented to see if the grantees were actually using the money to impermissibly advance a religious mission or goal. In other words, an establishment clause violation had to be found in the details and circumstances of the programs as administered, and not in some speculative or hypothetical fear based on the language of the law enacting the program. Charitable choice, like the statute at issue in *Bowen*, is neutral on its face toward religious and secular social welfare agencies, requiring the government to treat the two groups evenhandedly. *Bowen* insists that programs funded under charitable choice be analyzed as they actually operate to see if they advance religious ends. To this extent, *Bowen* leaves the government with plenty of room to fund religious organizations engaged in secular enterprises.

On the flip side, charitable choice does not ensure that any faith-based program will necessarily pass constitutional muster. The creation of a program consistent with the provisions of charitable choice does not eliminate the need to analyze it under existing establishment clause precedent. As suggested in *Bowen*, questions of constitutionality will require delving into the details of a program's execution. In the past, the discussion of the constitutionality of church-state partnerships has generally taken place on a far too abstract level. The particulars of actual programs, rather than speculation or theorizing, must be used to prove an unacceptable religious establishment. For this reason, the litigation bubbling up from the trial courts and lower appellate courts will be pivotal in putting factual flesh on the establishment clause bones. Only through such decisions will the parameters of what constitutes acceptable interaction between religious groups and the government in real-world settings be shaped.

One of the first legal challenges to a faith-based program was *American Jewish Congress and Texas Civil Rights Project v. Bost*. In the summer of 2000, the American Jewish Congress (AJC) sued the state of Texas to recoup $8,000 in state funds given to the Jobs Partnership of Washington County. The lawsuit charged that the job training and placement program, funded by the Texas Department of Human Services, was "permeated" by Protestant evangelical Christianity in violation of both the Texas and U.S. constitutions. The Jobs Partnership's curriculum intertwined basic employment skills with biblical teaching and study, and funds went to purchasing Bibles for participating clients. The money also paid part of the salary of the director, who supervised both the religious and the nonreligious aspects of the program. The plaintiff claimed that the religious parts of the program could not be extricated from the secular parts. Even proponents of faith-based programs agreed that the mixing of religious and secular aspects of the program probably exceeded the constitutional limits. However, the case was dismissed as moot, since the program ended before the lawsuit was filed. The AJC appealed to the Fifth Circuit Court of Appeals, seeking repayment of the $8,000. While the amount is relatively insignificant, the principle at stake is not. Were the agency required to repay the funds, the precedent could be a real disincentive to faith-based providers entering into partnerships with the government in the first place.

The American Jewish Congress also initiated an action in California in January 2001 challenging a faith-based initiative administered by the state's Department of Employment Development under a welfare provision in place since 1996 (*AJC v. Michael Bernick et al.*). The lawsuit charged that the state-funded Faith-Based Initiative Solicitation Proposal, intended to provide workforce development programs for high-risk individuals, was restricted to "interested nonprofit faith-based organizations." The AJC claimed that the program violated principles of governmental neutrality because it preferred religiously affiliated providers over secular ones. The proposal specifically earmarked $5 million in funds for faith-based groups alone. The AJC termed the program "affirmative action for religious groups," constituting an unacceptable "establishment" of religion by the state.

ACLU of Louisiana v. Foster was filed in May 2002 in U.S. district court. The lawsuit challenged the Louisiana Governor's Program on Abstinence, which included federal subsidies made available via the 1996 welfare bill. The program required that cities, states, and private organizations receiving federal grants teach abstinence as the only reliable way to prevent pregnancy and sexually transmitted diseases. Louisiana receives approximately $1.6 million in block grants each year to lower the state's teenage pregnancy rate; the ACLU argued in the suit that the funds were applied to support "Christ-centered" skits, religious youth revivals, biblical instruction, and other overtly religious methods. A federal judge ruled against Louisiana, ordering it to cease paying money to those organizations that "convey religious messages or otherwise advance religion" with tax dollars.[48]

Probably the most significant of the lower court cases are a pair of decisions in *Freedom from Religion Foundation v. McCallum*, involving the FaithWorks program in Milwaukee, Wisconsin. Two separate parts of this program conveniently frame the contrasting legal merits of direct streams of payment versus indirect voucher systems. In October 2000, the Freedom from Religion Foundation sued the state of Wisconsin, challenging its funding of FaithWorks, a residential treatment program for drug and alcohol addicts. FaithWorks received an initial grant of $600,000 from the state's welfare funds, and has been the recipient of subsequent grants as well. A self-described "inherently Christian" organization, FaithWorks employed a faith-based approach to treating addiction. The program provided its participants with Bible classes and a "faith-enhanced" twelve-step recovery program, requiring attendance at, but not participation in, the spiritual discussions that went on. By their own estimates, FaithWorks counselors spent about 20 percent of their time addressing matters of spirituality with the residents.

The first decision in the case struck down the direct-funding element of the program. The judge found that "the FaithWorks program indoctrinates its participants in religion, primarily through its counselors. . . . Religion is so integral to the FaithWorks program that it is not possible to isolate it from the program as a whole." She also found it significant that the funds from the state were not linked to the number of individuals served by FaithWorks, but came in a settled grant. While the judge took care to note that her decision did not directly implicate charitable choice, she made it clear that direct aid had to be limited to "financially segregated, secular activities" of the funded organizations.[49]

That decision, however, did not cover one piece of the FaithWorks program, a voluntary residential treatment option for those on probation and parole, paid for by vouchers. With *Zelman* pending before the Supreme Court at the time, the judge chose to defer her decision on this piece of the program until the high court had rendered its decision. Unsurprisingly, once the Court approved of school vouchers in *Zelman*, the judge in *McCallum* likewise upheld the residential treatment program of FaithWorks. Though FaithWorks was recommended for individual clients by probation and parole agents, the judge found that the program safeguarded the independent choice of the participants. First, it was only one of several options available for offenders in need of treatment and counseling. Moreover, agents were required to inform offenders of the religious content of FaithWorks, and had to obtain each offender's consent to participate in the program; they also informed the offender that he or she could not be forced to participate in a religious treatment program. Finally, the policy expressly required that the choices include secular alternatives to the recommended program if it had religious content. These safeguards, the judge said, indicated that offenders "participate[d] in the FaithWorks program as the result of their own private, independent choice." She further opined that the actions of those who chose Faith-Works nullified "any appearance of government endorsement through true private choice programs under which government aid reaches the religious program."

Another pair of lawsuits broached the sensitive issue of hiring and personnel rights of publicly funded religious organizations. *Pedreira v. Kentucky Baptist Homes for Children* (2001) was brought by Alicia Pedreira, a therapist at the Kentucky Baptist Homes for Children, an institution that receives most of its funding from the state, and is the state's biggest provider of services for troubled youth. Pedreira, a lesbian, was admittedly discharged on grounds that her lifestyle violated the core values of her Baptist employer. Pedreira charged that, since her position was partially funded with state money, her dismissal on grounds that her sexual orientation ran contrary to the Home's religious tenets violated the establishment clause.

The trial judge dismissed the lawsuit, concluding that Baptist Homes was only insisting upon conduct from its employees consistent with the Home's religious affiliation; Baptist Homes required employees to "exhibit values in their professional conduct and personal lifestyles that are consistent with the Christian mission and purpose of the institution." There was no condition that employees join the Baptist church or adopt its teachings; they were free to follow the religion of their choice. "While Baptist Homes seeks to employ only persons who adhere to a behavioral code consistent with its religious mission, the absence of religious requirements leaves their focus on behavior, not religion." The trial court concluded that the "civil rights statutes protect religious freedom, not personal lifestyle choices."[50] Pedreira appealed the decision to the Sixth Circuit Court of Appeals, where it is currently pending.

The *Pedreira* case stoked the furor over hiring issues, especially when paired with a much-publicized *Washington Post* story charging that the Salvation Army had lobbied the White House for an exemption from local antidiscrimination laws.[51] For those fearful that an expansion of

charitable choice would lead to widespread discrimination against employees by religious service providers, *Pedreira* provided ample ammunition.
A spokesman for the lesbian and gay rights project at the ACLU called
the decision "shocking stuff," warning that it "sets off alarm bells" and
"ups the ante on the Bush faith-based initiative."[52]

In the summer of 2002, a similar lawsuit was brought in Georgia state
court against the United Methodist Children's Home of Decatur, Georgia
(*Bellmore v. United Methodist Children's Home*). One of the two plaintiffs
had applied for a job as a psychological therapist at the United Methodist
Children's Home. He was one of the top candidates until his application
was terminated when the Home found out he was Jewish. The other
plaintiff had worked at the Home as a counselor for eight months before
being fired for being a lesbian. The plaintiffs sued the Home and the
Georgia Department of Human Resources, which provided about 40
percent of the Home's funds. The parties eventually settled out of court
on terms favorable to the plaintiff.

These cases might well clarify the hiring rights of publicly subsidized
religious providers. They raise fundamental issues about how broadly to
define the religious tenets of the organizations. That is, was Pedreira's
firing a discriminatory dismissal based upon her sexual orientation or was
it due to her being unable to uphold the religious mission or principles
of her employer? While dismissals based on sexual orientation generate
political motivation for intensely active gay and lesbian groups, personal
lifestyle choices are not entitled to civil rights protection. For these reasons, the employers claim that the firings occurred not because of the
employees' religious beliefs, but because their sexual orientation was in-
compatible with the religious identity and mission of the organization.
Even if these cases eventually serve to resolve the complex legal issues
enveloping organizations' hiring rights, the outcomes will surely contribute to the political volatility of the issue as well.

Finally, two lawsuits filed in February 2003 took aim at a program
greatly admired by President Bush. *Ashburn v. Maples* and *Americans United
for Separation of Church and State v. Prison Fellowship Ministries* challenge
the InnerChange Freedom Initiative of Iowa, a Bible-based program intended to prepare prison inmates for their return to society and to reduce
the likelihood of recidivism. While participation in the program is voluntary, the program is by its own admission overtly Christ-centered and

faith-based, seeking the "spiritual and moral transformation" of participating prison inmates. The program includes a rigorous course of Bible study, worship and prayer, and Christian counseling. Defenders claim that the spiritual elements of the program are run only with private donations, with state funds supporting the secular elements.

These lawsuits could produce important constitutional answers to key parts of President Bush's faith-based agenda. The InnerChange program was actually begun in Texas prisons in 1997, when Bush was governor of that state. It represents the type of intensely religious program that the president nevertheless envisions as eligible for public funding. Unlike the faith-based programs typically funded under charitable choice law in the context of welfare, InnerChange is religious at its core, and seeks the secular benefit—criminal rehabilitation—through religious and spiritual conversion. These cases revolve around the propriety of a pervasively religious program such as InnerChange operating with the benefit of public dollars. Complicating matters are studies that suggest the program has been remarkably successful in lowering the percentage of released inmates who return to criminal behavior.[53]

The true significance of the cases discussed here will be easier to determine once they work their way through the appeals process. But their importance is undeniable. Ultimately, the constitutional battle will be resolved in the courts. Current and future litigation will play an important part in establishing the constitutional parameters for future faith-based programs. This is inevitable in light of *Bowen*'s insistence that an improper blending of religion and social services be substantiated in programs as implemented, rather than on the face of the statute. To that extent, these cases are healthy and valuable exercises for giving shape to the establishment clause.

Conclusion

The public and political framing of the debate over the Bush faith-based initiative poisoned, distorted, and ultimately undermined constructive constitutional dialogue. The seeds of those distortions lay in the uncertainties that afflict the law of church-state relations, uncertainties that allowed for widely differing views on the correct interpretation and application of the establishment clause. Certainly those debating Bush's faith-based initiative had genuine and significant ideological differences over what the First Amendment allowed and proscribed. But the distance between those views was inflated dramatically as each side found its expression in the context of a high-intensity political battle with significant interests at stake. The complexity of the issues and genuine differences of perspective, inflamed by a desire to prevail in the arena of popular opinion, produced a public debate that often bore little relation to the actual constitutional status of the faith-based initiative. The mischaracterizations and distortions that marked the debate were more than mere ignorance or uncertainty about the law; they reflected intentional political strategies designed to ensure the defeat of the proposal.

The problems were amplified by a complicit media that tended to lack a sophisticated understanding of religion, an alien world to most of them. Guided by a propensity for conflict, journalists typically sought out polarizing and extreme voices rather than more moderate ones. While it is expected that those with deeply held convictions or interests at stake will resort to the most polarizing strategies to defeat a legislative initiative, democracy relies upon a free media to provide a more nuanced coverage. Finally, the constitutional issues were raised within and as part of a multifaceted and crosscutting policy debate. It proved impossible to keep the constitutional issues from becoming embroiled in the policy arguments. Questions of constitutionality and sound policy were thoroughly intertwined, blurred, and confused.

All of this illustrates what can happen when subtle and complex constitutional arguments become closely bound up in the politics of an issue. The demise of the Bush faith-based initiative demonstrates the potential dangers of waging a high-stakes political battle that implicates deeply held constitutional values. The nuances and complexities of church-state relations make it particularly ill-suited for a public debate. Distorting constitutional arguments becomes an easy way to exploit public anxieties and apprehensions for political gain.

The net effect in this case was to obfuscate the constitutionality of governmental partnerships with faith-based social service providers well beyond the experiences of the first five years of charitable choice. Ironically, the problems that charitable choice was meant to address may now be more pronounced than they were prior to its passage. If the tenor of the debate surrounding the Bush initiative is any indication, current public perceptions of the constitutional status of these partnerships seem more bewildered than before. If so, Bush's efforts may well have had the incongruous effect of heightening anxieties and apprehensions surrounding faith-based initiatives rather than easing them. Even as the Supreme Court grows friendlier to church-state interaction, the burden has shifted to supporters of faith-based initiatives to ease the anxieties of an ambivalent public.

Seven

Of Little Faith?

Lessons from the Faith-Based Saga

As we write this concluding chapter in early 2004, Congress seems close to agreement on a faith-based law. In early April of last year, a watered-down version of CARE cleared its final hurdle in the U.S. Senate, where it passed by an overwhelming margin of ninety-five to five. The House passed a similar version on September 17, 2003, by a vote of 408 to 13. Senate passage was made possible only by stripping the proposal of those provisions that gave any preference or special acknowledgment to religious organizations. What was left was a mere shadow of the original, and hardly qualified as a faith-based law. The slim remnant consisted largely of a benign set of tax breaks designed to encourage charitable contributions to all nonprofits, religious and secular alike. Efforts to ease religious groups' securing of public funding or protections of their hiring autonomy were nowhere to be seen. Backers of the faith-based initiative could claim victory, but it was at best a hollow one.

This closing chapter provides an opportune time to step back and consider the broader implications of the two-year saga of the faith-based initiative. The faith-based story is interesting on its own terms—intriguing campaign strategy, high legislative drama, important administrative actions, and detailed judicial decision making. But President Bush's faith-based initiative is also important for the insight its story provides for broader questions of American politics. To explore these, we return to the three lenses of politics, policymaking, and public religion set out in this book's opening pages. Considering the fate of the initiative through those lenses provides a useful framework for drawing larger lessons as to politics, policy, and legislative practice. Perhaps more significantly, we hope that post hoc reflection on the story of the initiative will enhance our ability in the future to better navigate the complex questions of the public role of religion in America.

The Original Appeal of Faith-Based Programs

The policy appeal of faith-based initiatives did not necessarily fit conventional ideological boundaries, its support coming from policy advocates with a variety of ideological inclinations. For liberals seeking to find ways to increase the government's commitment to providing for human needs, the faith-based initiative was a way to express increased interest in the poor that combined a focus on mainstream values with concerns about effectiveness and efficiency. For fiscal conservatives who still wanted to shrink the size of government, the initiative's rhetoric about increasing the role for faith-based and community providers sounded good. For communitarians with their concerns about civil society, enlarging the social service delivery universe to include small, grassroots, neighborhood-centered groups was attractive—for who better to integrate recipients into a supportive community network than churches and neighborhood religious organizations? For moral conservatives who attributed social problems at least in part to the erosion of personal behavior and responsibility, shifting service delivery to religious providers appeared more likely to generate programs that incorporated their values. For those who advocated more integrated programs that dealt with both material and nonmaterial needs, the faith-based initiative rested on a more holistic vision of the entire well-being of the client—physical, emotional, and spiritual.

From a political perspective, the faith-based initiative held similar promise in its ability to bridge traditional divides that too often sabotage the policymaking process. Its political potential lay in generating a broad, if new, coalition that one party could potentially capture. In the political environment of the 2000 campaign, candidates Bush and Gore and their respective parties had good reasons to sign on to the idea. For Bush and the Republicans, faith-based proposals provided tangible evidence that their "compassionate conservatism" was more than a catchy slogan, as skeptics claimed. By moving away from the more libertarian domestic welfare policies advocated by much of the GOP, Bush could soften perceptions of the Republican position on domestic policy and increase the party's attractiveness to minorities, Catholics, and other potential voting blocs. For Gore and the Democrats, their support for religious groups as service partners helped to counter the party's image as overly secularist, if not outright hostile to religion. Welcoming religiously based social services into the traditional Democratic project of safeguarding the social safety net was a way of embracing religion generally without abandoning the party's traditional commitments. In short, the potential political support was bipartisan, broad-based, and reflective of a variety of points on the political spectrum.

Finally, the faith-based proposals held special appeal to those who desired a greater role and presence for religious actors and convictions in the public and policy arenas, a highly popular proposition, at least when stated in general terms. By making government social service programs more inviting to religious groups and easing barriers to their entry, faith-based proposals made the broader point that the business of government need not be off-limits to the religious. Indeed, done well, cooperation could benefit both spheres.

These potentially broad coalitions of support ultimately unraveled, as the faith-based initiative fell prey to conventional forces in the spheres of policy, politics, and the debate over public religion. The legislative initiative, especially, got caught up in two debates difficult or impossible to win: the hiring discrimination/discretion controversy about retaining hiring and employee-benefit rights; and the efficacy/efficiency controversy about proving that faith-based social service approaches were equal or superior to currently funded programs before the religious approaches could be eligible for government funding. Once the proposal moved from the relatively friendly context of the campaign to the hothouse of governing, the interested parties and voices reverted to form, falling back into predictable political alliances and policy positions. Old debates and political battles resurfaced, as those who had muffled their opposition during the campaign regained their voice. The result was a lost opportunity, not only for an unambiguous Bush administration policy success, but for a rare bipartisan policy reform.

The Policy Lens

As we noted in the introduction, textbooks segment the policy process into several steps. Following one standard set of steps, we found it helpful to describe the promotion of the faith-based initiative as involving simultaneous efforts toward *legitimization* in the legislative arena (and to some extent in the judiciary) and *implementation* in the executive branch. Public policy texts go on to describe models or conceptualizations of how political power actually gets exercised in all the steps of the process. Thomas Dye, for example, lists nine different models such as institutional, process, group, elite, and public choice, in trying to explain how power is allocated in the process.[1] In discussing the real power of agenda-setting for public policies, Guy Peters identifies three basic theoretical approaches: pluralist, elitist, and state-centric.[2] To be useful, a model and approach should simplify and clarify what happens in a particular policy study. One model or approach may be more useful than the others for any particular policy story, but they need not be mutually exclusive. Different models and approaches can be usefully applied in the same study.

For our examination of the president's faith-based initiative, we found the process and group models and the state-centric theoretical approach most helpful. The *processes* of legitimization and implementation describe broadly what the faith-based initiative was facing in the legislative, executive, and judicial branches of government. The actions and interactions of existing interest *groups* with crowded issue agendas, and the failure of proponents to build a stable coalition of groups with a focused priority on the president's faith-based ideas, explain much of the initiative's ups and downs. The *state-centric* approach turns on its head the typical assumption that outside forces push government, by asserting that existing interest groups are pressured into activity by persons in government. This relatively novel assumption fits faith-based well, shining the spotlight on President Bush's personal interest in faith-based, Representative J. C. Watts's larger agenda to attract African Americans to the GOP, Senator Joe Lieberman's desire to make the Democratic Party more open to religious voices and voters, John DiIulio's willingness to serve in a Republican White House, and the actions of many other government officials with smaller roles in the faith-based story.

Congress and the Executive Branch

For many reasons, it is a complex task to measure the success of President Bush's faith-based policy initiatives in his first two years in office. One reason is that none of the three branches actually considered his initiative as he originally proposed it. In the House, H.R. 7 differed significantly from what Bush faith-based staff envisioned as a good initial legislative proposal. Because of Republican leadership support, the passage of H.R. 7 in the House was virtually assured the day it was introduced. Equally assured, however, was its characterization as a highly partisan bill. That characterization lingered, diminishing the legitimization that usually accrues to a bill successfully making its way through the legislature. The legitimization process also fared poorly in the Senate. The two faith-based tax bills introduced by Lieberman and Rick Santorum in 2001, and the CARE Act introduced in early 2002, had little overt opposition, but also little strong support. The Senate faith-based bills died mostly from bipartisan indifference and inattention, although the hiring and efficiency debates also helped slow them down. CARE, especially, failed to ignite a new public debate about a vastly different legislative approach (which the bill arguably was) to dispel impressions created during House debate on H.R. 7. The continued activism of opponents to the House bill, especially representatives Bobby Scott and Chet Edwards, perpetuated the partisan impression of the initiative; CARE supporters could not or did not do enough in response.

In the executive branch, policy implementation made steady progress, sometimes slowed by media attention but more often on track when members of the public interested in the issue got distracted by the legislative battles or more important extraneous events. The *Unlevel Playing Field* report seemed to rise out of nowhere in August 2001; in fact, however, the satellite faith-based offices were working quietly while most everyone was distracted by the noise of the House debate on H.R. 7. With the policy consequences of September 11 drawing everyone's attention, Bush faith-based staff members were able to act on the August report by making a series of changes to programs, rules, and contracts. They were even able to gain from Congress, and later distribute to faith-based groups, a relatively meager sum of compassion capital funds.

Legislative Failures

The proposal's legislative failure gives credence to the truism that intensity trumps size when it comes to the fate of legislation. The faith-based initiative as a poll-tested idea enjoyed broad public support; sizable majorities of Americans were sympathetic to the notion of publicly funding religious providers. But that support was diffuse and lukewarm. Few existing interest groups or other actors in the Washington, D.C., policy community actually liked the initiative as the president described it. Different sets of preexisting groups fought for changes from the administration's first day, one set successfully getting the House bill to move "right" upon introduction as H.R. 7, and another set getting it to move "left" when introduced in the Senate as CARE. In both chambers, however, the few groups supporting the respective bills were unwilling to expend significant political capital working for their enactment. When the respective legislative proposals reached crunch time, each lacked an energized, loyal base. House Republicans overcame this weakness on the strength of the leadership's willingness to move the process along at the president's request. In the Senate, party leaders have less power than in the House, and neither party's Senate leadership particularly cared for CARE. As a result, the Senate faith-based bill never made it to the floor for consideration.

The Perils of Partisanship
Labeling H.R. 7 as a payoff to purist Christian groups mischaracterized both the bill's intent and its content, even though some friends and foes were happy with the description. Simultaneously, however, that characterization doomed the bill's chances of enactment. In the House, its assumed strong proponents, the most conservative religious groups, had other issue priorities. Large intensely religious social services operated by national organizations, such as Prison Fellowship and Teen Challenge, were part of this coalition, and most of those groups did not want to make the compromises necessary to tamp down the partisanship. Another portion of the bill's potential direct beneficiaries, needy inner-city and minority churches operating social services, also provided little help. Such groups are not well-organized politically and, further, their main objective, a compassion capital fund, was left out of the original House bill and only added as a last-minute gesture. As the House bill moved further into the legislative process, the opposition intensified even though in the Judiciary Committee the bill was modified to attract centrists. Instead, a diverse array of groups, motivated by differing goals, mobilized against the initiative at every turn. Especially when the hiring discretion issue surfaced as the most potent argument against the bill, groups that represented gays and lesbians, racial and ethnic minorities, and others cohered into a galvanized, energized, and organized opposition.

The Dangers of Indifference
Thinking that they had learned their lesson, White House and Senate negotiators took a different legislative tack once the House finished its

work in July 2001. Devising a new text was actually quite simple—by early October of that year, the White House, Santorum, and Lieberman had pretty much settled on the outlines of a new bill. They almost succeeded in passing that compromise through the Senate before the end of the year but could not overcome a crowded Senate calendar, indifferent conservatives, and determined but quiet resistance from liberal groups and a handful of Democrats.

Early in 2002, Santorum and Lieberman tweaked the previous fall's compromise and introduced it as CARE. At first, it seemed that they had overcome their colleagues' doubt and distrust. But the broad support for CARE was not intense. Purist and pragmatic conservative groups were slightly more positive than indifferent, not many Republican senators were enthusiastic, and no White House offices seem to place it among their top priorities. At the same time, hostility to CARE seemed almost as intense as opposition to H.R. 7. The few House members and groups active against H.R. 7 were equally active, if not more so, against CARE. The broad support and narrow opposition to CARE in February 2002 quickly changed to much broader indifference and more intense opposition, dooming the bill after its financial provisions barely squeaked through the Finance Committee.

Legislative Lessons

Watching a popular campaign promise disintegrate into a pair of legislative proposals with few friends and many enemies provides a telling reminder of the difference between campaigning and governing. A well-received campaign plank cast in appealing generalities is no guarantee of success once its translation to specific policy proposals meets the legislative process. The devil clearly exists in the details, and many detailed legislative proposals generate far greater opposition than broad campaign ideas. The faith-based legislative proposals turned into Rorschach tests—different constituencies projected onto them their worst fears and concerns. When it came to the nitty-gritty of the legislative details, there seemed to be something for every interest to dislike.

The sum of those concerns doomed passage. On the right, some religious conservatives found the very notion of neutrality unpalatable, objecting to the possibility that public funds would be available for non-Christian faiths or religions outside the mainstream. Others in this group feared that limits on proselytizing or witnessing would remove from faith-based programs the very dimensions that made them so effective. For libertarians, the initiative was one more government intrusion into a place it did not belong; public funding of religious groups could only damage religious institutions and their work. On the left, the absence of new money led liberals to view the plan as empty rhetoric rather than a genuine effort to help the needy. Secular providers and larger religious groups that had long benefited from public dollars saw a threat that spelled more competition for already too limited resources. Finally, the hiring protections for religious groups provoked a storm among civil libertarians and gay rights activists.

The complexities of the faith-based proposal should have led its White House supporters to devise a carefully calibrated, closely coordinated legislative policy approach. They should have known that any number of technical details could alienate friends, confuse everyone, and ignite media firestorms. The initiative demanded a go-slow approach, with success contingent upon carefully laying a public relations foundation that might eventually lead to a consensus around a bill that could pass both House and Senate. Rather than striving for that unified and coherent strategy, Republicans in the House, Senate, and White House not only failed to work closely together, but most of them neglected Democrats all along the way.

Providing evidence that perhaps political scientists know something after all, the measured approach advocated by some proponents, such as former WHOFBCI director John DiIulio, probably would have better served the cause. That strategy depended upon a new and unusual coalition of religious conservatives joining moderate and liberal proponents for the poor. Creating such a coalition in the post-2000 election climate required a much more concerted and time-consuming effort.

Administrative Success

The proposal's administrative progress proves the truism that "slow and steady wins the race." A policy implementation strategy of relatively small incremental steps has the best chance of success. Once the Bush administration's faith-based staff got past the initial preoccupations with the House legislative battle, the *Unlevel Playing Field* report, and the long vacancy at the head of the WHOFBCI, they quietly focused on their primary task—creating a more receptive atmosphere for faith-based and community groups seeking to work with the federal government in delivering social services. Unfortunately for the faith-based staff, of course, those three initial preoccupations lasted more than a year, and no doubt delayed their achievements. Nevertheless, the faith-based initiatives of the executive branch have started to become integrated into the agencies and institutionalized in their routines. The five original faith-based offices, along with the two added in December 2002, are quietly changing regulations, earmarking program monies for faith-based organizations, and slowly transforming the relationship between executive branch agencies and religious groups.

Political Pitfalls:
Distrust, Polarization, and Public Opinion

There are a host of lessons to be learned from the faith-based story when looking through the political lens. Perhaps the starkest lesson is the central importance of the existing political environment. For any new policy to succeed, proponents must assess the political climate, measure the extent and scope of potential opposition, and design a plan to minimize the opposition and backlash. Even the simplest, seemingly uncontroversial proposal will have enemies. In a highly charged partisan environment, the political motives for blocking policy often eclipse the desire to meet even the noblest public need.

The dominant characteristic of the political environment at the beginning of the Bush administration was mistrust: mistrust between the two political parties and, especially, between the two sets of interest groups traditionally aligned with each party. Trust, a prerequisite for any meaningful bipartisan accomplishment, is a rarity if not a thing of the past in today's Washington. Certainly, the aftermath of the historic and unparalleled 2000 presidential election depleted any reservoir of trust between the two major political parties, poisoning relations even beyond the usual partisanship. The Florida imbroglio left a residue of bitterness and rancor, with a Republican ascending to the White House whose very legitimacy as president large numbers of Democrats questioned. The magnitude of Democratic distrust and suspicion made it difficult for them to cooperate with Bush on the faith-based initiative, especially since it was a signature part of his agenda. Given the strength of the black Democratic vote nationwide and the charges of suppression of black voting in Florida, Democrats could not help but be deeply wary of the motives behind a policy seemingly aimed at making political inroads with African Americans. Republican efforts to woo black leaders—Bush's meetings with select black clergy, an exclusively Republican faith-based summit on Capitol Hill attended primarily by black religious leaders—appeared to many Democrats to be a blatant effort to use the faith-based initiative for political gains in the most solid of Democratic voting blocs.

This case study also highlights the extreme difficulty of creating new public policy in an era of close party competition. Virtual parity between the two major parties amplifies the tendency to view every policy through the prism of its potential political and electoral consequences. The 2000 congressional election was the latest in a string of close and contested elections that have left the parties even more vigilant in protecting the key constituencies in their respective voting coalitions.

When President Bush began to translate his faith-based campaign promises into policy proposals, Democrats had strong political incentives to oppose any high-profile initiative that would move forward a Republican president's agenda. The faith-based initiative was a particularly important political target. If perceived as a genuine effort to attract minorities and put meat on the bones of compassionate conservatism, it could mean large Republican gains and Democratic losses. Republicans might also win over important votes among moderate suburban women and Catholics. Conversely, if it was perceived as a transparent effort to gain votes, its political objectives could be turned on their head.

Another political lesson is how important political rhetoric is in the battle for public opinion. Probably the critical factor that derailed faith-based legislation was the stir that arose over a religious group's freedom to hire on religious criteria when receiving public funds. Opponents labeled the entire faith-based initiative as government-funded religious discrimination. It worked marvelously. Proponents never united on an effective counterargument.

The faith-based initiative is a complex issue that does not easily distill into a convenient sound bite. Supporters never found a sharp, concise, and pointed phrase to explain what the proposal would do and why it was needed. Opponents, in contrast, found a simple phrase that captured one of their concerns in a powerful and incendiary way: religious discrimination. Once they discovered its rhetorical power, opponents rallied around the issue of civil rights and pounded the message home, altering the public debate and turning Congress against a notion it had seemed likely to approve. Survey data demonstrate how the discrimination issue stuck with an ambivalent public: three of four Americans approve of religious service providers receiving public funds, yet an even higher percentage disapproves of giving those same service providers the freedom to hire on religious criteria.[3] Until proponents of faith-based initiatives effectively address the hiring discretion issue in ways the public can digest, legislative success for a broad faith-based initiative is not likely. Those voting blocs who might otherwise respond positively to a successful and popular faith-based initiative—deeply religious African Americans and other racial and ethnic minorities, observant Catholics, "soccer moms," and others—will continue to vote by present patterns.

Reflections on the Public Dimensions of Religion

The most significant implications of the faith-based initiative are in the debate over the proper public role of religion in the realm of policy, politics, and government. After the initiative's rapid rise and fall, fundamental questions of religion and the public square loom even larger. Did the faith-based initiative ultimately help or hinder efforts to clarify the relationship between religion and government? For those who favor greater interaction between government and religion, is the playing field more or less favorable? For those suspicious of such interaction, are we closer to or farther from a dangerous church-state paradigm?

There are no conclusive answers to these questions. Americans remain ambivalent and divided about mixing religion and government. Indeed, the authors of this book disagree among themselves. We can, however, reflect upon how best to collectively negotiate the church-state divide in the wake of the faith-based initiative and hope that the lessons learned enhance the capacity for constructive future dialogue.

The End Game:
Moving the Ball Forward, or Thrown for a Loss?

What has been the net impact of the policy battle over the faith-based initiative? Is the country better off for having endured an undeniably nasty debate, or has the debate been destructive of church-state relations in this country? A case can be made for either side.

The Arguments for a Loss

Some would argue that church-state relations have only been damaged by the faith-based fiasco. Prior to the Bush initiative, charitable choice was safely embedded in four federal statutes; it was gradually, albeit modestly, gaining currency. The ambiguity of the constitutional issues had resulted in something of a truce by which many public officials tacitly allowed religious providers admittance to publicly funded programs while conveniently looking the other way when religious views arose. With few the wiser, substantial dealings between governmental entities and religious providers transpired beneath the constitutional radar screen.

To many, this status quo of uneven ambivalence was better than the repercussions of the failed faith-based legislative fight. The legislative debate arguably was akin to poking a stick into a hornet's nest. Opposition to religious-government collaboration in the social services had previously been diffused and disorganized, if not outright dormant. The Bush plan managed to thoroughly rouse and roil that opposition. The results were intense lobbying and public relations efforts against the legislation. That opposition will surely be on high alert if and when religious rights legislation is reintroduced in Congress, making its prospects equally difficult in the future.

At least as significant in the long term, however, are the legal challenges that have been provoked by the public debate. Lawsuits involving publicly funded faith-based social programs were rare before Bush made it an issue. Charitable choice had existed for five years without a direct challenge to its constitutionality. In contrast, a flurry of lawsuits has arisen since the summer of 2000. More cases are sure to come, with advocacy groups aggressively turning to litigation to stem the tide of greater church-state interaction. These lawsuits could eventually yield precedents that draw a stricter line of unacceptable religious establishment. Whatever the outcome of current and future suits, the threat of litigation is no longer merely hypothetical. While legal uncertainties have existed for some time, the likelihood of their metastasizing into a time-consuming and expensive lawsuit for a particular faith-based contractor is now significantly greater.

It is not unreasonable for some supporters of close cooperation to think that it might well have been better to let sleeping dogs lie.

The Arguments for Gaining Ground

On the other hand, proponents may have lost the faith-based battle but won the religion-in-government war. They can take no small consolation in the extent to which faith-based social programs have advanced in the wake of the president's plan. If one of their central aims was to increase the presence of religious groups in the delivery of government social services, the initiative must be judged at least a qualified success.

Notwithstanding the failings on the legislative side, a number of signs suggest that the public is far more attuned and agreeable to religious agencies becoming partners with government in meeting social needs. One such measure is simply the degree to which people have been made aware of charitable choice. Prior to the 2000 presidential campaign, the sheer magnitude of the ignorance that enveloped charitable choice was truly stunning. One 1999 study indicated that 80 percent of those in congregational leadership positions knew nothing of charitable choice, while studies in early 2000 put the level of clergy who were familiar with it as low as 8 to 3 percent. This widespread ignorance existed even as large majorities of Americans expressed their support for the basic idea of government funding of social services through religious groups.[4] The high-profile debate undeniably increased public awareness of the potential of religious agencies as collaborators with the government in delivering social services.

Nor was the unfamiliarity with charitable choice limited to private religious leaders. It could be found in equal measure among public officials responsible for implementing the law. Organizations assessing charitable choice implementation efforts meted out failing marks to the vast majority of states. Only a handful of states had taken tangible steps to put charitable choice into action. Many government administrators were unfamiliar with the statute; others chose to ignore or misinterpret its requirements. One assessment of implementation efforts stated that charitable choice was characterized by "vast ignorance both in the government sector and the faith sector."[5]

The Bush initiative and the tempest it set off did much to remedy this ignorance. The focus on charitable choice had the salutary effect of informing large numbers of actors, both public and private, that such laws are already on the books. As a result, those seeking to advance religious-based social welfare service delivery under the auspices of charitable choice are likely to find a far more informed and intelligent audience within and outside of government.

A second measure of success is found in the favorable developments in the executive branch. Legislation was only one facet of the administration's plan. Even as CARE stalled in the Senate at the end of 2002, the White House continued to press its case through executive orders and other administrative action. The initial orders creating the White House Office of Faith-Based and Community Initiatives in January 2001 identified five agencies where faith-based programs might naturally flourish, and efforts to promote such programs have proceeded on those fronts. Faith-based offices in the Department of Agriculture and at USAID were added in late 2002. As detailed in chapter 5, much of what the Bush administration hopes to accomplish can be done without legislation. Indeed, while new laws would make more secure the legal status of government/religious sector partnerships, the greater battle may well be against the contracting and grant-making culture ingrained in national, state, and local bureaucracies. On this front, the Bush administration will surely continue to push agencies to partner with religious organizations.

More than two years of concerted administrative efforts have yielded significant gains for faith-based proponents. Again, tangible evidence indicates that bureaucratic cultures have begun to look differently at faith-based organizations. Amy Sherman's 2002 survey cataloguing new publicly funded faith-based programs in fifteen states revealed a sizable upswing in the numbers of faith-based programs operating with government funds.[6] That study revealed more than 700 contracts totaling $125 million. While this may seem relatively modest within the universe of all government social spending, it was a considerable increase over past amounts. Moreover, the creation of new faith-based programs continues unabated. Hardly a week went by in late 2002 and early 2003 without a report of some new state program that melded public dollars with faith-based delivery. Indeed, when President Bush furthered his faith-based agenda with two executive orders in December 2002, the *lack* of public outcry was palpable. Collaborations between the government and the religious sector are commonplace, and are sure to continue with or without additional federal charitable choice legislation.

The Faith-Based Policy Debate: Clarifying or Confusing?

Whatever the growing impact "on the ground" of religious-government cooperation, the faith-based debate in Washington was hardly a model of nuanced or enlightened political dialogue. It did little to clarify or advance the debate about religion in the public square. Framed by the legislative battle, the debate was susceptible to, and dominated by, sound bites, distortion, mischaracterization, and manipulation.

One possible outcome of a debate about charitable choice and the subsequent faith-based initiative would be to clarify applicable church-state law. Proponents of faith-based believed that the ambiguities and misperceptions of establishment clause jurisprudence generated unjustified obstacles to a more vibrant and dynamic church-state relationship. They anticipated that clarifying the jurisprudence through new law would ease unwarranted barriers to helpful (and legal) collaborative efforts between public officials and religious nonprofits.

Arguably, the Bush plan ended up having precisely the opposite effect, serving only to further obscure the status of relevant law. The high-profile sound bite exchanges only muddied the constitutional waters with sweeping claims backed by one-sided constitutional analysis. In the minds of many, the permissibility of religious-government co-ventures is even more in question now and the perils of entering into such programs have increased. The faith-based initiative failed to prompt a meaningful collective exploration of "religion in the public square," no matter one's particular view of the question.

The 2000–2002 debate over the faith-based initiative, however, may have set the stage for a more meaningful discussion later. The initiative undoubtedly engaged the role of religion in public policy in a new and unprecedented fashion. Though legislation failed in the 107th Congress, administrative action proceeded. The underlying church-state dilemmas still exist, and the debate has begun. It may take years or even decades, but many disagreements over religion and its place in matters of public concern will be resolved.

All signs indicate that this issue will be with us for the foreseeable future. First, faith-based proponents in the House and the Senate will continue to introduce legislation. In addition, President Bush continues to advance the faith-based agenda via executive action. Even the WHOFBCI, created by a presidential executive order, will be difficult for subsequent administrations to abolish. Future presidents with less sympathy for the initiative may lower the profile of the White House office, but may be disinclined to eliminate it completely. The push for more faith-based partnerships in the Bush administration has also produced longer-lasting change in the culture of how agencies interact with religious organizations. While legal questions abound, legal decisions like *Zelman* mean that school voucher and other social service "choice" efforts will continue. With lawsuits proliferating in lower courts, the task of defining the constitutional propriety of state/religious sector partnerships is far from over and will keep the courts busy for years.

Which Venue? Facilitating a Constructive Public Square Dialogue

Our dissatisfaction with the quality of the church-state debate in the faith-based controversy raises the question of how to ensure a more edifying and productive dialogue in the future. One challenge is to identify the best forum in which to conduct such a debate. The saga of the Bush faith-based initiative demonstrated in no uncertain terms the problems with broaching the topic predominantly in the acrimonious legislative arena. The interests at stake, the need to mobilize one's supporters, and the importance of public opinion all made it too tempting to demagogue, distort, and disparage the opponent's arguments and positions. Especially with an issue as multifaceted and complicated as this one, the rough-and-tumble political arena rarely produces fair-minded and forthright analysis. The dynamics of the public fray—the politicians' desire to win an important legislative fight, the involvement of intensely engaged private interests, the channeling of the events to the public through media sound bites—render thoughtful discussion of the issues elusive at best. The backers of faith-based social services are well-advised to give pause before resuming an aggressive legislative strategy. Opponents, too, might think again about the arguments they used against legislation if, as is likely, administrative implementation brings with it broad public approbation. At the very least, a substantively honest legislative debate will require far greater care and attention to timing, strategy, and other circumstances.

The administrative approach presents different problems, many of them mirror images of the legislative difficulties. While legislation brings too much public and political pressure, executive orders may not bring enough. Executive action operates almost completely out of the public eye, rarely allowing for adequate exploration of the public square arguments necessary to legitimate faith-based programs. As President Bush faced legislative setbacks, he moved the faith-based agenda forward with unilateral executive orders as was within his rights and authority. But this strategy left important issues unaddressed. Because regulatory changes received little public scrutiny until they were announced or leaked to the media, they undermined substantive supporting arguments regarding faith-based effectiveness, efficiency, and professionalism.

The best forum for a thorough examination of the faith-based initiative, then, is not readily apparent. It even divides the authors of this book. David Ryden contends that the courts and the litigation process are the least encumbered by debilitating political pressures and thus provide the best venue for a constructive and thoughtful resolution of issues. While our judicial figures are not the contemporary versions of platonic philosopher kings, the judicial context has its advantages. A fully briefed and argued appellate case before a panel of experienced and sophisticated judges is arguably the closest thing to an adequate forum for exploring the appropriate place for religious groups in public policy making. Following the present course will eventually lead to the courts. As the legal challenges to the Bush administration's executive moves mature, we hope reasoned legal analysis without demagoguery will inform the debate. In the courts, there is at least a chance that the constitutional merits and failings can be weighed reflectively and insightfully.

Authors Amy Black and Douglas Koopman contend that political battles within the legislative branch are the preferred means of resolving the faith-based debate. The most democratic of the three branches, the legislature seeks to translate popular will into pragmatic policy. Although the faith-based debate has been undeniably messy and often misleading, eventually cooler heads will prevail, even in Congress. The wheat of each argument will be sifted from its chaff and, quite likely, a new view of the proper relationship between organized religion and government will emerge. The legislative process will legitimate that new view while leaving space for dissenting opinions to refine the new status quo.

The Neglected Theme of "Community"

Other significant questions relating to the propriety of religion in the public square rarely entered the faith-based discussion. We hope future debates on faith-based issues will address them. One of these questions is the connection between the specific issue of faith-based service delivery and the broader goal of strengthening and energizing civil society generally. The name given to the office by the Bush administration—the White House Office of Faith Based and *Community* Initiatives—is illustrative. Including "community" in the title admittedly was an attempt to broaden the political base and appeal of the proposal. But it was not solely politics. Rather, the name reflected important theoretical and intellectual roots from which the proposal grew.

Including faith-based providers in publicly subsidized social services is an important piece of a larger program generated by communitarian critiques of liberal social policy. Those critiques decry solutions to social problems that treat recipients as atomistic, isolated, self-contained units, as government programs tend to do. Communitarians, on the contrary, emphasize a person's need for social connectedness and belonging. They call for greater attention to the cultivation of civil society, the strengthening of intermediate organizations and associations that would better meet holistic needs. Communitarians have long criticized government social policy as in fact depleting and displacing small, local, social institutions that formerly served this purpose. Rather than enervate social institutions, the government should effectuate, energize, and engender civil society.

One way to accomplish this goal is to encourage small neighborhood-level organizations, many of which are faith-based, to deliver publicly subsidized programs. Churches and other small religious nonprofits are often unparalleled in how much volunteerism and participation they elicit from their members and how steadfastly they keep to a mission to care for those in need.

The explicit linking of "faith" and "community" in the White House office acknowledged these benefits. Moreover, the initiative made a special effort to highlight those religious groups that served as grassroots community building blocks but that had heretofore been neglected in government-funded programs. Before the Bush administration, government collaboration with religious entities had been limited mostly to larger agencies like Catholic Charities and Lutheran Social Services, organizations with the institutional infrastructure that enabled them to secure and administer government grants and contracts. Those agencies were not the model for grassroots service delivery, however. The faith-based initiative targeted smaller, autonomous, neighborhood-based groups that might not have the expertise or networks to help them partner with the government, but have the local credibility.

The efforts to persuade African American churches and clergy to support the initiative made sense, not just in terms of partisan politics, but from the perspective of communitarian social theory as well. The case for black churches' participation in government-sponsored social programs was especially compelling. The communitarian "connectedness" to the grass roots is embodied especially in the form of black churches and religious institutions, which occupy a unique and unparalleled position of social activism and outreach in African American communities. Black churches serve in many communities as the catalyst and backbone of black cultural identity, making them natural vehicles through which to channel social services. In addition to their role as spiritual centers and houses of worship, black churches are a central source of neighborhood stability and social structure. They provide a base for social, political, and economic empowerment. Study after study reveals that social mission and activism by black churches are unmatched by their white counterparts. In short, black churches are "centers of neighborhood and community life."[7]

Supporters of the Bush initiative argued from this understanding that black religious institutions are especially well-situated to work with government to get social services into the hands of those who need them. Charlene Turner Johnson of the Michigan Neighborhood Partnership in Detroit described the church as "ideally suited for neighborhood-based work. . . . We're real, human, touching. . . . "[8] John DiIulio, the one-time head of the White House Office of Faith-Based and Community Initiatives, has echoed that sentiment, asserting that their attentiveness to all the needs of the community gives black churches a unique community-building power.[9]

Certainly the Bush team had political reasons for courting high-profile evangelical black clergy. But politics dovetailed with policy based on the argument that, as the most permanent institutional presence in urban neighborhoods, black churches have a capacity to build community and serve as the glue of the social structure in ways that neither the state nor secular providers can hope to replicate. Disregarding the political and constitutional controversies for a moment, faith-based programs make sense from a community-building perspective, and perhaps from that perspective they make the most sense of all.

The Loss of the Prophetic Voice?

A long-standing concern about greater church-state collaboration is the loss of independence and integrity that recipient religious groups might experience. By bringing religious groups into a formal relationship with the state, one runs the risk of sapping them of that vitality and mission that are the very keys to their success. Opponents raise the specter that over time charitable choice would lead to the co-optation by the state of the core identity and mission of churches and faith-based groups. They argue that the traits that the government hopes to tap are those most likely to be muted, dampened, and eviscerated by the process of accepting government money and acceding to whatever demands or conditions government sets.

Again, the black churches provide the starkest and most compelling example to explore both sides of that argument. The flip side of the community-building capacity of black churches is their historic role as a prophetic presence. Black churches have not only served as the social and economic center of urban black communities, but also have been a locus of political mobilization and empowerment. Black churches have provided a forum for voices of opposition and conscience, holding society and the state to account for their disregard for the needs of black communities. In light of this history, charitable choice generated understandable wariness and suspicion among black leaders and religious figures, who adamantly opposed the 1996 welfare bill to which it was attached, and which they thought harmed the interests of blacks. They feared that collaboration with the government might in fact mute churches' forcefulness in condemning ongoing injustices or policy shortcomings affecting black communities. Would charitable choice funds and the contracting of social services go to those clergy and congregations willing to endorse and politically support those in power? Would accepting funds dilute the church's role as moral conscience for government's treatment of society's dispossessed?[10] Was charitable choice merely a precursor to, or a pretext for, the state dumping its responsibility for care of the poor on an already overburdened faith community?

These arguments were essentially the ones made by Representative Bobby Scott in his action against H.R. 7 in the House and CARE in the Senate. The other side, for whatever reason, really did not engage these concerns. But it would have been a debate worth having. There were good-faith arguments on each side that never found a voice. Many had good reason to doubt that collaboration with government could ever exist without compromising the moral and prophetic voice of the church. Others justifiably saw faith-based support from the government as an attractive and legitimate way to increase their capacity for serving the poor and needy as well as enhancing the political influence of their views. The actual experience of charitable choice collaborators revealed little cause for concern about being co-opted, but the political charges and suspicions drowned out all else.

Discomfort with Religious Transformation

Perhaps the most significant question hovering over the debate but never really addressed was the public utility, not just of religious institutions, but of religion itself. From the time Founding Father James Madison flatly declared in his *Memorial and Remonstrance against Religious Assessments* that government simply could not "employ religion as an instrument of civil policy," religious conviction has largely been consigned to a private role with respect to public policy.[11] But the implicit premise underlying charitable choice and the subsequent Bush faith-based effort represented a remarkable divergence from Madison's position. Among pioneers of the faith-based movement, the desire to facilitate government's partnering with religious service providers rested upon an assumption that religious *content* itself would play an instrumental role in faith-based social service. This is why the "pervasively sectarian" standard the Supreme Court seems ready to set aside is so problematic; it is a bar to truly effective treatment. Money should be able to go to overtly and intensively religious institutions precisely because of their inseparable religious character. Indeed, it was that religious dimension to treatment that the early supporters of the faith-based movement saw as central to healing and helping people. For these supporters, religious conviction was an unparalleled means of addressing problems and dysfunctions.

From this perspective, there was no problem with overt religiosity intermingling with government. President Bush himself, who had experienced the behavior-altering impact of religious conversion, was presumably in this camp. As governor of Texas, he stood fully behind state-sponsored drug treatment and correctional programs for convicted felons that made explicit use of religious methods such as Bible study, prayer, and worship. It seemed only natural to tap into this spiritual dimension of faith-based organizations, since it was precisely what made them so effective.

Yet the propriety of this approach was never fully addressed, and in this sense, the fundamental issue was never joined. Both sides ducked the central questions of overt religion's presence in publicly funded programs. On one side, charitable choice backers skirted the issue, pretending that the law only reinforced existing Supreme Court precedent. In reality, an honest reading of charitable choice laws and a sense of their underlying spirit reveals a tension, if not an outright contradiction. The laws claim fidelity to the establishment clause and take care to deny funds for "sectarian worship, instruction, or proselytization." But they simultaneously ensure and safeguard the rights of participating religious organizations to fully practice and express their religious beliefs. For evangelical groups, where witnessing and proselytizing are essential components of their religious practice, that leads to an obvious contradiction. Charitable choice expressly prohibits religious dissemination, but the idea of subsidizing religious groups in social welfare programs is based on acknowledging the transformative power of religion. As one pair of scholars noted, "the obvious difficulty in limiting government assistance to religious social activism lies in the most important reason why church-based institutions achieve good results: they convert people."[12] The notion that religious groups have a special capacity to effectively address destructive behavior, a capacity that warrants their inclusion in publicly funded programs, presumes that those religious values will be conveyed in the services these groups deliver.

On the other side, the intensity of the opposition to the Bush plan was motivated by a distinct sense that it marked a qualitative shift in the role of faith-based providers. The earlier arguments had largely revolved around the objective of tapping into religious social service agents because of the high motivation of deeply religious people. The perceived benefits in increased efficiency and effectiveness were seen as flowing from faith-motivated social service workers driven by religious *conviction*. But opponents saw in Bush and his initiative something larger and, to them, more invidious. The benefits that President Bush wanted to help fund stemmed from the religious *content* of the service itself and, usually, in clearly religious *circumstance*s. Sharing of religious convictions *by* openly religious persons *in* openly religious settings was at the core of effective treatment and rehabilitation. This struck an ominous note not only with secularists, but with civil libertarians who saw genuine threats to the religious freedom of program recipients.

Here lies the crux of the matter. At issue are fundamental and deep-seated philosophical differences that divide religionists and secularists on the question of religion as a source of public authority. For secularists, religion is seen as a negative, something that is essentially intolerant and oppressive, authoritarian and coercive. This view was captured in a moment of rare honesty by Annie Laurie Gaylor of the Freedom from Religion Foundation, who commented that "all these state-faith partner-ships will do more harm than good. . . . They promote religion as the 'cure-all' to our social problems and divert attention away from the real actions needed to achieve social and economic justice."[13] At the center of the distrust of Bush and his faith-based initiative is the implicit assumption that it ultimately would mean public dollars used for religious transforma-tion and conversion.

In contrast, people of faith point to religion's power at both ends of the social service equation. At the beginning point of service delivery, faith motivates those in service to go further in their efforts to help persons in need. And on the receiving end of social services, religious conviction is often correlated with program success. Faith has a transform-ative dimension that truly empowers beneficiaries to kick the addiction, live more productive lives, and so on. To cut religion out of the picture is to eviscerate the treatment. Whether public funds actually serve to advance religion is, in fact, beside the point. If a conversion-centered treatment "works," fund it, for the effectiveness, not the faith.

This central divide is illustrated by the recent lawsuits filed challenging InnerChange, the prison correctional and rehabilitation program that George W. Bush promoted as governor of Texas and praised as an ideal example of a faith-based program. InnerChange is qualitatively different from the charitable choice–related programs affected by the 1996 welfare reform bill. In welfare programs, the prime benefit typically was in recruiting people of faith to offer assistance to welfare recipients in their job search. Religion, to the extent it was part of the mix, was ancillary. In contrast, InnerChange is a program where the religious aspect is at the center of the service delivery. It seeks to fundamentally transform those in the program, through an intensely religious curriculum of rigorous daily Bible study, worship, prayer, and mentoring with volunteers from nearby churches. Once released from prison, program participants are placed within a mentoring church. The undeniable emphasis of Inner-Change is to transform participants spiritually, and that religious focus is advanced with the benefit of public funds. At the same time, the secular benefits realized from this intensely religious program are equally undeniable. No secular or government-run program seems to match the strikingly low rates of recidivism among those who have gone through InnerChange.

The InnerChange program brings into focus the fundamental question: Can the government utilize religion to its own secular ends even if it advances religion in the process? Can a program that is both religious at its core and successful in serving larger societal goals be supported by the government? Provided that other First Amendment criteria are met—the program is genuinely voluntary, it offers true choice for recipients, and it respects the religious exercise rights of participants—can a government-subsidized program use an intensely religious provider to realize public aims even as it clearly advances religion along the way?

This vital question cannot be answered without contemplating key elemental issues of religion, its place in the public realm, and its standing relative to the government. It also raises a host of auxiliary questions. One of these is the challenge of identifying the religious actors who qualify to participate in public programs. The government admittedly lacks the competency to judge or rank the authenticity of the ever-expanding universe of religious groups and faiths. Does this mean that the government simply ought to dismiss all religious groups from consideration for public funds? Or should it adopt a stance of formal neutrality that makes no distinctions between religious actors or between religious and secular ones, where all have equal admittance to policy involvement contingent on a record of program effectiveness? If the latter, what criteria of success must religious actors meet to qualify for participation in publicly funded programs? What demonstrable level of effectiveness on the part of religious providers is necessary? Must they show a solid empirical track record supported by established social science principles?

Those who worry about the potential for division and conflict flowing from religious participation would require a clearer showing of at least equal, if not better, effectiveness before allowing faith-based groups in. Others contend that setting a higher bar for faith-based effectiveness than that demanded of secular providers only demonstrates an ongoing bias against religion. Neutrality means judging by the same standards of effectiveness—or perhaps more accurately, *refusing* to judge by the same *lack* of effectiveness standards by which most current programs are *not* judged.

Objective analysis of faith-based social services has been hampered by the lack of hard data on their efficacy. The paucity of empirical studies on the effectiveness or success rate of actual faith-based programs has allowed each side to caricature the other. In the absence of a more detailed track record for faith-intensive programs, proponents are free to proclaim that faith-based agencies are superior providers whose quality of programs is unrivaled by their governmental or secular counterparts. The opponents argue, with equal conviction and similarly unfettered by fact, that faith-centered programs substitute religion for accepted treatment methods, emphasize volunteers over social work professionals, and are characterized by ineffectiveness. After two years of rancorous national debate over faith-based initiatives, these empirical shortcomings are only starting to be addressed. At the same time, however, the academic and media elites conducting and reporting on empirical research are, in general, unfamiliar with the language and norms of the faith-based community.

Conclusion: Framing a Better Debate

The church-state arrangement in our country is badly in need of updating. Our understandings are distorted by outdated historical assumptions, crabbed notions of faith, and the failure of public policy to reflect broad social consensus that exists among average Americans. Ongoing efforts to negotiate the role of religious nonprofits in publicly sponsored service delivery would benefit greatly from acknowledging and correcting these deficiencies.

For example, one striking dimension to the "public square" debate is the chasm between the perceptions of faith among elites compared to those among mainstream citizens. Elite opinion, among Democrats and

Republicans alike, is marked by a palpable lack of enthusiasm for collaboration between the public and religious sectors. It is well-documented that
strong religious conviction is less frequent among political elites than it
is among the population as a whole. It is difficult, even among high-ranking
policy officials within the Bush administration itself, to find someone who
will speak passionately about faith as the answer to ineffectual social
service programs, with the president himself being the exception that
proves the rule.

While many elites may pay lip service to the faith-based initiative,
there is a degree of jaded skepticism that undermines their credibility.
Many seem far more interested in the issue as a political bonanza than
for its intrinsic merit. In contrast, the typical American might well wonder
what the fuss is about in letting religious groups have a hand in government's efforts to address social problems. Sizable majorities in public
opinion polls accept the argument that the power of religion can change
people's lives: a Pew Forum on Religion and Public Life survey in April
2001 put the figure at 62 percent.[14] People of faith accept intuitively that
religion is an influence for good in helping individuals overcome addiction,
avoid the temptation to yield to crime, and alter other destructive behavior.
For those of faith, it goes without saying that a program that tends to
the spiritual and emotional needs of participants is going to be more
effective than one that merely feeds them, clothes them, and sees to their
physical needs.

A second, and perhaps more destructive, distortion stems from the
history of the separation of church and state. The nation would have a
far more productive exploration of the philosophical differences on
church-state interaction if combatants were to acknowledge that contemporary debates differ dramatically from those concerns that occasioned
the inclusion of the establishment clause in the Bill of Rights in the late
eighteenth century or that led to the key separationist decisions of the
mid-twentieth century. Contemporary establishment clause concerns are
of a fundamentally different nature. The focus of the original establishment clause was to avoid a dominant, government-sanctioned religion at
the national level while leaving states free to establish, or disestablish,
particular faiths. Well into the separationist jurisprudence of the 1960s
and 1970s, the focal point was the same: the concern was with the governments of a highly religious nation showing special favor to a particular

faith or denomination—usually a dominant mainstream Protestantism— over the rights of Catholics, Jehovah's Witnesses, or adherents of other smaller religious groups.

The explosion of religious pluralism in America during the past half-century has rendered those older concerns mostly antiquated and irrelevant. Nevertheless, they continue to dominate the rhetoric on church-state issues. The current divide over the public presence of religion is more fundamental; it is more accurately a deep-seated cultural rift between the deeply religious and the relentlessly secular. Barring the fervently religious from the public gate, as is implied by invoking yesteryear's separationist language in today's secular world, is not likely to mute these conflicts. If anything, it will only intensify the fighting and amplify the deep resentment that underpins it. The arguments and justifications that were developed in response to the earlier sectarian divide do not fit this new deeper rift. Indeed, the old language only obfuscates what is really at stake, making ultimate solutions that much more elusive.

Doubts about the legal status of faith-based services suggest another weakness in our church-state understanding, one that goes to the very nature of religious conviction and the actions it inspires. Offering social services via religious providers suggests a more expansive view of religion and how it is practiced publicly and collectively. This view runs counter to the commonplace treatment of religion. There has always been a discernible bias in our legal and constitutional understandings of what comprises legitimate religious belief and practice, a bias that undermines the legal standing of faith-based social service. In short, the essence of religious life was thought to be personal and individual in nature, rather than collective or corporate. To the extent there was a collective dimension worthy of recognition, it was in the context of worship. Religion was inward-looking and introspective, rather than outwardly or externally manifested. It was reflective and spiritually experiential, rather than active and behavioral.

Indeed, for secularists this crabbed version of religion was a key to constraining and controlling what they saw as the negative repercussions of religious conviction. If religion was in fact an intolerant, narrow, divisive force in society, its deleterious consequences could be managed by confining religion to private and personal boundaries. But recognizing social service as a legitimate form of religious exercise born of genuine spiritual conviction challenges the basic definition of religion. It raises the need for an enriched, enhanced mode of thinking about religious practice and exercise. For many people of faith, religion has undeniable and unavoidable public manifestations. It is not merely contemplative in orientation; it includes outward acts of social service as well. The reality for many who are devoutly religious is that social service is every bit as much an imperative of their faith as prayer, meditation, or other aspects of their personal spiritual walk.

Nor is religious devotion practiced only in isolation. It is not done merely by oneself, but has collective dimensions, through that body called the church. Unfortunately, our constitutional law is geared to individual rights and liberties; it generally lacks a nuanced and well-articulated understanding of rights as applied to and held by groups and associations. Clearly those religious exercise rights are implicated by the issues surrounding the faith-based initiative. Does a secular voluntary association that is engaged in social services, say the United Way, have a greater right to public acknowledgment than a religious voluntary organization like First Baptist Church that decides God is calling it to the same practice? The public square debate has the real opportunity to capture a truer understanding of religion, one that is more reflective of religious realities.

The constitutional and policy implications that would flow from this enhanced perspective are not self-evident. It may mean that the task of determining what constitutes the core of someone's faith, or a group's faith, is simply beyond the competence of our legal and judicial institutions. If so, this might compel an approach of strict neutrality and even-handedness that makes no distinction between religious and secular providers. Others might claim that the only approach, in light of this, is to err on the side of caution, and take a strict stance against any and all interaction between the state and the religious. Whatever the ramifications, the result of a modernized and enlightened debate would do far greater justice to belief systems that are central to millions of people in this country.

Appendix A

Interview Methodology

The story of the faith-based initiative is ongoing; even as we write, changes in the political environment are affecting the development and implementation of these proposals. As we embarked upon the project of assessing the first two years of George W. Bush's faith-based proposals, two things were very clear. First, the only way to discover what was really happening was to talk with individuals directly involved in the process. Although newspaper accounts can be helpful, the issue is incredibly complex and the rhetoric and spin surrounding this issue are quite intense. We knew that journalists' accounts would, by their very nature, have to simplify the complexities, and we also recognized that some stories might not provide an accurate account of events. Second, we realized the extremely sensitive nature of speaking with individuals directly involved in an ongoing policy debate. We understood that our sources, particularly those currently working in Congress or the White House, took risks to speak with us about a continuing controversy. We also knew that we needed to hear their stories and record their perspectives to even begin to understand the politics of the faith-based initiative.

We chose our initial interview subjects after compiling a list of important actors in the faith-based debate deemed central to the story because of their position or by recommendation of policy experts who had followed the issue. Our goal was to talk with current and former staff of the White House Office of Faith-Based and Community Initiatives and its satellites, congressional aides involved in the House and Senate processes, interest group activists who worked on both sides of the debate, and people involved in the early development of charitable choice. In each interview, we asked our subjects for suggestions of other people we should interview, and we noted those individuals whose names surfaced in several conversations.

Most of the people we wanted to interview agreed to speak with us, and almost everyone was very cooperative and forthcoming. Although we recognize that our interviews will not capture every detail of the story, we were impressed with our subjects' willingness to cooperate and their candor when discussing difficult or politically sensitive topics. The men and women with whom we met are dedicated to their tasks, take their jobs very seriously, and demonstrate professionalism. We are indebted to them for their willingness to share their experiences and impressions with us.

Amy Black and/or Doug Koopman conducted all of the interviews cited in this project. Whenever possible, we interviewed the subjects in person, typically at their place of business. In a few instances, we were unable to schedule a personal interview and relied on telephone interviews instead. The interviews ranged in length from about thirty minutes to over three hours, with the typical interview lasting approximately one hour. As warranted, we followed up the interviews with clarification questions via phone or e-mail.

Recognizing the sensitive nature of these interviews, we chose not to tape-record them. We took notes during the interviews and transcribed them as soon as possible after the meetings for the purpose of accuracy. Some of the people with whom we met agreed to speak on the record; most chose to speak on the record if we would clear quotes with them; a few spoke with us off the record or on background. In order to preserve anonymity, we assigned a unique identifying letter to each individual whom we quoted without direct attribution. The notes will reference such interviewees by their assigned pseudonyms.

Appendix B

List of Interviews

Ralph Benko, Americans for Community and Faith-Centered Enterprise

Annie Billings White, Former Legislative Counsel, Senator John Ashcroft (R-Missouri)

Stuart Bowen, Deputy Assistant to the President and Deputy Staff Secretary

Randy Brandt, Counsel, Senator Rick Santorum (R-Pennsylvania)

John Bridgeland, Assistant to the President and Director, USA Freedom Corps; Former Director, Domestic Policy Council

Stanley Carlson-Thies, Center for Public Justice; Former Associate Director for Law and Policy, White House Office of Faith-Based and Community Initiatives

John J. DiIulio, Jr., University of Pennsylvania; Former Director, White House Office of Faith-Based and Community Initiatives

Don Eberly, United States Agency for International Development (USAID); Former Deputy Director, White House Office of Faith-Based and Community Initiatives

Denise Edwards, Legislative Assistant, Office of Representative Chet Edwards (D-Texas)

Carl Esbeck, University of Missouri Law School; Former Director, Justice Department Faith-Based and Community Initiatives Taskforce

Max Finberg, Senior Legislative Assistant, Representative Tony Hall (D-Ohio)

William Galston, University of Maryland; Al Gore Campaign Adviser

Michael Gerson, Assistant to the President and Director of Speechwriting

Dan Gerstein, Director of Communications, Senator Joseph Lieberman (D-Connecticut)

Tim Goeglein, Special Assistant to the President and Deputy Director, White House Office of Public Liaison

Stephen Goldsmith, Chair, Corporation for National Service; George W. Bush Campaign Adviser

Kevin "Seamus" Hasson, President, The Becket Fund for Religious Liberty

Major George Hood, Public Affairs Director, National Headquarters, Salvation Army

Jack Horner, Legislative Director, Representative J. C. Watts (R-Oklahoma)

Rebecca Jones Hunt, Legislative Assistant, Representative Pete Hoekstra (R-Michigan)

Daniel Katz, Director of Legislative Affairs, Americans United for Separation of Church and State

KiKi Kless, Assistant to the Speaker for Policy, House Speaker Dennis Hastert (R-Illinois)

David Kuo, Deputy Director, White House Office of Faith-Based and Community Initiatives

Joseph Loconte, William E. Simon Fellow in Religion and a Free Society, Heritage Foundation

Will Marshall, President, Progressive Policy Institute

Chip Mellor, President, Institute for Justice

Phyllis Berry Myers, President and CEO, Center for New Black Leadership

Lauren Richardson Noyes, Former Legislative Director, Representative Joseph Pitts (R-Pennsylvania)

Brent Orrell, Director, Department of Labor Center for Faith-Based and Community Initiatives

Bobby Polito, Director, Department of Health and Human Services Center for Faith-Based and Community Initiatives

Meg Riley, Director of Advocacy and Witness, Unitarian Universalist Association of Congregations

Elizabeth Seale, Former Director, Department of Health and Human Services Center for Faith-Based and Community Initiatives

Duane Shank, Director of Outreach, Call to Renewal

Jim Skillen, President, Center for Public Justice

Ryan Streeter, Department of Housing and Urban Development Center for Faith-Based and Community Initiatives

Paul Taylor, Counsel, House Judiciary Committee, Constitution Subcommittee

Theresa Tilling Thompson, Senior Legislative Assistant, Representative Bobby Scott (D-Virginia)

Jim Towey, Director, White House Office of Faith-Based and Community Initiatives

Bill Wichterman, Chief of Staff, Representative Joseph Pitts (R-Pennsylvania)

Jim Wilkinson, White House Deputy Director of Communications

Don Willett, Former Director of Law and Policy, White House Office of Faith-Based and Community Initiatives

Appendix C

Executive Orders Affecting Faith-Based Policies, 2001–2002

I. Executive Order 13198; January 29, 2001

Establishment of White House Office of Faith-Based and Community Initiatives

By the authority vested in me as President of the United States by the Constitution and the laws of the United States of America, and in order to help the Federal Government coordinate a national effort to expand opportunities for faith-based and other community organizations and to strengthen their capacity to better meet social needs in America's communities, it is hereby ordered as follows:

Section 1. Policy.

Faith-based and other community organizations are indispensable in meeting the needs of poor Americans and distressed neighborhoods. Government cannot be replaced by such organizations, but it can and should welcome them as partners. The paramount goal is compassionate results, and private and charitable community groups, including religious ones, should have the fullest opportunity permitted by law to compete on a level playing field, so long as they achieve valid public purposes, such as curbing crime, conquering addiction, strengthening families and neighborhoods, and overcoming poverty. This delivery of social services must be results oriented and should value the bedrock principles of pluralism, nondiscrimination, evenhandedness, and neutrality.

Sec. 2. Establishment.

There is established a White House Office of Faith-Based and Community Initiatives (White House OFBCI) within the Executive Office of the President that will have lead responsibility in the executive branch to establish policies, priorities, and objectives for the Federal Government's comprehensive effort to enlist, equip, enable, empower, and expand the work of faith-based and other community organizations to the extent permitted by law.

Sec. 3. Functions.

The principal functions of the White House OFBCI are, to the extent permitted by law:

(a) to develop, lead, and coordinate the Administration's policy agenda affecting faith-based and other community programs and initiatives, expand the role of such efforts in communities, and increase their capacity through executive action, legislation, Federal and private funding, and regulatory relief;

(b) to ensure that Administration and Federal Government policy decisions and programs are consistent with the President's stated goals with respect to faith-based and other community initiatives;

(c) to help integrate the President's policy agenda affecting faith-based and other community organizations across the Federal Government;

(d) to coordinate public education activities designed to mobilize public support for faith-based and community nonprofit initiatives through volunteerism, special projects, demonstration pilots, and public-private partnerships;

(e) to encourage private charitable giving to support faith-based and community initiatives;

(f) to bring concerns, ideas, and policy options to the President for assisting, strengthening, and replicating successful faith-based and other community programs;

(g) to provide policy and legal education to State, local, and community policymakers and public officials seeking ways to empower faith-based and other community organizations and to improve the opportunities, capacity, and expertise of such groups;

(h) to develop and implement strategic initiatives under the President's agenda to strengthen the institutions of civil society and America's families and communities;

(i) to showcase and herald innovative grassroots nonprofit organizations and civic initiatives;

(j) to eliminate unnecessary legislative, regulatory, and other bureaucratic barriers that impede effective faith-based and other community efforts to solve social problems;

(k) to monitor implementation of the President's agenda affecting faith-based and other community organizations; and

(l) to ensure that the efforts of faith-based and other community organizations meet high standards of excellence and accountability.

Sec. 4. Administration.

(a) The White House OFBCI may function through established or ad hoc committees, task forces, or interagency groups.

(b) The White House OFBCI shall have a staff to be headed by the Assistant to the President for Faith-Based and Community Initiatives. The White House OFBCI shall have such staff and other assistance, to the extent permitted by law, as may be necessary to carry out the provisions of this order. The White House OFBCI operations shall begin no later than 30 days from the date of this order.

(c) The White House OFBCI shall coordinate with the liaison and point of contact designated by each executive department and agency with respect to this initiative.

(d) All executive departments and agencies (agencies) shall cooperate with the White House OFBCI and provide such information, support, and assistance to the White House OFBCI as it may request, to the extent permitted by law.

(e) The agencies' actions directed by this Executive Order shall be carried out subject to the availability of appropriations and to the extent permitted by law.

Sec. 5. Judicial Review.

This order does not create any right or benefit, substantive or procedural, enforceable at law or equity by a party against the United States, its agencies or instrumentalities, its officers or employees, or any other person.

GEORGE W. BUSH
THE WHITE HOUSE,
January 29, 2001.

II. Executive Order 13199; January 29, 2001

Agency Responsibilities with Respect to Faith-Based and Community Initiatives

By the authority vested in me as President by the Constitution and the laws of the United States of America, and in order to help the Federal Government coordinate a national effort to expand opportunities for faith-based and other community organizations and to strengthen their capacity to better meet social needs in America's communities, it is hereby ordered as follows:

Section 1. Establishment of Executive Department Centers for Faith-Based and Community Initiatives.

(a) The Attorney General, the Secretary of Education, the Secretary of Labor, the Secretary of Health and Human Services, and the Secretary of Housing and Urban Development shall each establish within their respective departments a Center for Faith-Based and Community Initiatives (Center).

(b) Each executive department Center shall be supervised by a Director, appointed by the department head in consultation with the White House Office of Faith-Based and Community Initiatives (White House OFBCI).

(c) Each department shall provide its Center with appropriate staff, administrative support, and other resources to meet its responsibilities under this order.

(d) Each department's Center shall begin operations no later than 45 days from the date of this order.

Sec. 2. Purpose of Executive Department Centers for Faith-Based and Community Initiatives.

The purpose of the executive department Centers will be to coordinate department efforts to eliminate regulatory, contracting, and other programmatic obstacles to the participation of faith-based and other community organizations in the provision of social services.

Sec. 3. Responsibilities of Executive Department Centers for Faith-Based and Community Initiatives.

Each Center shall, to the extent permitted by law: (a) conduct, in coordination with the White House OFBCI, a department-wide audit to identify all existing barriers to the participation of faith-based and other community organizations in the delivery of social services by the department, including but not limited to regulations, rules, orders, procurement, and other internal policies and practices, and outreach activities that either facially discriminate against or otherwise discourage or disadvantage the participation of faith-based and other community organizations in Federal programs;

(b) coordinate a comprehensive departmental effort to incorporate faith-based and other community organizations in department programs and initiatives to the greatest extent possible;

(c) propose initiatives to remove barriers identified pursuant to section 3(a) of this order, including but not limited to reform of regulations, procurement, and other internal policies and practices, and outreach activities;

(d) propose the development of innovative pilot and demonstration programs to increase the participation of faith-based and other community organizations in Federal as well as State and local initiatives; and

(e) develop and coordinate department outreach efforts to disseminate information more effectively to faith-based and other community organizations with respect to programming changes, contracting opportunities, and other department initiatives, including but not limited to Web and Internet resources.

Sec. 4. Additional Responsibilities of the Department of Health and Human Services and the Department of Labor Centers.

In addition to those responsibilities described in section 3 of this order, the Department of Health and Human Services and the Department of Labor Centers shall, to the extent permitted by law: (a) conduct a comprehensive review of policies and practices affecting existing funding streams governed by so-called "Charitable Choice" legislation to assess the department's compliance with the requirements of Charitable Choice; and (b) promote and ensure compliance with existing Charitable Choice legislation by the department, as well as its partners in State and local government, and their contractors.

Sec. 5. Reporting Requirements.

(a) Report. Not later than 180 days after the date of this order and annually thereafter, each of the five executive department Centers described in section 1 of this order shall prepare and submit a report to the White House OFBCI.

(b) Contents. The report shall include a description of the department's efforts in carrying out its responsibilities under this order, including but not limited to:

(1) a comprehensive analysis of the barriers to the full participation of faith-based and other community organizations in the delivery of social services identified pursuant to section 3(a) of this order and the proposed strategies to eliminate those barriers; and

(2) a summary of the technical assistance and other information that will be available to faith-based and other community organizations regarding the program activities of the department and the preparation of applications or proposals for grants, cooperative agreements, contracts, and procurement.

(c) Performance Indicators. The first report, filed 180 days after the date of this order, shall include annual performance indicators and measurable objectives for department action. Each report filed thereafter shall measure the department's performance against the objectives set forth in the initial report.

Sec. 6. Responsibilities of All Executive Departments and Agencies.

All executive departments and agencies (agencies) shall: (a) designate an agency employee to serve as the liaison and point of contact with the White House OFBCI; and

(b) cooperate with the White House OFBCI and provide such information, support, and assistance to the White House OFBCI as it may request, to the extent permitted by law.

Sec. 7. Administration and Judicial Review.

(a) The agencies' actions directed by this Executive Order shall be carried out subject to the availability of appropriations and to the extent permitted by law.

(b) This order does not create any right or benefit, substantive or procedural, enforceable at law or equity against the United States, its agencies or instrumentalities, its officers or employees, or any other person.

GEORGE W. BUSH
THE WHITE HOUSE,
January 29, 2001.

III. Executive Order 13279; December 12, 2002

Equal Protection of the Laws for Faith-Based and Community Organizations

By the authority vested in me as President by the Constitution and the laws of the United States of America, including section 121(a) of title 40, United States Code, and section 301 of title 3, United States Code, and in order to guide Federal agencies in formulating and developing policies with implications for faith-based organizations and other community organizations, to ensure equal protection of the laws for faith-based and community organizations, to further the national effort to expand opportunities for, and strengthen the capacity of, faith-based and other community organizations so that they may better meet social needs in America's communities, and to ensure the economical and efficient administration and completion of Government contracts, it is hereby ordered as follows:

Section 1. Definitions.

For purposes of this order:

(a) "Federal financial assistance" means assistance that non-Federal entities receive or administer in the form of grants, contracts, loans, loan guarantees, property, cooperative agreements, food commodities, direct appropriations, or other assistance, but does not include a tax credit, deduction, or exemption.

(b) "Social service program" means a program that is administered by the Federal Government, or by a State or local government using Federal financial assistance, and that provides services directed at reducing poverty, improving opportunities for low-income children, revitalizing low-income communities, empowering low-income families and low-income individuals to become self-sufficient, or otherwise helping people in need. Such programs include, but are not limited to, the following:

(i) child care services, protective services for children and adults, services for children and adults in foster care, adoption services, services related to the management and maintenance of the home, day care services for adults, and services to meet the special needs of children, older individuals, and individuals with disabilities (including physical, mental, or emotional disabilities);

(ii) transportation services;

(iii) job training and related services, and employment services;

(iv) information, referral, and counseling services;

(v) the preparation and delivery of meals and services related to soup kitchens or food banks;

(vi) health support services;

(vii) literacy and mentoring programs;

(viii) services for the prevention and treatment of juvenile delinquency and substance abuse, services for the prevention of crime and the provision of assistance to the victims and the families of criminal offenders, and services related to intervention in, and prevention of, domestic violence; and

(ix) services related to the provision of assistance for housing under Federal law.

(c) "Policies that have implications for faith-based and community organizations" refers to all policies, programs, and regulations, including official guidance and internal agency procedures, that have significant effects on faith-based organizations participating in or seeking to participate in social service programs supported with Federal financial assistance.

(d) "Agency" means a department or agency in the executive branch.

(e) "Specified agency heads" mean the Attorney General, the Secretaries of Agriculture, Education, Health and Human Services, Housing and Urban Development, and Labor, and the Administrator of the Agency for International Development.

Sec. 2. Fundamental Principles and Policymaking Criteria.

In formulating and implementing policies that have implications for faith-based and community organizations, agencies that administer social service programs supported with Federal financial assistance shall, to the extent permitted by law, be guided by the following fundamental principles:

(a) Federal financial assistance for social service programs should be distributed in the most effective and efficient manner possible;

(b) The Nation's social service capacity will benefit if all eligible organizations, including faith-based and other community organizations, are able to compete on an equal footing for Federal financial assistance used to support social service programs;

(c) No organization should be discriminated against on the basis of religion or religious belief in the administration or distribution of Federal financial assistance under social service programs;

(d) All organizations that receive Federal financial assistance under social services programs should be prohibited from discriminating against beneficiaries or potential beneficiaries of the social services programs on the basis of religion or religious belief. Accordingly, organizations, in providing services supported in whole or in part with Federal financial assistance, and in their outreach activities related to such services, should not be allowed to discriminate against current or prospective program beneficiaries on the basis of religion, a religious belief, a refusal to hold a religious belief, or a refusal to actively participate in a religious practice;

(e) The Federal Government must implement Federal programs in accordance with the Establishment Clause and the Free Exercise Clause of the First Amendment to the Constitution. Therefore, organizations that engage in inherently religious activities, such as worship, religious instruction, and proselytization, must offer those services separately in time or location from any programs or services supported with direct Federal financial assistance, and participation in any such inherently religious activities must be voluntary for the beneficiaries of the social service program supported with such Federal financial assistance; and

(f) Consistent with the Free Exercise Clause and the Free Speech Clause of the Constitution, faith-based organizations should be eligible to compete for Federal financial assistance used to support social service programs and to participate fully in the social service programs supported with Federal financial assistance without impairing their independence, autonomy, expression, or religious character. Accordingly, a faith-based organization that applies for or participates in a social service program supported with Federal financial assistance may retain its independence and may continue to carry out its mission, including the definition, development, practice, and expression of its religious beliefs, provided that it does not use direct Federal financial assistance to support any inherently religious activities, such as worship, religious instruction, or proselytization. Among other things, faith-based organizations that receive Federal financial assistance may use their facilities to provide social services supported with Federal financial assistance, without removing or altering religious art, icons, scriptures, or other symbols from these facilities. In addition, a faith-based organization that applies for or participates in a social service program supported with Federal financial assistance may retain religious terms in its organization's name, select its board members on a religious basis, and include religious references in its organization's mission statements and other chartering or governing documents.

Sec. 3. Agency Implementation.

(a) Specified agency heads shall, in coordination with the White House Office of Faith-Based and Community Initiatives (White House OFBCI), review and evaluate existing policies that have implications for faith-based and community organizations in order to assess the consistency of such policies with the fundamental principles and policymaking criteria articulated in section 2 of this order.

(b) Specified agency heads shall ensure that all policies that have implications for faith-based and community organizations are consistent with the fundamental principles and policymaking criteria articulated in section 2 of this order. Therefore, specified agency heads shall, to the extent permitted by law:

(i) amend all such existing policies of their respective agencies to ensure that they are consistent with the fundamental principles and policymaking criteria articulated in section 2 of this order;

(ii) where appropriate, implement new policies for their respective agencies that are consistent with and necessary to further the fundamental principles and policymaking criteria set forth in section 2 of this order; and

(iii) implement new policies that are necessary to ensure that their respective agencies collect data regarding the participation of faith-based and community organizations in social service programs that receive Federal financial assistance.

(c) Within 90 days after the date of this order, each specified agency head shall report to the President, through the Director of the White House OFBCI, the actions it proposes to undertake to accomplish the activities set forth in sections 3(a) and (b) of this order.

Sec. 4. Amendment of Executive Order 11246.

Pursuant to section 121(a) of title 40, United States Code, and section 301 of title 3, United States Code, and in order to further the strong

Federal interest in ensuring that the cost and progress of Federal procurement contracts are not adversely affected by an artificial restriction of the labor pool caused by the unwarranted exclusion of faith-based organizations from such contracts, section 204 of Executive Order 11246 of September 24, 1965, as amended, is hereby further amended to read as follows:

"SEC. 204 (a) The Secretary of Labor may, when the Secretary deems that special circumstances in the national interest so require, exempt a contracting agency from the requirement of including any or all of the provisions of Section 202 of this Order in any specific contract, subcontract, or purchase order.

(b) The Secretary of Labor may, by rule or regulation, exempt certain classes of contracts, subcontracts, or purchase orders (1) whenever work is to be or has been performed outside the United States and no recruitment of workers within the limits of the United States is involved; (2) for standard commercial supplies or raw materials; (3) involving less than specified amounts of money or specified numbers of workers; or (4) to the extent that they involve subcontracts below a specified tier.

(c) Section 202 of this Order shall not apply to a Government contractor or subcontractor that is a religious corporation, association, educational institution, or society, with respect to the employment of individuals of a particular religion to perform work connected with the carrying on by such corporation, association, educational institution, or society of its activities. Such contractors and subcontractors are not exempted or excused from complying with the other requirements contained in this Order.

(d) The Secretary of Labor may also provide, by rule, regulation, or order, for the exemption of facilities of a contractor that are in all respects separate and distinct from activities of the contractor related to the performance of the contract: provided, that such an exemption will not interfere with or impede the effectuation of the purposes of this Order: and provided further, that in the absence of such an exemption all facilities shall be covered by the provisions of this Order."

Sec. 5. General Provisions.

(a) This order supplements but does not supersede the requirements contained in Executive Orders 13198 and 13199 of January 29, 2001.

(b) The agencies shall coordinate with the White House OFBCI concerning the implementation of this order.

(c) Nothing in this order shall be construed to require an agency to take any action that would impair the conduct of foreign affairs or the national security.

Sec. 6. Responsibilities of Executive Departments and Agencies.

All executive departments and agencies (agencies) shall:

(a) designate an agency employee to serve as the liaison and point of contact with the White House OFBCI; and

(b) cooperate with the White House OFBCI and provide such information, support, and assistance to the White House OFBCI as it may request, to the extent permitted by law.

Sec. 7. Judicial Review.

This order is intended only to improve the internal management of the executive branch, and it is not intended to, and does not, create any right or benefit, substantive or procedural, enforceable at law or in equity by a party against the United States, its agencies, or entities, its officers, employees or agents, or any person.

GEORGE W. BUSH
THE WHITE HOUSE,
December 12, 2002.

Cases Cited

ACLU of Louisiana v. Foster (E.D. Louisiana 2002)

Agostini v. Felton, 521 U.S. 203 (1997)

Aguilar v. Felton, 473 U.S. 402 (1985)

American Jewish Congress v. Michael Bernick et al. (California 2001)

American Jewish Congress and Texas Civil Rights Project v. Bost (S.D. Texas 2002)

Ashburn and Americans United for Separation of Church and State v. Maples, Prison Fellowship Ministries, InnerChange Freedom Initiative, et al. (S.D. Iowa 2003)

Bellmore v. United Methodist Children's Home, and Department of Human Resources, State of Georgia (Superior Court, Fulton County, Georgia, 2002)

Board of Education v. Mergens, 496 U.S. 226 (1990)

Board of Ed. of Central School Dist. No. 1 v. Allen, 392 U.S. 236 (1968)

Board of Ed. of Westside Community Schools (Dist. 66) v. Mergens, 496 U.S. 226 (1990)

Bowen v. Kendrick, 487 U.S. 589 (1988)

Bradfield v. Roberts, 175 U.S. 291 (1899)

Committee for Public Ed. & Religious Liberty v. Nyquist, 413 U.S. 756 (1973)

Corporation of the Presiding Bishop v. Amos, 483 U.S. 327 (1987)

Everson v. Board of Education of Ewing Township, 330 U.S. 1 (1947)

Freedom from Religion Foundation v. McCallum and FaithWorks Milwaukee, 179 F. Supp. 2d 950 (W.D. Wisconsin 2002)

Freedom from Religion Foundation v. McCallum and FaithWorks Milwaukee, 2002 U.S. Dist., Lexis 14177 (W.D. Wisconsin 2002)

Freedom from Religion Foundation v. McCallum and FaithWorks Milwaukee, 2003 U.S., Lexis 6301 (7th Cir. 2003)

Good News Club v. Milford Central School, 533 U.S. 98 (2001)

Lamb's Chapel v. Center Moriches Union Free School Dist., 508 U.S. 384 (1993)

Lemon v. Kurtzman, 403 U.S. 602 (1971)

Levitt v. Committee for Public Education, 413 U.S. 472 (1973)

Locke v. Davey, 299 F.3d 748 (9th Cir. 2002)

McCollum v. Board of Education, 333 U.S. 203 (1948)

Meek v. Pittenger, 421 U.S. 349 (1975)

Mitchell v. Helms, 530 U.S. 793 (2000)

Mueller v. Allen, 463 U.S. 388 (1983)

Pedreira v. Kentucky Baptist Homes for Children (E.D. Kentucky 2001)

Rosenberger v. Rector and Visitors of Univ. of Va., 515 U.S. 819 (1995)

Widmar v. Vincent, 454 U.S. 263 (1981)

Witters v. Washington Department of Services for the Blind, 474 U.S. 481 (1986)

Wolman v. Walter, 433 U.S. 229 (1977)

Zelman v. Simmons-Harris, 536 U.S. 639 (2002)

Zobrest v. Catalina Foothills School Dist., 509 U.S. 1 (1993)

Notes

Introduction: The Faith-Based Initiatives through Three "Lenses"

1. See, for example, Jake Tapper, "Fade to White: The Only African American Republican in Congress Is Headed Home," *Washington Post Magazine*, 5 January 2003, W06.

2. Sheryl Gay Stolberg and Elisabeth Bumiller. "Divisive Words: The Overview; Powell Criticizes Lott for Remarks; Jeb Bush Joins In," *New York Times*, 19 December 2002, A1.

3. Associated Press, "Inhofe, Watts Back Off Defense of Trent Lott," 20 December 2002, http://web.lexis-nexis.com (accessed 10 March 2003).

4. J. C. Watts, interview with Tim Russert, *Meet the Press*, NBC, 15 December 2002.

5. Mary Leonard, "President Eases Way for Religious Charities," *Boston Globe*, 13 December 2002, A1.

6. Bill Sammon, "President Rolls Back 'Secular' Rules on Faith-based Groups," *Washington Times*, 13 December 2002, A1.

7. David L. Green and Susan Baer, "Faith Groups Get Boost in Bush Order," *Baltimore Sun*, 13 December 2002, A1; Richard W. Stevenson, "In Order, President Eases Limits on U.S. Aid to Religious Groups," *New York Times*, 13 December 2002, A1.

8. Dana Milbank, "Bush Issues 'Faith-Based Initiative' Orders," *Washington Post*, 13 December 2002, A4.

9. Nicholas M. Horrock, "Bush to Push Faith-Based Initiative," United Press International, 29 November 2002, www.up.com/print.cfm?StoryID=20021129-051337-4212r (accessed 2 December 2002).

10. Amy Fagan, "Watts to Support Narrower Faith Bill," *Washington Times*, 14 October 2002, A4.

11. Associated Press, "Bush Enacts 'Faith-Based' Measure," 12 December 2002, www.freedomforum.org/templates/document.asp?documentID=17353 (accessed 11 March 2003).

12. Barry Lynn, "Educate Public about Religious Right Agenda," ProChoice Online, 1999, www.wcla.org/99-spring/lynn.html (accessed 3 January 2003).

13. Horrock, "Bush to Push Faith-Based Initiative."

14. Sammon, "President Rolls Back 'Secular' Rules."

15. Green and Baer, "Faith Groups Get Boost."

16. Most general public policy textbooks contain roughly the same outline of the policymaking process. Two good examples that are primary sources of our understanding are Thomas R. Dye, *Understanding Public Policy*, 8th ed. (Englewood Cliffs, N.J.: Prentice Hall, 1995), and Guy B. Peters, *American Public Policy*, 5th ed. (Chatham, N.J.: Chatham House, 1999).

17. *Zelman v. Simmons-Harris*, 536 U.S. 639 (2002).

18. See, for example, Anna Greenberg and Stanley B. Greenberg, "Adding Values," *The American Prospect* 11, no. 19 (28 August 2000): 28. This journal has been an

especially lively forum for the Democratic Party's debate on how it should interact with more traditional and often explicitly religious themes and policies.

19. This argument is made by Geoffrey Layman in *The Great Divide: Religious and Cultural Conflict in American Party Politics* (New York: Columbia University Press, 2001). We find the general outlines of his argument quite helpful in explaining some of the partisan aspects of the faith-based story.

20. Paul Clorey, "Total Raised by Elite 100 Include Two $2 Billion Organizations and Four Generating at Least $1 Billion," *NonProfit Times* 39 (November 1997).

21. As a succinct example of this line of argument, see Ronald Sider, "Evaluating the Faith-Based Initiative: Is Charitable Choice Good Public Policy?" paper delivered as the Sorensen Lecture at Yale Divinity School, 15 October 2002.

22. Lynn, "Educate Public about Religious Right Agenda."

23. For one recent and representative defense of this view, see James W. Skillen, *Recharging the American Experiment: Principled Pluralism for Genuine Civic Community* (Grand Rapids, Mich.: Baker, 1994).

Chapter One. Before the Faith-Based Initiative: Background and Disputes

1. This portion of the chapter is an interpretation and summary of a variety of sources, including Ram Cnaan, "The Challenge of Devolution and the Promise of Religious-Based Social Services: An Introduction," in Ram Cnaan, Stephanie Boddie, and Robert Wineburg, eds., *The Newer Deal* (New York: Columbia University Press, 1999); Kathy Koch, "Child Poverty," *CQ Researcher* (Washington, D.C.: Congressional Quarterly, 2000), 283–300; Stephen V. Monsma, *When Sacred and Secular Mix: Religious Nonprofit Organizations and Public Money* (Lanham, Md.: Rowman and Littlefield, 1996); David Nather, "Bush's House Win on 'Faith-Based' Charity Clouded by Bias Concerns in Senate," *Congressional Quarterly Weekly Report* 59 (21 July 2001): 1774–75; Marvin Olasky, *The Tragedy of American Compassion* (Lanham, Md.: Regnery Gateway, 1992); Kurt C. Schaefer, "The Privatizing of Compassion: A Critical Engagement with Marvin Olasky," in David Gushee, ed., *Toward a Just and Caring Society: Christian Reponses to Poverty in America* (Grand Rapids, Mich.: Baker Books, 1999); Amy L. Sherman, *A Survey of Church-Government Anti-Poverty Partnerships* (Washington, D.C.: American Enterprise Institute, 2000), www.aei.org/e%20drive/web/public/tae/taejune00i.htm (accessed 14 February 2003); and Robert J. Wineburg, *A Limited Partnership: The Politics of Religion, Welfare, and Social Service* (New York: Columbia University Press, 2001).

2. This brief history draws heavily from Ira Lupu's excellent "Government Messages and Government Money: *Santa Fe, Mitchell v. Helms*, and the Arc of the Establishment Clause," Public Law and Legal Theory Working Paper 010, 2000. Lupu divides establishment clause litigation into two basic categories: cases that involve government support in the form of money for religious institutions (parochial school aid, charitable choice, grants to religious social service agencies), and those that entail government action that endorses religious messages (prayers at school football games or graduation ceremonies). It is only the former with which we concern ourselves here. Lupu sketches the contrasting directions of the Supreme Court jurisprudence in each case. With respect to money support, the Court has become increasingly accommodationist, moving from separation toward a

standard of neutrality in allowing public funds to flow to religious organizations. With respect to government support of religious messages, however, the Court has become more steadfastly separationist in seeking to avoid the state's imprimatur on religious messages in public settings.

3. One rare exception was the Supreme Court's decision in *Bradfield v. Roberts*, 175 U.S. 291 (1899). In that case, the Court approved of a federal subsidy for a hospital owned and operated by the Catholic Church. The Court determined the hospital to be a secular entity rather than a religious one, thereby avoiding the clause question.

4. One exception to the rule was *Board of Ed. of Central School Dist. No. 1 v. Allen*, 392 U.S. 236 (1968), when a divided Supreme Court upheld a New York state program which allowed for the lending of public school textbooks to the parents of children enrolled in private, sectarian schools.

5. *Committee for Public Ed. & Religious Liberty v. Nyquist*, 413 U.S. 756 (1973).

6. Similarly, the Court in *Committee for Public Ed. & Religious Liberty v. Nyquist*, 413 U.S. 756 (1973), disallowed a New York state program of tax credits for tuition assistance predominantly used by parents of students in Catholic schools.

7. In *Aguilar v. Felton*, 473 U.S. 402 (1985)—later to be overruled by *Agostini v. Felton*, 521 U.S. 203 (1997), the Supreme Court found unconstitutional a federal aid program that aided public and private school students alike. The disqualified program provided for public school teachers to teach remedial education to children residing in low-income areas who were failing to meet state educational performance standards.

8. The move from separation toward neutrality was further evidenced in other areas of establishment clause jurisprudence, particularly in a bloc of cases that dealt with access to school space and resources. See, e.g., *Zobrest v. Catalina Foothills School Dist.*, 509 U.S. 1 (1993). In *Widmar v. Vincent*, 454 U.S. 263 (1981), the Court extended to a student group that was organized for religious purposes the same rights of access to meeting space on a state university campus as other, nonreligious groups. Similar principles governed the decisions in *Board of Ed. of Westside Community Schools (Dist. 66) v. Mergens*, 496 U.S. 226 (1990); *Lamb's Chapel v. Center Moriches Union Free School Dist.*, 508 U.S. 384 (1993); and *Rosenberger v. Rector and Visitors of Univ. of Va.*, 515 U.S. 819 (1995). Each of these cases confronted efforts by the government to use the establishment clause as a shield against claims of equal access by religiously motivated groups to government resources. In each instance, the Court rejected the establishment clause argument in favor of equal access claims. (See Lupu, "Government Messages and Government Money," 43.)

9. William Bennett termed it "the most important book on welfare and social policy in a decade"; see Eyal Press, "Lead Us Not into Temptation," *The American Prospect* 12, no. 6 (9 April 2001), www.prospect.org/print/V12/6/press-e.html (accessed 19 June 2003).

10. Religious providers were included in correctional, welfare, and substance abuse programs, among others. More generally, Bush pushed through "a law freeing all faith-based groups in Texas from state oversight and licensing requirements" (Press, "Lead Us Not into Temptation").

11. This portion of the chapter is based on review, summary, and interpretation of a variety of congressional documents related to the passage of four charitable choice laws, most importantly committee reports and floor debate recorded in the *Congressional Record*. These four laws are Public Law 104-193, the Personal Responsibility and Work Opportunity Reconciliation Act of 1996, better known as the 1996 welfare reform law, enacted August 22, 1996; Public Law 105-285, enacted October 27, 1998, which reauthorized the community services block grant program; Public Law 106-310, enacted October 17, 2000, which included the Children's Health Act; and Public Law 106-544, an omnibus appropriations measure enacted December 21, 2000, which included the Community Renewal Tax Relief Act. The charitable choice provisions in each law differ slightly from each other, but in general they seek the same objectives in similar legislative language. Interpretation of the above-referenced written record was aided by a number of persons, especially David Ackerman, a legislative attorney in the American Law division of the Congressional Research Service, during the spring of 2001. Information about the congressional debate comes from interviews conducted with several primary actors, and is supplemented by other accounts, most notably Julie A. Segal's essay "A Holy Mistaken Zeal: The Legislative History and Future of Charitable Choice," in Derek Davis and Barry Hankins, eds., *Welfare Reform and Faith-Based Organizations* (Waco, Tex.: J. M. Dawson Institute of Church-State Studies, 1999).

12. Anne Billings White, interview by Amy Black, 22 July 2002.

13. Richard Ostling, "Protestants Key in Charity Concept," Associated Press, 8 February 2001.

14. James Skillen, interview by Amy Black, 18 July 2002.

15. Daniel Katz, interview by Amy Black, 19 July 2002.

16. Confidential portion of interview "B." (On our use of anonymous/confidential interviews, see appendix A.)

17. Katz, interview.

18. Ibid.

19. Billings White, interview.

20. U.S. Congress, House, Office of U.S. Representative Bobby Scott, "Current Federal Programs Containing Charitable Choice: Welfare Reform Act (P.L. 104-93)," 2000, www.house.gov/scott/c_choice/fp_welfare_reform_act.htm (accessed 11 June 2003).

21. AU Bulletin, *Church and State*, no. 243 (December 1998): 3.

22. U.S. Congress, Senate, Committee on Health, Education, Labor, and Pensions, *The Youth Drug and Mental Health Services Act of 1999*, Senate Report 106-196, 19 October 1999.

23. Billings White, interview.

24. Stanley Carlson-Thies, "'Don't Look to Us': The Negative Responses of Churches to Welfare Reform," *Notre Dame Journal of Law, Ethics, and Public Policy* 11, no. 2 (1997): 667.

25. Monsma, *When Sacred and Secular Mix*.

26. Amy L. Sherman, *Fruitful Collaboration between Government and Christian Social Ministries: Lessons Learned from Virginia and Maryland*, Center for Public Justice, January 1998.

27. Amy L. Sherman, *The Growing Impact of Charitable Choice: A Catalogue of New Collaborations between Government and Faith-Based Organizations in Nine States* (Annapolis, Md.: Center for Public Justice, 2000), www.cpjustice.org/stories/storyreader$315; and Amy L. Sherman, *A Survey of Church-Government Anti-Poverty Partnerships* (Washington, D.C.: American Enterprise Institute, 2000), www.theamericanenterprise.org/taejune00i.htm (accessed 30 June 2002).

28. Laurie Goodstein, "Religious Groups Slow to Accept Government Money to Help Poor," *New York Times*, 17 October 2000, A22.

29. Amy L. Sherman, "Tracking Charitable Choice: A Study of the Collaboration between Faith-Based Organizations and the Government in Providing Social Services in Nine States," *Social Work and Christianity* 27, no. 2 (fall 2002): 112–29.

30. Ira C. Lupu and Robert W. Tuttle, *Government Partnerships with Faith-Based Service Providers: The State of the Law* (Washington, D.C.: The Roundtable on Religion and Social Welfare Policy, 2002).

Chapter Two. On the Trail: Campaigning on Faith-Based Issues

1. Michael Gerson, interview by Amy Black, 19 July 2002.

2. Ron Brownstein, "Greater Role for Religious Charities Urged," *Los Angeles Times*, 25 May 1999, A14.

3. Christopher Shea, "Gore Gets Religion," Salon.com, www.salon.com/news/feature/1999/06/15/faith/print.html (accessed 15 June 1999).

4. Andrew Kohut, John C. Green, Scott Keeter, and Robert C. Toth, *The Diminishing Divide: Religion's Changing Role in American Politics* (Washington, D.C.: Brookings Institution, 2000).

5. Ibid., 123.

6. Ibid.

7. On differences between the views of the general public and those of elites, see Ted Jelen and Clyde Wilcox, *Public Attitudes toward Church and State* (Armonk, N.Y.: M. E. Sharpe, 1995). On the issue of banning a moment of silence in public schools, see ibid., 78, 100.

8. Ray Suarez and Elizabeth Arnold, *Talk of the Nation*, National Public Radio, 23 June 1999.

9. Jill Zuckman, "In N.H., Gore Puts Focus on Religion," *Boston Globe*, 23 May 1999, A1.

10. Jonathan G. S. Koppell, "Charity: When Private Hands Do the Public's Work," *Los Angeles Times*, 19 December 1999, M2.

11. Joe Frolik, "Using Faith to Find Solutions to Poverty," *Cleveland Plain Dealer*, 28 November 1999, 1A.

12. Outside observers can never know with certainty the complete array of factors that motivate the decision-making process. In the following sections, we rely

upon analysis from the campaign advisers directly involved in the process and discuss the possible motivations that were widely attributed to both candidates.

13. Gerson, interview.
14. Ibid.
15. Rev. Meg Riley, interview by Amy Black, Washington, D.C., 23 July 2002.
16. Jeffrey Rosen, "Is Nothing Secular?" *New York Times Magazine*, 30 January 2000, 40.
17. Peter Beinart, "Faith-Based Altercation," *The New Republic*, 5 February 2001, www.tnr.com/punditry/beinart020501.html (accessed 28 October 2003).
18. Quoted in Ken Herman, "Bush's Faith-Based Initiatives: Black Clergy Could Add Surprising Support," *Atlanta Journal-Constitution*, 11 March 2001, C7.
19. John Green and John DiIulio, "How the Faithful Voted," *Center Conversations*, no. 10 (March 2001): 10.
20. Ann McFeatters, "Presidential Candidates Saying Something of Values," *Pittsburgh Post-Gazette*, 30 May 1999, A11.
21. William Galston, interview by Amy Black, telephone conversation, 5 July 2002.
22. See, e.g., Zuckman, "In N.H., Gore Puts Focus on Religion," A1.
23. Galston, interview.
24. Sandra Sobieraj, "Gore: Church Should Get Government Funds," Associated Press, 24 May 1999.
25. Dan Katz, Americans United for Separation of Church and State, interview by Amy Black, Washington, D.C., 19 July 2002.
26. Lewis Solomon and Matthew J. Vlissides, Jr., "In God We Trust? Assessing the Potential of Faith-Based Social Services," *Policy Report*, Progressive Policy Institute, February 2001, 1.
27. Albert A. Gore, Jr., speech delivered to the Salvation Army, 25 May 1999, www.cpjustice.org/stories/storyreader$384 (accessed 12 February 2003).
28. Ibid.
29. Joseph Loconte. "Bush vs. Gore on Faith-Based Charity," *American Enterprise*, June 2000.
30. George W. Bush, "Duty of Hope," speech delivered in Indianapolis, Ind., 22 July 1999, www.cpjustice.org/stories/storyreader$383 (accessed 12 February 2003).
31. Brownstein, "Greater Role for Religious Charities Urged," A13.
32. Terry M. Neal, "Bush Outlines Charity-Based Social Service Policies," *Washington Post*, 23 July 1999, A2.
33. Joseph Loconte, interview by Amy Black, telephone conversation, 9 January 2003.
34. Galston, interview.
35. Gerson, interview.
36. George W. Bush, presidential nomination acceptance speech, Philadelphia, Pa., 3 August 2000.
37. Green and DiIulio, "How the Faithful Voted," 5.
38. Will Marshall, interview by Amy Black, Washington, D.C., 23 July 2002.
39. The factors that contribute to the polarization and legislative struggles are myriad and complex. This section makes no attempt to be comprehensive but provides

an overview of several trends and developments that hindered the prospects for faith-based legislation. We will develop these concepts further in the following chapters as we examine the political battles in all three branches of government.

40. Max Finberg, Senior Legislative Assistant for Representative Tony Hall (D-Ohio), interview by Amy Black, Washington, D.C., 27 June 2002.

41. Dan Rather and Jim Axelrod, "President-Elect George W. Bush's Efforts to Win Over African-Americans," *CBS Evening News*, 20 December 2000.

42. Andrew Sullivan, "The Drag Race," *The New Republic*, 18 December 2000, 16.

43. Galston, interview.

44. Katz, interview.

45. Dana Milbank and Thomas Edsall, "Faith Initiative May Be Revised," *Washington Post*, 12 March 2001, A01.

46. Rebecca Carr, "Bush's Faith-Based Initiatives," *Atlanta Journal-Constitution*, 11 March 2001, 7C.

47. Pat Robertson, "Faith-Based Initiatives Pose Some Problems," www.pat robertson.com/NewsCommentary/FaithBasedInitiatives.asp (accessed 25 February 2003).

48. Ralph Benko, interview by Amy Black, Washington, D.C., 19 July 2002.

49. Lauren Richardson Noyes, former Legislative Director for Representative Joseph Pitts (R-Pennsylvania), interview by Amy Black, Washington, D.C., 28 June 2002.

50. John DiIulio, Jr., "Supporting Black Churches: Faith, Outreach, and the Inner-City Poor," *Brookings Review*, spring 1999, 43.

51. "Leading African American Pastors Endorse Bush," George W. Bush campaign press release, 4 February 2000.

52. Julie Mason, "Black Ministers Back Bush Plan," *Houston Chronicle*, 20 March 2001, A6.

53. Herman, "Bush's Faith-Based Initiatives," 7C.

54. Kevin "Seamus" Hasson, The Becket Fund for Religious Liberty, interview by Amy Black, 23 July 2002.

55. The religious discrimination argument is absolutely central to the ongoing political story of the faith-based initiative and is discussed in much greater detail in the following chapters.

56. Katz, interview.

Chapter Three. Partisan Appeal: Faith-Based in a Republican House

1. This introductory section on Representative Hall is drawn chiefly from *CQ Politics in America 2002*, pp. 780–81, and *Almanac of American Politics 2002*, 1198–1200.

2. Max Finberg, interview by Amy Black and Douglas Koopman, 27 June 2002.

3. U.S. Congress, House, Office of Representative Tony Hall, "Faith/Community-Based Initiative Could Help Clinch Victory in Fight against Hunger, Hall Says," press release, 30 January 2001.

4. Finberg, interview.

5. Confidential portion of interview with "S." (On our use of anonymous/confidential interviews, see appendix A.)

6. Some of the observations in this chapter are derived from one of the author's journal notes written while serving as a volunteer legislative fellow to U.S. Representative J. C. Watts (R-Oklahoma) from late January 2001 to early May 2001. The interpretations are solely those of the authors.

7. Confidential portion of interview with "S."

8. Ibid.

9. Confidential portion of interview with "M."

10. "Rallying the Armies of Compassion," speech delivered by George W. Bush, 30 January 2001.

11. David Nather, "Bush Plan to Promote Faith-Based Charities Creates Dilemma for Both Parties," *Congressional Quarterly Weekly Report* 59 (3 February 2001): 283–85.

12. Business Wire, "ACLJ Calls President Bush's Faith-Based Plan 'Creative' and 'Constitutionally Sound'," 29 January 2001; and Sean Scully, "Faith-Based Initiatives Office Opens to Many Calls," *Washington Times*, 21 February 2001, A1.

13. Confidential portion of interview with "T."

14. Confidential portion of interview with "P."

15. Confidential portion of interview with "S."

16. Ibid.

17. Confidential portion of interview with "M."

18. Fred Kammer, S.J., "Partners against Poverty," *Washington Post*, 10 February 2001, A23; Sue Anne Pressley, "Faith-Based Groups under Fresh Scrutiny," *Washington Post*, 11 February 2001, A3; Lutheran Services of America, "Largest Nonprofit Challenges President Bush to Follow Through for the Nation's Most Vulnerable," press release, 29 January 2001; Alliance for Children and Families, "The Alliance for Children and Families Reacts to President Bush's Faith-Based Initiative," press release, 1 February 2001.

19. United Jewish Communities, "United Jewish Communities Statement on Bush Administration's Faith-Based Programs Initiative," press release, 5 February 2001.

20. Thomas Edsall, "Jewish Leaders Criticize 'Faith-Based' Initiative," *Washington Post*, 27 February 2001, A4.

21. Laura Meckler, "Religious Groups Wary of Bush Plan," Associated Press, 20 February 2001.

22. Jack Horner, interview by Douglas Koopman, 27 June 2002.

23. Confidential portion of interview with "J."

24. John Leland, "Some Black Pastors See New Aid under Bush," *New York Times*, 2 February 2001, A12; Andrea Billups, "Watts Announces Outreach to Blacks," *Washington Times*, 24 February 2001, 4.

25. Finberg, interview.

26. Laurie Goodstein, "For Religious Right, Bush's Charity Plan Is Raising Concerns," *New York Times*, 3 March 2001, A1.

27. Thomas Edsall, "Robertson Joins Liberals in Faulting Bush's 'Faith-Based' Plan," *Washington Post*, 22 February 2001, A5.

28. For a discussion of this dispute from the point of view of one of the purists, see Marvin Olasky, "Rolling the Dice," *World*, 4 August 2001, 18–24.

29. Edsall, "Robertson Joins Liberals," A5.

30. Goodstein, "Raising Concerns," A1.
31. Marvin Olasky, "Sounds of Silence: Bush Initiative Gets through the House, but What Now?" *World*, 4 August 2001, www.worldmag.com/world/issue/08-04-01/closing_2.asp (accessed 2 December 2002).
32. Confidential portion of interview with "S."
33. Edsall, "Robertson Joins Liberals," A5; Goodstein, "Raising Concerns," A1.
34. Goodstein, "Raising Concerns," A1.
35. Marvin Olasky, "Let Faith-Based Programs Solve Our Social Problems," in Robert M. Huberty and Christopher Yablonski, eds., *Mandate for Charity: Policy Proposals for the Bush Administration* (Washington, D.C.: Capital Research Center, 2001), 17–21.
36. Joseph Loconte, "Faith-Based Skepticism," *Weekly Standard* 6, no. 27 (26 March 2001): 10–12; and Franklin Foer and Ryan Lizza, "Holy War," *The New Republic*, 2 April 2001, 14, 16–17.
37. Confidential portion of interview with "J."
38. Jim VandeHei and Laurie McGinley, "Bush Team Falls behind Schedule in Its Nominations," *Wall Street Journal*, 22 March 2001, A1; and Foer and Lizza, "Holy War," 16.
39. Thomas Edsall and Dana Milbank, "Blunt Defense of 'Faith-Based' Aid," *Washington Post*, 8 March 2001, A8.
40. Billups, "Watts Announces Outreach."
41. Meghan Twohey, "Limelight Scorching 'Charitable Choice'?" *National Journal*, 28 April 2001, 1236–37.
42. VandeHei and McGinley, "Bush Team Falls behind Schedule"; Milbank and Edsall, "Blunt Defense"; and confidential portion of interviews with "P" and "T."
43. Finberg, interview.
44. Stanley Carlson-Thies, interview by Amy Black, 22 July 2002.
45. Confidential portion of interview with "P."
46. Confidential portion of interview with "S."
47. Confidential portion of interview with "T."
48. Billups, "Watts Announces Outreach."
49. Confidential portion of interview with "O."
50. Larry Witham, "Faith-Based Plan Shows Cultural Split," *Washington Times*, 26 March 2001, 4.
51. David Nather, "House GOP Bets on Passing Aid to 'Faith-Based' Groups: Senate Keys on Tax Incentives," *Congressional Quarterly Weekly Report* 59 (24 March 2001): 661–62.
52. Confidential portion of interview with "J."
53. Confidential portion of interview with "T."
54. Thomas Ferraro, "Bush's Faith-Based Measures Ready for Congress," Reuters, 20 March 2001.
55. Confidential portion of interview with "A."
56. Laurie Goodstein, "Battle Lines Grow on Plan to Assist Religious Groups," *New York Times*, 12 April 2001, A22.

57. Laura Meckler, "Conservatives Rally around Bush Plan," Associated Press, 11 April 2001.

58. Goodstein, "Battle Lines Grow," A22.

59. Steven Benen, " 'Faith-Based' Fanaticism? Watts' Religious Advisory Committee Sparks Criticism," *Church and State*, June 2001, www.au.org/churchstate/cs6012.htm (accessed 14 December 2001).

60. Elizabeth Becker, "Republicans Hold Forum with Blacks in Clergy," *New York Times*, 26 April 2001, A18; Laura Meckler, "GOP Summit Pumps Up Pastors on Bush Religion Plan," Associated Press Online, 25 April 2001.

61. Susan Crabtree, "Faith-Based Initiative Off to a Rocky Start," *Roll Call*, 11 June 2001, 1; Becker, "Republicans Hold Forum," A18.

62. Finberg, interview.

63. Confidential portion of interview with "O."

64. Ibid.

65. Twohey, "Limelight Scorching," 1237.

66. Laura Meckler, "DiIulio: Programs Should Have Grants," Associated Press Online, 26 April 2001.

67. Confidential portion of interview with "U."

68. Ibid.

69. Denise Edwards, interview by Douglas Koopman, 7 February 2003.

70. Dana Milbank and Glenn Kessler, "Charities Decry Tax Bill Setback," *Washington Post*, 30 May 2001, A1.

71. Confidential portion of interview with "O."

72. Crabtree, "Rocky Start," A18.

73. Dana Milbank, "Bush Assails 'Faith-Based Initiative' Critics," *Washington Post*, 6 June 2001, A6.

74. Confidential portion of interviews with "R" and "T."

75. U.S. Newswire, "Two New Groups Founded to Extend President Bush's Vision of Faith-Based and Community Enterprise," 6 June 2001; Mike Allen, "Bush Aims to Get Faith Initiative Back on Track," *Washington Post*, 25 June 2001, A1.

76. Confidential portion of interview with "L."

77. U.S. Congress, House, Committee on Ways and Means, H.R. 7, *The Community Solutions Act of 2001*, hearing before the Subcommittee on Human Resources and Subcommittee on Select Revenue Measures of the Committee on Ways and Means, House of Representatives, 107th Congress, 1st sess., 14 June 2001, Serial 107-34.

78. Ibid.

79. Ibid.

80. U.S. Congress, House, Committee on Ways and Means, Subcommittees on Human Resources and Select Revenue Measures, testimony, 17 July 2001, www.house.gov/ways_means/humres/107cong/6-14-01/6-14scott.htm (accessed 15 August 2002).

81. Ibid.

82. Ibid.

83. Theresa Tilling Thompson, interview by Douglas Koopman, 12 February 2003.

84. Lori Nitschke, "Bush's 'Faith-Based' Initiative Hobbled by Growing Disputes over Final Form, Constitutionality," *Congressional Quarterly Weekly Report* 59 (23 June 2001): 1520.

85. Laura Meckler, "Faith-Based Bill Moves Forward," Associated Press Online, 19 June 2001.

86. U.S. Congress, House, Committee amendment to H.R. 7, Document S6301, House Legislative Counsel, 28 June 2001.

87. Mark Kukis, "House Reshapes Stalled Faith-Based Bill," United Press International, 27 June 2001, www.vny.com/f/news/upidetail.cfm?QUI=198020 (accessed 3 July 2001).

88. David Nather, "Diminished 'Faith-Based Initiative' Heads toward House Floor," *Congressional Quarterly Weekly Report* 59 (14 July 2001): 1687–89.

89. Confidential portion of interview with "O."

90. Lori Nitschke, "Ways and Means Scales Back Bush Plan for Fostering Charitable Donations," *Congressional Quarterly Weekly Report* 59 (14 July 2001): 1688.

91. Dana Milbank, "Charity Cites Bush Help in Fight against Hiring Gays," *Washington Post*, 10 July 2001, A1.

92. Reuters, "White House Denies Helping Charity on Gays," 10 July 2001, www.cnn.com/2001/ALLPOLITICS/07/10/bush.salarmy.reut/index.html (accessed 20 July 2001).

93. Dana Milbank and Mike Allen, "Rove Heard Charity Plea on Gay Bias," *Washington Post*, 12 July 2001, A1; Dana Millbank, "Story of Charity Plea Changes Again," *Washington Post*, 13 July 2001, A2.

94. Nather, "Diminished 'Faith-Based Initiative'," 1689.

95. Ibid.

96. David Nather, "Bush's House Win on 'Faith-Based' Charity Clouded by Bias Concerns in Senate," *Congressional Quarterly Weekly Report* 59 (21 July 2001): 1774–75; Don Eberly, interview by Amy Black, 1 July 2002.

97. Congressional Record, 19 July 2001, H4273, 3274.

98. Nather, "Bush's House Win Clouded," 1774–75; confidential portion of interview with "R."

99. A *Wall Street Journal* version of the House legislative post-mortem, obviously promoted by WHOFBCI insiders, appeared on January 25, 2002 (Jim VandeHei, "Bush Moves to Resurrect His Faith-Based Initiative," *Wall Street Journal*, 25 January 2002, A16). The main point of the story was that Bush "badly miscalculated when he allowed conservative Republicans to carry the legislative torch. . . . [T]hey wrote a bill that was needlessly partisan and arguably unconstitutional." House Republican staff persons were upset about the story and drafted a response on the constitutionality question, but interestingly omitted any discussion of partisanship.

100. Confidential portion of interview with "U."

101. Confidential portion of interview with "T."

102. Ibid.

103. Confidential portion of interview with "S."

104. Will Marshall, interview by Amy Black, 23 July 2002.

105. Confidential portion of interview with "O."

106. James Skillen, interview by Amy Black, 18 July 2002.

107. Confidential portion of interview with "S."

Chapter Four. Who CAREs? Faith-Based in a Divided Senate

1. *Congressional Quarterly's Politics in America 2002* (Washington, D.C.: Congressional Quarterly Press, 2002), 851–52.

2. Michael Barone, Richard E. Cohen, and Charles E. Cook, Jr., *Almanac of American Politics 2002* (Washington, D.C.: National Journal, 2002), 1296.

3. *Congressional Quarterly's Politics in America 2002*, 186.

4. Ibid., 187.

5. *Almanac of American Politics 2002*, 326.

6. Dana Milbank, "Charity Bill Compromise Is Reached," *Washington Post*, 6 February 2002, A1.

7. Federal Document Clearing House Political Transcripts, "President Bush Holds Media Availability with Senator Lieberman," 7 February 2002, http://web.lexis-nexis.com (accessed 6 February 2003); Mei-Ling Hopgood, "Senate Introduces Faith-Based Initiative Compromise Plan," Cox News Service, 7 February 2002, http://web.lexis-nexis.com (accessed 6 February 2003); U.S. Congress, Senate, Office of Senator Rick Santorum, "Lieberman, Santorum Announce Bipartisan Compromise on President's Faith-Based Initiative; Unveil Consensus Charity Bill at White House Event," http://santorum.senate.gov/pressreleases/record.cfm?id=181168 (accessed 12 June 2003).

8. Quoted in Hopgood, "Senate Introduces Faith-Based Initiative Compromise Plan."

9. Quoted in ibid.

10. Dana Milbank, "Bush Unveils 'Faith-Based' Initiative," *Washington Post*, 30 January 2001, A1.

11. Rebecca Carr, "Bush Unveils Legislation for Faith-Based Charities," Cox News Service, 31 January 2001.

12. White House faith-based staff person, memorandum to authors, 1 March 2003.

13. David Nather, "Bush Plan to Promote Faith-Based Charities Creates Dilemma for Both Parties," *Congressional Quarterly Weekly Report* 59 (3 February 2001): 283–85; Thomas Edsall, "Lieberman May Back Faith Initiative Bill," *Washington Post*, 2 March 2001, A7.

14. Confidential portion of interview with "N."

15. Dana Milbank and Thomas Edsall, "Faith Initiative May Be Revised," *Washington Post*, 12 March 2001, A01.

16. Laura Meckler, "Critics Protest Bush Religion Plan," Associated Press Online, 13 March 2001.

17. Steve Holland, "Bush Religious Charity Plan Faces Drawn-Out Path," Reuters, 14 March 2001.

18. David Nather, "Lieberman-Santorum Bill Would Widen Tax Deductions for Charitable Contributions," *Congressional Quarterly Weekly Report* 59 (17 March 2001): 609.

19. David Nather, "House GOP Bets on Passing Aid to 'Faith-Based' Groups: Senate Keys on Tax Incentives," *Congressional Quarterly Weekly Report* 59 (24 March 2001): 661–62.

20. Elizabeth Becker, "Republicans Hold Forum with Blacks in Clergy," *New York Times*, 26 April 2001, A18.

21. Confidential portion of interview with "N."

'2. David Morgan, "Advisor: Bush's Faith-Based Plan Poses No Threat," Reuters, 1 April 2001.

23. Larry Witham, "Senate Democrats Assail Faith-Based Bill," *Washington Times*, 7 June 2001, 4.

24. Ibid.

25. Ibid.

26. Mark Benjamin, "Faith-Based Charity Plan under Scrutiny," United Press International, 6 June 2001, www.vny.com/cf/news/upidetail.cfm?QID=191844 (accessed 7 June 2001).

27. Joseph Lieberman and Rick Santorum, "Unite to Bolster Faith-Based Efforts," *Philadelphia Inquirer*, 19 June 2001, A15.

28. Dan Balz, "Democrats Criticize Their Own—and Bush," *Washington Post*, 17 July 2001, A4.

29. Associated Press, "Lieberman to Draft Faith-Based Bill," Associated Press Online, 22 July 2001.

30. Arshad Mohammed, "Bush Hints at Compromise in Faith-Based Initiative," Reuters, 26 July 2001.

31. Ibid.

32. "Faith-Based Initiative Faces Delays in Senate," *CQ Daily Monitor*, 1 August 2001; Thomas Ferraro, "Senate Backer Offers Concession on Bush Faith Plan," Reuters, 1 August 2001.

33. U.S. Congress, Senate, Office of Senator Rick Santorum, "Senate Floor Statement. Santorum and Lieberman Introduce Phase II of President's Faith-Based Initiatives," 3 August 2001.

34. *Unlevel Playing Field: Barriers to Participation by Faith-Based and Community Organizations in Federal Social Service Programs*, WhiteHouse.gov, 16 August 2001, www.whitehouse.gov/new/releases/2001/08/unlevelfield.html (accessed 29 April 2002).

35. Mike Allen, "'Faith-Based' Backup Plan," *Washington Post*, 17 August 2001, A2.

36. Nicholas M. Horrock, "Faith-Based Chief Quits," United Press International, 17 August 2001, www.vnycom/cf/news/upidetail.cfm?QID=212815 (accessed 18 August 2001).

37. Dana Milbank, "DiIulio Resigns from Top 'Faith-Based' Post," *Washington Post*, 18 August 2001, A4.

38. Horrock, "Faith-Based Chief Quits"; U.S. Newswire, "DiIulio Departure Raises Danger of More Ideological Direction for White House Government Funding of Religion Program, Says Group," 17 August 2001.

39. Milbank, "DiIulio Resigns," A4.
40. Claude Marx, "Santorum Doubts Government Charity Aid," Associated Press, www.washingtonpost.com/wp-srv/aponline/20011009/aponline185258_000.htm (accessed 10 October 2001).
41. Pew Forum on Religion and Public Life, and Pew Research Center for the People and the Press, "Post 9-11 Attitudes: Religion More Prominent, Muslim-Americans More Accepted" (Washington, D.C.: Pew Forum, 6 December 2001).
42. Mary Leonard, "Faith Bill Advances Amid Religious Mood," *Boston Globe*, 18 November 2001, A1.
43. U.S. Newswire, "Text of a Letter from the President to the Senate Majority Leader and the Senate Republican Leader," 7 November 2001.
44. U.S. Newswire, "Nation's Leading Interfaith Organization Tells President: Now Is Not the Time to Advance Divisive Faith-Based Initiative," 8 November 2001.
45. David Nather, "Faith-Based Initiatives, Now More Than Ever?" *Congressional Quarterly Weekly Report* 59 (10 November 2001): 2654.
46. Confidential portion of interview with "N."
47. Search for Common Ground, *Finding Common Ground: Twenty-Nine Recommendations of the Working Group on Human Needs and Faith-Based and Community Initiatives* (Washington, D.C.: Search for Common Ground, 2001).
48. Amy Fagan, "Panel Releases Suggestions for Senate's Faith-Based Proposal," *Washington Times*, 16 January 2002, A6.
49. Ron Sider, "Implacable Foes Find (Some) Common Ground on Faith-Based Initiatives," *Christianity Today*, 30 January 2002, www.christianitytoday.com/ct/2002/103/32.0.html (accessed 1 February 2002).
50. Confidential portion of interview with "U."
51. Hervey Colette, "Panel Reports to Senator on the Faith-Based Initiative," Cox News Service, 15 January 2002, http://web.lexis-nexis.com (accessed 20 August 2002); Associated Press, "Group: U.S. Needs to Support Religion," Associated Press Online, 15 January 2002; Fagan, "Panel Releases Suggestions."
52. Elisabeth Bumiller, "Accord Reached on Charity Aid Bill after Bush Gives In on Hiring," *New York Times*, 8 February 2002, A19.
53. Dana Milbank, "Bush Endorses Compromise in Senate on Aid to Charities," *Washington Post*, 8 February 2002, A4.
54. Laura Meckler, "Compromise Reached on Charity Bill," Associated Press Online, 7 February 2002.
55. Bennet Roth, "Faith-Based Effort Gains Ground; Most Controversial Issues Not Included in Bid to Help Charities," *Houston Chronicle*, 8 February 2002, A3; Tom Daschle, "Compromise Good for South Dakota, America," *Rapid City Journal*, 15 February 2002; Milbank, "Bush Endorses Compromise," A4; Bumiller, "Accord Reached on Charity Aid Bill," A19.
56. "President Agrees to Compromise on Faith-Based Initiative Bill," *Christian Times*, March 2002, www.christiantimes.com/Articles/Articles%20Mar02/Art_Mar02_02.html (accessed 28 May 2002).
57. "Shortchanging Charities," *Christianity Today*, 7 March 2002, www.christianity today.com/ct/2002/003/32.35.html (accessed 12 June 2003); "President Agrees to Compromise on Faith-Based Initiative Bill."

58. Jennifer Loven, "Religious Charities Able to Use Space," Associated Press, 14 March 2002; Larry Witham, "Labor Debuts Bush's Faith Plan," *Washington Times*, 18 April 2002.

59. Grover Norquist, "The Classic Coalition for CARE," United Press International, 27 May 2002, www.upi.com/print.cfm?storyID=26052002-064722-8290r (accessed 30 May 2002).

60. Confidential portion of interview with "U."

61. Confidential portion of interview with "O."

62. Elisabeth Bumiller, "Bush Rallies Faithful in Call for Passage of Charity Bill," *New York Times*, 12 April 2002, A20.

63. "Lieberman, Santorum Press for Markup of Charity Tax Breaks," *CQ Daily Monitor*, 7 June 2002.

64. David Hess, "Senate Tax Bill Markup Bogs Down amid Unusual Procedure," *Congress Daily*, 14 June 2002.

65. Amy Fagan, "Senate Panel OKs Charity Part of Bush's Faith-Based Initiative," *Washington Times*, 19 June 2002, A6.

66. Mary Leonard and Sue Kirchhoff, "Faith-Based Bill May Be Windfall for Universities," *Boston Globe*, 21 June 2002, A1.

67. Anjetta McQueen, "Bush May Settle for Narrower Scope on Faith-Based Initiatives," *Congressional Quarterly Weekly Report* 60 (22 June 2002): 1662–63.

68. Reuters, "Bush Calls on Senate to Pass Faith-Based Initiative," Reuters, 2 July 2002.

69. Sandra Kerr, "CARE Update," personal e-mail, National Committee on Planned Giving, 13 September 2002; Amy Fagan and Dave Boyer, "Faith-Based Bill Close to Senate Floor," *Washington Times*, 18 September 2002, A7.

70. Amy Fagan, "Senate Looks for Faith-Based Deal," *Washington Times*, 11 September 2002, A5.

71. Congressional Record, 19 September 2002, S8914.

72. "Loss of Faith," *Weekly Standard*, 30 September 2002, 2.

73. Alan K. Ota, "Anti-Discrimination Battle May Tie Up Faith-Based Bill," *CQ Daily Monitor*, 25 September 2002.

74. Congressional Record, 24 September 2002, S9093–S9095.

75. Ota, "Anti-Discrimination Battle."

76. Mary Leonard, "CARE Act Opposition," *Boston Globe*, 25 September 2002, A10.

77. Ibid.

78. Amy Fagan, "Watts to Support Narrower Faith Bill," *Washington Times*, 14 October 2002, A4.

79. Laura Meckler, "Senate Still Trying to Move Scaled-Back 'Faith-Based' Legislation," Associated Press, 15 October 2002, www.sfgate.com/cgi-bin/article.cgi?f=news/archive/2002/10/15/national1751EDT0748.DTL (accessed 16 October 2002).

80. Confidential portion of interview with "M."

81. Larry Witham, "Towey Said Faith-Based Bill 'Held Hostage' by Reed," *Washington Times*, 24 October 2002, A6.

82. U.S. Congress, Senate, Office of Senator Rick Santorum, "Statement on the CARE Act," 14 November 2002, http://santorum.senate.gov/statement november14.html (accessed 14 January 2003).

83. U.S. Congress, Senate, Office of Senator Rick Santorum, *Charity Aid, Recovery, and Empowerment Act of 2002*, http://santorum.senate.gov/crsnovember14.html (accessed 14 January 2003).

84. Ibid.

85. Larry Witham, "Amendments Kill CARE in Senate," *Washington Times*, 15 November 2002, A10.

86. Kevin Eckstrom, "Faith-Based Funding Dead in Senate," *Baptist Standard*, 25 November 2002, www.baptiststandard.com/2002/11_25/print/faithbased.html (accessed 26 November 2002).

87. Confidential portion of interview with "E."

88. Marvin Olasky, "Faith-Based Initiative: Officials Should Not Weaken It to Appease the Left," *World*, 23 November 2002, www.worldmag.com/world/issue/11-23-02/opening_2.asp (accessed 2 December 2002).

89. Laura Meckler, "'Faith-Based' Bill Falls Short," Associated Press, 15 November 2002.

Chapter Five. Rocky Roads: Faith-Based Efforts in the Executive Branch

1. Richard Morin, "Leading with His Right; John DiIulio, Ready to Go to the Mat with a Faith-Based Approach to Crime," *Washington Post*, 26 February 2001, C01.

2. William Galston, interview by Amy Black, telephone conversation, 5 July 2002.

3. Franklin Foer and Ryan Lizza, "Holy War," *The New Republic*, 2 April 2001, 14.

4. John DiIulio, personal communication with Amy Black, 26 February 2003.

5. John DiIulio, interview by Amy Black, Philadelphia, Pa., 28 September 2002.

6. Terry Mattingly, "God Is in the Church-State Details," Gospelcom.net, 18 August 1999, http://tmatt.gospelcom.net/column/1999/08/18 (accessed 10 June 2002).

7. "Executive Order: Establishment of White House Office of Faith-Based and Community Initiatives," 29 January 2001, www.whitehouse.gov/news/releases/2001/01/20010129-2.html (accessed 3 March 2003). See appendix C.

8. "Executive Order: Agency Responsibilities with Respect to Faith-Based and Community Initiatives," 29 January 2001, www.whitehouse.gov/news/releases/2001/01/20010129-3.html (accessed 3 March 2003). See appendix C.

9. *Unlevel Playing Field: Barriers to Participation by Faith-Based and Community Organizations in Federal Social Service Programs*, WhiteHouse.gov, 16 August 2001, www.whitehouse.gov/news/releases/2001/08/unlevelfield.html (accessed 30 August 2001).

10. Stuart Bowen, interview by Amy Black, Washington, D.C., 13 September 2002.

11. DiIulio, interview, 28 September 2002.

12. Don Willett, interview by Amy Black, telephone conversation, 15 August 2002.

13. Confidential interview "G," interview by Amy Black.

14. David Nather, "Bush Plan to Promote Faith-Based Charities Creates Dilemma for Both Parties," *Congressional Quarterly Weekly Report* 59 (3 February 2001): 283–85.

15. Kathryn Dunn Tenpas, "Can an Office Change a Country? The While House Office of Faith-Based and Community Initiatives," preliminary report for the Pew Forum, Washington, D.C., February 2002, 5.

16. David Kuo, interview by Amy Black, Washington, D.C., 20 September 2002.

17. Confidential interview "O," interview by Amy Black and Douglas Koopman.

18. Sebastian Mallaby, "DiIulio's Good-Faith Effort," *Washington Post*, 20 August 2001, A15.

19. Julie Elliott, "Falwell to Bush: Pick Director with Care," *Dallas Morning News*, 20 August 2001, 14A.

20. Tenpas, "Can an Office Change a Country?" 11.

21. Jim VandeHei, "Bush Moves to Resurrect His Faith-Based Initiative," *Wall Street Journal*, 25 January 2002, A25.

22. John J. DiIulio, Jr., "Compassion 'In Truth and Action': How Sacred and Secular Places Serve Civic Purposes, and What Washington Should—and Should Not— Do to Help," speech delivered before the National Association of Evangelicals, Dallas, Tex., 7 March 2001, www.whitehouse.gov/news/releases/2001/03/20010307-11.html (accessed 22 April 2002).

23. Ibid.

24. Thomas Edsall and Dana Milbank, "Blunt Defense of 'Faith-Based' Aid," *Washington Post*, 8 March 2001, A8.

25. John J. Miller and Ramesh Ponnuru, "DiIulio's Bully Pulpit," *National Review Online*, 8 March 2001, www.nationalreview.com/daily/nr030801.shtml (accessed 28 February 2003).

26. Foer and Lizza, "Holy War," 16.

27. The faith-based satellite office in the Department of Justice is called the Faith-Based and Community Initiatives Task Force. The other four agencies established "Centers for Faith-Based and Community Initiatives." To minimize confusion, however, we will refer to the five offices collectively as "centers" or "satellite offices."

28. Stanley Carlson-Thies, interview by Amy Black, Washington, D.C., 22 July 2002.

29. Meghan Twohey, "Bush Cleans House, Takes Charge of Faith Team," *The Federal Paper*, 23 September 2002, 24.

30. Bobby Polito, interview by Amy Black, Washington, D.C., 9 August 2002.

31. Brent Orrell, interview by Amy Black, Washington, D.C., 1 July 2002.

32. George W. Bush, "Rallying the Armies of Compassion," January 2001, p. 17

33. DiIulio, "Compassion 'In Truth and Action'."

34. *Unlevel Playing Field*.

35. Elizabeth Seale, interview by Amy Black, Washington, D.C., 23 September 2002.

36. Tenpas, "Can an Office Change a Country?," 5.

37. Jim Wilkinson, interview by Amy Black, Washington, D.C., 13 September 2002.

38. Bradley H. Patterson, Jr., *The White House Staff: Inside the West Wing and Beyond* (Washington, D.C.: Brookings Institution Press, 2000), 326.

39. Confidential interview "T," interview by Amy Black.

40. Confidential interview "R," interview by Amy Black.

41. Jim Towey, interview by Amy Black, Washington, D.C., 20 September 2002.
42. Carlson-Thies, interview.
43. Confidential interview "V," interview by Amy Black.
44. Confidential interview "W," interview by Amy Black.
45. Confidential interview "O," interview by Amy Black and Douglas Koopman.
46. Seale, interview.
47. John J. DiIulio, interview by Amy Black, Philadelphia, Pa., 9 December 2002.
48. Lori Nitschke, "Faith-Based Charity Bill Advances in House with Little Democratic Support," *Congressional Quarterly Weekly Report* 59 (30 June 2002): 1586–87.
49. Carlson-Thies, interview.
50. Confidential interview "J," interview by Amy Black.
51. Ibid.
52. Confidential interview "R," interview by Amy Black.
53. Will Marshall, interview by Amy Black, Washington, D.C., 19 July 2002.
54. Mike Allen, "Bush Aims to Get Faith Initiative Back on Track," *Washington Post*, 25 June 2001, A1.
55. Confidential interview "A," interview by Amy Black.
56. Allen, "Bush Aims," A1.
57. Confidential interview "J," interview by Amy Black.
58. Meg Riley, interview by Amy Black, Washington, D.C., 23 July 2002.
59. David Nather, "Bush's House Win on 'Faith-Based' Charity Clouded by Bias Concerns in Senate," *Congressional Quarterly Weekly Report* 59 (21 July 2001): 1774–75.
60. Confidential interview "T," interview by Amy Black.
61. Confidential interview "W," interview by Amy Black.
62. Ralph Benko, interview by Amy Black, Washington, D.C., 19 July 2002.
63. Foer and Lizza, "Holy War," 17.
64. Dana Milbank, "Charity Cites Bush Help in Fight against Hiring Gays," *Washington Post*, 10 July 2001, A1.
65. Confidential interview "O," interview by Amy Black and Douglas Koopman.
66. Confidential interview "R," interview by Amy Black.
67. Milbank, "DiIulio Resigns," A4.
68. Rebecca Carr, "Bush Losing Key Aide," *The Atlanta Journal and Constitution*, 17 August 2001, 1A.
69. Foer and Lizza, "Holy War," 17.
70. Dana Milbank, "DiIulio Resigns from Top 'Faith-Based' Post," *Washington Post*, 18 August 2001, A4.
71. "Reform Jewish Movement Reacts to DiIulio's Departure," Religious Action Center for Reform Judaism.
72. John Bridgeland, interview by Amy Black, Washington, D.C., 6 December 2002.
73. Robert Putnam, testimony before U.S. House Subcommittee on Select Education hearing on "The Corporation for National and Community Service," 11 April 2002.
74. Michael Gerson, interview by Amy Black, Washington, D.C., 19 July 2002.

75. Rebecca Jones, interview by Amy Black, Washington, D.C., 2 July 2002.

76. George W. Bush, "Remarks by the President and Jim Towey in Announcement of the New Director of the Office of Faith-Based and Community Initiatives," 2 February 2002, www.politicsandvirtue.com/faithbased.htm (accessed 3 March 2003).

77. Towey, interview.

78. Mike Allen, "'Faith-Based' Initiative to Get Push," *Washington Post*, 31 August 2002, A1.

79. Twohey, "Bush Cleans House," 1.

80. Ibid, 24.

81. "Executive Order: Equal Protection of the Laws for Faith-Based and Community Organizations," 12 December 2002, www.whitehouse.gov/news/releases/2002/12/20021212-6.html (accessed 12 December 2002). See appendix C.

82. Pew Forum for Religion and Public Life, "Faith-Based Initiatives and the Bush Administration," http://pewforum.org/issues/display.php?IssueID=3 (accessed 4 March 2003).

Chapter Six. Pervasive Confusion: The Federal Courts and Faith-Based Initiatives

1. For a more detailed background of the path of modern establishment clause doctrine, see chapter 1.

2. For an explanation of the *Lemon* test, see the discussion of *Lemon v. Kurtzman* in chapter 1.

3. *Widmar v. Vincent*, 454 U.S. 263 (1981); *Board of Education v. Mergens*, 496 U.S. 226 (1990); *Zobrest v. Catalina Foothills School District*, 509 U.S. 1 (1993); *Lamb's Chapel v. Center Moriches Union Free School District*, 508 U.S. 384 (1993); *Rosenberger v. Rector and Visitors of the University of Virginia*, 515 U.S. 819 (1995).

4. Ira C. Lupu, "Government Messages and Government Money: *Santa Fe, Mitchell v. Helms*, and the Arc of the Establishment Clause," Public Law and Legal Theory Working Paper 010, 2002, available at www.papers.ssrn.com/paper.taf?abstract_id=241736 (accessed 22 October 2003).

5. Those taking a more supportive stance toward charitable choice and faith-based initiatives included Carl Esbeck, "A Constitutional Case for Governmental Cooperation with Faith-Based Social Service Providers," *Emory Law Journal* 46 (1997): 1; Stephen V. Monsma, *When Sacred and Secular Mix: Religious Nonprofit Organizations and Public Money* (Lanham, Md.: Rowman and Littlefield, 1996); and Douglas Laycock, "The Underlying Unity of Separation and Neutrality," *Emory Law Journal* 46 (1997): 43. Those critical of charitable choice and faith-based initiatives included Alan Brownstein, "Constitutional Questions about Charitable Choice," in *Welfare Reform and Faith-Based Organizations*, ed. Derek Davis and Barry Hawkins (Waco, Tex.: J. M. Dawson Institute of Church-State Studies, 1999); and Martha Minow, "Choice or Commonality: Welfare and Schooling after the End of Welfare as We Know It," *Duke Law Journal* 49 (1999): 493.

6. Center for Public Justice, "A Guide to Charitable Choice" (Washington, D.C.: Center for Public Justice, 18 December 2000), available at www.cpjustice.org/charitablechoice (accessed 23 October 2003).

7. Carl Esbeck, "Charitable Choice and the Critics," *New York University Annual Survey of American Law* (2000), available at www.nyu.edu/pubs/annualsurvey/archive/57_1_17.pdf (accessed 23 October 2003).

8. Center for Public Justice, "A Guide to Charitable Choice."

9. Center for Public Justice, "Charitable Choice: Constitutional Issues" (2001), available at www.cpjustice.org/charitablechoice/constitution (accessed 23 October 2003).

10. President Clinton continued to take this position even after the *Mitchell v. Helms* decision came down in the summer of 2000. In signing into law the Children's Health Act in October 2000, he commented that government funding would be limited under the act's charitable choice language to groups willing and able to "separate their religious activities from their substance abuse treatment and prevention activities." Bill Clinton, statement on signing the Children's Health Act of 2000, Weekly Compilation of Presidential Documents, 23 October 2000, 2504.

11. David Ackerman, "Charitable Choice: Constitutional Issues and Developments through the 106th Congress," report prepared for the Congressional Research Service of the U.S. Congress, Washington, D.C., 2000.

12. One analysis characterized the recent developments in the direction of neutrality as "pathbreaking." Ira Lupu and Robert Tuttle, "The Distinctive Place of Religious Entities in Our Constitutional Order," *Villanova Law Review* 47 (2000): 37.

13. *Liberty Online*, January/February 2001, www.libertymagazine.org/article/articleview/240/1/31 (accessed 23 October 2003).

14. David Saperstein, "Testimony before the U.S. House of Representatives Constitution Subcommittee," 7 June 2001, www.rac.org/news/060701testimony.html (accessed 23 October 2003).

15. David Saperstein, "Public Accountability and Faith-based Organizations: A Problem Best Avoided," *Harvard Law Review* 116 (2003): 1353; see also Alex J. Luchenitser, "Casting Aside the Constitution: The Trend toward Government Funding of Religious Social Service Providers," Americans United for Separation of Church and State, www.au.org/luchenitser.htm (accessed 23 October 2003).

16. Institute for Public Affairs, "The Constitutionality of 'Charitable Choice'," 2001, available at www.ou.org/public/publib/constit.htm (accessed 23 October 2003); see also the discussion of *Mitchell* earlier in this chapter.

17. Elizabeth Palmer, "Charitable-Choice Supporters Put Faith in Court's Judgment," *Congressional Quarterly Weekly Report* 59 (3 March 2001): 475; Michael D. Goldhaber, "Bush's Church Idea Illegal?" *National Law Journal*, 15 January 2001, A1.

18. Wendy Kaminer, "Faith-Based Favoritism," *The American Prospect*, 9 April 2001, www.prospect.org/print/V12/6/kaminer-w.html (accessed 23 October 2003).

19. Ackerman, "Charitable Choice: Constitutional Issues."

20. David K. Ryden, "Faith-Based Initiatives and the Constitution: Black Churches, Government, and Social Services Delivery," in Drew Smith, ed., *New Day Begun: African American Churches and Civic Culture in Post-Civil Rights America* (Durham, N.C.: Duke University Press, 2003).

21. Ackerman, "Charitable Choice: Constitutional Issues."

22. Lupu and Tuttle, *Government Partnerships*.

23. Ibid.

24. Ibid.

25. Stephen V. Monsma, "The 'Pervasively Sectarian' Standard in Theory and Practice," *Notre Dame Journal of Law, Ethics & Public Policy* 13 (1999): 321; Ronald Sider, "Evaluating the Faith-Based Initiative: Is Charitable Choice Good Public Policy?" paper delivered as the Sorensen Lecture at Yale Divinity School, 15 October 2002.

26. This is reflected in the academic debate, which is phrased essentially in terms of the neutrality/pervasive sectarianism dichotomy. For illustrative works, see Stephen V. Monsma, "The 'Pervasively Sectarian' Standard in Theory and Practice," *Notre Dame Journal of Law, Ethics, & Public Policy* 13 (1999): 321; Laycock, "Underlying Unity"; and Brownstein, "Constitutional Questions." A thorough canvassing of the competing positions is contained in Stephen V. Monsma, ed., *Church-State Relations in Crisis: Debating Neutrality* (Lanham, Md.: Rowman and Littlefield, 2002).

27. Justices Scalia, Thomas, Rehnquist, and Kennedy are reliable conservative votes for a more accommodationist view of the First Amendment. Justices Stevens, Breyer, Souter, and Ginsburg, in contrast, can be counted on to take a more separationist view.

28. Ira Lupu and Robert Tuttle, "*Zelman*'s Future: Vouchers, Sectarian Providers, and the Next Round of Constitutional Battles," *Notre Dame Law Review* 76 (2003): 99.

29. Laurie Goodstein, "Voucher Ruling Seen as Further Narrowing Church-State Division," *New York Times*, 28 June 2002, A24.

30. Ibid.

31. Lupu and Tuttle, "*Zelman*'s Future"; Lupu and Tuttle, *Government Partnerships*.

32. "Government Relationships with Faith-based Providers," *Roundtable on Religion and Social Welfare Policy: The State of the Law*, transcript, 11 December 2002.

33. For a detailed analysis of the constitutionality of Blaine amendments, see the discussion in Lupu and Tuttle, "*Zelman*'s Future."

34. The 2003–2004 term may clarify how the U.S. Supreme Court will resolve questions surrounding the constitutionality of Blaine amendments. On the Court's docket is *Locke v. Davey*, a Pennsylvania case pitting the state's prohibition on the funding of religious instruction against the free exercise clause of the federal Constitution.

35. Stephen Lazarus, "An Uphill Climb to True Tolerance," *Capital Commentary*, 13 August 2001, www.cpjustice.org/stories/storyReader$564 (accessed 23 October 2003).

36. A survey conducted in March 2001 by the Pew Forum found heavy resistance to the protection of hiring rights of religious groups. Of those surveyed, 78 percent said they opposed funded religious groups being able to hire those of the same religious faith or beliefs. Laurie Goodstein, "Support for Religion-Based Plan Is Hedged," *New York Times*, 11 April 2001.

37. Betsy Rothstein, "GOP 'Charitable Choice' Unnerves Dems," 28 June 2000, www.house.gov/scott/c_choice/ar_Hill_Article_06_28_00.htm (accessed 23 October 2003).

38. Dana Milbank and Thomas Edsall, "Faith Initiative May Be Revised," *Washington Post*, 12 March 2001, A01; Lazarus, "Uphill Climb."

39. Nathan Diament, "A Slander against Our Sacred Institutions," *Washington Post*, 28 May 2001, A23; Nancy Zirkin, "Statement of Nancy Zirkin, Director of Public Policy and Government Affairs, American Association of University Women on The Community Solutions Act (H.R. 7)," 17 July 2001; Barry Lynn, quoted in Dennis R. Hoover, "Charitable Choice and the New Religious Center," *Religion in the News*, spring 2000: 4.

40. Jeffrey Rosen, "Religious Rights," *The New Republic*, 26 February 2001: 16.

41. Carl Esbeck, "Isn't Charitable Choice Government-Funded Discrimination?" Center for Public Justice, 2001, www.cpjustice.org/stories/storyreader$375 (accessed 23 October 2003).

42. Lazarus, "Uphill Climb."

43. See John Orr, "Religion-Based Employment Discrimination in Charitable Choice: A Guide for the Perplexed," The Center for Religion and Civic Culture, 2002, www.usc.edu/dept/LAS/religion_online/welfare/discrimination.html (accessed 23 October 2003); see also Lupu and Tuttle, *Government Partnerships*.

44. Orr, "Religion-Based Employment Discrimination."

45. Ibid.

46. Lupu and Tuttle, *Government Partnerships*, 48.

47. The CARE legislation introduced in the Senate was stripped of those provisions lending explicit protection to the hiring autonomy of funded religious groups. This proved inadequate for the initiative's opponents, who insisted on language prohibiting the right to discriminate in hiring based on religious compatibility.

48. Ceci Connolly, "Judge Orders Changes in Abstinence Program," *Washington Post*, 26 July 2002, A3.

49. Lupu and Tuttle, *Government Partnerships*, 26–29. The decision drew widely differing opinions on what it meant for charitable choice. Daniel Kelly, the attorney representing FaithWorks, contends that it renders charitable choice a "dead letter." Not so, according to Stephen Lazarus of the Center for Public Justice, who argues that it simply means that states will need to be more careful in how they channel money to faith-based agencies and how those agencies are run.

50. "Government Funded Charities Can Fire Homosexuals, Says Federal Court," *Christianity Today*, 25 July 2001, www.christianitytoday.com/ct/2001/130/32.0.html (accessed 23 October 2003).

51. See the discussion of this episode in chapter 5.

52. The Pedreira lawsuit also asserts that the state money going to Baptist Homes violates the establishment clause, on grounds that the defendant is a "pervasively sectarian" organization. The defendant also threatened not to renew its contract if the state imposed an anti-bias rule on hiring and firing. The state eventually backed down.

53. "Changing Bad Habits," *Houston Chronicle*, 10 April 2003, 1.

Chapter Seven. Of Little Faith? Lessons from the Faith-Based Saga

1. Thomas R. Dye, *Understanding Public Policy*, 8th ed. (Englewood Cliffs, N.J.: Prentice Hall, 1995).

2. Guy B. Peters, *American Public Policy*, 5th ed. (Chatham, N.J.: Chatham House, 1999).

3. Pew Forum on Religion and Public Life, "Faith-Based Initiatives and the Bush Administration," http://pewforum.org/issues/display.php?IssueID=3 (accessed 4 March 2003).

4. Mark Chaves, "Religious Congregations and Welfare Reform: Who Will Take Advantage of 'Charitable Choice'?" *American Sociological Review*, December 1999: 836–46.

5. Amy L. Sherman, *The Growing Impact of Charitable Choice: A Catalogue of New Collaborations between Government and Faith-Based Organizations in Nine States*, 2000, www.cpjustice.org/stories/storyreader$315 (accessed 14 February 2003).

6. Amy L. Sherman, "Tracking Charitable Choice: A Study of the Collaboration between Faith-Based Organizations and the Government in Providing Social Services in Nine States," *Social Work and Christianity* 27, no. 2 (fall 2002): 112–29; Center for Public Justice, *Charitable Choice: Gaining Momentum*, 2001, www.cpjustice.org/stories/storyreader$277 (accessed 23 October 2003).

7. Harold Dean Trulear, *Faith-Based Institutions and High-Risk Youth* (Philadelphia, Pa.: Public/Private Ventures Field Report Series, Spring 2000), 10.

8. Charlene Turner Johnson, interview by David K. Ryden, 19 October 1999.

9. John J. DiIulio, Jr., "Supporting Black Churches: Faith, Outreach, and the Inner-City Poor." *Brookings Review*, spring 1999.

10. Some evidence of these arguments surfaced early in President Bush's tenure, when he appeared to selectively woo more conservative evangelical black leaders, while ignoring or neglecting others representing sizable African American constituencies. The concerns worsened when the Republican-organized faith-based summit in April 2001 did likewise.

11. James Madison, *Memorial and Remonstrance against Religious Assessments*, http://religiousfreedom.lib.virginia.edu/sacred/Madison_M81_1785.html (accessed 23 October 2003).

12. Isaac Kramnick and R. Laurence Moore, "Can the Churches Save the Cities? Faith-Based Services and the Constitution," *The American Prospect*, November/December 1997: 47–53.

13. Annie Laurie Gaylor, "Bush's 'Faith-Based' Plans Assault Constitution," Freedom from Religion Foundation, Madison, Wisconsin, 29 January 2001, http://archive.aclu.org/congress/ffrfRelease.pdf (accessed 23 October 2003).

14. Pew Forum on Religion and Public Life, "Faith-Based Initiatives and the Bush Administration."

Bibliography

Ackerman, David. "Charitable Choice: Constitutional Issues and Developments through the 106th Congress." Report prepared for the Congressional Research Service of the U.S. Congress. Washington, D.C., 2000.

Allen, Mike. "Bush Aims to Get Faith Initiative Back on Track." *Washington Post*, 25 June 2001, A1.

———. "'Faith-Based' Backup Plan." *Washington Post*, 17 August 2001, A2.

———. "'Faith-Based' Initiative to Get Push." *Washington Post*, 31 August 2002, A1.

Alliance for Children and Families. "The Alliance for Children and Families Reacts to President Bush's Faith-Based Initiative." Press release, 1 February 2001.

Associated Press. "Lieberman to Draft Faith-Based Bill." 22 July 2001.

———. "Group: U.S. Needs to Support Religion." *New York Times*, 15 January 2002.

———. "Bush Enacts 'Faith-Based' Measure." 12 December 2002.

———. "Inhofe, Watts Back Off Defense of Trent Lott." 20 December 2002.

AU Bulletin. *Church and State*, no. 243 (December 1998): 3.

Balz, Dan. "Democrats Criticize Their Own—and Bush." *Washington Post*, 17 July 2001, A4.

Barone, Michael, Richard E. Cohen, and Charles E. Cook, Jr. *Almanac of American Politics 2002*. Washington, D.C.: National Journal, 2002.

Becker, Elizabeth. "Republicans Hold Forum with Blacks in Clergy." *New York Times*, 26 April 2001, A18.

Beinart, Peter. "Faith-Based Altercation." *The New Republic*, 5 February 2001.

Benen, Steven. "'Faith-Based' Fanaticism? Watts' Religious Advisory Committee Sparks Criticism." *Church and State*, June 2001. www.au.org/churchstate/cs6012.htm (accessed 14 December 2001).

Benjamin, Mark. "Faith-Based Charity Plan under Scrutiny." UPI Wire Service, 6 June 2001.

Billups, Andrea. "Watts Announces Outreach to Blacks." *Washington Times*, 24 February 2001, 4.

Broder, David S. "More Risk Than Reward?" *Washington Post*, 11 July 2001, A19. Available at www.house.gov/scott/c_choice/more_risk_than_reward.htm (accessed 14 February 2003).

Brownstein, Alan E. "Constitutional Questions about Charitable Choice." In *Welfare Reform and Faith-Based Organizations*, edited by Derek Davis and Barry Hawkins, 219–65. Waco, Tex.: J. M. Dawson Institute of Church-State Studies, 1999.

Brownstein, Ron. "Greater Role for Religious Charities Urged." *Los Angeles Times*, 25 May 1999, A13–A14.

Bumiller, Elisabeth. "Accord Reached on Charity Aid Bill after Bush Gives In on Hiring." *New York Times*, 8 February 2002, A19.

———. "Bush Rallies Faithful in Call for Passage of Charity Bill." *New York Times*, 12 April 2002, A20.

Busby, John A. "Open Letter from National Commander." *Salvation Army*, 13 July 2001.

Bush, George W. "Duty of Hope." Speech delivered in Indianapolis, Ind., 22 July 1999. www.cpjustice.org/stories/storyreader$383 (accessed 12 February 2003).

———. Presidential Nomination Acceptance Speech. Philadelphia, Pa., 3 August 2000.

———. "Rallying the Armies of Compassion." 30 January 2001.

———. Executive Order. "Agency Responsibilities with Respect to Faith-Based and Community Initiatives." 29 January 2001. www.whitehouse.gov/news/releases/2001/01/20010129-3.html (accessed 3 March 2003).

———. Executive Order. "Establishment of White House Office of Faith-Based and Community Initiatives." 29 January 2001. www.whitehouse.gov/news/releases/2001/01/20010129-2.html (accessed 3 March 2003).

———. "Remarks by the President and Jim Towey in Announcement of the New Director of the Office of Faith-Based and Community Initiatives." 2 February 2002. www.politicsandvirtue.com/faithbased.htm (accessed 3 March 2003).

———. Executive Order. "Equal Protection of the Laws for Faith-Based and Community Organizations." 12 December 2002. www.whitehouse.gov/news/releases/2002/12/20021212-6.html (accessed 12 December 2002).

Business Wire. "ACLJ Calls President Bush's Faith-Based Plan 'Creative' and 'Constitutionally Sound'." 29 January 2001.

Carlson-Thies, Stanley. "'Don't Look to Us': The Negative Responses of Churches to Welfare Reform." *Notre Dame Journal of Law, Ethics, and Public Policy* 11, no. 2 (1997): 667.

———. "Charitable Choice: Bringing Religion Back into American Welfare." *Journal of Policy History* 13, no. 1 (2001): 109.

Carr, Rebecca. "Bush Unveils Legislation for Faith-Based Charities." Cox News Service, 31 January 2001.

———. "Bush's Faith-Based Initiatives." *Atlanta Journal-Constitution*, 11 March 2001, 7C.

———. "Bush Losing Key Aide." *Atlanta Journal-Constitution*, 17 August 2001, 1A.

Center for Public Justice. "Charitable Choice Compliance: A National Report Card." Washington, D.C.: Center for Public Justice, 19 November 2000. www.cpjustice.org/stories/storyreader$296.

———. "A Guide to Charitable Choice." Washington, D.C.: Center for Public Justice, 18 December 2000. www.cpjustice.org/charitablechoice.

———. "Charitable Choice: Constitutional Issues." www.cpjustice.org/charitablechoice/constitution (accessed 15 April 2003).

———. "Charitable Choice: Gaining Momentum." www.cpjustice.org/stories/storyreader$277 (accessed 15 April 2003).

———. About the Center. www.cpjustice.org/about.html (accessed 15 April 2003).

———. Our Purpose. www.cpjustice.org/purpose. (accessed 15 April 2003).

"Changing Bad Habits." *Houston Chronicle*, 10 April 2003, 1.

Chaves, Mark. "Religious Congregations and Welfare Reform: Who Will Take Advantage of 'Charitable Choice'?" *American Sociological Review*, December 1999: 836–46.

Christian Legal Society Center for Law and Religious Freedom. "Litigation." www.clsnet.org/clrfPages/litigation/litigation_Overview.php3 (accessed 15 April 2003).

Clinton, Bill. Statement on Signing the Children's Health Act of 2000. Weekly Compilation of Presidential Documents, 23 October 2000, 2504.

Clorey, Paul. "Total Raised by Elite 100 Include Two $2 Billion Organizations and Four Generating at Least $1 Billion." *NonProfit Times*, November 1997, 37.

Cnaan, Ram. "The Challenge of Devolution and the Promise of Religious-Based Social Services: An Introduction." In *The Newer Deal*, edited by Ram Cnaan, Stephanie Boddie, and Robert Wineburg, 1–22. New York: Columbia University Press, 1999.

———. "Keeping the Faith in the City: How 401 Urban Religious Congregations Serve Their Neediest Neighbors." Philadelphia, Pa.: Center for Research on Religion and Urban Civil Society, 2000.

Colette, Hervey. "Panel Reports to Senator on the Faith-Based Initiative." Cox News Service, 15 January 2002.

Congressional Quarterly's Politics in America 2002. Washington, D.C.: Congressional Quarterly Press, 2002.

Connolly, Ceci. "Judge Orders Changes in Abstinence Program." *Washington Post*, 26 July 2002, A3.

Crabtree, Susan. "Faith-Based Initiative Off to a Rocky Start." *Roll Call*, 11 June 2001, 1.

———. "Bush's Faith-Based Initiatives." *Atlanta Journal-Constitution*, 11 March 2001, 7C.

Cushman, Clare, ed. *The Supreme Court Justices: Illustrated Biographies*. 2d ed. Washington, D.C.: Congressional Quarterly, 1995.

Daschle, Tom. "Compromise Good for South Dakota, America." *Rapid City Journal*, 15 February 2002.

Diament, Nathan J. "A Slander against Our Sacred Institutions." *Washington Post*, 28 May 2001, A23.

DiIulio, John J., Jr. "Supporting Black Churches: Faith, Outreach, and the Inner-City Poor." *Brookings Review*, spring 1999.

———. "Compassion 'In Truth and Action': How Sacred and Secular Places Serve Civic Purposes, and What Washington Should—and Should Not—Do to Help." Speech delivered before the National Association of Evangelicals, Dallas, Tex., 7 March 2001. www.whitehouse.gov/news/releases/2001/03/20010307-11.html (accessed 22 April 2002).

Dionne, E. J., Jr. "Al Gore Speaks for Himself." *Washington Post*, 28 May 1999, A35.

Dye, Thomas R. *Understanding Public Policy*. 8th ed. Englewood Cliffs, N.J.: Prentice Hall, 1995.

Eckstrom, Kevin. "Faith-Based Funding Dead in Senate." *Baptist Standard*, 25 November 2002. www.baptiststandard.com/2002/11_25/print/faithbased.html (accessed 26 November 2002).

Edsall, Thomas. "Robertson Joins Liberals in Faulting Bush's 'Faith-Based' Plan." *Washington Post*, 22 February 2001, A5.

———. "Jewish Leaders Criticize 'Faith-Based' Initiative." *Washington Post*, 27 February 2001, A4.

———. "Lieberman May Back Faith Initiative Bill." *Washington Post*, 2 March 2001, A7.

Edsall, Thomas, and Dana Milbank. "Blunt Defense of 'Faith-Based' Aid." *Washington Post*, 8 March 2001, A8.

Elliott, Julie. "Falwell to Bush: Pick Director with Care." *Dallas Morning News*, 20 August 2001, 14A.

Esbeck, Carl H. "A Constitutional Case for Governmental Cooperation with Faith-Based Social Service Providers." *Emory Law Journal* 46, no. 1 (1997): 1–42.

———. "Charitable Choice and the Critics." *New York University Annual Survey of American Law* (2000). www.nyu.edu/pubs/annualsurvey/archive/57_1_17.pdf (accessed 20 January 2003).

———. "Isn't Charitable Choice Government-Funded Discrimination?" Center for Public Justice, 2001. www.cpjustice.org/stories/storyreader$375 (accessed 14 February 2003).

Fagan, Amy. "Panel Releases Suggestions for Senate's Faith-Based Proposal." *Washington Times*, 16 January 2002, A6.

———. "Senate Panel OKs Charity Part of Bush's Faith-Based Initiative." *Washington Times*, 19 June 2002, A6.

———. "Senate Looks for Faith-Based Deal." *Washington Times*, 11 September 2002, A5.

———. "Watts to Support Narrower Faith Bill." *Washington Times*, 14 October 2002, A4.

Fagan, Amy, and David Boyer. "Faith-Based Bill Close to Senate Floor." *Washington Times*, 18 September 2002, A7.

"Faith-Based Initiative Faces Delays in Senate." *CQ Daily Monitor*, 1 August 2001, 4.

Farber, Daniel, William Eskridge, and Philip Frickly, eds. *1996 Supplement to Cases and Materials on Constitutional Law: Themes for the Constitution's Third Century*. St. Paul. Minn.: West, 1996.

Fernandez, Manny, and April Lynch. "Salvation Army Cuts S.F. Programs; Charity Spurns City's Domestic Partner Law." *San Francisco Chronicle*, 4 June 1998.

Ferraro, Thomas. "Bush's Faith-Based Measures Ready for Congress." Reuters Wire, 20 March 2001.

———. "Senate Backer Offers Concession on Bush Faith Plan." Reuters, 1 August 2001.

Fleischer, Ari. "Statement by the Press Secretary on the Request by the Salvation Army for an OMB Circular." Office of the Press Secretary, 10 July 2001. www.whitehouse.gov/news/releases/2001/07/20010710-12.html.

Foer, Franklin, and Ryan Lizza. "Holy War." *The New Republic*, 2 April 2001, 14, 16–17.

Fransley, Arthur E., II. "Faith-Based Action." *Christian Century*, 14 March 2001, 12–15.

Frolik, Joe. "Using Faith to Find Solutions to Poverty." *Cleveland Plain Dealer*, 28 November 1999, 1A.

Gaylor, Annie Laurie. "Bush's 'Faith-Based' Plans Assault Constitution." Freedom from Religion Foundation, Madison, Wisconsin, 29 January 2001. http://archive. aclu.org/congress/ffrfRelease.pdf (accessed 23 October 2003).

Goldhaber, Michael D. "Bush's Church Idea Illegal?" *National Law Journal*, 15 January 2001, A1.

Goodstein, Laurie. "Religious Groups Slow to Accept Government Money to Help Poor." *New York Times*, 17 October 2000, A22.

———. "For Religious Right, Bush's Charity Plan Is Raising Concerns." *New York Times*, 3 March 2001, A1.

———. "Support for Religion-Based Plan Is Hedged." *New York Times*, 11 April 2001, A14.

———. "Battle Lines Grow on Plan to Assist Religious Groups." *New York Times*, 12 April 2001, A22.

———. "Voucher Ruling Seen as Further Narrowing Church-State Division." *New York Times*, 28 June 2002, A24.

Gore, Albert A., Jr. Speech delivered to the Salvation Army, 25 May 1999. www.cp justice.org/stories/storyreader$384 (accessed 12 February 2003).

"Government Funded Charities Can Fire Homosexuals, Says Federal Court." *Christianity Today*, 25 July 2001. www.christianitytoday.com/ct/2001/130/32.0.html (accessed 14 February 2003).

"Government Relationships with Faith-Based Providers." *Roundtable on Religion and Social Welfare Policy: The State of the Law*. Transcript of roundtable held in Washington, D.C., 11 December 2002.

Green, David L., and Susan Baer. "Faith Groups Get Boost in Bush Order," *Baltimore Sun*, 13 December 2002, A1.

Green, John, and John DiIulio. "How the Faithful Voted." *Center Conversations*, no. 10 (March 2001).

Greenberg, Anna, and Stanley B. Greenberg. "Adding Values." *The American Prospect* 11, no. 19 (28 August 2000): 28.

Hacker, Jacob S. "Faith Healers." *The New Republic*, 28 June 1999, 16.

Hanks, Liza W. "Justice Souter: Defining Substantive Neutrality in an Age of Religious Politics." *Stanford Law Review* 48, no. 4 (April 1996): 903–37.

Herman, Ken. "Bush's Faith-Based Initiatives: Black Clergy Could Add Surprising Support." *Atlanta Journal-Constitution*, 11 March 2001, C7.

Hess, David. "Senate Tax Bill Markup Bogs Down amid Unusual Procedure." *Congress Daily*, 14 June 2002.

Holland, Steve. "Bush Religious Charity Plan Faces Drawn-Out Path." Reuters, 14 March 2001.

Hoover, Dennis R. "Charitable Choice and the New Religious Center." *Religion in the News*, spring 2000, 4.

Hopgood, Mei-Ling. "Senate Introduces Faith-Based Initiative Compromise Plan." Cox News Service, 7 February 2002. Lexis-Nexis, accessed 6 February 2003.

Horowitz, Michael, and Marvin Olasky. "Statement of Principles: Government Financing of Faith-Based Institutions." In *Mandate for Charity: Policy Proposals for the Bush Administration*, edited by Robert M. Huberty and Christopher Yablonski, 23–26. Washington, D.C.: Capital Research Center, 2001.

Horrock, Nicholas M. "Faith-Based Chief Quits." UPI Wire, 17 August 2001.

———. "Bush to Push Faith-Based Initiative." United Press International, 29 November 2002. www.up.com/print.cfm?StoryID=20021129-051337-4212r (accessed 2 December 2002).

Huberty, Robert M., and Christopher Yablonski, eds. *Mandate for Charity: Policy Proposals for the Bush Administration*. Washington, D.C.: Capital Research Center, 2001.

Institute for Public Affairs. "The Constitutionality of 'Charitable Choice'." 2001. www.ou.org/public/publib/constit.htm.

Jelen, Ted, and Clyde Wilcox. *Public Attitudes toward Church and State*. Armonk, N.Y.: M. E. Sharpe, 1995.

Johnson, Byron. "The InnerChange Freedom Initiative: A Preliminary Evaluation of a Faith-Based Prison Program." Center for Research on Religion and Urban Civil Society at the University of Pennsylvania, Philadelphia, Pa., June 2003.

Jones, Jim. "Unique Prison Program Serves as Boot Camp for Heaven." *Christianity Today* 42, no. 2 (9 February 1998): 88.

Kaminer, Wendy. "Faith-Based Favoritism." *The American Prospect*, 9 April 2001. www.prospect.org/print/V12/6/kaminer-w.html (accessed 14 February 2003).

Kammer, Fred, S.J. "Partners against Poverty." *Washington Post*, 10 February 2001, A23.

Kirkpatrick, David. "A Blaine Amendment Update." www.schoolreport.com/school report/articles/blaine_7_00.htm (July 2000).

Klein, Joe. "The Men in the Mirror," *New Yorker*, 14 June 1999.

Koch, Kathy. "Child Poverty." *CQ Researcher*. Washington, D.C.: Congressional Quarterly, 2000, 283–303.

Kohut, Andrew, John C. Green, Scott Keeter, and Robert C. Toth. *The Diminishing Divide: Religion's Changing Role in American Politics*. Washington, D.C.: Brookings Institution, 2000.

Komer, Richard, and Clint Bolick. "School Choice: The Next Step: The State Constitutional Challenge." www.ij.org/editorial/choice_next.shtml (1 July 2002).

Koppell, Jonathan G. S. "Charity: When Private Hands Do the Public's Work." *Los Angeles Times*, 19 December 1999, M2.

Kramnick, Isaac, and R. Laurence Moore. "Can the Churches Save the Cities? Faith-Based Services and the Constitution." *The American Prospect*, November/December 1997, 47–53.

Kukis, Mark. "House Reshapes Stalled Faith-Based Bill." United Press International, 3 July 2001. www.vny.com/f/news/upidetail.cfm?QUI=198020 (accessed 3 July 2001).

Lardner, Lynford. "How Far Does the Constitution Separate Church and State?" *American Political Science Review* 45, no. 1 (March 1951): 121.

Laycock, Douglas. "The Underlying Unity of Separation and Neutrality." *Emory Law Journal* 46 (1997): 43.

Layman, Geoffrey. *The Great Divide: Religious and Cultural Conflict in American Party Politics.* New York: Columbia University Press, 2001.

Lazarus, Stephen. "An Uphill Climb to True Tolerance." *Capital Commentary*, 13 August 2001. www.cpjustice.org/stories/storyreader$564 (accessed 14 February 2003).

"Leading African American Pastors Endorse Bush." George W. Bush campaign press release, 4 February 2000.

Leland, John. "Some Black Pastors See New Aid under Bush." *New York Times*, 2 February 2001, A12.

Leonard, Mary. "The Real Issue Is Trust." *Boston Globe*, 29 April 2001, D1.

———. "Faith Bill Advances Amid Religious Mood." *Boston Globe*, 18 November 2001, A1.

———. "CARE Act Opposition." *Boston Globe*, 25 September 2002, A10.

———. "President Eases Way for Religious Charities." *Boston Globe*, 13 December 2002, A1.

Leonard, Mary, and Sue Kirchhoff. "Faith-Based Bill May Be Windfall for Universities." *Boston Globe*, 21 June 2002, A1.

Liberty Online. January/February 2001. www.libertymagazine.org/article/articleview/240/1/31 (accessed 23 October 2003).

Lieberman, Joseph, and Rick Santorum. "Unite to Bolster Faith-Based Efforts." *Philadelphia Inquirer*, 19 June 2001, A15.

"Lieberman, Santorum Press for Markup of Charity Tax Breaks." *CQ Daily Monitor*, 7 June 2002.

Loconte, Joseph. "Bush vs. Gore on Faith-Based Charity." *American Enterprise*, June 2000.

———. "Faith-Based Skepticism." *Weekly Standard* 6, no. 27 (26 March 2001): 10–12.

"Loss of Faith." *Weekly Standard*, 30 September 2002, 2.

Loven, Jennifer. "Religious Charities Able to Use Space." Associated Press, 14 March 2002.

Luchenitser, Alex J. "Casting Aside the Constitution: The Trend toward Government Funding of Religious Social Service Providers." Americans United for the Separation of Church and State. www.au.org/luchenitser.htm.

Lupu, Ira C. "Government Messages and Government Money: *Santa Fe, Mitchell v. Helms*, and the Arc of the Establishment Clause." Public Law and Legal Theory Working Paper 010, 2002, available at www.papers.ssrn.com/paper.taf?abstract_id=241736 (accessed 22 October 2003).

Lupu, Ira. C., and Robert W. Tuttle. "Government Partnerships with Faith-Based Service Providers: The State of the Law." Washington, D.C.: The Roundtable on Religion and Social Welfare Policy, 2002.

———. "The Distinctive Place of Religious Entities in Our Constitutional Order." *Villanova Law Review* 47 (2002): 37.

————. "*Zelman*'s Future: Vouchers, Sectarian Providers, and the Next Round of Constitutional Battles." *Notre Dame Law Review* 76 (2003): 917ff.

Lutheran Services of America. "Largest Nonprofit Challenges President Bush to Follow Through for the Nation's Most Vulnerable." Press release, 29 January 2001.

Lynn, Barry. "Educate Public about Religious Right Agenda." ProChoice Online (1999). www.wcla.org/99-spring/lynn.html (accessed 3 January 2003).

Mallaby, Sebastian. "DiIulio's Good-Faith Effort." *Washington Post*, 20 August 2001, A15.

Marks, Alexandra. "A Spiritual Approach to Time behind Bars." *Christian Science Monitor*, 16 April 2001. www.csmonitor.com/durable/2001/04/16/fp1s4csm.shtml.

Marx, Claude. "Santorum Doubts Government Charity Aid." Associated Press, 9 October 2001.

Mason, Julie. "Black Ministers Back Bush Plan." *Houston Chronicle*, 20 March 2001, A6.

Mattingly, Terry. "God Is in the Church-State Details." Gospelcom.net, 18 August 1999. http://tmatt.gospelcom.net/column/1999/08/18 (accessed 10 June 2002).

McFeatters, Ann. "Presidential Candidates Saying Something of Values." *Pittsburgh Post-Gazette*, 30 May 1999, A11.

McQueen, Anjetta. "Bush May Settle for Narrower Scope on Faith-Based Initiatives." *Congressional Quarterly Weekly Report* 60 (22 June 2002): 1662.

Meckler, Laura. "Religious Groups Wary of Bush Plan." Associated Press, 20 February 2001.

————. "Critics Protest Bush Religion Plan." Associated Press, 13 March 2001.

————. "Conservatives Rally around Bush Plan." Associated Press, 11 April 2001.

————. "GOP Summit Pumps Up Pastors on Bush Religion Plan." Associated Press, 25 April 2001.

————. "DiIulio: Programs Should Have Grants." Associated Press, 26 April 2001.

————. "Faith-Based Bill Moves Forward." Associated Press, 19 June 2001.

————. "Compromise Reached on Charity Bill." Associated Press, 7 February 2002.

————. "Senate Still Trying to Move Scaled-Back 'Faith-Based' Legislation." Associated Press, 15 October 2002.

————. "'Faith-Based' Bill Falls Short." Associated Press, 15 November 2002.

Media Transparency. "Robert Bork." www.mediatransparency.org/people/robert_bork.htm (accessed 16 October 2002).

Milbank, Dana. "Bush Unveils 'Faith-Based' Initiative." *Washington Post*, 30 January 2001, A1.

————. "Defending 'Faith-Based' Plan." *Washington Post*, 6 March 2001.

————. "Bush Assails 'Faith-Based Initiative' Critics." *Washington Post*, 6 June 2001, A6.

————. "Charity Cites Bush Help in Fight against Hiring Gays." *Washington Post*, 10 July 2001, A1.

————. "Story of Charity Plea Changes Again." *Washington Post*, 13 July 2001, A2.

————. "DiIulio Resigns from Top 'Faith-Based' Post." *Washington Post*, 18 August 2001, A4.

———. "Charity Bill Compromise Is Reached." *Washington Post*, 6 February 2002, A1.

———. "Bush Endorses Compromise in Senate on Aid to Charities." *Washington Post*, 8 February 2002, A04.

———. "Bush Issues 'Faith-Based Initiative' Orders." *Washington Post*, 13 December 2002, A4.

Milbank, Dana, and Mike Allen. "Rove Heard Charity Plea on Gay Bias." *Washington Post*, 12 July 2001, A1.

Milbank, Dana, and Thomas Edsall. "Faith Initiative May Be Revised." *Washington Post*, 12 March 2001, A01.

Milbank, Dana, and Glen Kessler. "Charities Decry Tax Bill Setback." *Washington Post*, 30 May 2001, A1.

Miller, John. J., and Ramesh Ponnuru. "DiIulio's Bully Pulpit." *National Review Online*, 8 March 2001. www.nationalreview.com/daily/nr030801.shtml (accessed 28 February 2003).

Minow, Martha. "Choice or Commonality: Welfare and Schooling after the End of Welfare as We Know It." *Duke Law Journal* 49 (1999): 493.

Mockler, Rick. "Faith-Based Social Welfare." Catholic Charities of California website, www.cccalifornia.org/articles/2001/article10131.html (accessed 20 January 2003).

Mohammed, Arshad. "Bush Hints at Compromise in Faith-Based Initiative." Reuters, 26 July 2001.

Monsma, Stephen V. *When Sacred and Secular Mix: Religious Nonprofit Organizations and Public Money.* Lanham, Md.: Rowman and Littlefield, 1996.

———. "The 'Pervasively Sectarian' Standard in Theory and Practice." *Notre Dame Journal of Law, Ethics & Public Policy* 13 (1999): 321.

———, ed. *Church-State Relations in Crisis: Debating Neutrality.* Lanham, Md.: Rowman and Littlefield, 2002.

Morgan, David. "Advisor: Bush's Faith-Based Plan Poses No Threat." Reuters, 1 April 2001.

Morin, Richard. "Leading with His Right; John DiIulio, Ready to Go to the Mat with a Faith-Based Approach to Crime." *Washington Post*, 26 February 2001, C01.

Nather, David. "Bush Plan to Promote Faith-Based Charities Creates Dilemma for Both Parties." *Congressional Quarterly Weekly Report* 59 (3 February 2001): 283–85.

———. "Lieberman-Santorum Bill Would Widen Tax Deductions for Charitable Contributions." *Congressional Quarterly Weekly Report* 59 (17 March 2001): 609.

———. "House GOP Bets on Passing Aid to 'Faith-Based' Groups: Senate Keys on Tax Incentives." *Congressional Quarterly Weekly Report* 59 (24 March 2001): 661–62.

———. "Diminished 'Faith-Based Initiative' Heads toward House Floor." *Congressional Quarterly Weekly Report* 59 (14 July 2001): 1687–89.

———. "Bush's House Win on 'Faith-Based' Charity Clouded by Bias Concerns in Senate." *Congressional Quarterly Weekly Report* 59 (21 July 2001): 1774–75.

———. "Faith-Based Initiatives, Now More Than Ever?" *Congressional Quarterly Weekly Report* 59 (10 November 2001): 2654.

Neal, Terry M. "Bush Outlines Charity-Based Social Service Policies." *Washington Post*, 23 July 1999, A2.

Nitschke, Lori. "Bush's 'Faith-Based' Initiative Hobbled by Growing Disputes over Final Form, Constitutionality." *Congressional Quarterly Weekly Report* 59 (23 June 2001): 1520.

———. "Faith-Based Charity Bill Advances in House with Little Democratic Support." *Congressional Quarterly Weekly Report* 59 (30 June 2001): 1586–87.

———. "Ways and Means Scales Back Bush Plan for Fostering Charitable Donations." *Congressional Quarterly Weekly Report* 59 (14 July 2001): 1688.

Norquist, Grover. "The Classic Coalition for CARE." UPI Wire, Washington Politics and Policy Desk, 27 May 2002.

Olasky, Marvin. *The Tragedy of American Compassion*. Lanham, Md.: Regnery Gateway, 1992.

———. "Let Faith-Based Programs Solve Our Social Problems." In *Mandate for Charity: Policy Proposals for the Bush Administration*, edited by Robert M. Huberty and Christopher Yablonski, 17–21. Washington, D.C.: Capital Research Center, 2001.

———. "Rolling the Dice." *World*, 4 August 2001, 18–24.

———. "Sounds of Silence: Bush Initiative Gets through the House, but What Now?" *World*, 4 August 2001. www.worldmag.com/world/issue/08-04-01/closing_2.asp (accessed 2 December 2002).

———. "Faith-Based Initiative: Officials Should Not Weaken It to Appease the Left." *World*, 23 November 2002. www.worldmag.com/world/issue/11-23-02/opening _2.asp (accessed 2 December 2002).

Orr, John. "Religion-Based Employment Discrimination in Charitable Choice: A Guide for the Perplexed." The Center for Religion and Civic Culture, 2002. www.usc.edu/dept/LAS/religion_online/welfare/discrimination.html (accessed 22 October 2003).

Ostling, Richard. "Protestants Key in Charity Concept." AP Wire, 8 February 2001.

Ota, Alan K. "Anti-Discrimination Battle May Tie Up Faith-Based Bill." *CQ Daily Monitor*, 25 September 2002.

Palmer, Elizabeth A. "Charitable-Choice Supporters Put Faith in Court's Judgment." *Congressional Quarterly Weekly Report*, 3 March 2001: 475.

Patterson, Bradley H., Jr. *The White House Staff: Inside the West Wing and Beyond*. Washington, D.C.: Brookings Institution Press, 2000.

Peters, B. Guy. *American Public Policy: Promise and Performance*. 5th ed. Chappaqua, N.Y.: Seven Bridges Press, 1999.

Pew Forum on Religion and Public Life. "Faith-Based Initiatives and the Bush Administration." http://pewforum.org/issues/display.php?IssueID=3 (accessed 4 March 2003).

———. "In Good Faith: A Dialogue on Government Funding of Faith-Based Social Services." http://pewforum.org/publications/reports/ingoodfaith.pdf (accessed 10 April 2003).

Pew Forum on Religion and Public Life, and Pew Research Center for the People and the Press. "Post 9-11 Attitudes: Religion More Prominent, Muslim-Americans More Accepted." Washington, D.C., 6 December 2001.

"President Agrees to Compromise on Faith-Based Initiative Bill." *Christian Times*, March 2002. www.christiantimes.com/Articles/Articles%20Mar02/Art_ Mar02_02.html (accessed 28 May 2002).

"President Commends House for Action on Faith-Based and Community Initiative." White House news release, 19 July 2001. www.whitehouse.gov/news/releases/2001/07/20010719-9.html (accessed 3 March 2003).

Press, Eyal. "Faith-Based Furor." *New York Times*, 1 April 2001, section 6, p. 62.

———. "Lead Us Not into Temptation." *The American Prospect* 12, no. 6 (9 April 2001): 20.

Pressley, Sue Anne. "Faith-Based Groups under Fresh Scrutiny." *Washington Post*, 11 February 2001, A3.

Putnam, Robert. Testimony. U.S. House of Representatives, Education and Workforce Committee, Subcommittee on Select Education, Hearing on "The Corporation for National and Community Service." 11 April 2002.

Quaid, Libby. "Welfare Provision Challenge Planned." Associated Press Online, 9 January 1998.

Rather, Dan, and Jim Axelrod. "President-Elect George W. Bush's Efforts to Win Over African-Americans." *CBS Evening News*, 20 December 2000.

"Reform Jewish Movement Reacts to DiIulio's Departure." Religious Action Center for Reform Judaism press release, 17 August 2001. http://uahc.org/reform/rac/news/081701.html (accessed 3 March 2002).

Reuters. "White House Denies Helping Charity on Gays." 10 July 2001. CNN.com (accessed 20 July 2001).

———. "Bush Calls on Senate to Pass Faith-Based Initiative." Reuters, 2 July 2002.

Robertson, Pat. "Faith-Based Initiatives Pose Some Problems." www.patrobertson.com/NewsCommentary/FaithBasedInitiatives.asp (accessed 25 February 2003).

Rosen, Jeffrey. "Is Nothing Secular?" *New York Times Magazine*, 30 January 2000, 40.

———. "Religious Rights." *The New Republic*, 26 February 2001, 16.

Rosin, Hanna, and Terry M. Neal. "Converting Convicts to Christians: Texas Blesses Use of Strict 'Christ-Centered' Agenda at Small Prison." *Washington Post*, 27 November 1999, A1.

Roth, Bennet. "Faith-Based Effort Gains Ground; Most Controversial Issues Not Included in Bid to Help Charities." *Houston Chronicle*, 8 February 2002, A3.

Rothstein, Betsy. "GOP 'Charitable Choice' Unnerves Dems." 28 June 2000. www.house.gov/scott/c_choice/ar_Hill_Article_06_28_00.htm.

Ryden, David K. "Faith-Based Initiatives and the Constitution: Black Churches, Government, and Social Services Delivery." In *New Day Begun: African American Churches and Civic Culture in Post-Civil Rights America*, edited by Drew Smith, 248–77. Durham, N.C.: Duke University Press, 2003.

Sammon, Bill. "President Rolls Back 'Secular' Rules on Faith-Based Groups." *Washington Times*, 13 December 2002, A1.

Saperstein, David. "Testimony before the U.S. House of Representatives Constitution Subcommittee." 7 June 2001. www.rac.org/news/060701testimony.html.

———. "Public Accountability and Faith-Based Organizations: A Problem Best Avoided." *Harvard Law Review* 116 (2003): 1353.

Schaefer, Kurt C. "The Privatizing of Compassion: A Critical Engagement with Marvin Olasky." In *Toward a Just and Caring Society: Christian Reponses to Poverty in America*, edited by D. Gushee, 144–61. Grand Rapids, Mich.: Baker Books, 1999.

Scully, Sean. "Faith-Based Initiatives Office Opens to Many Calls." *Washington Times*, 21 February 2001, A1.

Search for Common Ground. *Finding Common Ground: Twenty-Nine Recommendations of the Working Group on Human Needs and Faith-Based and Community Initiatives.* Washington, D.C.: Search for Common Ground, 2001.

Segal, Julie A. "A Holy Mistaken Zeal: The Legislative History and Future of Charitable Choice." In *Welfare Reform and Faith-Based Organizations*, edited by Derek Davis and Barry Hankins, 9–27. Waco, Tex.: J. M. Dawson Institute of Church-State Studies, 1999.

Shea, Christopher. "Gore Gets Religion." Salon.com, June 1999. www.salon.com/news/feature/1999/06/15/faith (accessed 15 June 1999).

Sherman, Amy L. *Fruitful Collaboration between Government and Christian Social Ministries: Lessons Learned from Virginia and Maryland.* Center for Public Justice, January 1998.

———. *The Growing Impact of Charitable Choice: A Catalogue of New Collaborations between Government and Faith-Based Organizations in Nine States.* 2000. www.cpjustice.org/stories/storyreader$315 (accessed 14 February 2003).

———. *A Survey of Church-Government Anti-Poverty Partnerships.* Washington, D.C.: American Enterprise Institute, 2000.

———. "Tracking Charitable Choice: A Study of the Collaboration between Faith-Based Organizations and the Government in Providing Social Services in Nine States." *Social Work and Christianity* 27, no. 2 (fall 2002): 112–29.

"Shortchanging Charities." *Christianity Today*, 7 March 2002. www.christianitytoday.com/ct/2002/003/32.35.html (accessed 12 June 2003).

Sider, Ronald. "Implacable Foes Find (Some) Common Ground on Faith-Based Initiatives." *Christianity Today*, 28 January 2002.

———. "Evaluating the Faith-Based Initiative: Is Charitable Choice Good Public Policy?" Paper delivered as the Sorensen Lecture at Yale Divinity School, 15 October 2002.

Skillen, James. *Recharging the American Experiment: Principled Pluralism for Genuine Civic Community.* Grand Rapids, Mich.: Baker, 1994.

Sobieraj, Sandra. "Gore: Church Should Get Government Funds." Associated Press, 24 May 1999.

Solomon, Lewis D., and Matthew J. Vlissides, Jr. "In God We Trust? Assessing the Potential of Faith-Based Social Services." Policy report, Progressive Policy Institute, February 2001.

Stevenson, Richard W. "In Order, President Eases Limits on U.S. Aid to Religious Groups." *New York Times*, 13 December 2002, A1.

Stolberg, Sheryl Gay, and Elisabeth Bumiller. "Divisive Words: The Overview; Powell Criticizes Lott for Remarks; Jeb Bush Joins In." *New York Times*, 19 December 2001, A1.

Suarez, Ray, and Elizabeth Arnold. *Talk of the Nation.* National Public Radio, 23 June 1999.

Sullivan, Andrew. "The Drag Race." *The New Republic*, 18 December 2000.

Tapper, Jake. "Fade to White: The Only African American Republican in Congress Is Headed Home." *Washington Post Magazine*, 5 January 2003, W06.

Tenpas, Kathryn Dunn. "Can an Office Change a Country? The White House Office of Faith-Based and Community Initiatives." Preliminary report for the Pew Forum, Washington, D.C., February 2002.

Trulear, Harold Dean. *Faith-Based Institutions and High-Risk Youth*. Philadelphia, Pa.: Public/Private Ventures Field Report Series, Spring 2000, 10.

Twohey, Meghan. "Limelight Scorching 'Charitable Choice'?" *National Journal*, 28 April 2001, 1236–37.

———. "Bush Cleans House, Takes Charge of Faith Team." *The Federal Paper*, 23 September 2002.

United Jewish Communities. "United Jewish Communities Statement on Bush Administration's Faith-Based Programs Initiative." Press release, 5 February 2001.

Unlevel Playing Field: Barriers to Participation by Faith-Based and Community Organizations in Federal Social Service Programs. WhiteHouse.gov, 16 August 2001. www.whitehouse.gov/new/releases/2001/08/unlevelfield.html (accessed 29 April 2002).

Urofsky, Melvin, ed. *The Supreme Court Justices: A Biographical Dictionary*. New York: Garland, 1994.

U.S. Congress. House. Committee amendment to H.R. 7. 2001, S6301. House Legislative Counsel for the House Judiciary Committee. 28 June 2001.

U.S. Congress. House. Committee on Ways and Means. H.R. 7. *Community Solutions Act of 2001*. Hearing before the Subcommittee on Human Resources and Subcommittee on Select Revenue Measures of the Committee on Ways and Means, House of Representatives, 107th Congress, 1st sess., 14 June 2001, Serial 107-34.

U.S. Congress. House. Committee on Ways and Means, Subcommittees on Human Resources and Select Revenue Measures. Testimony, 17 July 2001. www.house.gov/ways_means/humres/107cong/6-14-01/6-14scott.htm.

U.S. Congress. House. Office of Representative Tony Hall. "Faith/Community-Based Initiative Could Help Clinch Victory in Fight against Hunger, Hall Says." Press release, 30 January 2001.

U.S. Congress. House. Office of Representative Bobby Scott. "Current Federal Programs Containing Charitable Choice: Welfare Reform Act (P.L. 104-93)." · www.house.gov/scott/c_choice/fp_welfare_reform_act.htm (accessed 11 June 2003).

U.S. Congress. Senate. Committee on Health, Education, Labor, and Pensions. *The Youth Drug and Mental Health Services Act of 1999*. Senate Report 106-196. 19 October 1999.

U.S. Congress. Senate. Office of Senator Rick Santorum. Senate Floor Statement. Santorum and Lieberman Introduce Phase II of President's Faith-Based Initiatives. 107th Congress, 1st sess. Washington, D.C.: Government Printing Office, 3 August 2001.

———. *Charity Aid, Recovery, and Empowerment Act of 2002*. http://santorum.senate.gov/crsnovember14.html (accessed 14 January 2003).

———. Statement on the CARE Act, 14 November 2002. http://santorum.senate.gov/statementnovember14.html (accessed 14 January 2003).

———. "Lieberman, Santorum Announce Bipartisan Compromise on President's Faith-Based Initiative; Unveil Consensus Charity Bill at White House Event." Press release, 2002. http://santorum.senate.gov/pressreleases/record.cfm?id= 181168 (accessed 12 June 2003).

U.S. Newswire. "New Groups Founded to Extend President Bush's Vision of Faith-Based and Community Enterprise." 6 June 2001.

———. "DiIulio Departure Raises Danger of More Ideological Direction for White House Government Funding of Religion Program, Says Group." 17 August 2001.

———. "Text of a Letter from the President to the Senate Majority Leader and the Senate Republican Leader." 7 November 2001.

———. "Nation's Leading Interfaith Organization Tells President: Now Is Not the Time to Advance Divisive Faith-Based Initiative." 8 November 2001.

VandeHei, Jim. "Bush Moves to Resurrect His Faith-Based Initiative." *Wall Street Journal*, 25 January 2002.

VandeHei, Jim, and Laurie McGinley. "Bush Team Falls behind Schedule in Its Nominations." *Wall Street Journal*, 22 March 2001, A1.

Watts, J. C. Interview with Tim Russert. *Meet the Press*. NBC, 15 December 2002.

Wineburg, Robert J. *A Limited Partnership: The Politics of Religion, Welfare, and Social Service*. New York: Columbia University Press, 2001.

Witham, Larry. "Faith-Based Plan Shows Cultural Split." *Washington Times*, 26 March 2001, 4.

———. "Senate Democrats Assail Faith-Based Bill." *Washington Times*, 7 June 2001, 4.

———. "Labor Debuts Bush's Faith Plan." *Washington Times*, 18 April 2002, A11.

———. "Towey Said Faith-Based Bill 'Held Hostage' by Reed." *Washington Times*, 24 October 2002, A6.

———. "Amendments Kill CARE in Senate." *Washington Times*, 15 November 2002, A10.

Working Group on Human Needs and Faith-Based and Community Initiatives. *Harnessing Civic and Faith-Based Power to Fight Poverty*. April 2003. www.workinggroup. org/Documents/SFCGbook2003Final.pdf (accessed 11 April 2003).

Zirkin, Nancy. "Statement of Nancy Zirkin, Director of Public Policy and Government Affairs, American Association of University Women, on The Community Solutions Act (H.R. 7)." AAUW press release, 17 July 2001.

Zuckman, Jill. "In N.H., Gore Puts Focus on Religion." *Boston Globe*, 23 May 1999, A1.

Index